A GUIDE TO FACULTY DEVELOPMENT

A GUIDE TO FACULTY DEVELOPMENT

Second Edition

Kay J. Gillespie,
Douglas L. Robertson,
and Associates

○

Afterword by
William H. Bergquist

Professional and Organizational Development
Network in Higher Education

JOSSEY-BASS
A Wiley Imprint
www.josseybass.com

Published by Jossey-Bass
A Wiley Imprint
989 Market Street, San Francisco, CA 94103-1741—www.josseybass.com

Readers should be aware that Internet Web sites offered as citations and/or sources for further information may have changed or disappeared between the time this was written and when it is read.

Limit of Liability/Disclaimer of Warranty: While the publisher and author have used their best efforts in preparing this book, they make no representations or warranties with respect to the accuracy or completeness of the contents of this book and specifically disclaim any implied warranties of merchantability or fitness for a particular purpose. No warranty may be created or extended by sales representatives or written sales materials. The advice and strategies contained herein may not be suitable for your situation. You should consult with a professional where appropriate. Neither the publisher nor author shall be liable for any loss of profit or any other commercial damages, including but not limited to special, incidental, consequential, or other damages.

Jossey-Bass books and products are available through most bookstores. To contact Jossey-Bass directly call our Customer Care Department within the U.S. at 800-956-7739, outside the U.S. at 317-572-3986, or fax 317-572-4002.

Jossey-Bass also publishes its books in a variety of electronic formats. Some content that appears in print may not be available in electronic books.

Library of Congress Cataloging-in-Publication Data

Gillespie, Kay Herr.
    A guide to faculty development/Kay Gillespie, Douglas L. Robertson & Associates; foreword by William H. Bergquist. — 2nd ed.
       p.   cm. — (The Jossey-Bass higher and adult education series)
    Includes bibliographical references and index.
    ISBN 978-0-470-40557-4 (cloth)
       1. College teachers—Training of.   2. Universities and colleges—United States—Faculty.   I. Douglas L. Robertson & Associates   II. Title.
    LB2331.72.G55   2010
    378.1'2—dc22

                                                                        2009042686

Printed in the United States of America
SECOND EDITION
HB Printing   10 9 8 7 6 5 4 3 2 1

The Jossey-Bass Higher and Adult Education Series

CONTENTS

Preface   ix
About the Authors   xiii

Part One Establishing and Sustaining a Faculty Development Program

1. Overview of Faculty Development: History and Choices   3
   Mathew L. Ouellett
2. Program Types and Prototypes   21
   Virginia S. Lee
3. Establishing an Educational Development Program   35
   Douglas L. Robertson
4. Working with a Faculty Development Committee   53
   Kim M. Mooney
5. Listen, Learn, Lead: Getting Started in Faculty Development   67
   Margaret W. Cohen
6. Important Skills and Knowledge   83
   Todd D. Zakrajsek
7. Promoting Your Program and Grounding It in the Institution   99
   Ed Neal and Iola Peed-Neal
8. Practical Suggestions for Programs and Activities   117
   Donna E. Ellis and Leslie Ortquist-Ahrens

Part Two Key Priorities in Faculty Development: Assessment, Diversity, and Technology

9. Program Assessment for Faculty Development   135
   Kathryn M. Plank and Alan Kalish
10. Assessing Teaching Practices and Effectiveness for Formative Purposes   151
    Michael Theall and Jennifer L. Franklin

11. Assessment Practices Related to Student Learning:
   Transformative Assessment   169
   Catherine M. Wehlburg
12. Overview of Diversity Issues Relating to Faculty
   Development   185
   Mathew L. Ouellett
13. Conceptualizing, Designing, and Implementing Multicultural
   Faculty Development Activities   203
   Christine A. Stanley
14. Working with Underrepresented Faculty   225
   Franklin Tuitt
15. International Faculty Development: Pursuing Our Work with
   Colleagues Around the World   243
   *Nancy Van Note Chism, David Gosling, and Mary
   Deane Sorcinelli*
16. Issues in Technology and Faculty Development   259
   Sally Kuhlenschmidt

**Part Three Faculty Development Across Institutional
Types, Career Stages, and Organizations**

17. Effective Practices at Research Universities: The Productive
   Pairing of Research and Teaching   277
   Constance Ewing Cook and Michele Marincovich
18. Effective Practices in the Context of Small Colleges   293
   Michael Reder
19. Faculty Development in the Context of the
   Community College   309
   Helen Burnstad and Cynthia J. Hoss
20. Graduate and Professional Student Development Programs   327
   Laura L. B. Border and Linda M. von Hoene
21. Working with Adjunct Faculty Members   347
   Terri A. Tarr
22. Supporting Faculty Members Across Their Careers   363
   Ann E. Austin
23. Organizational Development   379
   Kay J. Gillespie

Afterword by William H. Bergquist   397
Epilogue   419
Name Index   421
Subject Index   429

PREFACE

In the mid 1980s, the Professional and Organizational Development (POD) Network in Higher Education recognized that there was a need for a handbook for the field; the present work represents the third such volume in an evolving line of POD-sponsored publications. The previous edition of this book (Gillespie, 2002) represented a significant expansion of the earlier *Handbook for New Practitioners* (Wadsworth, Hilsen, & Shea, 1988). Higher education and the field are sufficiently dynamic that this second edition has been needed in less than a decade after the first edition, and requests to translate this new edition were received even prior to its publication. Representing a significant revision and expansion, this second edition has been completely rewritten and includes new authors and eighteen new chapters.

Purposes and Audience

The volume is designed to help educational developers, novice and expert alike, to provide valuable service, counsel, and leadership to their colleges and universities. The book presents a detailed description of the field of educational development for administrators, faculty, trustees, legislators, and students of higher education who may want, or need, to understand the nature, utility, and promise of the relatively young but quickly maturing field of educational development.

Overview of Contents

The book's twenty-three chapters are grouped into three parts. Part One, "Establishing and Sustaining a Faculty Development Program," comprises eight chapters that provide an introduction to the field, its history, literature, and key themes; an identification of basic issues, decisions, and practicalities in establishing and sustaining successful educational development programs; and a discussion of essential knowledge and skills that one needs in order to excel as an educational developer. Part

Two, "Key Priorities in Faculty Development: Assessment, Diversity, and Technology," consists of eight chapters that address the assessment of programs, teaching, and student learning; explore what educational developers must know to become multiculturally and interculturally competent and to help faculty, students, and staff to do the same; and discuss how educational developers can help faculty to use technology effectively in their teaching as well as how educational developers can use technology effectively in their own work. Finally, Part Three, "Faculty Development Across Institutional Types, Career Stages, and Organizations," includes seven chapters that explore educational development in various institutional types—for example research universities, small colleges, and community colleges; examine ways in which educational developers can support faculty at various stages across their careers; and discuss the vital role that educational developers can play in organizational development at their institutions. Multiple points of entry exist for this book, and readers should feel encouraged to move around its linked chapters as fits their needs and interests.

Naming the Field

Readers of this volume will see the field referred to by a number of terms, including *educational development, faculty development,* and *professional development.* Indeed, readers will notice that this book retains its former title, which refers to the field by its traditional but increasingly inaccurate name, "faculty development." What *not* to call the field is clear: its interests, expertise, and core purposes include much more than faculty development. However, our professional community has not achieved consensus on what its name should be. As volume editors, we believe that imposing a common term on the contributing authors is inappropriate at this time because the current conversation about what to call the field remains productive. Therefore, as editors, we have chosen not to restrict this conversation prematurely; and readers will encounter the varying terms in this volume. Having said that, we strongly believe that, when the third edition of this volume is published, a naming consensus will have been achieved and the book must have an updated title.

Conclusion

Across the book's twenty-three chapters written by its thirty-one authors, some points are repeated and emphasized by different authors; some authors voice different positions on identical issues; and of course all authors present original points on issues that only they discuss. This complexity represents well the field of educational development at the present moment, with its points of convergence, divergence, and growth. We hope that readers will experience in this book the field's rich accumulation of all that it has been and the considerable potential of all that it may become.

August 2009   *Kay J. Gillespie*
                  CKF Associates in Higher Education Development

                                                    Douglas L. Robertson
                                Florida International University

REFERENCES

Gillespie, K. H. (Ed.). (2002). *A guide to faculty development: Practical advice, examples, and resources.* Bolton, MA: Anker.

Wadsworth, E. C., Hilsen, L., & Shea, M. A. (Eds.). (1988). *A handbook for new practitioners.* Stillwater, OK: New Forums.

ABOUT THE AUTHORS

The Editors

Kay J. Gillespie works independently as a higher education consultant and editor. She is professor emerita at Colorado State University, where she was a tenured faculty member in the Department of Foreign Languages and Literatures, holding the PhD degree in Germanic languages and literatures from the University of Colorado at Boulder. Her discipline-specific research specialties were the work of the Swiss dramatist Friedrich Dürrenmatt and literary and artistic expression of Roma in the time of National Socialism. In 1976, she began working in faculty development and held the position of associate director of the Office of Instructional Services at Colorado State University from 1986 to 1995. Dr. Gillespie has served on the Core Committee (board of directors) and as the president of the Professional and Organizational Development (POD) Network in Higher Education, which is an international association focusing on faculty, instructional, and organizational development. She served on numerous committees within the association and had extensive involvement in conference planning and presentation. She also served as the executive director of the association from 2001 to 2006. She has written and presented on a variety of topics relating to faculty, instructional, and organizational development. She can be contacted at kaygi2@aol.com.

Douglas L. Robertson, PhD in cultural geography, Syracuse University, is dean of undergraduate education and professor of higher education at Florida International University. He has been involved in promoting innovation in U.S. higher education for more than thirty-three years and has twenty-four years of administrative experience in undergraduate and graduate education. In addition, he has held the rank of tenured full professor at five universities. Dr. Robertson has helped to start or reorganize four university professional development centers and has directed three of them. He is a member of the Professional and Organizational Development (POD) Core Committee and chair of its

Publication Committee. He serves as senior editor of a book series on college teaching (New Forums Press) and is a current or past member of the editorial boards for *Innovative Higher Education,* the *Journal for Excellence in College Teaching,* and the *Kentucky Journal for Excellence in College Teaching and Learning.* Recently he completed a five-year appointment as a Fulbright Senior Specialist Candidate. He has provided more than 150 consultations to educational, health care, human service, governmental, and business organizations. He has authored or coedited six books, including *Making Time, Making Change: Avoiding Overload in College Teaching* and *Self-Directed Growth.* In total, he has authored or coauthored more than 110 academic articles, books, chapters, and presentations as well as assorted poems. He can be reached at drobert@fiu.edu.

The Authors

Ann E. Austin is the Dr. Mildred B. Erickson Distinguished Professor of Higher, Adult, and Lifelong Education at Michigan State University. She received her PhD in higher education from the University of Michigan. She is co-principal investigator for the Center for the Integration of Research, Teaching, and Learning (CIRTL) and directs an institute at Michigan State that focuses on higher education issues in the global context. Professor Austin's research interests concern faculty careers and professional development, organizational change and transformation in higher education, reform in graduate education, and the improvement of teaching and learning processes in higher education. She can be reached at aaustin@msu.edu.

William H. Bergquist is an international coach and consultant. He has authored forty-four books and served as president of a graduate school. Bergquist consults on and writes about personal, group, organizational, and societal transformations. He spent many years working in the field of faculty development, helped to found the Professional and Organizational Development (POD) Network, and published a three-volume series of handbooks on faculty development. Other publications over the past three decades focus on issues in higher education, including curriculum design, program development, quality and access, and the subcultures that operate in the academy. In recent years, he has focused on the processes of organizational coaching, having written several books on the topic; and he cofounded the *International Journal of Coaching in Organizations* and the International Consortium for Coaching in Organizations. He can be reached at whbergquist@aol.com.

Laura L. B. Border, director of the Graduate Teacher Program, University of Colorado at Boulder, received her doctorate in French Literature from the University of Colorado at Boulder and has coauthored five editions of *Collage and Montage.* She served on the Professional and Organizational Development (POD) Network in Higher Education's Core Committee and as president of the organization from 2002 to 2004. She is currently a campus leader for the National Center for the Integration of Research Teaching and Learning (CIRTL) Network. Her interests include learning styles, nonbiased teaching, and the preparation of graduate students in all disciplines as current teaching assistants and as future faculty. She can be reached at laura.border@colorado.edu.

Helen Burnstad is director emerita of staff and organizational development at Johnson County Community College; she now consults with community colleges on staff and organizational development matters. She received her EdD in higher education administration with an emphasis on community college teaching and staff development from the University of Arkansas in Fayetteville. Her research interests are in community college staff development programs, adjunct faculty development, development of mid-level managers in community colleges, and organizational development. She can be reached at helenb@jccc.edu.

Nancy Van Note Chism is professor of higher education and student affairs in the Indiana University School of Education, Indianapolis. She received her PhD in educational policy and leadership from The Ohio State University and led professional and organizational development activities there and at Indiana University-Purdue University Indianapolis for more than twenty years. Her research interests are educational development, especially in international contexts; the faculty profession; peer review of teaching; and college teaching and learning topics such as multicultural teaching, the impact of physical space on learning, and instructional technology. She can be reached at nchism@iupui.edu.

Margaret W. Cohen is associate professor of educational psychology and associate provost for professional development and founding director of the Center for Teaching and Learning at the University of Missouri–St. Louis. She earned her PhD in educational psychology from Washington University in St. Louis. Her scholarship focuses on professional development and teaching and learning processes, including faculty and student engagement. She can be contacted at Peggy_Cohen@umsl.edu.

Constance Ewing Cook is associate vice provost and executive director of the Center for Research on Learning and Teaching at the University of Michigan, where she also serves as clinical professor of education. She received her PhD in political science from Boston University. Her research interests are institutional transformation strategies, with a focus on creating a culture of teaching, and educational development strategies, with a focus on department chairpersons and international higher education leaders. She can be contacted at cecook@umich.edu.

Donna E. Ellis is the associate director of the Centre for Teaching Excellence at the University of Waterloo. She received her MA from the University of Waterloo in language and professional writing and is a doctoral candidate in Waterloo's Management Sciences program. Her research interests include students' responses to innovative teaching and assessment methods and the professional development of new educational developers and graduate students. She can be contacted at donnae@uwaterloo.ca.

Jennifer L. Franklin is senior consultant for faculty and course evaluation in the Office of Institutional Research and Planning Support, University of Arizona (UA), and is also instructional development and assessment specialist at UA's Learning Technologies Center. She received her PhD in instructional systems technology from Indiana University. Her research interests include effective teaching and learning across the disciplines, teacher and course evaluation, and online instructional practices. As proprietor of Instructional Development and Evaluation Services, she has consulted on teacher-course evaluation systems at a wide range of postsecondary institutions. She can be contacted at jennyfra@email.arizona.edu.

David Gosling is an independent higher education consultant and visiting research fellow at the University of Plymouth, United Kingdom. He received his PhD from Leeds University in the philosophy of education and was head of educational development at the University of East London until 2002. His current research interests are the role and functions of faculty development centers internationally, the Centres for Excellence in Teaching and Learning (in the United Kingdom), peer-supported review of teaching and learning, and critical histories of academic development (an international study). He can be contacted at dwg@davidgosling.net.

Cynthia J. Hoss is provost/chief academic officer at Grantham University. Her EdD in curriculum, instruction, and administration is from the University of Nebraska–Lincoln. Dr. Hoss has served for thirty-four years in public and private two-year and four-year institutions of higher education. She has served two terms as president of the North American Council for Staff, Program, and Organizational Development (NCSPOD) and is a Higher Learning Commission consultant evaluator.

Her research interests are faculty development, instruction/academic assessment, institutional effectiveness, and leadership. She can be reached at choss@grantham.edu.

Alan Kalish is director of the University Center for the Advancement of Teaching and adjunct assistant professor of education policy and leadership at The Ohio State University. He received his PhD in English and American literature from Indiana University. He teaches in the Graduate Interdisciplinary Specialization in College and University Teaching. His research interests include qualitative and quantitative studies of transitions from graduate school to faculty life, teaching and learning in higher education, peer review of teaching, preparing future faculty, support for scholarship of teaching and learning, and assessment of academic support units. He can be reached at kalish.3@osu.edu.

Sally Kuhlenschmidt has been the director of the Faculty Center for Excellence in Teaching at Western Kentucky University since 1994. She received her PhD in clinical psychology from Purdue University and has been engaged with technology for instruction since her teaching career began in 1986, including teaching online since 1997. She initiated the original Professional and Organizational Development (POD) Network conference Web site and is a long-term member of POD's electronic communications and resources committee. Her center has received repeated recognition for innovation from POD. Her current research interests include assessment of faculty development and using technology to enhance development. She can be reached at sally.kuhlenschmidt@wku.edu.

Virginia S. Lee is senior consultant and managing member of Virginia S. Lee & Associates, a higher education consulting firm based in Durham, North Carolina, focusing on teaching, learning, and assessment. Special areas of expertise include course and curriculum development, inquiry-guided learning, and institution-wide education reform efforts including quality enhancement plans. Lee is the editor of *Teaching and Learning Through Inquiry: A Guidebook for Institutions and Instructors* (Stylus, 2004). She was the 2008 president of the Professional and Organizational Development (POD) Network in Higher Education. She received her PhD in educational psychology from the University of North Carolina at Chapel Hill. She can be reached at vslee@virginiaslee.com.

Michele Marincovich is associate vice provost for undergraduate education and director of the Center for Teaching and Learning at Stanford University. She received her PhD in (East Asian) history from Georgetown University. A former executive director of the Professional and Organizational Development Network, she has written and presented on the improvement of teaching at research universities, teaching assistant training, the design and evaluation of faculty development programs, teaching evaluation approaches, and the role of disciplinary differences in higher education. She can be reached at marin@stanford.edu.

Kim M. Mooney is interim provost and vice president for academic affairs at her undergraduate alma mater, Franklin Pierce University. She earned her PhD in social psychology from the University of New Hampshire. Dr. Mooney is the founding director of the Center for Teaching and Learning and former special assistant to the president for assessment at St. Lawrence University. Her recent publications address the results of a national survey on the professional experiences of women psychologists, the exploration of key professional development issues at liberal arts colleges, and a set of strategies for starting faculty development programs at small colleges. She can be reached at mooneyk@ franklinpierce.edu.

Ed Neal holds the PhD in adult and higher education from the University of North Carolina at Chapel Hill and was the founding director of the Office of Faculty Development at the University of North Carolina at Chapel Hill. He served in that capacity for thirty-two years but recently retired and continues as a professional consultant in higher education, working with his partner, Iola Peed-Neal, to provide faculty development services to colleges and universities across the United States. He can be reached at Ed_Neal@unc.edu.

Leslie Ortquist-Ahrens is associate professor of foreign languages and founding director of the Center for Teaching and Learning at Otterbein College in Westerville, Ohio. She received her PhD in comparative literature with emphases in German, film, and mass culture studies from Indiana University. In addition to German, she has taught literature and writing for the Integrative Studies core curriculum and cotaught a Senior-Year Experience about global citizenship at Otterbein. Her research interests include mass culture in Germany in the 1920s and faculty development topics including facilitation, faculty learning communities, critical reflection, and collaborative learning. She can be reached at LOrtquist-Ahrens@otterbein.edu.

Mathew L. Ouellett is director of the Center for Teaching at the University of Massachusetts Amherst. He received his EdD in social justice education from the University of Massachusetts Amherst. He directs a full complement of faculty development programs at the center and holds an adjunct appointment in the Smith College School for Social Work, where he teaches graduate courses on the implications of race and racism and social work practice in the United States.

His research interests include issues of inclusive teaching and learning and diversity and systemic change in higher education. He can be reached at mlo@acad.umass.edu.

Iola Peed-Neal earned the MFA from the University of North Carolina at Greensboro and served as a faculty developer and associate director of the Center for Teaching and Learning at the University of North Carolina at Chapel Hill for thirty-two years. She retired in 2008 and now consults on administrative and practical issues associated with teaching improvement programs. She also works with Ed Neal on projects and services for institutions of higher education and can be reached at Iola_Peed-Neal@unc.edu.

Kathryn M. Plank is associate director of the University Center for the Advancement of Teaching and adjunct assistant professor of educational policy and leadership at The Ohio State University. She received her PhD in English from The Pennsylvania State University. She teaches a graduate course on college teaching and coordinates faculty learning community programs. Her research interests include program assessment, teaching consultation, diversity, educational technology, critical thinking, and team teaching. She can be reached at plank.28@osu.edu.

Michael Reder directs Connecticut College's Joy Shechtman Mankoff Faculty Center for Teaching & Learning, where he runs a variety of programs designed to support faculty and improve student learning. He holds the PhD in English Literature from the University of Massachusetts Amherst. He serves on the advisory boards for the Professional and Organizational Development (POD) Network publication *Essays on Teaching Excellence* and for the POD series published in *Thriving in Academe* and is an editorial review board member for the journal *Innovative Higher Education*. He serves as a Teagle Assessment Scholar on the Wabash National Study of Liberal Arts Education and consults regularly with small liberal arts colleges starting or enhancing their faculty development programs. He can be reached at reder@conncoll.edu.

Mary Deane Sorcinelli is associate provost and professor of educational policy, research, and administration, University of Massachusetts Amherst. She received her EdD in educational policy, research, and administration from the University of Massachusetts Amherst and has led professional and organizational development activities at Indiana University Bloomington and the University of Massachusetts Amherst for more than two decades. Her research interests include the academic career development process, from new to senior faculty; mentoring programs for new and underrepresented faculty; faculty development in North America and international contexts; and a range of topics related to the improvement and evaluation of college teaching. She can be reached at msorcinelli@acad.umass.edu.

Christine A. Stanley is vice president and associate provost for diversity and professor of higher education at Texas A & M University. She received her PhD in curriculum and instruction from Texas A & M University. Her research interests include college teaching, diversity, and professional development in higher education. Since 2003, most of her research has focused on the experiences of faculty of color in predominantly white colleges and universities. She served as president of the Professional and Organizational Development Network in Higher Education from 2000 to 2001. She can be reached at cstanley@tamu.edu.

Terri A. Tarr is the associate director of the Center for Teaching and Learning and an adjunct faculty member in the Department of Psychology at Indiana University-Purdue University Indianapolis (IUPUI). She earned a PhD in developmental psychology from Purdue University as well as an MA in school psychology and a BA in psychology from Ball State University. She has written and presented on part-time faculty issues and served as the director of the Associate Faculty Office at IUPUI from 1998 to 2006. She can be reach at tatarr@iupui.edu.

Michael Theall is associate professor of teacher education at Youngstown State University (YSU), Youngstown, Ohio, and 2009 president of the Professional and Organizational Development Network in Higher Education. He received his PhD from Syracuse University with a focus on instructional design, development, and evaluation. He teaches graduate education courses and first-year college survival courses, and he coordinates the professional development program for YSU's Beeghley College of Education. His research interests are the professoriate, faculty evaluation, student ratings of teaching, faculty professional development, higher education organizational development, college teaching and learning, and motivational issues. He can be reached at mtheall@ysu.edu.

Franklin Tuitt is assistant professor and director of the Higher Education Program in the Morgridge College of Education at the University of Denver. He received his doctorate from the Harvard Graduate School of Education. His research and scholarship explore a range of topics related to access and equity in higher education, teaching and learning in racially diverse college classrooms, and diversity and organizational transformation. Dr. Tuitt serves as a consultant and trainer for education-related organizations across the country. He can be reached at ftuitt@du.edu.

Linda M. von Hoene is the director of the Graduate Student Instructor (GSI) Teaching and Resource Center at the University of California (UC), Berkeley. She received her PhD in German studies from UC Berkeley.

She teaches courses for graduate students at UC Berkeley on teaching and learning in higher education, designing courses to enhance student motivation, and mentoring in higher education. Her research interests are in the professional development of graduate students and future faculty; course design and motivation; and feminist, psychoanalytic, and postcolonial perspectives on the teaching and learning of foreign languages. She can be reached at vonhoene@berkeley.edu.

Catherine M. Wehlburg is the executive director of the Office for Assessment and Quality Enhancement at Texas Christian University. She received her PhD in educational psychology from the University of Florida. Dr. Wehlburg is interested in the use of assessment data as a means for transforming teaching and learning. She works with the Commission on Colleges of the Southern Association of Colleges and Schools as an accreditation visitor focusing on institutional effectiveness issues. She can be reached at c.wehlburg@tcu.edu.

Todd D. Zakrajsek is the executive director of the Center for Faculty Excellence at the University of North Carolina at Chapel Hill. Prior to his current appointment, he established both the Faculty Center for Innovative Teaching at Central Michigan University and the Center for Teaching and Learning at Southern Oregon University. While at Southern Oregon, he taught in the psychology department as a tenured associate professor. Dr. Zakrajsek publishes and presents widely on the topic of student learning and faculty development. He directs two conferences devoted to teaching and learning, one national and one international. He can be reached at tzak@email.unc.edu.

A GUIDE TO FACULTY DEVELOPMENT

PART ONE

ESTABLISHING AND SUSTAINING A FACULTY DEVELOPMENT PROGRAM

This part of the book consists of eight chapters that provide an introduction to the field, its history, literature, and key themes; an identification of basic issues, decisions, and practicalities in establishing and sustaining successful educational development programs; and a discussion of essential knowledge and skills that one needs in order to excel as an educational developer.

OVERVIEW OF FACULTY DEVELOPMENT

HISTORY AND CHOICES

Mathew L. Ouellett

MY PURPOSE IN THIS CHAPTER is to set the stage broadly for the chapters that follow; to call readers' attention to some of the literature, both body of practice and research based, upon which much of this book is built; and to suggest key questions that await further pursuit as we continue to expand and refine the work of faculty development. For both seasoned and beginning practitioners, the good news is that during the past several decades our colleagues have steadily contributed to a rich body of knowledge that serves to illuminate why we pursue our work in the ways we do, how we do what we do, and what the principles and values are that undergird what we do.

A Note on Language and Scope

In the Preface of this volume, the volume editors address common confusion that stems from our currently fuzzy and interchangeable use of terms, including *educational development, faculty development,* and *professional development.* As the editors point out, our community is in the process of building consensus on what words best describe our work, but we are not there yet. Therefore, readers of this volume will see the field named by a number of terms. I invite readers to join this ongoing conversation.

In order to provide a broad foundation for the topics covered in depth by specific chapters, my goal here is twofold: to summarize the historical context and to introduce topics and questions addressed in later chapters of this volume. The test is to achieve these two goals succinctly and without "stealing the thunder" or unnecessarily repeating the efforts of my colleagues. Their chapters provide the best in research, practice, and innovative approaches and offer an in-depth exploration of the implications of these issues from the perspective of educational developers.

A Brief History of Faculty Development

Colleges and universities in the United States have a long history of commitment to the development and success of faculty members related to their disciplinary expertise and research. Lewis (1996) pointed out that the sabbatical leave instituted at Harvard University in 1810 is probably the oldest form of faculty development. The primary goal of this early program was to support faculty members' further development as scholars within their fields. Well into the 1960s, this focus on increasing research expertise was the standard of support in colleges and universities.

Faculty development, as we understand it today, began to emerge in U.S. higher education in the social and economic turbulence of the late 1950s and 1960s (Bergquist, 1992; Rice, 2007; Sorcinelli, Austin, Eddy, & Beach, 2006). With the advent of the student rights movement across higher education in the United States, students began to demand more control over what they studied (for example, the emergence of ethnic studies programs) and to assert the right to give teachers feedback on what they found to be boring and irrelevant courses (Gaff & Simpson, 1994). Additionally, students began to demand a role in the determination of the content of the curriculum, expecting that courses would be, in their perceptions, more relevant to their experiences, concerns, and aspirations.

The reimagination of faculty life in the 1960s and 1970s encompassed the broadening of what should constitute the central work of faculty. This was the recognition that success for faculty members had been defined almost exclusively by research and publication success. The expansion to include a more holistic focus on, and concomitant rewards for, excellence in teaching and service was a dramatic departure from what had been a generally accepted standard. Faculty members increasingly advocated that institutional and career rewards, particularly tenure and promotion standards, should reflect a broad understanding of the nature of their work. These shifting perspectives on the roles and rewards for faculty members in higher education intertwined with two concurrent important social movements: the human potential and the student rights movements (Bergquist, 1992; Gaff & Simpson, 1994; Lewis, 1996, Rice, 2007). This era launched a reevaluation of the traditional focus on the role of researcher and introduced a reappraisal of the value of and rewards for faculty members who focused on excellence in teaching. This dialogue continues on college and university campuses and within professional associations as well.

Stages of Faculty Development Work

A number of authors have suggested models for understanding the stages in the evolution of the research and practices in faculty development during the past several decades (Rice, 2007; Sorcinelli et al., 2006; Tiberius, 2001). In *Creating the Future of Faculty Development: Learning from the Past, Understanding the Present,* Sorcinelli et al. (2006) categorized the evolution of faculty development into four past ages (scholar, teacher, developer, and learner) and one new one (the age of the networker).

In their conceptualization, Sorcinelli et al. described the first stage (roughly the mid-1950s into the early 1960s) as the Age of the Scholar, indicating that during this time faculty development efforts intended to improve scholarly competence. In the 1950s and early 1960s, few institutions had formal programs addressing teaching improvement. The focus of support was on the development of scholarly expertise as indicated by research success and publication rates. Heiss (1970) noted that the pervasive norms of the time honored the development of research skills through "rigorous exposure to theory and practice" (p. 229) but held that teaching skills came "naturally" or automatically as one's scholarship increased. Not surprisingly, researchers at the time noted that few doctoral programs included any formal pedagogical training (Nowlis, Clark, & Rock, 1968). In practical terms, faculty members understood that the pathway to success was based upon research and publication records.

The second stage, the Age of the Teacher, spanned the mid-1960s through the 1970s and witnessed an extension to include faculty, instructional, and organizational components of the improvement of teaching effectiveness. This period saw increased numbers of faculty members becoming dissatisfied with the narrowing of resources and sole focus on research as the definitive benchmark of faculty accomplishment. Recognizing the changing landscape, individuals and foundations began to argue for a broadening of the definition of scholarship and an exploration of other venues for faculty fulfillment and vitality (Astin, Comstock, Epperson, Greeley, Katz, & Kaufman, 1974; Rice, 2007). At this same time, research institutions began to respond to these changing demands by establishing faculty development opportunities (Eble & McKeachie, 1985). Melnik and Sheehan (1976) described three key forms of "teaching improvement programs" that began to emerge at this time as "one-shot" programs, expert centers, and financial incentive programs. The one-time programs included workshops, colloquia, and other opportunities of relatively brief duration. Examples of the "expert center" include the Center for Research on Learning and Teaching established at the University of Michigan, Ann Arbor, in 1962 and the Clinic to Improve Teaching at the University of Massachusetts Amherst established in 1972 (Melnik & Sheehan, 1976; Tiberius, 2001). Such centers offered sustained teaching improvement services and advice often delivered by faculty colleagues who had been granted release time. The financial incentive programs were small grants for individual faculty members to develop and implement teaching improvement projects. During this period, a group of faculty members and higher education scholars founded the Professional and Organizational Development Network in Higher Education (POD) in 1974, which was a pivotal event in the evolution of what we now call faculty or educational development.

Sorcinelli et al. (2006) then defined the 1980s as the Age of the Developer. This period saw a number of faculty development units emerge formally on campuses and a greater institutionalization of the role of faculty developers (Eble & McKeachie, 1985; Erickson, 1986; Sorcinelli et al., 2006). Initiatives on changing the state of undergraduate education from private foundations (for example, the Bush, Ford, and Lilly Foundations) helped provide the resources and motivation for innovation and experimentation with new approaches to teaching and faculty development (Sorcinelli et al., 2006).

The 1990s was the Age of the Learner. In a dramatic paradigm shift, the focus of teaching and instructional development moved from what had been a singular focus on the development of the pedagogical expertise and platform skills of teachers (the "sage on the stage") to include a focus on student learning (teachers as the "guide on the side"). This shift caused a surge of interest in student-centered pedagogical methods such as active and collaborative approaches and problem and inquiry-based learning strategies that brought students directly into the teaching and learning equation (Barr & Tagg, 1995; Sorcinelli et al., 2006). This decade also saw a profusion of new, more complex options and resources for initiatives in faculty, instructional, and organizational development. The relatively fast evolution of faculty support programs—from periodic sabbatical leaves to extend one's disciplinary expertise to comprehensive institution-wide programs that address faculty needs for growth and development across career stages and roles—is perhaps the greatest testament to the resonance and value of a more systemic approach to educational development.

Finally, Sorcinelli et al. (2006) proposed that we have now entered a new stage, the Age of the Networker. In this age, faculty developers will be called upon to "preserve, clarify, and enhance the purposes of faculty development, and to network with faculty and institutional leaders to respond to institutional problems and propose constructive solutions as we meet the challenges of the new century . . ." (p. 28).

Data gathered by Sorcinelli et al. (2006) indicate a rapidly growing constellation of individuals responsible for education development activities on campuses. The majority of survey respondents identified their primary roles as administrative, and they were relatively new to the field (that is, ten or fewer years); but more than three-fifths of respondents indicated they held faculty appointments. Additionally, some centers may now have staff positions, especially in centers located within larger institutional settings. Thus, we now have a pipeline of practitioners who may not have followed traditional faculty career pathways but bring specific expertise, such as instructional technology, to educational development. "As a group they [faculty developers] tend to be relatively new to the field with only one-quarter reporting that they have been in faculty development for a decade or more" (p. 36). This surge has created great interest in strengthening the dialogue between seasoned faculty development practitioners and relative newcomers, with the idea that there is much to be learned from each other. Not surprisingly, our articulation of what we do has evolved, too.

Building a Common Lexicon

Early on, Francis (1975) defined *faculty development* as a primarily classroom-based, individualized endeavor: a "process which seeks to modify the attitudes, skills, and behavior of faculty members toward greater competence and effectiveness in meeting student needs, their own needs, and the needs of the institution" (p. 720). Nearly twenty years later, Lewis (1996) noted that the term *faculty development* had evolved, as had the field, into a more expansive term meant to encompass three key areas of effort: personal development (self-reflection, vitality, and growth), instructional development (course and student-based initiatives), and organizational development (program, departmental, and institution-wide efforts). Diamond (2002) pointed out that these approaches are not mutually exclusive, but that, in combination, they allow for a tailoring of programs and resources best suited to the questions and goals at hand.

Diamond (2002) offered a further analysis of roles by presenting them as interdependent domains of faculty, instructional, organizational, and professional development. In his perspective, these roles parse out as follows. Faculty development focuses on the improvement of the individual instructor's teaching skills; instructional development on students' learning by improving the course and curriculum experience; and organizational development on the interrelationship and effectiveness of units within the institution; finally, educational development refers to the overall interaction resulting from the prior three efforts (Diamond, 1988, 2002).

Faculty development, professional development, organizational development, and the *scholarship of teaching and learning* interchangeably refer to aspects of the wide array of duties taken on by faculty developers. In international contexts, the more encompassing term *educational development* is used to cover the related initiatives for academic development, staff development, and quality enhancement. Recently, Felten, Kalish, Pingree, and Plank (2007) have argued for the adoption of the term *educational development* as the most inclusive term to describe "a profession dedicated to helping colleges and universities function effectively as teaching and learning communities" (p. 93). These several terms, and the accompanying confusion about when and how to use them accurately, are indicative of the fast-paced, international growth of the field and the complexity of competing demands arising from these often overlapping functions (Gosling, Sorcinelli, & Chism, 2008).

Today, the demands placed upon faculty members and the complexity of their roles and responsibilities continue to evolve at an astonishing pace. Consequently, our understanding of what constitutes "faculty development" and our language to articulate these changes in perspective will continue to evolve to reflect new conceptualizations.

Expanding the Horizon of Faculty Development

Changes in higher education and in the expectations of faculty members, including paradigm shifts in our approaches to teaching and learning and emergent research on the stages of faculty life, contribute significantly to the scope and breadth of faculty development. In their comprehensive research study, Sorcinelli et al. (2006) polled faculty developers to discern the three top challenges they saw facing the faculty and higher education institutions. As one would expect, respondents reported a range of priorities, but five emerged across institution type and size as central. These five concerns were

1. Balancing increasingly complex and demanding faculty roles
2. Assessment of teaching and student learning (especially in the context of increasingly diverse students)
3. The impact of technology
4. Addressing the needs of part-time faculty
5. The demands of interdisciplinary leadership development for chairs and institutions (pp. 104–105)

Response to the study to date indicates that these challenges resonate internationally as well (Gosling, Sorcinelli, & Chism, 2008).

Chism (2006) indicated that there is utility in approaching the work of educational development from multiple perspectives. She explained that one benefit of such an approach is that it prompts us to identify the strategies, theoretical perspectives, and consultation practices best suited for the challenge at hand. Inarguably, there is reason to respond to the priorities and unique needs of one's institution. However, as faculty developers, we often have an institution-wide platform from which to work; and this perspective offers an opportunity to introduce new ideas, models, and practices that influence the development and progress of the institution.

In the chapters that follow, our colleagues address the specific content knowledge, skills, and values needed for success in promoting effective educational development. Some of these chapters dovetail neatly with the historical development of the field of faculty or educational development, and others point to emergent priorities. Collectively, they contribute to helping both new and experienced educational developers think more creatively, act more holistically, and meet the complex needs of diverse constituents more successfully in the future. Next, I briefly highlight four key topics that are of universal concern for educational developers: (1) the increasingly complex roles of faculty members, (2) the focus assessment of student learning and curricular innovations, (3) technology, and (4) diversity.

Complex Roles of Faculty Members

The definition of the scope of faculty work traditionally involved research, teaching, and service. The common wisdom used to be that the more expert you were within your disciplinary concentration (in other words, the better your research), the better your teaching. While it is true that great teachers can be great researchers and great researchers can be great teachers, it is not necessarily so for all. Consequently, efforts to apply adult development, educational psychology, and learning theories to the faculty development context have helped practitioners to determine when to use different strategies to bring about professional growth and development (Herbert & Loy, 2001; McKeachie, 1991; Menges & Rando, 1989). Faculty developers have long been familiar with the usefulness of theories of learning (Kolb, 1984), reflective practice (Brookfield, 1995; Schön, 1983), adult education (Saroyan, Amundsen, & Li, 1997), and adult learning theories (King & Lawler, 2003).

However, as research documents, the needs and values of the faculty are changing at every stage of the career path; our guiding theories and practices must do so, too. We will benefit from approaching these needs with creativity and generosity (Rice, Sorcinelli, & Austin, 2000; Sorcinelli & Austin, 2006; Trower, 2000). Chapter Twenty-Two, entitled "Supporting Faculty Members Across Their Careers," directly addresses these issues.

For example, with new and junior faculty members we now see an increased demand for better balance between work and life, support for the challenges of dual-career couples, and an acknowledgment of the demands of parenting as well as taking care of aging parents. We already see innovative efforts to rethink traditional support mechanisms. Gonzales and Baran (2005) have written eloquently about how their sustained multicultural dialogue between senior and junior faculty members in the same department became a mutually rewarding exchange of expertise and skills and how their relationship became a model of interracial dialogue for students. Another example is the complete reenvisioning of mentoring moving from top-down, individualized models to mutual mentoring (peer-to-peer) communities to meet the socialization needs of new and junior faculty and faculty of color (Yun & Sorcinelli, 2007, 2008).

Additionally, there is growing interest in addressing the pre-professional needs of senior graduate students, especially those who expect to pursue careers in academia. The Council of Graduate Schools in partnership with the Association of American Colleges formed the Preparing Future Faculty initiative in 1993 as an early effort to develop resources and programmatic models to prepare students for faculty careers within a wide array of institutional settings (Council of Graduate Schools, 2008). However, we know that much remains to be done to establish healthier and more transparent models of graduate education and preparation for the professoriate (Gaff, Pruitt-Logan, Sims, & Denecke, 2003; Golde & Dore, 2001; Lovitts, 2001). While this topic has been of particular interest to developers located in research universities (Nyquist, Austin, Sprague, & Wulff, 2001; Nyquist & Sprague, 1998; Wulff & Austin, 2004), in truth many graduate students will become junior colleagues at institutions of varying types and sizes. Border and von Hoene provide guidance on these issues in their chapter entitled "Graduate and Professional Student Development Programs" (Chapter Twenty).

Finally, the exponential growth in the numbers of both part-time faculty appointments and adjunct faculty members, specifically addressed in Tarr's chapter on "Working with Adjunct Faculty Members" (Chapter Twenty-One), presents educational developers with the challenge of addressing the needs of these often under-acknowledged members of the academic community.

Assessment of Student Learning and Curricular Innovations

Faculty development emerged partially out of a need to alleviate concerns of parents and legislators and to assure them that students could experience an optimal teaching and learning environment (Lewis, 1996). Today, due to a range of pressures, including budgetary concerns, legislative activism, and changing accreditation standards, the assessment and accountability movements have sharpened the interests of the faculty and academic administrators in finding methods for informing parents, legislators, citizens, prospective students, and alumni how well students are doing in achieving course-based, program, and institutional learning goals (Wehlburg, 2006). Such efforts apply to a wide array of academic development initiatives beyond the classroom.

Faculty developers can make important contributions in this area by facilitating key discussions, providing empirical evidence based on evaluation and assessment data of current curricula, and assisting in the review of existing programs (Diamond, 2005). Developers have the skills, neutrality, and understanding of technology needed to help organize and facilitate meetings before faculty members and key administrators finalize major decisions. They also can provide expertise and resources to help design and pilot course innovations and assess program enhancements. Additionally, developers continually acquire data useful in the assessment and evaluation of new curricula. For example, Cook (2001) offered a useful description of instructional consultants' involvement in a recent curriculum reform effort on the campus of the University of

Michigan, and Smith (2000) described a program sponsored by the Fund for the Improvement of Postsecondary Education to promote faculty use of inquiry-based learning methods. Chapters in this book address these matters in detail.

Technology

Instructional technology is now ubiquitous in most colleges and universities. For many faculty members the central issues related to technology have moved from questions about whether or not to use the technologies to questions of when, to what degree, and to what ends to use them. As we know, when implemented appropriately, the emerged and emerging technologies can act as a great accelerator to the teaching and learning process. For example, on my campus, students often cite course Web sites as one of the most useful instructional resources for them, enabling them to keep up with course announcements, check due dates for assignments, and retrieve course presentations or notes.

The good news is that faculty members are often willing to admit they need assistance when implementing instructional technologies. The rewards can be immediate when students demonstrate that such uses can make a positive difference in their classroom experiences. The bad news is that linking good teaching practices with effective use of instructional technology can be frustratingly labor intensive, unpredictable, and expensive. Issues commonly cited are the cost of hardware and software, lack of clarity about copyright and fair use practices, and the social implications of the role of technology in the teaching and learning relationship (Shih & Sorcinelli, 2000). What is clear is that it takes a steady hand to guide instructors in using technology to enhance instead of to replace existing pedagogies. It is especially effective when the choices of applications clearly suit a professor's teaching style or can be seen to accommodate a student's learning style needs (Gibbs, Major, & Wright, 2003; Shih & Sorcinelli, 2000).

A knotty but pervasive issue on campuses today is the role of hybrid and distance education courses. For some, such courses are an expedient cost-cutting or revenue-producing measure or a strategy to maximize usage of limited classroom space rather than a conscious pedagogical preference. However, as any faculty member who has taught online will attest, it is rarely true that online or hybrid courses are less effort for the instructor than ones taught face to face. It will continue to be important for faculty developers to help facilitate the dialogue between instructors and administrators as they explore the underlying assumptions, values, and beliefs about teaching embedded in such online initiatives (Chickering

& Ehrmann, 1996). On the plus side, conversations about technology initiatives create opportunities for networking across campus. The chapter "Issues in Technology and Faculty Development" by Sally Kuhlenschmidt (Chapter Sixteen) provides more discussion of these issues.

Diversity of Faculty and Students

Since the 1970s, faculty developers have paid close attention to the importance of reviews of organizational structures (Diamond, 1988; Graf, Albright, & Wheeler, 1992; Lindquist, 1978). Such efforts have generally focused on the effectiveness of programmatic efforts and innovations along the three common dimensions described earlier: individual consultation and support services, instructional development initiatives at program and department levels, and organizational development. More recently, however, practitioners and scholars have called for more sustained analysis at the organizational level (Baron, 2006; Chism, 1998). What has been neglected is how deeply diversity and multicultural dynamics embed these issues at every level of our practice (Jacobson, Borgford-Parnell, Frank, Peck, & Reddick, 2001; Lieberman, 2007).

However, as complex new issues confront us, new research and practice models for understanding organizations can be essential (Jackson, 2005; Lockhart & Borland, 2001). Marchesani and Jackson (2005) have applied the theory and practice of multicultural organization development (MCOD) to educational institutions. This data-driven model is a tool for supporting social justice and diversity goals in the context of a systemic change initiative. Unlike other organizational change systems, in the MCOD model a level of social justice must be present in order to pursue social diversity. Our field would benefit from an expansion of research paradigms to include data-driven multicultural organization development models in order to expand our understanding of the unique contributions and challenges in different institutional settings, such as community colleges, Historically Black Colleges and Universities (HBCUs), predominately Hispanic Serving Institutions (HSIs), and Tribal Colleges.

Faculty development within community colleges is of concern because faculty members at such institutions are increasingly held accountable for student learning outcomes, adjusting to a learner-centered focus, and learning to incorporate technology in the classroom; they are being asked to teach effectively in far more diverse classroom environments than had been the case (Eddy, 2005). Quick growth in student populations, competition for resources, heavy teaching loads, and a lack of resources are often cited challenges. However, there is an increasingly strong effort to address these needs via organizations like the North American Council for Staff, Program and Organization Development (NCSPOD). Because community colleges are often feeder schools for nearby four-year colleges and universities, our workplaces, student populations, and the health and well-being of our institutions are increasingly tied together. (See Chapter Nineteen, "Faculty Development in the Context of the Community College," by Burnstad and Hoss).

Clearly, different types of institutions have their own faculty development needs (Sorcinelli et al., 2006). Historically Black Colleges and Universities have a unique historical tradition, culture, and mission in the context of higher education; and, just like other higher education institutions, they are responding to changing demands from faculty, students, and staff. The HBCU Faculty Development Network, founded in 1994, has been instrumental in facilitating the institutionalization of faculty development at these institutions as well as in highlighting their innovations in teaching and learning (Dawkins, Beach, & Rozman, 2006).

As with the relationships between community colleges and neighboring four-year institutions, faculty developers may overlook the benefits that may come from closer alignment with the work of colleagues across institutional type and mission. When feasible, we ought to look for ways to sustain dialogues that encourage and extend each other's work. A recent example of this became evident when members of the HBCU Faculty Development Network surveyed their members to determine what faculty development opportunities were offered on their campuses and what members saw as important future priorities. They were able to collaborate with a research team that had administered a similar survey to members of the predominately white organization, the POD Network (Sorcinelli, Austin, Eddy, & Beach, 2006). Ultimately, this allowed both research teams to compare data sets and to extend their projects' resources in important new directions (Dawkins, Beach, & Rozman, 2006).

Conclusion

This chapter ends as it began, with an understanding that not all issues carry the same salience for every faculty developer or in every institutional context. The task for practitioners, new or experienced, is to find the right balance and most useful array of programmatic offerings based on institutional needs, level of support, and faculty expectations. In fact, such diversity of perspectives, expectations, and effort contributes to the richness of the field of faculty development. Our charge is to identify and address those issues most central to the faculty and institutions we call home. Additionally, as the number of educational development practitioners continues to grow and as the field becomes increasingly professionalized, we need to give special attention to how we welcome a diverse group of practitioners to the field and support their preparation and training.

REFERENCES

Astin, A. W., Comstock, C., Epperson, D., Greeley, A., Katz, J., & Kaufman, R. (1974). *Faculty development in a time of retrenchment.* Washington, DC: Group for Human Development in Higher Education and Change.

Baron, L. (2006). The advantages of a reciprocal relationship between faculty development and organizational development in higher education. In S. Chadwick-Blossey & D. R. Robertson (Eds.), *To improve the academy: Vol. 24. Resources for faculty, instructional, and organizational development* (pp. 29–43). Bolton, MA: Anker.

Barr, R. B., & Tagg, J. (1995). From teaching to learning: A new paradigm for undergraduate education. *Change, 27*(6), 13–25.

Bergquist, W. H. (1992). *The four cultures of the academy: Insights and strategies for improving leadership in collegiate organizations.* San Francisco: Jossey-Bass.

Brookfield, S. (1995). *Becoming a critically reflective teacher.* San Francisco: Jossey-Bass.

Chickering, A., & Ehrmann, S. (1996, October). Implementing the seven principles: Technology as lever. *AAHE Bulletin,* 3–6.

Chism, N.V.N. (1998). The role of educational developers in institutional change: From the basement office to the front office. In M. Kaplan & D. Lieberman (Eds.), *To improve the academy: Vol. 17. Resources for faculty, instructional, and organizational development* (pp. 141–153). Bolton, MA: Anker.

Chism, N.V.N. (2006). POD connections: Faculty development theories. *NEFDC Exchange, 17*(1), 8.

Cook, C. E. (2001). The role of a teaching center in curriculum reform. In D. Lieberman & C. Wehlburg (Eds.), *To improve the academy: Vol. 19. Resources for faculty, instructional, and organizational development* (pp. 217–231). Bolton, MA: Anker.

Council of Graduate Schools. (2008). *The preparing future faculty program.* Retrieved November 5, 2008, from http://www.cgsnet.org

Dawkins, P. W., Beach, A. L., & Rozman, S. L. (2006). Perceptions of faculty developers about the present and future of faculty development at Historically Black Colleges and Universities. In S. Chadwick-Blossey

& D. R. Robertson (Eds.), *To improve the academy: Vol. 24. Resources for faculty, instructional, and organizational development* (pp. 104–120). Bolton, MA: Anker.

Diamond, R. M. (1988). Faculty development, instructional development, and organizational development: Options and choices. In E. C. Wadsworth (Ed.), *A handbook for new practitioners* (pp. 9–11). Stillwater, OK: New Forums.

Diamond, R. M. (2002). Faculty, instructional, and organizational development: Options and choices. In K. Gillespie, L. Hilsen, & E. Wadsworth (Eds.), *A guide to faculty development: Practical advice, examples, and resources* (pp. 2–8). Bolton, MA: Anker.

Diamond, R. M. (2005). The institutional change agency: The expanding role of academic support centers. In S. Chadwick-Blossey & D. R. Robertson (Eds.), *To improve the academy: Vol. 23. Resources for faculty, instructional, and organizational development* (pp. 24–37). Bolton, MA: Anker.

Eble, K. E., & McKeachie, W. J. (1985). *Improving undergraduate education through faculty development.* San Francisco: Jossey-Bass.

Eddy, P. L. (2005). Faculty development in community colleges: Surveying the present, preparing for the future. *Journal of Faculty Development 20*(3), 143–152.

Erickson, G. (1986). A survey of faculty development practices. In M. Svinicki, J. Kurfiss, & J. Stone (Eds.), *To improve the academy: Vol. 5. Resources for faculty, instructional, and organizational development* (pp. 182–196). Stillwater, OK: New Forums.

Felten, P., Kalish, A., Pingree, A., & Plank, K. (2007). Toward a scholarship of teaching and learning in educational development. In D. R. Robertson & L. B. Nilson (Eds.), *To improve the academy: Vol. 25. Resources for faculty, instructional, and organizational development* (pp. 93–108). Bolton, MA: Anker.

Francis, J. B. (1975). How do we get there from here? Program design for faculty development. *Journal of Higher Education, 46*(6), 719–732.

Gaff, J. G., Pruitt-Logan, A. S., Sims, L. B., & Denecke, D. (2003). *Preparing future faculty in the humanities and social sciences: A guide for change.* Washington, DC: American Association of Colleges and Universities, Council of Graduate Schools.

Gaff, J. G., & Simpson, R. D. (1994). Faculty development in the United States. *Innovative Higher Education, 18*(3), 167–176.

Gibbs, J. E., Major, C. H., & Wright, V. H. (2003). Faculty perception of the costs and benefits of instructional technology: Implications for faculty work. *Journal of Faculty Development, 19*(2), 77–88.

Golde, C. M., & Dore, T. M. (2001). *At cross purposes: What the experiences of doctoral students reveal about doctoral education.* A report prepared for The Pew Charitable Trusts. Retrieved December 8, 2008, from http://www.phd-survey.org

Gonzales, D., & Baran, J. (2005). Breaking the silence: Innovative approaches for promoting dialogue about diversity issues within a communication disorders department. In M. L. Ouellett (Ed.), *Teaching inclusively: Resources for course, department & institutional change in higher education* (pp. 225–240). Stillwater, OK: New Forums.

Gosling, D., Sorcinelli, M. D., & Chism, N.V.N. (2008, June). *The future of faculty/educational development: An international perspective.* Presentation at the biennial meeting of the International Consortium for Educational Development, Salt Lake City, UT.

Graf, D. L., Albright, M. J., & Wheeler, D. W. (1992). Faculty development's role in improving undergraduate education. In M. J. Albright & D. L. Graf (Eds.), *New directions for teaching and learning, no. 51. Teaching in the information age: The role of educational technology* (pp. 101–109). San Francisco: Jossey-Bass.

Heiss, A. M. (1970). *Challenges to graduate schools.* San Francisco: Jossey-Bass.

Herbert, F., & Loy, M. (2001). The evolution of a teacher professor: Applying behavior change theory to faculty development. In D. Lieberman & C. Wehlburg (Eds.), *To improve the academy: Vol. 20. Resources for faculty, instructional, and organizational development* (pp. 197–207). Bolton, MA: Anker.

Jackson, B. (2005). The theory and practice of multicultural organization development in education. In M. L. Ouellett (Ed.), *Teaching inclusively: Resources for course, department and institutional change in higher education* (pp. 3–20). Stillwater, OK: New Forums.

Jacobson, W., Borgford-Parnell, J., Frank, K., Peck, M., & Reddick, L. (2001). Operational diversity: Saying what we mean, doing what we say. In D. Lieberman & C. Wehlburg (Eds.), *To improve the academy: Vol. 20. Resources for faculty, instructional, and organizational development* (pp. 128–149). Bolton, MA: Anker.

King, K. P., & Lawler, P. A. (Eds.). (2003). *New directions for adult and continuing education, no. 98. New perspectives on designing and implementing professional development of teachers of adults.* San Francisco: Jossey-Bass.

Kolb, D. (1984). *Experiential learning: Experience as the source of learning and development.* Upper Saddle River, NJ: Prentice-Hall.

Lewis, K. G. (1996). A brief history and overview of faculty development in the United States. *International Journal for Academic Development, 1*(2), 26–33.

Lieberman, D. (2007). Diversity initiatives, institutional change, and curricular reform in higher education. In D. A. Brunson, B. Jarmon, & L. L. Lampl (Eds.), *Letters from the future: Linking students and teaching with the diversity of everyday life* (pp. 3–25). Sterling, VA: Stylus.

Lindquist, J. (1978). Approaches to collegiate teaching improvement. In J. Lindquist (Ed.), *Designing teaching improvement programs* (pp. 3–22). Berkeley, CA: Pacific Soundings.

Lockhart, M., & Borland Jr., K. (2001). Incorporating diversity in all faculty/staff development programs . . . Regardless of the content. *Journal of Faculty Development, 18*(2), 57–64.

Lovitts, B. E. (2001). *Leaving the ivory tower: The causes and consequences of departure from doctoral study.* Lanham, MD: Rowman & Littlefield.

Marchesani, L. M., & Jackson, B. W. (2005). Transforming higher education institutions using multicultural organizational development: A case study of a large northeastern university. In M. L. Oullett (Ed.), *Teaching inclusively: Resources for course, department, and institutional change in higher education* (pp. 214–251). Stillwater, OK: New Forums.

McKeachie, W. J. (1991). What theories underlie the practice of faculty development? In K. Zahorski (Ed.), *To improve the academy: Vol. 10. Resources for faculty, instructional, and organizational development* (pp. 3–8). Stillwater, OK: New Forums.

Melnik, M. A., & Sheehan, D. S. (1976). Clinical supervision elements: The clinic to improve university teaching. *Journal of Research and Development in Education, 9*(2), 67–76.

Menges, R., & Rando, W. (1989). What are your assumptions? Improving instruction by examining theories. *College Teaching, 37*(2), 54–60.

Nowlis, V., Clark, K. E., & Rock, M. (1968). *The graduate student as teacher.* Washington, DC: American Council on Education.

Nyquist, J. D., Austin, A. E., Sprague, J., & Wulff, D. H. (2001). *The development of graduate students as teaching scholars: A four-year longitudinal study, final report.* Seattle: University of Washington, Center for Instructional Development and Research.

Nyquist, J. D., & Sprague, J. (1998). Thinking developmentally about TAs. In M. Marincovich, J. Prostko, & F. Stout (Eds.), *The professional development of graduate teaching assistants* (pp. 61–88). Bolton, MA: Anker.

Polich, S. (2008). Assessment of a faculty learning community program: Do faculty members really change? In L. B. Nilson & J. E. Miller (Eds.), *To improve the academy: Vol. 26. Resources for faculty, instructional, and organizational development* (pp. 106–118). San Francisco: Jossey-Bass.

Rice, R. E. (2007). It all started in the sixties: Movements for change across the decades—a personal journey. In D. R. Robertson & L. B. Nilson (Eds.), *To improve the academy: Vol. 25. Resources for faculty, instructional, and organizational development* (pp. 3–17). Bolton, MA: Anker.

Rice, R. E., Sorcinelli, M. D., & Austin, A. E. (2000). *Heeding new voices: Academic careers for a new generation.* New Pathways Working Paper Series, no. 7. Washington, DC: American Association for Higher Education.

Saroyan, A., Amundsen, C., & Li, C. (1997). Incorporating theories of teacher growth and adult education in a faculty development program. In D. DeZure (Ed.), *To improve the academy: Vol. 16. Resources for faculty, instructional, and organizational development* (pp. 93–116). Stillwater, OK: New Forums.

Schön, D. A. (1983). *The reflective practitioner: How professionals think in action.* New York: Basic Books.

Shih, M., & Sorcinelli, M. D. (2000). TEACHnology: Linking teaching and technology in faculty development. In M. Kaplan & D. Lieberman (Eds.), *To improve the academy: Vol. 18. Resources for faculty, instructional, and organizational development* (pp. 151–163). Bolton, MA: Anker.

Smith, K. S. (2000). Faculty development that transforms the undergraduate experience at a research university. In D. Lieberman & C. Wehlburg (Eds.), *To improve the academy: Vol. 19. Resources for faculty, instructional, and organizational development* (pp. 193–204). Bolton, MA: Anker.

Sorcinelli, M. D., & Austin, A. E. (2006). Developing faculty for new roles and changing expectations. *Effective Practices for Academic Leaders, 1*(11), 1–16.

Sorcinelli, M. D., Austin, A. E., Eddy, P. L., & Beach, A. L. (2006). *Creating the future of faculty development: Learning from the past, understanding the present.* Bolton, MA: Anker.

Tiberius, R. G. (2001). A brief history of educational development: Implications for teachers and developers. In D. Lieberman & C. Wehlburg (Eds.), *To improve the academy: Vol. 20. Resources for faculty, instructional, and organizational development* (pp. 20–37). Bolton, MA: Anker.

Trower, C. A. (Ed.). (2000). *Policies on faculty appointment: Standard practices and unusual arrangements.* Bolton, MA: Anker.

Wehlburg, C. (2006). *Meaningful course revision: Enhancing academic engagement using student learning data*. Bolton, MA: Anker.

Wulff, D., & Austin, A. E. (Eds.). (2004). *Pathways to the professoriate: Strategies for enriching the preparation of future faculty*. San Francisco: Jossey-Bass.

Yun, J., & Sorcinelli, M. D. (2007). From mentors to mentoring networks: Mentoring in the new academy. *Change, 39*(6), 58–61.

Yun, J., & Sorcinelli, M. D. (2008). When mentoring is the medium: Lessons learned from a faculty development initiative. In L. B. Nilson & J. E. Miller (Eds.), *To improve the academy: Vol. 27. Resources for faculty, instructional, and organizational development* (pp. 365–384). San Francisco: Jossey-Bass.

2

PROGRAM TYPES AND PROTOTYPES

Virginia S. Lee

THE FIRST TEACHING CENTER IN THE UNITED STATES, the Center for Research on Learning and Teaching at the University of Michigan, Ann Arbor, was founded in 1962. It was followed shortly thereafter by the Clinic to Improve University Teaching at the University of Massachusetts Amherst. Since then, there has been a steady increase in the number of educational development centers in the United States and Canada, as well as beyond, with a flurry of start-ups early in the millennium. A barometer of this growth is the membership level in the Professional and Organizational Development (POD) Network, which has increased from twenty individuals in 1976 to nearly 1,800 members in 2007 and represents a range of institutions of higher education in the United States, Canada, and abroad.

Over the decades the field of faculty development has also changed. Lacking its own distinctive base of theory, research, and practice, in the 1950s and 1960s the field sought inspiration from the work of researchers and practitioners in elementary and secondary school environments. As a distinctive field, faculty development then found a toehold in the social ferment of the 1960s and 1970s; according to Bergquist (1992), it is the most conspicuous exemplar of the developmental culture that tried to address the perceived inadequacies of the collegial culture, the legacy of Oxford and Cambridge Universities on the one hand and the German research university on the other. During the same period, the research base on student development during the college years and teaching in colleges and universities grew; a variety of avenues to share best practices emerged and included conferences of professional organizations, journals devoted to college teaching, and publishing companies.

Over the same period, a dramatic transformation of the teaching and learning agenda occurred in higher education. With the erosion of the manufacturing base and the consolidation of the agricultural sector of the U.S. economy, the college degree replaced the high school diploma as a requirement of the knowledge economy. Student enrollments in colleges and universities increased, along with a steady democratization of higher education: today's student body includes more first-generation college students, more students of color, more international students, and more nontraditional students than ever before. The assessment movement caught hold, and with it came a growing demand for accountability from the American public as so-called consumers of higher education. Simultaneously, the academic disciplines evolved; new fields of study appeared, including alternative epistemologies arising from feminism, African American studies, critical theory, postmodernism, and multidisciplinary approaches. Instructional technologies became more pervasive and varied than ever before with the rise of the personal computer, software packages including the Microsoft Office suite, the World Wide Web, online environments, distance education, smart classrooms, wireless connectivity, cell phones, and mp3 players. Finally, with the increasing ubiquity of electronic technologies and the rise of the economies of India and China, for example, higher education has become increasingly global, exportable, competitive, and tied to national agendas.

Like a chameleon, the distinctive coloration, shadings, and features of the programs offered by teaching and learning centers have changed against this backdrop at the same time that the underlying structures and basic spheres of activity have remained true to the origins of the field. In 1975, the *Journal of Higher Education* published a major article on faculty development written by William Bergquist and Steven Phillips. In the article the authors proposed three levels for change—attitude, process, and structure, which quickly became professional (or "faculty"), instructional, and organizational development, respectively—the classic model of educational development that still influences the practices of teaching and learning centers today (Burdick, 2007). As the field of faculty (or educational) development has evolved, each of these three subfields has waxed and waned in importance: for a while early interest in instructional development receded as faculty development became more prominent, but recently organizational development has become more salient. The practices of centers and the kinds of programs they offer can vary substantially, however, depending on the type of institution (that is, research, comprehensive, liberal arts, community college, or specialized) and the interests and experience levels of its director and personnel.

As a matter of fact, the number of centers that have directors and key staff with less than five years of experience in the field is quite large (Sorcinelli, Austin, Eddy, & Beach, 2006) and, with the proliferation of centers in recent years, probably reflects the growing edge of the field. The relative inexperience of a sizeable portion of center leadership personnel is due to the peculiar nature of faculty development appointments, particularly in small colleges, but sometimes in larger universities as well. Often institutions recruit center directors from the faculty ranks, offering them partial or total release time from their customary duties for a limited term (for example, three to five years). While faculty directors typically have a strong interest in teaching and success in the classroom, they may have no formal background in faculty development and limited familiarity with the literature and research base that supports it. In contrast, some directors of large, well-established centers are faculty development pioneers with twenty to thirty years of experience in the field. As a result, the current practice of faculty development recapitulates the evolution of the field. At the same time that many newer centers offer primarily basic workshops on a range of teaching skills more typical of early practice in the field, other more mature centers are exploring emergent areas of practice.

In the remainder of this chapter, I describe, first, common variations in the organizational structure and programs and services offered by faculty (or educational) development centers in the United States and, second, emergent areas of practice in response to recent changes in the teaching and learning agenda in higher education.

Types of Centers

Despite the number of centers and the variety of institutions in which they reside, there are five basic organizational structures for educational development centers:

1. Single, centralized teaching and learning center

2. Individual faculty member, with or without a physical center

3. A committee that supports faculty development

4. A clearinghouse for programs and offerings

5. Structures such as system-wide offices (Sorcinelli et al., 2006).

Variations on these basic structures include centers that serve a particular population, such as graduate students; support a more specialized initiative such as problem-based learning or service learning; or reside in a school. The POD Network in Higher Education Web site (http://www.podnetwork.org) includes a very useful search function for hundreds of teaching center Web sites in the United States, Canada, and abroad.

Single, centralized teaching and learning centers are most common in research and comprehensive institutions, although they occur in all institution types (Sorcinelli et al., 2006). They are typically older and better established than other differently structured efforts, sometimes having evolved from other structures such as the center as individual faculty member director or faculty development committee.

Core professional staff may include a director; associate director; one or two assistant or program directors, sometimes with responsibility for a specific area (for example, a specialized population such as graduate students); a constellation of disciplines such as science, technology, engineering, and mathematics (STEM), social science, or humanities; and support staff such as an administrative assistant. The director may be a faculty member or a faculty development professional or both, with either a full- or part-time appointment. A part-time director drawn from the ranks of the senior, tenured faculty and an associate director, often with a faculty development background and a visiting faculty appointment in an academic department, is a common combination. Centralized centers often have a faculty advisory committee, which may be quite active if the center is new or if the director is a faculty development professional and desires additional credibility with the faculty and administration or assistance in navigating the politics of the institution. The center may supplement the efforts of its paid staff with graduate and/or undergraduate students in any number of areas including special projects, technology, or administrative assistance.

The center director typically reports to the Office of the Provost, often through an associate vice provost. A reporting line to academic affairs is highly desirable because it ensures access to higher administration and explicitly aligns the center with the academic mission of the institution. Depending upon their origin and evolution, some centers report to a graduate school dean, although this is far less common than the model discussed. Centralized offices typically offer an array of programs, some of which may serve special populations at the university or support specialized initiatives, as is further described following.

Core budgets vary widely, chiefly depending on the number of staff members and the degree to which the center supports instructional technology. The center may supplement its core budget with external support such as grants. A small number of centers are named centers supported through endowments.

An individual faculty member, with or without a physical center, is most typical of small, liberal arts colleges but is to a lesser extent also a model found at comprehensive universities (Sorcinelli et al., 2006). However, as noted previously, centralized centers in large universities may evolve from this model. Small college centers of this type have proliferated in recent years, and the POD Network now has an active Small College Committee serving this population.

Drawn most frequently from the ranks of the tenure-track faculty, the individual directing this kind of effort often has a part time appointment and no dedicated administrative staff or physical center. Less frequently the center is part of the portfolio of an associate dean or other administrator. This director may work with a faculty advisory committee in order to build support and stay in touch with the needs of the faculty. Working with an advisory committee also helps ensure the sustained success of faculty development beyond the tenure of the individual faculty member. Small college campuses may overly identify faculty development with the individual faculty member. Further, the fruits of such efforts can be short lived if the director goes on sabbatical or returns full time to the faculty ranks.

Program offerings are typically limited, in keeping with the more modest size of the center. Initially the center may focus on one or two programs, perhaps allied with other campus initiatives, and then expand over time. Activities may occur discretely or as part of regular meetings, committee work, and course and curriculum planning (Reder, Mooney, Holmgren, & Kuerbis, 2009). Budgets of centers organized in this way are typically quite small.

Committees that support faculty development—essentially an advisory committee without a director—are most typical of liberal arts and community colleges and share many attributes of the individual faculty member model. A similar model, *a clearinghouse for programs and offerings,* is most common in community colleges (Sorcinelli et al., 2006). These models may evolve into more formal structures over time, becoming part of the portfolio of an associate dean, the responsibility of an individual faculty member, or even a centralized center.

Systemwide offices, as the phrase implies, are found in larger state systems (for example, California and Georgia). They often support and coordinate the efforts of centralized centers or other faculty development efforts on individual campuses.

Whatever the institutional context, the initiative for the establishment of a center may come from any number of sources: grassroots agitation by faculty, administration, outgrowth of a reaccreditation effort, or support of a specific initiative such as problem-based learning or service learning. At the same time, centers can also be vulnerable to changes in administration; waning administrative support; tightening budgets; consolidations of units on campus; poor leadership; failure to address key constituencies; and the sudden absence of a key faculty member due to retirement, sabbatical, or acceptance of a position elsewhere.

Programs and Services

While the range and number of programs and services offered by individual centers varies considerably, normally the types of programs and services they offer fall within the categories below. The first three program types discussed following—workshops, individual consultations, and classroom observations—are characteristic of the earliest offerings in the field of faculty development and still the programs most commonly found in many centers. They emphasize the expertise of the faculty development professional as a resource for faculty members in the area of instructional development and as a facilitator of faculty development. Very generally, as the remainder of the list or programs and services presented following progresses, the faculty development professional serves less as an expert on instructional development and increasingly more as, first, a facilitator of faculty development and, second, as a change agent for organizational development. When orchestrated together, variations and combinations of these program strategies can have a significant impact on the institutions that the centers serve.

Workshops encompass a single event or a series of events offered by center staff, faculty or staff members, or external consultants on any number of topics. Common topic areas include course design, teaching strategies, evaluation of students, evaluation of teaching, and the use of various instructional technologies.

Individual consultations occur when a faculty member meets one on one with a center staff member or, less commonly, with a faculty fellow in strict confidence on some aspect of teaching including the introduction of a new teaching strategy, course and syllabus development, or strategies to address poor student evaluations in one or more areas of classroom practice. Consultation is a powerful strategy that can lead to important changes in the practice of faculty members who take advantage of them.

It is also quite resource intensive, however, and consequently a luxury for centers that are short staffed.

Classroom observations are conducted at the request of a faculty member, who invites a center staff member to observe one or more classroom sessions. Typically an individual consultation both precedes and follows the observation. During the pre-observation meeting the client and consultant together arrive at a common understanding of the client's concerns; in the post-observation meeting they discuss the session, and the consultant shares detailed observations, sometimes using a videotape of the session, with the idea of altering the client's practice in some way. A variation of the observation uses Small Group Instructional Diagnosis (SGID) in which a trained facilitator, whether a center staff member, faculty member, or graduate student, with the permission of the instructor, meets with students in a class without the faculty member present. The facilitator enables or guides small group discussions, arriving at a consensus of core strengths and areas for improvement that are subsequently shared with the instructor.

Orientations are often held at the beginning of the fall, or less commonly, in the spring semester for new faculty and graduate teaching assistants. The center often plans and coordinates this event, sometimes bringing in external consultants in addition to campus experts. The length and content of orientations varies from a one-day event during which attendees hear about campus resources in a talking-heads kind of format, often with lunch provided, to a one-day workshop on critical instructional skills and campus resources, to longer orientations that may extend for several days before the beginning of the semester. Sometimes the events of an orientation program are scheduled throughout an entire school year.

Grants to individual faculty members, groups of faculty members, or a department typically support an aspect of course or curriculum development, including the purchase of materials such as educational software, partial support of a graduate student, travel to a teaching-related conference, payment of an external consultant, or a working retreat for faculty.

Faculty fellows build relationships with the faculty and extend the influence of the center. Some centers support a limited number of faculty fellows. Fellows may secure partial release time from their teaching or other department duties to work on a project, develop a program, or perform a service negotiated with the center.

Teaching circles normally comprise six to eight faculty members who gather around a common topic of interest. The participants agree to meet regularly, usually for a fixed period of time, often an academic semester.

Common topics include active learning or a specific teaching strategy such as problem-based learning, teaching portfolios, course-based assessment, or course design; the possibilities are limitless. Participants may also read a book together, discuss it, and explore the implications for their teaching. Typically the center facilitates the organization of the circles and may supply some funding for books and other materials.

Faculty learning communities (FLCs) are a more extensive faculty development activity than teaching circles in both duration of time and the resources that support them. Faculty learning communities bring a group of eight to ten faculty members from a variety of disciplines together around some focal point of concern for a semester or, more commonly, for a full year. There are two main types of FLCs: cohort and topic based. The cohort-based FLC addresses the needs of a group of faculty such as new, senior, or female faculty members; faculty members of color; or administrators such as department chairs. The topic-based FLC focuses on a special campus teaching and learning need such as team teaching, diversity, or departmental assessment of general education. The center coordinates the organization of the FLCs and may provide funds to support gatherings around meals or other refreshments, off-campus retreats, travel to conferences, and materials such as books.

Management of grant-funded projects represents an expansion of a center's campus resources by partnering with other academic and support units or even other institutions to procure grants to support a project on its campus such as inquiry-guided learning; first-year seminars; reform in science, technology, engineering, and mathematics courses and curricula; teaching large-enrollment courses; the integration of instructional technology; or mentoring. Center staff may simply participate in the grant by offering extended programs and services supported by it, coordinating the grant, or both. Grants may also provide funds for the dissemination of findings during and following the grant period, thereby increasing the visibility of the institution nationally as well as the work of the center. Successful competition for grants can also enhance the status of the center on its own campus and enhance support from its administration.

Engagement in national projects is related to grant-funded projects. Centers may facilitate their institutions' participation in any number of national projects, such as the American Association of Colleges and Universities' (AAC&U's) Greater Expectations Project or the Carnegie Scholars Program sponsored by the Carnegie Foundation for the Advancement of Teaching. Center personnel generally find the engagement with other institutions stimulating and benefit from finding out more about their practices. As with grant projects, participation in national projects can enhance the visibility of the institution and the status of the center on its own campus.

Centers offer other programs and services as well. For example, centers may assist in the recognition of excellence in teaching through coordination of the selection process and the planning and publicizing of teaching awards ceremonies. In the interest of maintaining impartiality, however, they do not participate in the selection of teaching award winners. Also, most centers assemble resources on teaching such as a library of books and publications on teaching and learning in higher education; produce their own newsletters with helpful articles; and develop Web sites, sometimes with links to other teaching resources.

Center directors and staff also engage in a range of informal activities to enhance the visibility of the work of the centers, forge important alliances with faculty and administration, and broker partnerships with other campus units and constituencies. In addition, center directors and other key staff members may serve on committees related to the teaching and learning missions of their institutions as another strategy for enhancing teaching and learning on their campuses. Judiciously selected committee service can also contribute to the organizational development process and enhance the visibility and credibility of the educational development effort. Accrediting agencies have begun to recognize the importance of sound educational development efforts. Consequently, center directors and staff are increasingly playing an important role in reaccreditation efforts, including the development and implementation of quality enhancement plans, a relatively new requirement for colleges and universities accredited by the Southern Association of Colleges and Schools (SACS). They may also provide a fresh perspective on the revision of promotion, retention, and tenure guidelines, the configuration of physical space at the institution, including classroom renovation, and broad strategic planning issues such as student success and campus climate.

Emerging Program Types

As the teaching and learning agenda in higher education has become more complex and faculty development has matured as a field of practice, a small but growing number of centers are extending the types of programs and strategies they use to influence their institutions as well as their basic organizational structures. Further, many longtime faculty development professionals who are reaching the pinnacle of their careers are extending their practice into wider and wider spheres of influence. In the wake of center closings, tightening budgets, and a slowing economy, some centers are becoming far more deliberate in positioning themselves within broader institutional initiatives and in the context of their institutions' strategic plans. With increasing access to higher administration, centers are helping administrators see how faculty development, more enlightened approaches to teaching and learning, and the sustained development of human capital in their institutions can address larger strategic issues such as retention, swelling enrollments in an era of tightening resources, and the diversification of the student body. Organizational development is slowly coming into its own as a specialized and increasingly sophisticated area of practice.

Specifically, the following developments in higher education are challenging conventional structures and programs of teaching centers and bringing about new configurations of programs and areas of practice.

- The proliferation and growing sophistication of learning technologies, the increasing number of platforms for learning, the merging of institutional boundaries as courses offered asynchronously accommodate students from anywhere in the world, and students for whom electronic technologies have always been ubiquitous and who are very facile with these technologies

- The growing diversification of the student body; globalization and, with the rise of India and China in particular, the increasing competitiveness of higher education, internationally, particularly in the STEM disciplines; the exporting of U.S. higher education to Asia and the Middle East; and the increasing nationalization of the higher education agenda

- The growth of the assessment field and with it the emergence of the scholarship of teaching and learning

- The changing guidelines for reaccreditation by the regional accrediting bodies, including the heightened centrality of student learning in the reaccreditation process, outcomes-based program review, and the inclusion of quality enhancement plans in some regions

- The growing number of partners in the learning enterprise, including libraries, technology centers, student affairs and resident life professionals, and the wider communities in which institutions reside

- A growing consumerist orientation and the more vigilant role played by parents with ubiquitous telecommunications

- The rising number of part-time instructors, representing an outsourcing of aspects of the traditional faculty role

The result of all these changes has been an explosion of opportunities for faculty developers and centers to contribute to the enhancement of teaching and learning effectiveness and to the institution's overall mission, both within their institutions and outside them. In fact, finding the right balance between internal and external commitments is an ongoing challenge for many faculty developers. Without changing their fundamental organizational structure, more and more centers are becoming players in broader curricular issues such as general education or partnering with other professionals on campus in areas such as assessment. In addition, a slowly increasing number of seasoned practitioners are assuming roles in higher administration, whether as deans or associate vice provosts for faculty development. Further, like organisms adapting to new environments, a small but growing number of centers are adopting broader missions, entering into new partnerships, and creating new organizational structures, depending on local conditions. A few examples are described next.

Merging with an instructional technology unit has become more common as electronic instructional technologies have become more pervasive, as budgets of distance education units have swollen with the revenue-producing capacities of distance education programs, and as chief information officers have risen to high-ranking administrative positions. Although at times technology centers merge with educational development centers, sometimes the reverse occurs: the center becomes part of the technology unit. In my view, however, the absorption of the technology center into the teaching center is more appropriate because the teaching center reflects correctly the means–end relationships between and among learning, pedagogy, and technology. Pedagogical decisions based on intended student learning outcomes should precede decisions about which instructional technologies to use. Further, the use of sophisticated electronic technologies should not be a foregone conclusion. The Center for New Designs in Learning and Scholarship at Georgetown University and the Teaching and Learning Center at the University of Greensboro are two examples of centers conceived from their inception as units with a strong instructional technology component.

Consolidation describes the placement of an array of programs for the faculty in a single office so as to facilitate a cohesive approach to professional development. Constituent programs vary but can include programs related to teaching; technology; promotion and tenure policies and procedures related to teaching; faculty wellness; and programs for subgroups of faculty, such as women, new, and adjunct faculty members. Centers structured in this way include the Consortium for Learning and Scholarship (including the Center for Teaching and Learning) at

Indiana University-Purdue University Indianapolis (IUPUI) and the Office of Faculty Development (including the Center for Teaching) at the University of Massachusetts Amherst. The Hubbard Center for Faculty Development at Appalachian State University is an example of a center that has acquired and shed a variety of programs for faculty members throughout its history.

There are also a few centers that combine programs for faculty, staff, and administrators. For example, the Office of Faculty and Organizational Development at Michigan State University is structured in this way.

Reorganization of an existing center by the expansion of the center's mission is a recent, albeit isolated, development. For example, after a lengthy reexamination of faculty development needs by an independent task force in anticipation of the retirement of key staff people, the Center for Teaching and Learning at the University of North Carolina at Chapel Hill has reorganized as the Center for Faculty Excellence. Led by a half-time director appointed from the faculty and a full-time executive director with expertise in faculty development, the new center comprises three separate spheres of activity: teaching, research, and leadership. The center has new offices in the university's main library and an enhanced technology component, signaling a stronger and more explicit partnership among units in alignment with the broadened mission.

Whether these emerging organizational structures and program types represent the new face of faculty development is hard to say. Certainly, though, the broader missions of these centers stretch the traditional boundaries of faculty development and extend its reach. Coincidentally, the term *educational development,* long used in the United Kingdom, Canada, and Australia, has gained wider currency in the United States in the past several years. As compared to *faculty development,* the term more commonly used in the United States, educational development conveys a tighter integration of faculty, instructional, and organizational development strategies to affect the teaching and learning agenda in higher education. Broader still, the term *academic development* is catching on, recognizing development activities related to the broader mission of institutions of higher education including research, teaching, leadership, and service. In my view, academic development constitutes equal parts opportunity and peril: the embrace of teaching and learning as a legitimate sphere of faculty concern and activity or the eclipse of teaching and learning by the dominant sphere of research.

Conclusion

Since its inception, faculty development has grown as a field; and so have the number of educational development centers. Most centers fall into one of five basic organizational structures, offering combinations from a common palette of programs and services. These programs and services represent the three classic areas of educational development: faculty, instructional, and organizational development. More mature centers led by seasoned faculty development professionals sometimes evidence emerging areas of practices as do isolated centers that represent new models for educational development centers.

Faculty, or educational, development has since its inception been a field focused on change; and this focus continues. Given the centrality of the faculty in the life of colleges and universities and the acceleration of change in higher education, faculty development is more important than ever. While intimately tied to the teaching and learning agenda of institutions, faculty development plays a critical role in enhancing overall institutional effectiveness. More and more educational developers are partnering with higher administration to address broad strategic planning issues such as student success, faculty retention, cost effectiveness, and operational efficiencies. In fact, faculty development has emerged as a central player in the transformation of colleges, universities, and higher education today.

REFERENCES

Bergquist, W. H. (1992). *The four cultures of the academy: Insights and strategies for improving leadership in collegiate organizations.* San Francisco: Jossey-Bass.

Bergquist, W. H., & Phillips, S. R. (1975). Components of an effective faculty development program. *Journal of Higher Education, 46*(2), 177–212.

Burdick, D. (2007). *An outline of POD's history.* Nederland, CO: POD Network in Higher Education.

Reder, M., Mooney, K. M., Holmgren, R. A., & Kuerbis, P. J. (2009). Starting and sustaining successful faculty development programs at small colleges. *To improve the academy: Vol. 27. Resources for faculty, instructional, and organizational development* (pp. 267–286). San Francisco: Jossey-Bass.

Sorcinelli, M. D., Austin, A. E., Eddy, P. L., & Beach, A. L. (2006). *Creating the future of faculty development: Learning from the past, understanding the present.* Bolton, MA: Anker.

3

ESTABLISHING AN EDUCATIONAL DEVELOPMENT PROGRAM

Douglas L. Robertson

IN MANY COUNTRIES, EMERGENT NORMS in higher education press colleges and universities to attend explicitly to the development of their professional and organizational effectiveness. A common outcome of this pressure is the creation, resurrection, or reorganization of an institutional educational development program. This chapter serves as a resource for anyone interested in this task.

What is included in "establishing a program"? No benefit seems to come from drawing a strict distinction between conceptualizing a program and managing its formative early months. So the phrase "establishing a program" includes both overlapping sets of tasks. In addition, educational development programs have been around long enough that a new phenomenon has emerged: the resurrected program, a once functioning program that for whatever reason disappeared or was significantly diminished but that now is being reincarnated. Perhaps a new provost did not support the program, or a budget crisis forced a funding cut. Also, current educational development programs are occasionally being merged with other programs (for example, with programs in information technology or human resources), which creates the need to reorganize the educational development program fundamentally. All three of these endeavors—creating, resurrecting, and reorganizing a program— are included in this discussion of "establishing a program."

The objectives for this chapter are to increase readers' ability to do the following:

- Determine what decisions need to be made: focus fundamental considerations in creating, resurrecting, or reorganizing an educational development program at their institutions
- Make decisions on key issues: discern a desired position on these fundamental considerations
- Clarify the vision: integrate decisions with a clear and compelling vision for the educational development programs

To help achieve these objectives, a series of questions are identified and discussed. Readers' specific contexts influence how they respond to these questions, and this chapter avoids as much as possible delivering a decontextualized list of "principles of good practice." The goals are to identify important considerations, not to articulate imperatives, and also to help readers develop a position on those considerations that are germane to their context and then to combine those positions into a clear vision.

This chapter is intended to be practical; however, it is also informed by the literature of the field. A useful body of work exists on this topic for further study (see the selected bibliography at the end of this chapter). In addition, *To Improve the Academy* (the annual, peer-reviewed volume of the Professional and Organizational Development [POD] Network in Higher Education) is a twenty-seven-year cornucopia of intelligent, well-founded, practical ideas, a number of which relate to this chapter's topic of establishing an educational development program. Readers who have not done so already are encouraged to set aside sufficient time to browse the complete set, stopping where appropriate. Doing so is definitely worth the time and effort.

Decision Points in Building an Effective Program

Now the discussion turns to identifying fundamental questions in establishing an educational development program. The fourteen sets of questions that follow are not arranged in a strict linear sequence, as if a single proper sequence could be imposed on what is usually a fairly dynamic and idiosyncratic process. Readers should feel free to move around among the sets of questions as it suits their interests.

What are desirable preconditions for establishing an educational development program?

Building a broad constituent base for the program is a vital first step. Having all or even nearly all of an institution's faculty, staff, administrators, and students in favor of establishing an educational development program is not a realistic goal. However, having as many of them as possible desiring the establishment of such a program optimizes the prospects of success. For example, if a faculty task force has been charged by the provost or senate president with investigating the rationale for supporting faculty development and the task force then issues a report recommending a program, this garnered support contributes to the its establishment and ultimate success. The same is true for staff, if the program is to serve staff. Having the support of the president, provost, other appropriate vice presidents, deans, chairs, and directors also helps. Students are rarely aware of the issue of faculty or staff development. However, one could explore ways to get student government or other student groups involved in the discussions, perhaps issuing a statement in support of establishing the program.

Should there be a center?

The form that educational development programs take varies widely (see also Chapter Two, entitled "Program Types and Prototypes"). For example, Sorcinelli, Austin, Eddy, and Beach (2006) sent a survey to the entire POD Network 2001 membership asking, among other things, how faculty development programs were structured. At the three hundred institutions represented by the respondents, Sorcinelli et al. found the following array of structures (p. 37):

○ A centralized unit with dedicated staff (54 percent)

○ Individual faculty member or administrator (19 percent)

○ A committee that supports faculty development (12 percent)

○ A clearinghouse for programs and offerings (4 percent)

○ Other structures, such as system-wide offices or combinations (11 percent)

In this survey, the structure for faculty development programs varied significantly by institutional type. (See also Chapter Seventeen, "Effective Practices at Research Universities"; Chapter Eighteen, "Effective Practices in the Context of Small Colleges"; and Chapter Nineteen, "Faculty Development in the Context of the Community College.") The central unit (usually called a "center") was the most common structure at research universities, comprehensive universities, and community colleges (72 percent, 51 percent, and 34 percent, respectively), while the individual faculty or administrator was the most common form at liberal arts colleges (33 percent) (Sorcinelli et al., 2006, p. 38). Two rules of thumb with which to begin the discussion of what form a program should take in a specific context would be (1) a center is usually the preferable form, and (2) something is better than nothing.

What should the program's mission be?

Formulating the program's mission involves a number of critical choices. For example, whom will the program serve? The faculty, for sure, but will programming exist for staff as well? How about administrators? Adjunct faculty? Graduate assistants? The institutional resources invested in educational development programs should be aligned with clear goals. What should the goals be? Who should be served toward what end?

For nearly two decades now, since Senge (1990) popularized the phrase "learning organization," many colleges and universities have declared that they want to be one. This aspiration is odd because, in fact, every organization is a learning organization whether it wants to be or not. People who work in an organization are learning every day through their interactions, even without formal professional development programs. Sometimes what they learn is useful for the organization, and sometimes it is not. Because institutions are already learning organizations, it is probably more accurate for them to say that they aspire to be "*intentional* learning organizations," wherein learning resources are directed toward helping faculty, staff, and administrators to learn and develop in ways that are in alignment with the strategic directions of the institution.

In large organizations, the person who attends to this aligned intentional learning is sometimes called a "chief learning officer." Indeed, a journal has emerged by that name. The functional concept seems to make sense for colleges and universities. An educational developer may be the logical person to take responsibility for this intentional learning. If the educational developer and the program serve this important new function, it should be stated explicitly in the mission.

An alternative approach to guiding learning strategically is to develop programs in response to the expressed learning needs of those whom the center is to serve. Rather than programming aligned with strategic directions, this latter approach tends to produce a shotgun effect to educational programming.

The choice involved with these two alternatives is not unlike the choice faced by teachers who want to include learners in shaping a course while still understanding that they as teachers know more than their students about the topic and have a responsibility to be the learning leader. This choice is something that can be addressed in the mission statement of the educational development program.

Another important consideration in determining the program's mission is the kinds of development to which the program will attend. At least four choices exist:

1. Instructional development: helping those who teach to learn to do it ever more effectively

2. Faculty development: helping faculty members with all aspects of faculty work across their careers

3. Curriculum development: facilitating instructional design (integrated learning goals, activities, and assessment) in the contexts of course units up to whole programs such as general education or degree programs

4. Organizational development: helping the institution to develop as an intentional learning organization in order to enhance strategic institutional effectiveness, for example, through a new chairperson and staff development

An educational development program can be more than a teaching and learning center, and its entire scope should be expressed in its mission statement.

Here is a hypothetical mission statement that illustrates a professional development center conceptualized in broader terms than a faculty teaching and learning center and inclusive of technology training:

> The center's primary mission is to assist the university in realizing its full potential as an intentional learning organization by helping its faculty and staff, individually and collectively, to continue their rigorous and relevant ongoing development in coordination with the university's core values and strategic priorities. The center serves the university by helping faculty and staff in four areas:
>
> 1. Instructional development
>
> 2. Faculty development
>
> 3. Curricular development
>
> 4. Organizational development
>
> The center's programming and consultations integrate training in pertinent technological tools into these four related areas of development.

A program's mission statement involves a number of critical choices, and it should be formulated carefully and clearly with representative involvement of the stakeholders. Readers will benefit from examining the mission statements of existing educational development programs, which can be easily accessed by using the search engine on the front page of the POD Web site (http://www.podnetwork.org/search.htm#faculty).

What process should be used to formulate the mission and strategic plan?

Implementing a process that produces a statement of mission, vision, key values, and strategic plan (goals, activities, and assessment) for the educational development program can take a variety of forms. Whatever the form, the process generally benefits from providing a wide variety of opportunities (face to face, print, and electronic; individual and group) for all of the major stakeholders to participate. These stakeholders may include students, faculty, chairpersons, deans, executive administrators, academic support and student affairs staff, alumni, community members, or anyone else who might affect or be affected by the new educational development program, directly or indirectly.

The process of holding a series of meetings or conversations, perhaps inviting different categories of stakeholders to each meeting, not only provides invaluable data but also, as a result of each group's facilitated dialogue, generally serves to elevate the sophistication of the organization relative to the new educational development program and the pertinent issues. Iterative processes, through which the results and analysis of the conversations are shared with stakeholders, generally produce broader and deeper investment in the new program by those stakeholders.

Should the program include instructional technology?

Whether teaching face-to-face, online, or hybrid courses, faculty members frequently need to learn to use existing and emerging technological tools such as course management systems, presentation applications, smartboards, plagiarism programs, streaming media, Podcasting, and social networking tools (see also Chapter Sixteen, "Issues in Technology and Faculty Development"). Instructional technologists who help the faculty learn to use these technological tools can be located organizationally in information technology units, or they can be integrated into educational development programs.

The significance of the difference in these two cultures (information technology and educational development) should not be underestimated. Instructional technologists housed in an information technology organizational unit tend to treat the technology as their content and present workshops such as Blackboard I, II, and III, in which they run through all the Blackboard tools whether faculty members need them or not. They may secretly, or perhaps openly, harbor the belief that faculty members should be required to take their Blackboard training before they are allowed to use the course management system in a real course. Instructional technologists who are situated within an educational development program, where the enduring emphasis is on pedagogy rather than technology itself, tend to develop training and consultations around teaching problems, such as developing an online community or active learning in an online environment. With this latter approach, faculty members are supported in learning to use the technological tools; but they do so within the context of improving their teaching practices by solving a teaching problem. Needing to learn a new technological tool presents an opportunity to the instructional technologist to help faculty members reexamine their teaching practices and perspectives. Instructional technologists who work within the information technology organizational culture are more likely to run from these pedagogical distractions, whereas those who work in the context of an educational development program are more likely to relish these instructional development opportunities.

Integrating instructional technology into educational development programs is not without its challenges, however. For one thing, the salaries in these two organizational units (information technology and educational development) are generally structured differently; salaries are commonly higher for information technologists than for educational developers. Another issue relates to the market for instructional technologists, which is often robust, particularly in metropolitan areas. Consequently, an instructional technologist's tenure in an educational development program can be short. These challenges require a meaningful commitment by the institution's leadership to ensure that the salaries of instructional technologists in educational development programs are competitive with their counterparts in the institution's information technology unit so as to prevent internal raiding of highly performing personnel. Also, as much as possible, salaries for instructional technologists in educational development programs should attempt to be competitive with those in external markets, realizing that colleges and universities can rarely match corporations in this regard.

What should the budget be?

Remember that something is better than nothing; nonetheless, a general guideline does exist with which to begin this discussion of budget (Fink, personal communication, June 20, 2007). Former POD president Dee Fink, in his experience with faculty development programs at many different kinds of institutions, noticed that at centers that one could consider to be financially well supported, the center budget was between

½ to 1 percent of faculty salaries and benefits (or of whomever the center is designed to serve, perhaps also including adjunct faculty, graduate teaching assistants, and certain staff). For example, if the center is to serve full- and part-time faculty and their salaries and benefits total $70 million, a well-funded center budget would be between $350,000 and $700,000. An important consideration is whether or not the center includes instructional technology. Instructional technology staff and equipment are expensive relative to instructional consultants, and those costs demand a larger center budget.

Where should the program be positioned organizationally?

An important consideration in establishing an educational development program is situating that program in the organizational structure and determining the reporting line for its director or coordinator. Educational development programs are quite vulnerable to being marginalized. Therefore, the reporting line should be as high as possible and in academic affairs, preferably reporting directly to the chief academic officer.

What are the characteristics of the ideal director?

Directors or coordinators of educational development programs come in many forms. They can be full-time or part-time, faculty or staff, tenured or never tenured. However, no matter what the specifics may be, they need to have credibility with the key stakeholders, in particular with the specific clients for the educational development program.

Usually, faculty members constitute the primary client group for educational development programs. So the director benefits from having credibility with faculty. Optimal credibility arises when directors are perceived as colleagues who have added another area of expertise (educational development) to their disciplinary training as opposed to being considered faculty support staff. In other words, it helps if the director has been a successful faculty member before becoming a director. Although plenty of highly successful directors do not have this status and earn their credibility in different ways, significant credibility for the director can come from being a senior faculty colleague (terminal degree, previously obtained tenure, and rank of at least associate professor) with a solid teaching, research, and service background. It further helps if the directors receive faculty status as part of their appointment and are considered faculty colleagues. In a national study of educational developers, Mullinix (2008) found that four out of five (79 percent) of the educational developers who responded said that faculty status was important, and half of these (48 percent) said that it was critical or very important; slightly more than half of the respondents (54 percent) said that it added to their credibility; and about one quarter (28 percent) said that it impacted their effectiveness. Two quotes help to summarize the qualitative data from the study. An educational developer with faculty status explained as follows: "I believe that being a faculty colleague provides instant rapport and respect with other faculty. I can speak about promotion, tenure, classroom management, online teaching, electronic portfolios from personal experience rather than theory alone" (Mullinix, 2008, p. 184). An educational developer without faculty status commented, "I have never had faculty status, but I believe it would be *very* helpful in my work with faculty. I have been told (sometimes very directly) that my lack of faculty status makes me less qualified to help certain faculty members despite my credentials (Ph.D.) and teaching experiences" (p. 183).

Besides this fundamental consideration of faculty background, other important characteristics of the ideal director include the following (see Chapter Six, "Important Skills and Knowledge"):

- Knowledge of pertinent literatures, practices, and technologies
- Experience with educational development
- Clinical skills (for example, working confidentially in consulting relationships)
- Facilitation skills (for example, facilitating workshops, retreats, meetings, and events)
- Managerial skills
- Leadership skills (see Sidle, 2005)

We must remember, however, that an effective director certainly does not need to possess all these characteristics. Credibility and effectiveness emerge from all of the skills working in concert.

Should the program director be permanent or rotating?

On this topic, readers may benefit from reflecting on and discussing the comments of a senior faculty member and center director at a small liberal arts college regarding the merits of being a rotating center director: "We designed our Learning Center Coordinator position to be one for faculty to rotate through on three-year shifts. It seemed interesting at the time we designed it, but as the guinea pig for the new position, I'm finding a few flaws in the design. For instance, technically I'm entering my final year in the position (although I plan to stay on at least one year beyond that) and am just now feeling vaguely competent as a faculty developer" (anonymous, personal communication, April 10, 2007). Rotating directorships do not appear to be as desirable as permanent directorships. Educational development is an established professional field, and it is not reasonable or efficient to expect a faculty or staff member to master a new field in a year or so and then leave it a year or so later.

What services should the program provide?

Educational development programs often provide at least four sets of services (see Chapter Two, "Program Types and Prototypes," and Chapter Eight, "Practical Suggestions for Programs and Activities"):

- Events, such as workshops or special speakers
- Programs, such as peer-led communities of practice or innovative teaching grants
- Consultations, such as with a faculty member regarding a teaching and learning issue or with a department regarding its faculty evaluation system
- Process facilitations, such as retreats focused on, for example, the accreditation process or a department meeting in which learning outcomes for a major are discussed

A handy organizer for thinking about the issue of program services can be made by creating a 2 × 2 matrix that combines two considerations: (1) who the client is (individual or group) and (2) what generates the activity (client request or center initiative). Such a matrix is presented in Figure 3.1.

As in most things, balance is advisable; and so it is with the four quadrants. If a program's services are dominated by client-generated activities, then the program has little opportunity to provide proactive leadership for the institution. If a program largely pursues center-generated activities, it may be perceived as unresponsive to those it is supposed to serve; and the support of its stakeholders may wane. Similarly, with regard to individuals and groups, if too much emphasis is placed on working with individuals when one can see significant change and development over time, then the breadth of impact may be questioned. If a program's focus

Figure 3.1. Organizer for Program Services.

	Client-Generated	Center-Generated
Individuals		
Groups		

is largely on group activities, however, where the numbers with regard to participation can be quite high, the depth of impact may be suspect because significant behavioral change is unlikely within the context of large events and because these events often attract repeating participants who already "see the light." Again, each institution will have to make its own decision about what blend of services best serves their institution.

How should the services be delivered?

Quite understandably, educational developers often worry about "getting people to come." However, that is just part of the story. Delivery of services can be conceptualized in two fundamental ways:

1. Centripetally: bringing in clients, physically (for example, to workshops) and electronically (for example, to the Web site)
2. Centrifugally: going out to clients, physically (for example, making house calls) and electronically (for example, through Podcasting).

Readers may find it useful to create another 2 × 2 matrix as an organizer for thinking about the delivery of services, with centripetal and centrifugal on the top and physical and electronic on the side. Again, balance is a desirable goal.

In addition, because clients are often chronically overloaded (Robertson, 2003), developing services as a part of an ongoing "Just-in-Time 24/7 Support Initiative" is frequently useful. Developmental resources can be made available electronically (for example, Web-based tutorials and searchable databases) and in print (such as through books given to faculty members to build their personal teaching reference libraries), so that the faculty can receive developmental support when they need it. Also useful is providing for drop-in, face-to-face consultations or as-needed electronic consultations via phone, e-mail, or instant message. What each institution does will vary. However, the issue of providing just-in-time 24/7 developmental support for often extremely busy clients is important.

What are the ethical guidelines for educational developers?

Sometimes decision makers who are helping to establish an educational development program do not realize that the field of educational development has an established literature, mature professional associations, and long-standing leaders. Sometimes they are also unaware of the ethical guidelines for educational developers that have been developed by the Professional and Organizational Development Network in

Higher Education (http://www.podnetwork.org/faculty_development/ ethicalguidelines.htm). In particular, I strongly encourage readers to examine the part of the POD ethical guidelines that speak to confidentiality, which is one of the most important elements in encouraging clients to participate in programs that will help them to develop in profound rather than superficial ways. These confidentiality guidelines help educational developers navigate through the often difficult relationship that development programs can have with evaluation systems.

Should the program have an advisory board?

Effective advisory boards (or committees) serve as a two-way communication conduit, bringing information to the program from throughout the institution and sending out information throughout the institution from the program. Also, effective boards broaden ownership of the program. The educational developer should not, however, underestimate the time it takes to establish and maintain an effective board. (See also Chapter Four, "Working with a Faculty Development Committee.")

How can a program build its brand?

Branding is simply building people's positive association with and expectations for something, in this case, with a new educational development program. Of course, to build these positive associations and expectations (or its brand), a program must fulfill its claims to help clients and stakeholders in ways that they find meaningful. Having symbols (for example, a memorable name and logo) to which these experiences and perceptions can easily attach helps the program to build its positive identity. (See also Chapter Seven, "Promoting Your Program and Grounding It in the Institution".)

Promising people that they will benefit from the program's services and then delivering on that promise is an obvious task. Less obvious, and easy to trivialize, is the significance of the name given to the educational development program and the importance of its graphical expression or logo. There are hundreds of centers, and creating a name for a new unit is challenging. An informal analysis by the author reveals that the most common words in centers' names are as follows: *center, teaching, learning, enhancement, excellence, effectiveness, instructional, faculty, development*, and *technology*.

Establishing an educational development program creates a naming opportunity and perhaps also the possibility of a large gift. In fact, a number of U.S. centers are named after donors or iconic figures in an institution's history. Generally, prospective donors are reluctant to give support to faculty development programs and projects. However, these same donors often show enthusiasm for giving to programs that benefit students and their learning. Thus, it is worthwhile to explain to prospective donors that, by giving to a program that intends to help faculty to improve as teachers, they are ultimately giving to help students learn.

Creating a logo for the name may be a wonderful opportunity for an institution's graphic design students to work on a real-world project; it need not be expensive. No matter how the logo is developed, it should convey the professionalism of the educational development program that it represents. Clip art just will not do.

Conclusion

These fourteen questions stand out as important in creating, resurrecting, or reorganizing an educational development program. The hope is that this chapter helps readers to become clearer about what their major considerations are, where they stand in relation to those considerations, and how their positions on those considerations come together to create a vision for establishing an educational development program at their institution.

REFERENCES

Mullinix, B. B. (2008). Credibility and effectiveness in context: An exploration of the importance of faculty status for faculty developers. In D. R. Robertson & L. B. Nilson (Eds.), *To improve the academy: Vol. 26. Resources for faculty, instructional, and organizational development* (pp. 173–195). San Francisco: Jossey-Bass.

Professional and Organizational Development Network in Higher Education. (n.d.). *Ethical guidelines for educational developers.* Retrieved August 14, 2008, from http://www.podnetwork.org/faculty_development/ethicalguidelines.htm

Robertson, D. R. (2003). *Making time, making change: Avoiding overload in college teaching.* Stillwater, OK: New Forums.

Senge, P. M. (1990). *The fifth discipline: The art and practice of the learning organization.* New York: Doubleday.

Sidle, C. C. (2005). *The leadership wheel.* New York: Palgrave Macmillan.

Sorcinelli, M. D., Austin, A. E., Eddy, P. L., & Beach, A. L. (2006). *Creating the future of faculty development: Learning from the past, understanding the present.* Bolton, MA: Anker.

SELECTED BIBLIOGRAPHY

Ambrose, S. (1995). Fitting programs to institutional cultures: The founding and evolution of the university teaching center. In P. Seldin & Associates, *Improving college teaching* (pp. 77–90). Stillwater, OK: New Forums.

Bergquist, W. H., & Phillips, S. R. (1975). *A handbook for faculty development, Vol. I.* Washington, DC: Council for the Advancement of Small Colleges.

Bergquist, W. H., & Phillips, S. R. (1977). *A handbook for faculty development, Vol. II.* Washington, DC: Council for the Advancement of Small Colleges.

Bowman, M. A. (1993). The new faculty developer and the challenge of change. In D. L. Wright & J. P. Lunde (Eds.), *To improve the academy: Vol. 12. Resources for faculty, instructional, and organizational development* (pp. 247–259). Stillwater, OK: New Forums.

Centra, J. A. (1976). *Faculty development practices in U. S. colleges and universities.* Princeton, NJ: Educational Testing Service.

Chism, N.V.N., Fraser, J. M., & Arnold, R. L. (1996). Teaching academies: Honoring and promoting teaching through a community of expertise. *New Directions for Teaching and Learning, no. 65. Honoring exemplary teaching* (pp. 25–32). San Francisco: Jossey-Bass.

Crawley, A. L. (1995). Faculty development programs at research universities: Implications for senior faculty renewal. In E. Neal & L. Richlin (Eds.), *To improve the academy: Vol. 14. Resources for faculty, instructional, and organizational development* (pp. 65–90). Stillwater, OK: New Forums.

Diamond, R. M. (1984). Instructional support centers and the art of surviving: Some practical suggestions. In L. C. Buhl & L. A. Wilson (Eds.), *To improve the academy: Vol. 3. Resources for faculty instructional, and organizational development* (pp. 49–57). Stillwater, OK: New Forums.

Diamond, R. M. (2002). Faculty, instructional, and organizational development: Options and choices. In K. H. Gillespie, L. R. Hilsen, & E. C. Wadsworth (Eds.), *A guide to faculty development: Practical advice, examples, and resources* (pp. 2–8). Bolton, MA: Anker.

Eble, K. E., & McKeachie, W. J. (1985). *Improving undergraduate education through faculty development.* San Francisco: Jossey-Bass.

Erickson, G. (1986). A survey of faculty development practices. In M. Svinicki, J. Kurfiss, & J. Stone (Eds.), *To improve the academy: Vol. 5. Resources for faculty, instructional, and organizational development* (pp. 182–196). Stillwater, OK: New Forums.

Fink, L. D. (2002). Establishing an instructional development program: An example. In K. H. Gillespie, L. R. Hilsen, & E. C. Wadsworth (Eds.), *A guide to faculty development: Practical advice, examples, and resources* (pp. 35–44). Bolton, MA: Anker.

Frantz, A. C., Beebe, S. A., Horvath, V. S., Canales, J., & Swee, D. E. (2005). The roles of teaching and learning centers. In S. Chadwick-Blossey & D. R. Robertson (Eds.), *To improve the academy: Vol. 23. Resources for faculty, instructional, and organizational development* (pp. 72–90). Bolton, MA: Anker.

Gaff, J. C. (1975). *Toward faculty renewal: Advances in faculty, instructional, and organizational development.* San Francisco: Jossey-Bass.

Gillespie, K. H., Hilsen, L. R., & Wadsworth, E. C. (Eds.). (2002). *A guide to faculty development: Practical advice, examples, and resources.* Bolton, MA: Anker.

Gray, T., & Conway, J. (2007). Build it (right) and they will come: Boost attendance at your teaching center by building community. *Journal of Faculty Development, 21*(3), 179–184.

Hellyer, S., & Boschmann, E. (1993). Faculty development programs: A perspective. In D. L. Wright & J. P. Lunde (Eds.), *To improve the academy: Vol. 12. Resources for faculty, instructional, and organizational development* (pp. 217–224). Stillwater, OK: New Forums.

Kalivoda, P., Broder, J., & Jackson, W. K. (2003). Establishing a teaching academy: Cultivation of teaching at a research university campus. In C. M. Wehlburg & S. Chadwick-Blossey (Eds.), *To improve the academy: Vol. 21. Resources for faculty, instructional, and organizational development* (pp. 79–92). Bolton, MA: Anker.

Lang, H. G., & Conner, K. K. (1988). Some low-budget tips for faculty development programming. In E. Wadsworth (Ed.), *A handbook for new practitioners* (pp. 139–143). Stillwater, OK: New Forums.

Lewis, K. G. (1996). Faculty development in the United States: A brief history. *International Journal of Academic Development, 1*(2), 26–33.

Lewis, K., & Lunde, J. P. (Eds.). (2001). *Face to face: A source book of individual consultation techniques for faculty/instructional developers* (rev. ed.). Stillwater, OK: New Forums.

Lieberman, D. A., & Guskin, A. E. (2003). The essential role of faculty development in new higher education models. In C. M. Wehlburg & S. Chadwick-Blossey (Eds.), *To improve the academy: Vol. 21. Resources for faculty, instructional, and organizational development* (pp. 257–272). Bolton, MA: Anker.

Lindquist, J. (Ed.). (1979). *Designing teaching improvement programs.* Washington, DC: Council for the Advancement of Small Colleges.

Lindquist, J. (1981). Professional development. In A. W. Chickering & Associates, *The modern American college: Responding to the new realities of diverse students and a changing society* (pp. 730–747). San Francisco: Jossey-Bass.

Mooney, K. M., & Reder, M. (2008). Faculty development at small and liberal arts colleges. In D. R. Robertson & L. B. Nilson (Eds.), *To improve the academy: Vol. 26. Resources for faculty, instructional, and organizational development* (pp. 158–172). San Francisco: Jossey-Bass.

Mullinix, B. B. (2008). Credibility and effectiveness in context: An exploration of the importance of faculty status for faculty developers. In D. R. Robertson & L. B. Nilson (Eds.), *To improve the academy: Vol. 26. Resources for faculty, instructional, and organizational development* (pp. 173–195). San Francisco: Jossey-Bass.

Neal, E., & Peed-Neal, I. (2009). Experiential lessons in the practice of faculty development. In L. B. Nilson & J. Miller (Eds.), *To improve the academy: Vol. 27. Resources for faculty, instructional, and organization development* (pp. 14–31). San Francisco: Jossey-Bass.

Nelsen, W. C. (1980). Faculty development: Perceived needs for the 1980s. In W. C. Nelsen & M. E. Siegel (Eds.), *Effective approaches to faculty development* (pp. 145–149). Washington, DC: Association of American Colleges.

Nelsen, W. C., & Siegel, M. E. (Eds.). (1980). *Effective approaches to faculty development*. Washington, DC: Association of American Colleges.

Nemko, M., & Simpson, R. D. (1991). Nine keys to enhancing campus wide influence of faculty development centers. In K. J. Zahorski (Ed.), *To improve the academy: Vol. 10. Resources for student, faculty, and institutional development* (pp. 83–87). Stillwater, OK: New Forums.

Nyquist, J. (1986). CIDR: A small service firm within a research university. In M. Svinicki, J. Kurfiss, & J. Stone (Eds.), *To improve the academy: Vol. 5. Resources for student, faculty, and institutional development* (pp. 66–83). Stillwater, OK: New Forums.

O'Banion, T. (1972). *Teachers for tomorrow: Staff development in the community junior college.* Tucson: University of Arizona Press.

Rice, D. R. (1991). What every faculty development professional needs to know about higher education. In K. J. Zahorski (Ed.), *To improve the academy: Vol. 10. Resources for student, faculty, and institutional development* (pp. 89–96). Stillwater, OK: New Forums.

Rice, R. E. (2007). It all started in the sixties: Movements for change across the decades—A personal journey. In D. R. Robertson & L. B. Nilson (Eds.), *To improve the academy: Vol. 25. Resources for faculty, instructional, and organizational development* (pp. 3–17). Bolton, MA: Anker.

Schuster, J. H., Wheeler, D. W., & Associates (1990). *Enhancing faculty careers: Strategies for development and renewal.* San Francisco: Jossey-Bass.

Seldin, P., & Associates. (1990). *How administrators can improve teaching.* San Francisco: Jossey-Bass.

Senge, P. M. (1990). *The fifth discipline: The art and practice of the learning organization.* New York: Doubleday.

Siegel, M. E. (1980). Empirical findings on faculty development programs. In W. C. Nelsen & M. E. Siegel (Eds.), *Effective approaches to faculty development* (pp. 131–144). Washington, DC: Association of American Colleges.

Sorcinelli, M. D. (1988). Encouraging excellence: Long-range planning for faculty development. In E. Wadsworth (Ed.), *A handbook for new practitioners* (pp. 27–34). Stillwater, OK: New Forums.

Sorcinelli, M. D. (2002). Ten principles of good practice in creating and sustaining teaching and learning centers. In K. H. Gillespie, L. R. Hilsen, & E. C. Wadsworth (Eds.), *A guide to faculty development: Practical advice, examples, and resources* (pp. 9–23). Bolton, MA: Anker.

Sorcinelli, M. D., & Aitken, N. (1995). Improving teaching: Academic leaders and faculty developers as partners. In W. A. Wright & Associates (Ed.), *Teaching improvement practices: Successful strategies for higher education* (pp. 311–323). Bolton, MA: Anker.

Sorcinelli, M. D., Austin, A. E., Eddy, P. L., & Beach, A. L. (2006). *Creating the future of faculty development: Learning from the past, understanding the present.* Bolton, MA: Anker.

Tiberius, R. G. (2002). A brief history of educational development: Implications for teachers and developers. In D. Lieberman & C. Wehlburg (Eds.), *To improve the academy: Vol. 20. Resources for faculty, instructional and organizational development* (pp. 20–37). Bolton, MA: Anker.

Wadsworth, E. C., Hilsen, L., & Shea, M. A. (Eds.). (1988). *A handbook for new practitioners.* Stillwater, OK: New Forums.

Wheeler, D. W., & Schuster, J. H. (1990). Building comprehensive programs to enhance faculty development. In J. H. Schuster, D. W. Wheeler, & Associates, *Enhancing faculty careers: Strategies for development and renewal* (pp. 275–297). San Francisco: Jossey-Bass.

Wilkerson, L. (1984). Starting a faculty development program: Strategies and approaches. In L. C. Buhl & L. A. Wilson (Eds.), *To improve the academy: Vol. 3. Resources for faculty instructional, and organizational development* (pp. 25–43). Stillwater, OK: New Forums.

Wright, D. L. (2000). Faculty development centers in research universities: A study of resources and programs. In M. Kaplan & D. Lieberman (Eds.), *To improve the academy: Vol. 18. Resources for faculty, instructional, and organizational development* (pp. 291–301). Bolton, MA: Anker.

Wright, D. L. (2002). Program types and prototypes. In K. H. Gillespie,
    L. R. Hilsen, & E. C. Wadsworth (Eds.), *A guide to faculty development:
    Practical advice, examples, and resources* (pp. 24–34). Bolton, MA:
    Anker.
Zahorski, D. (1993). Taking the lead: Faculty development as institutional
    change agent. In D. L. Wright & J. P. Lunde (Eds.), *To improve the
    academy: Vol. 12. Resources for faculty, instructional, and organizational
    development* (pp. 227–245). Stillwater, OK: New Forums.

4

WORKING WITH A FACULTY DEVELOPMENT COMMITTEE

Kim M. Mooney

THE PURPOSE AND ACTIVITIES of a faculty development committee are highly dependent on institutional culture and context. The structure and charge of a faculty development committee may vary according to whether it is situated in or out of the institutional governance system; this positioning may determine whether its members serve in advisory capacities or as active participants in the planning of programming. In addition, the committee's activity may be guided by the presence or absence of a center for teaching and learning and a center director. The purpose of this chapter is to help coordinators of faculty development, chairs of faculty development committees, and directors of centers for teaching and learning organize their campus faculty development committees so as to engage in meaningful, shared ownership of professional development efforts on behalf of their colleagues. Whether working with an advisory board that has members of one's choosing or with a formal institutional committee the membership of which is predetermined, this chapter encourages creative and strategic planning for faculty developers. However, the suggestions provided here are directed toward committee members who fill substantive rather than just advisory roles on their committees. If your institution is in the initial stage of planning and starting a centralized faculty development effort, this chapter can enhance the understanding and effectiveness of doing so with the guidance of a faculty committee.

The results from a recent national survey of faculty developers' perceptions of their work (Sorcinelli, Austin, Eddy, & Beach, 2006) confirmed that, although faculty development programs are becoming more centralized and more frequently administered by dedicated staff lines, one of the primary influences on the planning, implementation, and administration of programs is still shaped by institutional type. Because liberal arts, faith-based, and specialized colleges are more likely than other institutional types to use a committee to promote and support faculty development activities and to envision faculty development as requiring faculty input (Sorcinelli et al., 2006), the ideas and advice offered in this chapter may be more directly pertinent to faculty development structures found on smaller college campuses. Certainly there are, however, exceptions to this model.

Given the multiple roles juggled by faculty developers at small and liberal arts colleges (Mooney & Reder, 2008), successfully guiding a committee's work may not only invigorate on-campus programs but lighten the developers' load as well. Ultimately, whether one is working at a large research university or a small college with a teaching mission, convening a committee invested in a collaborative vision for faculty development may be the first step in "putting an end to pedagogical solitude" (Shulman, 2004, p. 140). Once that vision is widely shared, Tierney (2002) suggested working on the second important element, that is, defining what matters to the work by developing a mission statement that inspires one's colleagues. If the new faculty developer inherits an established committee with longstanding members, using the first meeting to explore their perceptions of the strengths and challenges of the committee's charge is one way to determine how ready they are to reshape some of that ongoing work. Acknowledging and respecting the work the committee has accomplished in the past while invigorating its interest in new ideas is a balance worth pursuing. If the committee is just starting its work and has not received an articulated charge from an administrator or another group, such as a faculty senate, then the first task of the committee would be to develop its charge. This task is extremely important because it will begin to chart the directions the committee takes in the implementation of significant institutional effort. The resources of the Professional and Organizational Development (POD) Network in Higher Education can provide assistance in finding a place to start with the development of a committee charge; one can use the search engine on the POD Network Web site to find similar institutions with similar structures and then review examples of charges to their faculty development committees.

Institutional Context and Committee Goals

Although it is not unusual for a faculty development committee to exist in conjunction with a center for teaching and learning (Sorcinelli et al., 2006) and for its charge to be directly connected to the center's mission and chaired by the center's director, the structure and administration of faculty development is unique to each campus culture. The center director may be the chair of the committee or an ex officio member. At liberal arts and other types of small colleges, where centers are less predominant than at large research universities, the faculty development committee may be part of the formal governance system and have an established charge and predetermined number of faculty and administrative staff members. The annual goals and agenda of a committee are subject to the emerging needs and interests of faculty members, the particular campus culture and initiatives, and the broader institutional mission.

Faculty developers across all institutional types agree that a primary purpose for their work is to create and sustain cultures of teaching excellence (Sorcinelli et al., 2006). To be fully effective, ideally the faculty development committee is viewed as a politically neutral group coordinated in its efforts to advance effective teaching. According to Lunde and Healy (2002), the committee should not be cast in a reactive or simply bureaucratic role but should rather be viewed as and function as a group that generates creative, thoughtful programs and remains flexible in responding to the needs of its constituents.

Responsibilities of the Chairperson or Faculty Development Leader

A recent article outlining thirteen principles of effective practice for faculty developers, especially those at small colleges (Reder, Mooney, Holmgren, & Kuerbis, 2009), offered a number of suggestions with direct application to the productive ways faculty developers may work with their committees.

Committee Membership

Primary among these responsibilities, assuming that the coordinator of faculty development or the convener of the committee has influence over the committee membership, Reder et al. (2009) recommended including "*un*usual suspects." Inviting at least one or two faculty colleagues to membership who may initially seem disinterested in promoting teaching and learning discussions and workshops may not only challenge one's own thinking in productive ways but may also widen the circle of other faculty members who pay attention to and attend the committee-sponsored events.

Although faculty developers are less focused on creating recognition for excellent teaching than they are for positively influencing the teaching culture at the broadest level (Sorcinelli et al., 2006), involving faculty leaders known for their classroom and student learning successes lends another level of credibility to the committee's work. One model for engaging the outstanding teachers and scholars on a campus is to invite them to serve in the capacity of an "associate" or "fellow" and to give them a very specific programming idea to work with each semester. The associates, who may have other commitments outside the classroom, need not serve on the committee itself. The importance of diverse and representative committee membership, including key staff members (that is, a librarian and instructional technologist), cannot be overstated.

Some portion of the faculty development committee membership may change each year. To address the revolving membership and the attendant need to educate new members about the purposes of faculty development on your campus, one may consider distributing a FAQ (frequently asked questions) sheet along with a packet of general readings to new committee members. In addition, one may want to invite new committee members to peruse the faculty development Web site and then schedule a meeting with each new member to discuss the information found there and in the packets. Sharing the previous year's agendas or event schedule may also help shape the new members' expectations about the kind of work the faculty development committee is expected to accomplish.

Organizing the Committee's Work

In addition to serving as the primary person behind the planning, implementation, and facilitation for faculty development workshops and events, the faculty developer must learn how to make productive and efficient use of the committee's time, expertise, and energy. This basic advice for working effectively with a faculty development committee is foundational. An organized committee chairperson inspires participation through his or her own degree of commitment to the committee. The following list is not exhaustive but provides guidelines for putting one's best foot forward when organizing the faculty development committee's work.

○ If not already established, determine the committee size based on the projected number and scope of programs and events that are expected to be sponsored in any given academic year; incorporate new committee members based on the potential for creative coordination or cosponsorship of programs.

○ Survey members for a common meeting time; and, if possible, establish a predictable schedule and a regular meeting place.

○ Create a committee e-mail list, and use it to facilitate ease of communication and to create a sense of community among committee membership. Encourage all members to use the e-mail list if they have an idea to share prior to a formal meeting or to convey feedback about a recent program.

○ Solicit input for the primary goals and programs for a full semester to full year.

○ At least a few days before each meeting, use the e-mail list to solicit agenda items from members; provide an agenda in advance for every meeting.

○ Create subcommittees for major projects, and provide time during meetings for them to accomplish work and report back to the full committee. This approach to providing time for subcommittee meetings is most effective when every member of the full committee serves on one of the subcommittees.

○ Educate committee members on the broader issues in faculty development and higher education by providing relevant and timely articles from, for example, *Change* magazine, chapters from the POD Network publication *To Improve the Academy*, or the *POD Network Essays on Teaching Excellence*. Distribution and subsequent discussion of this kind of material not only expands the knowledge base of committee members; it can also contribute to building a sense of community among the committee members as they share their thoughts, reactions, and experiences with each other.

○ If the committee chair regularly attends the annual POD conference or intends to make that meeting a part of his or her own professional development, it is beneficial to invite at least one or two committee members to attend that conference as well. The practice of broadening committee members' perspective on the centrality of faculty development work to the many colleges and universities that also send representatives to the POD conference is a compelling message. The creative ideas that these committee members will subsequently contribute to program planning on the home campus is an additional benefit.

○ Whenever possible, provide clerical support for major projects; continue to garner tangible support for the committee's ideas and events from key administrators.

○ Manage the budget and communicate its availability for programming activities to the committee.

○ Continually pursue the best practices in the field and educate the committee about the creative work going on elsewhere. The faculty developer's enthusiasm and confidence offer tremendous potential for energizing a group of colleagues to exceed even their own expectations about how effective their efforts might be on behalf of their colleagues.

It is not uncommon for faculty developers to find themselves as ex officio members rather than chairpersons of faculty development committees. In this instance, it is important to be prepared for differing expectations than those just discussed and even possible tensions that may arise under these circumstances. If you do not chair the faculty development committee, the first problem you may encounter is the regularity with which the committee meets. The frequency of faculty development committee meetings, the richness of the agenda, and the productive facilitation of the meetings have direct bearing on the quality and degree to which your administrative responsibilities are accomplished. If circumstances allow, communicate with the chairperson early on to convey your preferences for the frequency of committee meetings and the variety of agenda items that would best serve the work. Certainly give the chairperson ample opportunity to weigh in, but continue to emphasize the need for a collaborative approach to the faculty development work on your campus.

Coordination with Others

The perspectives and insights of the committee membership are critical for the creation of an overall plan and calendar for the year's events, but the coordination of the committee's ideas and plans with other offices and programs is the responsibility of the person in the faculty developer role. Another Reder et al. (2009) recommendation for faculty development leaders is to "use the talent pool on your own campus" when considering event facilitators (p. 276); and the faculty development committee may be very helpful in deciding where this talent can be found. Inviting nationally known authors on teaching and learning to campus can be exciting and fruitful but may not be a viable financial option more than once a year. An invitation asking current faculty members on your own campus to facilitate teaching and learning discussions encourages shared owner-ship for this important work; this sense of ownership creates the likeli-hood that those attending the event will find the source of ideas credible. Coordination with other offices and units on campus, as appropriate for the mission and activities planned by the committee, is also likely to fall within the responsibilities of the faculty developer.

Management

That faculty development committees are more a phenomenon of a small college situation means that it is unlikely the faculty developer will have significant administrative tasks in such areas as financial or personnel management. However, there might be an annual amount budgeted for the work of the committee, and the faculty developer is probably the person responsible for determining the details of this budget. There might also be a staff person who is assigned to assist with the work of the com-mittee so the faculty developer can get involved with supervisory tasks. While these responsibilities are unlikely to be terribly demanding, if there are questions about how to handle them, one can always tactfully seek assistance from others who already have this kind of experience.

The Work of the Committee

Ideally, a faculty development committee generates, launches, supports, and implements successful, well-received faculty development programs on behalf of their colleagues. In addition to planning formal training workshops on specific teaching and learning topics—such as leading classroom discussions, effective feedback and grading, or writing and speaking across the disciplines—the components of developing program-ming are best decided upon through committee deliberation based on input and suggestions from faculty colleagues. The committee should be positioned for campuswide *communication* and *collaboration* on all teaching and learning issues; the membership strategies discussed earlier should facilitate this goal. One of the early assignments a faculty developer should work out with the committee is how and when they want to contact their colleagues about ideas for programming and how and when they should announce their program plans to the broader community. Asking the committee to consider the medium and the message that will make their efforts consistent with their mission but distinctive from other campus announcements is a good starting point for this discussion.

Program Ideas

A faculty development committee with continuing membership may be well prepared to offer specialized activities depending on members' time commitments and the committee's financial resources. The list below expands upon a few programming ideas offered by Svinicki (2002) that faculty development committees may wish to adapt and offer on their campuses. This brief listing should be understood, however, as offering just a few of what could be a very long list of programming ideas; other chapters in this book provide additional details and suggestions. The three possibilities suggested below illustrate how the faculty development committee can be involved in the planning, preparation, and implementation of programs that promote the improvement of teaching and learning.

PEER OBSERVATION OF CLASSROOM TEACHING. At a faculty member's request, a member of the committee may be asked to review a syllabus or other course materials or may be asked to sit in on a class in order to give feedback about a specific teaching issue. It must first be understood that these consultations are not evaluative and will not find their way into that faculty member's tenure and promotion dossier. Because the committee's work in this arena is intended to be supportive and formative and focused on what any individual faculty member wishes to discuss about classroom teaching, colleagues should be assured that classroom observations are voluntary. Working with committee members to prepare them for this kind of activity is essential, and this preparation should include a thorough review of the best practices (see, for example, Chism, 2008, and back issues of *To Improve the Academy*).

If the faculty development committee intends to develop a more regular and comprehensive classroom observation service, it may want to explain its philosophy and model fully through a newsletter or open forum involving the faculty. This disclosure would serve to alleviate any concerns faculty members might have about confidentiality, and they can also be assured that peer-to-peer discussions are not brought back to committee-level discussions.

PLANNING AND SUPPORTING NEW FACULTY ORIENTATION. Welcoming new colleagues to campus is an important role for any faculty developer and faculty development committee. A thoughtful, well-organized gathering in advance of the start of classes signals to new professors that they are valued and that the community wants them to succeed. Committee members may sponsor a panel on a variety of topics including the teaching and learning culture or on the resources available for teaching and scholarship. Facilitating new faculty orientation is also a good way to generate programming and workshop topics for the coming academic year.

In a short period of time at the beginning of the academic year, it is not possible or desirable to cover all of the important details and policies that new colleagues may want to know before they start their careers at your institution. A faculty development committee can be instrumental in the ongoing orientation of new colleagues by hosting monthly gatherings to discuss additional relevant policy and practice information. In addition to providing useful information, such meetings may offer a social outlet to new faculty, which they will also appreciate.

WORKSHOPS ON PREPARING A TENURE AND PROMOTION DOSSIER. In collaboration with the committee that reviews tenure and promotion cases, and perhaps even with the dean's or provost's office, the faculty development committee can perform a valuable service when it schedules time and space for informal or formal discussion about the kinds of information and materials to include or avoid in a tenure and promotion dossier. Of course, these discussions and their format vary across campuses; but the invitation of a politically neutral committee to participate in a discussion about portfolio development and suggestions about how to organize a coherent case affords the opportunity for a valuable exchange of information.

Effective Subcommittee Work

As a faculty development program matures and moves beyond one or two focused programs, the committee may need to compartmentalize its work in order to expand its reach and support for the faculty. If a faculty developer is working with a committee of nine or more individuals and finds that meetings are less productive as the programming expands, it may be time to consider establishing subcommittees. Assuming all committee members are serving on one of the subcommittees, it will be important for the chair to provide time for subcommittee conversations during the regular meeting time and to leave additional time for subcommittees to report back to the larger group before the end of the meeting.

Once the full committee determines the foci of two or three subcommittees, the faculty developer might write up a brief charge for each and convey these via e-mail so that members can freely choose their own assignments. It may be necessary to assign someone to lead or convene each subcommittee, especially if these smaller groups anticipate meeting independently, outside of regularly scheduled full committee meetings. The full faculty development committee may wish to send work to a particular subcommittee, and they may also assign deadlines for that work. As the chairperson of the full committee, you will want to facilitate a discussion about general expectations for subcommittee work before the members begin their assignments. Following are a few suggestions for the kind of subcommittees that might make substantive contributions to the larger faculty development committee effort.

TECHNOLOGY SUPPORT AND TRAINING. It may be surprising that the faculty development, support, and training category did not make the top-ten issues list of the annual EDUCAUSE Current Issues Survey (Allison & Deblois, 2008) completed by college and university instructional technology (IT) leaders. Security and funding issues continue to present more pressing challenges for IT personnel; but technology training for faculty is still an evolving enterprise on traditional, residential campuses. Therefore, it is an issue that must be considered within the specific campus culture.

Regardless of institutional type, however, mandates about the use of technology in the classroom will likely backfire and further delay advances in experimentation and training (Brown, 2003). A faculty development and teaching committee is poised to offer the guidance and venues that educational technologies staff members may lack if they work in isolation from the teaching faculty. The educational technology staff may be more aware of early adopters of new technology and bring this information to the committee's attention, while the faculty members on the committee may suggest productive approaches to introducing the new technology to the rest of their colleagues. This subcommittee may also serve in an advisory capacity if the educational technology staff considers purchasing new software or upgrading classroom spaces. Establishing a strong connection to the educational technology staff and inviting them into the committee structure is an important step to take early in the establishment of an advisory board or committee. It is also an example of how a faculty development committee can be well positioned to promote cooperation and collaboration between and among different institutional divisions.

INCORPORATING INSTITUTIONAL RESEARCH AND DATA ON TEACHING AND LEARNING. The Sorcinelli et al. (2006) national study indicated that priorities among faculty developers focus more on meeting individual faculty needs than on responding to the critical needs of the institution. So it is likely that faculty development programming responds to and emphasizes issues brought forth by the faculty. This may be especially true at liberal arts institutions. Yet, faculty development work that takes advantage of institutional data on teaching and learning can result in programming that speaks directly to specific national survey findings and institutional benchmarking. Many faculty colleagues will find information about the responses of students at the institution to the National Survey of Student Engagement (NSSE) or their own responses to a national faculty survey quite compelling and applicable to their classroom teaching, especially if they can consider campus results in direct comparison to national results. A subcommittee charged with collaborating with the office of institutional research on what surveys are administered on campus, the timing of the data availability, and maintaining a specific focus on teaching and student learning issues could beneficially inform the full committee's plans for the year as well as the work of other faculty and campus committees.

PRODUCING WEB RESOURCES AND NEWSLETTERS. Perennial time constraints do not allow faculty members to attend every campus function in which they might have interest. Once a faculty development program has matured and is known for offering regularly scheduled workshops, teaching circles, or technology training, the committee may be asked to make available the materials from its sponsored events. A subcommittee that anticipates these requests determines information to be posted to the faculty development Web site and obtains and posts those materials in a timely way provides a foundational service on behalf of the entire committee's efforts. Members of this subcommittee may consider using the Web site to showcase colleagues' successful innovative pedagogies and may also post reading lists or links to other Web sites that support teaching and learning.

Important questions about teaching and learning often arise in committee discussions, and they are either not easily addressed through a workshop or not possible to address because the semester's programming calendar does not allow for an additional gathering. Brief but regular publications from the faculty development committee may offer a venue for reflections by distinguished professors, book reviews on teaching and learning, emerging issues in higher education, or even a regular column featuring faculty-student interviews.

Questions and Answers About Faculty Development Committees

If the institution is just beginning a formal approach to faculty development or if one is a newly designated committee chairperson or center director, questions may arise about working with committees that extend beyond the faculty developer's leadership role or about the functioning of the committee. The questions below are common; and the answers should be considered within the context of your own faculty, teaching, and campus cultures.

What kind of administrative support should I seek for the faculty development committee's work?

Svinicki's (2002) summary of the kind and degree of administrative support that leads to the success of faculty development efforts is very helpful. For the most part, because administrators often hold the purse strings, it is important for a faculty development committee to propose and receive a realistic budget to achieve its goals. In the long run, however, administrators who are knowledgeable about the committee's work, who acknowledge when that work makes an impact on some aspect of the teaching culture, and who remember to include the committee or at least the chair of the committee in some aspect of strategic planning are all sending signals that the administration values the faculty development committee's work and contributes to the perception that the faculty should pay attention to the opportunity it affords.

How can we gain the attention of our colleagues and improve attendance and participation at our committee's events?

Reder et al. (2009, p. 277) suggested "generating grassroots interest in your programs before announcing them." If each member of the committee contacts two other faculty members to describe what the committee is planning and solicits ideas for feedback before the event is announced, this early contact may produce interest in and commitment to attending a specific event. Reder et al. (2009) also encouraged those planning workshops and programs to invite prominent faculty members to lead discussions. Another significant element to remember is that it is important to provide refreshments whenever possible. Certainly, the provisions of light refreshments of any kind signals that the faculty development committee values their colleagues' time and effort to attend the sponsored event. The implicit message in all of these suggestions is to promote excellence and inclusiveness as the committee's standards for its processes and for its results.

How important is the role of a center for teaching and learning for effective faculty development?

This question applies in all contexts for faculty development, as noted in the previous chapters of this volume; and a faculty development committee will also need to address the question. One important factor influencing the answer to the question is institutional mission and type (Mooney & Reder, 2008; Sorcinelli et al., 2006). Because larger, research-intensive universities serve more faculty members and graduate students, the success of their faculty development programs may depend on a centralized administrative structure that includes a physical space and a dedicated staff. Individuals responsible for faculty development committees and programs at smaller institutions work within a variety of models. For smaller colleges, a center, even if it is in name only or a virtual center, gives faculty development a tangible identity on campus. On the other hand, faculty development efforts at numerous, prominent small colleges operate out of a faculty member or administrator's office quite effectively. Exploring the answer to this question within the institutional context in a deliberate and inclusive way is a good first step to determining whether and how your institutional resources should be put toward establishing a center for teaching and learning or a centralized faculty development effort.

Conclusion

Faculty development goals and activities are never static. Working with a faculty development committee affords multiple voices and perspectives to shape the mission and programming for faculty development and its implementation. Providing effective leadership for such a committee requires ongoing attention to and balance of the needs of individual faculty colleagues and the institutional charge given to the committee. It also calls for the continuing professional development of the developer. There is abundant opportunity for the work of a faculty development committee to be accomplished in highly organized and collaborative ways that reach out to multiple faculty constituencies and even beyond the faculty itself to other divisions on campus. As a politically neutral committee, the faculty development group gains legitimacy as a source of valuable information and programming that serves the best interests of the faculty, and ultimately, the students.

REFERENCES

Allison, D. H., & Deblois, P. B. (2008). Top-ten IT issues, 2008. *EDUCAUSE Review, 43*(3), 36–61.

Brown, D. (2003). (Ed.). *Developing faculty to use technology: Programs and strategies to enhance teaching.* Bolton, MA: Anker.

Chism, N.V.N. (2008). *Peer review of teaching: A sourcebook.* Bolton, MA: Anker.

Lunde, J. P., & Healy, M. M. (2002). The basics of faculty development committees. In K. H. Gillespie (Ed.), *A guide to faculty development: Practical advice, examples, and resources* (pp. 251–257). Bolton, MA: Anker.

Mooney, K. M., & Reder, M. (2008). Faculty development at small and liberal arts colleges. In D. R. Robertson & L. Nilson (Eds.), *To improve the academy: Vol. 26. Resources for faculty, instructional, and organizational development* (pp. 158–172). Bolton, MA: Anker.

Reder, M., Mooney, K. M., Holmgren, R., & Kuerbis, P. (2009). Starting and sustaining successful faculty development programs at small colleges. In L. Nilson & J. Miller (Eds.), *To improve the academy: Vol. 27. Resources for faculty, instructional, and organizational development* (pp. 267–286). San Francisco: Jossey-Bass.

Shulman, L. S. (2004). *Teaching as community property: Essays on higher education.* San Francisco: Jossey-Bass.

Sorcinelli, M. D., Austin, A. E., Eddy, P. L., & Beach, A. L. (2006). *Creating the future of faculty development: Learning from the past, understanding the present.* Bolton, MA: Anker.

Svinicki, M. (2002). Faculty development: An investment for the future. In R. M. Diamond (Ed.), *Field guide to academic leadership* (pp. 211–222). San Francisco: Jossey-Bass.

Tierney, W. G. (2002). Mission and vision statements: An essential first step. In R. M. Diamond (Ed.), *Field guide to academic leadership* (pp. 49–58). San Francisco: Jossey-Bass.

5

LISTEN, LEARN, LEAD

GETTING STARTED IN FACULTY DEVELOPMENT

Margaret W. Cohen

READERS OF THIS VOLUME ARE LIKELY either preparing for the exciting work of faculty development or have just begun in this work. Whether the appointment is to a new faculty center or to an established office, making a transition is an important and luxurious time to explore new responsibilities and become acquainted with the institution and its community from a new or different perspective. This chapter offers suggestions for orienting to the role and responsibilities of a faculty developer by relying on the professional and personal strengths that led to one's selection for this role. Although the paths to faculty development are as varied as the initial concerns and questions new faculty developers have about their work, their strengths converge on two passions: faculty development professionals share expertise in and a keenness for teaching and inquiry. These two passions are the foundational competencies on which to focus the work of faculty development, reveal its direction, and discover the nearby resources to help attain and sustain successes.

Multiple Paths and Opportunities for Inquiry

Passions for teaching and inquiry are likely related to the reasons one pursues a shift or expansion to include faculty development on a career path. The rosters of faculty developers, also called "educational developers," include veteran faculty who, respected for their disciplinary and pedagogical expertise, are invited to focus their efforts on supporting their colleagues. The enthusiasm of others who enter this field is fueled by successes in mentoring junior colleagues, part-time faculty members, or graduate students. The ranks of educational developers include those who prepared as instructional designers, institutional researchers, librarians, and persons with background in traditional academic disciplines. Information technology staff members charged with training users in new technologies such as course management systems may hold staff positions in offices of educational development. Since 1993, when the Council of Graduate Schools partnered with the Association of American Colleges and Universities to initiate the Preparing Future Faculty program, more and more institutions have been augmenting traditional doctoral programs with opportunities that also prepare graduate students for the responsibilities of teaching and service (Colbeck, O'Meara, & Austin, 2008). As students earn graduate credentials in university and college teaching and explore teaching in a scholarly way, some are attracted to full-time work in faculty development centers. A developing option for doctoral students in higher education is in new programs that are preparing professionals interested in careers related to faculty and teaching assistant development.

The existence of these programs acknowledges the need for doctorally prepared faculty developers and testifies to the maturity of the field of educational development. That, in turn, is prescient confirmation that opportunities for research related to educational development are plentiful. Who, for example, chooses to prepare for this career focus in graduate school? What routes lead experienced faculty members from across the disciplines in higher education to shift their emphasis to educational development? What are effective supports for faculty developers, and how are they best provided? Questions like these will guide the research of future doctoral students and stimulate the research interests of others in the field. Currently, it is not possible to point to reports that document the percentages of individuals who move into educational development from various paths. Data are needed that explain how individuals acquired their expertise and what paths and experiences influenced them to choose this new career. An effort to respond to this void in the literature base brought together collaborators from Australia, Canada, England, Scotland, and the United States. This international group reported on the project "Pathways into Educational Development" at the 2008 meeting of the International Consortium for Educational Development (Stockley et al., 2008; McDonald & Stockley, 2008).

They created an online database with the goal of learning what attracts, supports, and sustains individuals who work in educational development. (Persons interested in contributing to this developing knowledge base are invited to visit the group's Web site at http://www.edpathways.com.)

We are beginning, however, to learn something about the developmental needs that drive new faculty developers in their early years on the job. Over a five-year period, fifty-six new developers, who were in their first four years of work, identified the "burning issues" that prompted them to seek consultations during a preconference workshop that I have organized and presented at the annual conference of the Professional and Organizational Development (POD) Network since 2003 (Cohen, 2003). The workshop is called "How's It Going? Reflecting on Our Work." Participants in this workshop are required to prepare in advance for the consultations by compiling a portfolio of their work in educational development and isolating one question on which they seek guidance from veteran developers. Over the years these questions, submitted in advance of the workshop, have ranged from practical to visionary concerns. On the practical end of the continuum, new faculty developers want to learn how to reach faculty members who teach on a part-time basis, how to attract greater attendance at programs and workshops, and where to secure more resources. They question how to construct mentoring programs for various groups of colleagues. They want to learn how to assess the impact of their work on their clients and on their institutions. They want to guide their colleagues in applying the Scholarship of Teaching and Learning to their instructional work (Shulman, 2004) and learn the best ways to communicate with colleagues outside of their own disciplines. These concerns reflect the preparatory experiences Jensen (2002) described as she began work as a faculty consultant and the questions Sorcinelli (2002) used as a foundation for a set of principles of good practice for newcomers to the field.

At the visionary end of the continuum, new faculty developers want to learn which strategies could change the value their institutional cultures place on teaching and learning effectiveness. They want to influence how their institutions prioritize their strategic goals. These issues reflect the changes in higher education that Sorcinelli, Austin, Eddy, and Beach (2006) anticipated would affect the work of faculty developers, that is, changes in the professoriate; in the student body; and in what we know about teaching, learning, and scholarship.

Responding with confidence to these issues necessitates that they be fashioned into researchable questions and hypotheses. These tasks may be the future work of faculty developers: to be attentive and responsive to changes in higher education and to be prepared to inquire systematically into its most compelling realities. The pressing issues of the 2010s will challenge faculty developers to work in environments where funding is dwindling, where new technologies enable alternative ways to deliver education, where interdisciplinary work becomes the new academic currency, and where faculty colleagues feel discouraged by an increasingly diverse and consumer-oriented student body. Demands for accountability, learning outcomes, and evidence of successful engagement come from taxpayers, legislators, governing boards, and accrediting bodies. Each demands that institutions chart their futures realistically and strategically and assess their efforts in ways that document continuous improvements. Institutional leaders expect that faculty developers will know how to be responsive to this agenda.

Applying Research and Inquiry Skills

The research and inquiry skills acquired in one's academic discipline are foundational to this new work in faculty development. Transition time will be well spent in investigating both the field of faculty development and one's institution. Most likely the former is new to the practitioner, and the latter is familiar. Nevertheless, even when a person has been at an institution for many years, one's perspective changes in a new role. While a new role in educational development may distance a person from colleagues and a familiar faculty role, it opens new vantage points and offers insights into decision making across the institution. Bridges (2003) emphasized that persons making transitions in an organization are not making those changes alone; when responsibilities and expectations change, the organization is also in transition. Researching one's institution from the viewpoint of a new assignment leads to different and expanded perspectives about a variety of matters, such as how workload or tenure policies are administered differently across departments of one institution. At times, new perspectives may offer access to privileged or confidential information from peers or about the institution. The new faculty developer may learn, for example, which campus opinion leaders influence academic leaders' decisions and which do not. Confidential exchanges about policy missteps or violations are indications of items to address in upcoming orientations and programs.

As you distill this information, consider conferring with others in educational development. Among the resources available is an expansive network of colleagues who will lend advice and offer support. Take the time to do these explorations early in a new appointment. Time spent in early exploration is significant for the information one acquires and the credibility one accrues, and the ability to use time in this way is likely to be a short-lived luxury.

Researching Faculty Development

Researching the field of faculty development leads new educational developers to a growing set of helpful resources. A primary recommendation is to meet those doing related work and to discover the organization upon which they rely for an abundance of useful assets. Then explore the volumes and journals that inform the field and become familiar with the variety of online resources that link organizations and institutions. Knowledge from these resources will accumulate quickly. It is easily available and readily shared.

A good starting place to research the field is to know the organizations that bind it together by serving as central clearinghouses, repositories, and information conduits for faculty developers. While there are several such organizations around the world, the POD Network is one very good example of such an association. Its Web site (http://www.podnetwork .org) links from its home page to a wealth of information about faculty, instructional, and organizational development, including related conferences, publications, grant opportunities, and other resources. Here one will find the *Ethical Guidelines for Educational Developers,* a resource to review often and consult as role conflicts arise or clarity is needed about an activity or request. The POD Network conference opens with half- and whole-day preconference workshops, which offer participants time with colleagues to consider their work, review their progress, learn new strategies or avenues for conveying information, and consult with veteran faculty developers. Two of these annual workshops are designed explicitly for those new to faculty development. The "Getting Started Workshop for New Faculty Developers" is a day-long event designed for those new to the field. The other is "How's It Going? Reflecting on Our Work" mentioned earlier. It offers opportunity to consult on a specific "burning issue" with veteran developers. Every odd year POD cosponsors the Institute for New Faculty Developers (INFD), a five-day program that introduces new educational developers to key topics and strategies for conveying them to others. These institutes generally include such topics as faculty consultations, creating faculty learning communities, designing and assessing courses and programs, and understanding faculty *and* student learning and motivation. Information about the institute is linked to the POD Network Web pages, where there are also links to join the

POD listserv, a forum for the frequent exchange of ideas, announcements of meetings, news, and open positions, and where members turn to seek information from one another.

What makes the POD Network an essential organization is immediately apparent when one reviews the listserv archives, the Web site, or attends the annual conference: this is an organization in and through which participants generously offer and share their ideas and products. An organization that values such collaboration contrasts sharply with the competitive spirit that defines success in many disciplines. Those who join POD, attend the workshops, and contribute to the meetings and listserv gain colleagues who support one another through transitional stress, uncertainty, and disappointment and who, in turn, celebrate each other's victories and successes.

Smaller regional or interest networks also offer valuable opportunities for connecting with educational development colleagues. For example, the HBCU (Historically Black Colleges and Universities) Faculty Development Network convenes in the fall. The Southern Regional Faculty and Instructional Development Consortium meets in March, and the New England Faculty Development Consortium regularly sponsors fall and spring conferences. Small, informal groups include the Great Plains Faculty Development Consortium, which generally meets annually in the late spring, and the Missouri Illinois Faculty Developers (MIFD), which meets twice a year at a different host institution. The MIFD includes faculty developers working at institutions close to the city of St. Louis, who routinely share information via e-mail. They support one another's programming endeavors by cosponsoring or promoting events. Colleagues take advantage of the "fifty-mile rule," which holds that an informative presentation by a faculty colleague may draw a more enthusiastic audience at another institution than at home. The MIFD group relies on its members' proximity to exchange resources—without spending dollars—in the spirit of a cooperative. A presentation given by one colleague is exchanged for a presentation by a colleague from another campus. Members are a phone call away for updates, information, or empathy. That kind of connection is critical because many faculty developers operate solo or in institutional offices with small staffs. Meeting colleagues from nearby institutions and organizations is the first step to creating a collegial network of professional support.

This openhanded and respectful exchange of resources and ideas that characterizes relationships among colleagues working in educational development also explains the wealth of material that is publicly shared on the Web sites you will explore as your research on faculty

development continues. For example, TeachingCoach.Org (http://www
.teachingcoach.org) provides a well-organized set of resources offering
advice, books, blogs, and online coaching for new faculty developers. The
Center for Teaching Excellence at the University of Kansas maintains a
comprehensive list of links to faculty development centers at institutions
on nearly every continent (http://www.cte.ku.edu/cteInfo/resources/web
sites.shtml). In itself, exploring how other centers construct their
Web pages and present their services and programs creates an opportunity
to consider what types of pages and organization will attract your faculty
colleagues. For realistic ideas and ways to present services and programs
that are offered at U.S. institutions similar to yours, consult the pages
of campuses within the same Carnegie classifications as your institution
(McCormick & Zhao, 2005). Carnegie classifications are available online
at http://www.carnegiefoundation.org/classifications. The POD Web site
also offers excellent search opportunities for such information.

Another organization with links to many published resources is the
Society for Teaching and Learning in Higher Education (STLHE), a
Canadian organization with Web pages offered in English and in
French. Linked to the organization's Web site are announcements
of events and awards; members' discounts from publishers; and a
range of informative publications including newsletters and *Green
Guides,* essays on topics that will interest instructors in higher education. Two journals, *Positive Pedagogy* and the *Canadian Journal for
the Scholarship of Teaching and Learning,* can be accessed from the
STLHE Web pages. The variety of resources on these pages will appeal
to both new and experienced faculty developers. Similar, bilingual Web
pages are also offered by Pathways to the Profession of Educational
Development at http://www.edpathways.com.

Many online resources include suggestions for books, journals,
and newsletters that inform the educational development community.
Exploring the printed literature is also important. Your library may be able
to help purchase materials that can then be widely shared. Consider which
volumes and which subscriptions to purchase for the office or center library
that will support your work and attract others for visits and consultations. Newsletters such as the *Teaching Professor, Department Chair,* and
Academic Leader are published in print and electronically; and subscriptions
offer various options for distributing copies to faculty and administrators. Two publications likely to be available in most faculty development
centers are the *Chronicle of Higher Education* and *Change* magazine.
Both are written to communicate news, innovations, trends, and best practices to a broad audience of faculty, staff, administrators, and students.

Two periodicals to consider for your growing professional development library that will appeal to faculty colleagues across the disciplines seeking classroom options and innovations are *College Teaching* and the *National Teaching and Learning Forum*. Peer-reviewed articles and monographs presenting effective, research-based practices are published in *Innovative Higher Education, New Directions for Teaching and Learning,* and the *Journal on Excellence in College Teaching*. These materials can demonstrate to colleagues how their instructional decisions and practices can be based on the body of literature about teaching and learning in higher education. Note also that the POD Web site offers a list of important periodicals.

Researching Your Institution

Since the goals of the instructional and organizational work of educational development include creating inviting environments for learning, it is important to discover what is already in place and what interests others and drives their goals for learning. Researching the institution requires many of the same skills used to explore faculty development. If you are new to faculty development, even if most of your academic experience is at the same institution, taking time to research it from your new perspective is vitally important. (See also Chapter Seven, "Promoting Your Program and Grounding It in the Institution.") One might liken this exploration to that of an anthropologist. Meeting others on their own turf is crucial for acquiring an understanding of how they regard the institution and for establishing yourself as a credible colleague interested in others, their work, and where they do it. What one learns from this research will be reflected in one's own work. It will be evident in the office or center that the new faculty developer is joining or creating and in the reputation that one cultivates about one's role and work. It will be apparent in how the values of the institution are conveyed from the new faculty developer's office and how one models the citizenship skills expected by the organization. The recommendations in the following sections of this chapter suggest how to develop a research strategy for examining the institution's culture, contexts, and infrastructure and for beginning to chart the direction of one's work.

EXAMINING THE INSTITUTION. Although every institution provides formal documents to review, most of your exploration will be in face-to-face meetings with faculty and staff colleagues. Complete the reading research first since key documents will help to identify informants to interview. Review the institution's mission and vision statements and strategic plan. Accreditation bodies are requiring that these formal documents be publicly accessible; but, if they are not available online, request them and request access to the password-protected software through which institutional data and documents are uploaded. The most recent institutional self-study prepared for accreditation or reaccreditation will likely be found there. Review the guidelines and procedures in place for the cyclical reviews of programs and centers. The documents prepared for these reviews will provide insights into how program goals and outcomes are aligned and how educational development is regarded in departments and colleges. They will offer hints of what units need or think they need, and they may also contribute to the list of individuals you can meet in individual meetings as your research continues.

If the faculty developer is creating a new office, it is advisable to select a broad sample of persons to interview from each division, academic and nonacademic. If one is joining an existing office, one should seek recommendations for key supporters and detractors whose vantage points will be informative. Other things one can do are as follows.

1. Create a list of individuals to interview that includes academic and nonacademic administrative leaders, deans and directors, department chairs, faculty members of all ranks and status (tenure-track, non-tenure track, part-time, early career, tenured) across all disciplines, and teaching assistants and graduate students who are planning for academic roles.

2. Request a meeting in their offices; doing so will help you learn more about the physical setting of the campus if it is new to you. Prepare for these interviews by constructing a list of questions that will guide you to learn others' perceptions of the institution, its needs, their unit's (college, department, program, center) needs, and their expectations of a faculty developer.

3. Listen carefully for the feedback and "pushback" that provoked the "burning issues" identified by new faculty developers. As you inquire about these expectations, you will learn about the needs and concerns of various individuals and groups. You will learn how each understands and perceives the workplace as you listen for their explanations of the institution's mission, strategic plans and goals, and attitudes about accreditation. Inquire about how each understands and participates in the faculty governance structure, and listen for answers that can help in your work. For example, a program revising its degree requirements may need help aligning

a new curriculum with campus goals or developing an assessment plan for its outcomes. An instructional technology committee may be charged with recommending designs for renovating classroom spaces. A strategic planning committee may recognize that it has not developed a mechanism for informing the institutional community of its plans.

4. Analyze the responses you hear for opportunities. These interviews are not intended for instant problem solving. Rather, they are intended to help you understand the institution, and they require you to listen and be empathic. Loquacity may have been important as you interviewed for this job; listening skills are needed to do it well.

In addition to listening for personal and group perceptions, needs, and expectations, listen for and develop an understanding of the initiatives adopted or under consideration. How much focus on student learning is expressed during the interviews? Higher education institutions are challenged today to adopt a continuous improvement model (Massy, 2003) to assess their impact and focus the organization on learning (Senge, 2006). Massy's quality principles elucidate Senge's concept by showing that learning organizations define quality by identifying outcomes, providing evidence of outcomes, and adopting collaborative processes that are compatible with the organization's mission and values. As new initiatives are discussed during the interviews, are they understood as supports for student learning and success, or are they regarded with mistrust? Are processes in place to evaluate their successes? What processes were used to select initiatives such as first-year experiences, learning communities, interdisciplinary work, and the Scholarship of Teaching and Learning? Who is leading the recruitment and retention initiatives that respond to data from the National Survey of Student Engagement (Kuh, 2003) by promoting active and collaborative learning and enriching academic experiences such as service learning, undergraduate research, and study abroad? How does the institution intend to assess the impact of such initiatives?

This time of transition creates an invitation to learn about the institution and learn from its citizens. It is a luxurious time to discover the uniqueness of the institution and to learn which services and resources will be welcomed by the community. The data you collect will validate the direction of your work.

ANALYZING THE DATA AND PRIORITIZING YOUR WORK. The patterns in the interview data provide direction and priorities for future work. As you look for themes in the data, consider what you will do to create a center and a reputation that complements and reflects the institutional context. Be attentive to possible partners and allies across the divisions with whom you can confer as you plan and make decisions. Identify allies in the organization whose priorities and interests align with yours. These will be individuals upon whom you can call for advice or leads to talented faculty presenters or cosponsors for a seminar series. Be attentive to potential partners who may offer human, financial, or material resources that can be tapped as contributions to your work. These supporters include influential faculty members and opinion leaders whom you may invite to serve on a faculty advisory group or development committee. This concept is further developed in Chapter Four, "Working with a Faculty Development Committee."

From the documents reviewed and the interview data collected you will discover how the institution identifies itself. Knowing which factors make the institution unique (for example, ranked programs, student body, urban mission, award-winning researchers and teachers) allows you to tailor priorities so that they are congruent with the institutional culture. Consider the pressing needs identified by each group with whom you have met. Responding to the suggestions of early career faculty members entails supporting their effectiveness as academicians. They may crave an orientation or a mentoring program that truly introduces them to colleagues and offices in the institutional community. They may be eager to learn new instructional technologies, or they may want to know how to research their teaching effectiveness. What pressing needs did the administrative leaders identify? How do their concerns align with those of their faculty colleagues? As you plan to respond to the needs they articulated, call upon these deans and directors to be program partners and cosponsors. Consider developing programs that bring divisions together so that those in one administrative unit can meet colleagues and learn about the supports available in another unit. Those in the divisions of student affairs and information technology are potential partners. Since they cannot easily draw faculty members to their initiatives without support from the academic units, you may be the catalyst for initiating new conversations. Use the data you have collected to explain why the institution should invest in its graduate students and faculty members at every stage of their careers (Morrison-Shetlar & Hohenleitner, 2008). Document and assess your efforts to ensure that you have the evidence needed to demonstrate the impact of your work. (See Chapter Nine, "Program Assessment for Faculty Development.")

Finally, use the data to define how you will become a stellar and valued citizen of the institution. Show your respect for the institution's values by integrating them into the work you do. If the challenge is to become a learning-focused institution, rely on the vocabulary of student engagement to design seminars and invite speakers to present. If the organization is focused on meeting the needs of individual learners, focus on the values of diversity and inclusiveness as you offer consultations and share resources with instructors. If the campus elects to be known as an inspiring steward of the environment, programming that increases global awareness and the responsibilities of citizenship will help faculty and staff members under-stand how to meet these responsibilities in the classroom and through their scholarship and service. In short, the outcomes of your research and inquiry lead to synchronizing your priorities and goals with the most pressing needs and the most prominent initiatives at your institution.

Maintaining and Sustaining Success

Achieving and maintaining success in your new role requires trusting your intrapersonal and interpersonal strengths as you manage the transition, continue to learn and grow, and become comfortable in the role of an educational developer. In addition to learning a new role, your transition may be to a new institution with new colleagues and staff. It may require moving to a new locale, finding a new home, and ensuring that others in your family make smooth transitions. Recognizing the emotions that accom-pany these changes provides clues for introspection. Robertson (1988) referred to three transformation patterns that accompany transitions: resistance to leaving one's former role and environment, grieving that loss, and courageously moving forward to learn about and master the new role and environment. Applying your inquiry and teaching skills to research your new role and to prioritize your strategies requires the cour-age to use your interpersonal skills in new ways. It also takes courage to reflect upon and analyze how your personal strengths and weaknesses are supporting your growth in this new role. Robertson argued that, since this is a change you sought, achieving success includes recognizing that there are personal goals you want to develop in this new environment and that you will need a plan to develop them. Think of this as applying to your-self the strategies used to assess needs and to plan systematically. This is addressed in Chapter Six, "Important Skills and Knowledge."

Build on Your Intrapersonal and Interpersonal Strengths

This chapter began with the suggestion that the passions for teaching and research that brought you to faculty development are competencies that are foundational to your new work. These are the springboards from which to consider both your strengths and weaknesses. Maintaining this passion sustains your credibility as a faculty member even though you may lament the loss of that full-time role. By continuing to teach—or acquiring new classroom experiences if you have not taught before—you gain genuine examples of teaching in the same context as your faculty colleagues. You will draw on these experiences during consultations and seminars. If you do not have a departmental affiliation, consider requesting a courtesy appointment in your discipline. This provides you with an academic home, and the department is likely to turn to you to teach an occasional course. By continuing to seek research opportunities, you bring your own experiences to conversations about making time to collect and analyze data, write, and publish. What may change is that you maintain these strengths in new ways and with new campus collaborators. From teaching well, you may begin to reflect on your own teaching and learning processes in ways that will help others. From the research perspective, your scholarship may refocus on an aspect of your current professional work or on questions provoked by colleagues' innovations, successes, and questions. Building on your strengths in new ways requires introspection and planning to identify behaviors and skills you want to acquire.

Making plans to build new competencies or strengthen developing skills can be challenging. Disclosing fragile skill areas is risky in a new environment where you may not have peers. Although you may develop new behaviors and competencies by observing carefully what strong models say and do, learning is also enhanced by feedback from others. This is when you can call upon your counterparts at other institutions to be your sounding boards. They will empathize with the puzzles you are working out. You can also seek consultations or seminars at professional meetings such as POD and the Institute for New Faculty Developers, where you can take advantage of networking and leadership development opportunities in a comfortable environment.

Interpersonal skills and competencies also contribute to how you focus your work and maintain your successes. Stay in touch with those you meet as you research the institution by inviting their input into planning and welcoming their feedback as you assess the effectiveness of an event. Gathering input from diverse groups of colleagues sends a message that their interests and needs are influencing the direction of your work. These small groups may help you identify talented colleagues whom you can involve in your programs. Some of these contacts will become allies upon whom you can depend for feedback and clarity. Being present and observant at campus events such as convocations, meetings, productions, or departmental colloquia is another way to meet and discover colleagues whose gifts and skills may complement your planning. At these events you may hear about new initiatives under consideration in various divisions of the institution. Be alert to how your work can support these opportunities, and create avenues to inform others about the concepts and innovations you have learned through your contacts and professional literature. At least once a year you will be expected to report on your activities and account for how you used the resources allocated to your office. Chapter Nine, "Program Assessment for Faculty Development," will give you valuable thoughts and ideas on how to assess and evaluate your program.

Conclusion

The strengths and competencies you bring to the role of a faculty developer will be complemented by the new skills you develop. As an educator you have a passion for teaching and guiding others to develop their strengths. As a researcher you have the skills of a keen observer and careful listener. Apply these skills to all you do: research your environment, document and assess each endeavor, listen to the feedback you solicit and receive, and systematically convey what you are learning to others at your own institution and to those in your professional networks. The puzzles are plentiful; the learning is continuous; and the outcomes will strengthen you, your colleagues, and the institution.

REFERENCES

Bridges, W. (2003). *Managing transitions: Making the most of change* (2nd ed.). Cambridge, MA: Da Capo Press.

Cohen, M. W. (2003, November). *How's it going? Reflecting on our work as new faculty developers.* Preconference workshop at the annual meeting of the Professional and Organizational Development Network in Higher Education, Denver, CO.

Colbeck, C. L., O'Meara, K. A., & Austin, A. E. (Eds.). (2008). *New directions for teaching and learning, no. 113. Educating integrated professionals: Theory and practice on preparation for the professoriate.* San Francisco: Jossey-Bass.

Jensen, J. D. (2002). If I knew then what I know now: A first-year faculty consultant's top ten list. In K.H. Gillespie (Ed.), *A guide to faculty development: Practical advice, examples, and resources* (pp. 92–100). Bolton, MA: Anker.

Kuh, G. D. (2003). What we're learning about engagement from NSSE: Bookmarks for effective educational practices. *Change, 35*(2), 24–32.

Massy, W. F. (2003). *Honoring the trust: Quality and cost containment in higher education.* Bolton, MA: Anker.

McCormick, A., & Zhao, C. (2005). Rethinking and reframing the Carnegie classification. *Change, 37*(5), 52–57.

McDonald, J., & Stockley, D. (2008). Pathways to the profession of educational development: An international perspective. *International Journal for Academic Development, 13*(3), 213–218.

Morrison-Shetlar, A. I., & Hohenleitner, K. (2008). Investing in faculty at every career stage. *Project Kaleidoscope Volume I: What works, what matters, what lasts* (pp. 1–6). Retrieved December 22, 2008, from http://www .pkal.org/documents/Vol4InvestingInFacultyAtEveryCareerStage.cfm

Pathways to the Profession of Educational Development. (n.d.). Retrieved December 30, 2008, from http://www.iathe.org/pathways/

Pathways to the Profession of Educational Development. (n.d.). *New developers' resources.* Retrieved December 22, 2008, at http://www.edpathways.com

Professional and Organizational Development Network in Higher Education. (n.d.). Retrieved December 30, 2008, from http://www.podnetwork.org/

Robertson, D. L. (1988). *Self-directed growth.* Muncie, IN: Accelerated Development.

Senge, P. M. (2006). *The fifth discipline: The art and practice of the learning organization.* New York: Doubleday.

Shulman, L. S. (2004). *Teaching as community property: Essays on higher education.* San Francisco: Jossey-Bass.

Sorcinelli, M. D. (2002). Ten principles of good practice in creating and sustaining teaching and learning centers. In K. H. Gillespie (Ed.), *A guide' to faculty development: Practical advice, examples, and resources* (pp. 9–23). Bolton, MA: Anker.

Sorcinelli, M. D., Austin, A. E., Eddy, P. L., & Beach, A. L. (2006). *Creating the future of faculty development: Learning from the past, understanding the present.* Bolton, MA: Anker.

Stockley, D., Mighty, J., McDonald, J., Taylor, L., Sorcinelli, M. D., Ouellett, M. L., et al. (2008, June). *Mapping our pathway into the field of educational development.* Presentation at the biennial meeting of the International Consortium for Educational Development, Salt Lake City, UT.

TeachingCoach.Org (n.d.). *Support for new faculty developers in higher education.* Retrieved December 22, 2008, from http://www.teachingcoach.org

University of Kansas, Center for Teaching Excellence. (n.d.). *CTE information: Other teaching centers.* Retrieved December 22, 2008, from http://www .cte.ku.edu/cteInfo/resources/web sites.shtml

6

IMPORTANT SKILLS AND
KNOWLEDGE

Todd D. Zakrajsek

AS A PROFESSIONAL FIELD, educational development is a relatively new phenomenon. Unlike in most disciplines within higher education, many individuals in educational development do this work as a result of a passion for student learning and a desire to assist others rather than by undertaking a systematic study of a specific area with the intent of becoming an expert in that field. As a result, many educational developers find themselves working in an area in which they have little training or specific background. That said, most educational developers have a strong set of foundational skills and implicit knowledge.

The context for this work is an important consideration in how it is done; and context involves a number of factors, such as the size of institution, longevity of current educational development center or effort, support for the program, the resources allocated to the effort, and the current ability level of the developer. As Lee has indicated in Chapter Two, "Program Types and Prototypes," educational development efforts are now extending beyond traditional assistance with pedagogical issues and including development in areas such as leadership and research. As a consequence of being a relatively new field, with individuals from varied backgrounds and with a sometimes ill-defined job description, no universally adopted guidelines can describe what knowledge must be acquired or skills developed to become a successful educational developer or director of a center. There are, however, a few fundamental areas of knowledge and a set of skills that are widely accepted as valid and necessary for those working in educational development.

General Skills and Knowledge

Higher education is an interesting field in that many individuals within the academy are prepared for only some of their day-to-day responsibilities. To receive a terminal degree, graduate students must demonstrate expertise in scholarly or creative endeavors in their disciplines; however, they then likely find themselves teaching with little or no background in pedagogy, applying for large grants with limited budget and project management training, or serving as institutional leaders with no disciplinary under-standing of business administration. Most of what we know today about educational development was amassed by a dedicated group of individuals who learned from the pedagogical literature, conducted research on teaching and learning, pulled together information from relevant disciplines, implemented practices, and shared this information with one another. This shared information has created a foundation of skills and knowledge that supports developers in assisting faculty members in a wide variety of academic duties and responsibilities.

Understanding the Field

There is a growing body of literature dedicated to the enhancement of effective teaching and learning in higher education and exploring other areas that support the work of faculty members, such as leadership development and the submission of grant proposals. Perhaps the most important knowledge an educational developer can possess is where information currently exists related to a variety of academic disciplines, a basic understanding of the wide variety of current pedagogical approaches, and an awareness that the field of educational development is growing at an exponential rate.

PUBLISHED LITERATURE. A great deal can be learned about teaching, learn-ing, and leadership through published literature. For example, there are many publications pertaining specifically to the Scholarship of Teaching and Learning (SoTL), including those by Boyer (1990), Hatch (2005), and Naylor (2006). In addition, publishers such as Jossey-Bass, Stylus, and New Forums offer extensive print resources in many areas related to educational development and student learning. For new developers, two particularly worthwhile introductory sources are the books *How People Learn* by Bransford et al. (1999) and the *Jossey-Bass Reader on the Brain and Learning* (2007). These two sources provide just a sampling of the massive amount of work that currently exists to support educational development. With so many publications in print, it is difficult to know where to begin. As is emphasized elsewhere in this volume, the best place to start is the Professional and Organizational Development (POD) Network Web site (http://podnetwork.org/). Among the resources on the Web site are the POD-IDEA (Center) notes on specific teaching and learning topics; these short pieces arose from a collaboration between the two organizations and address topics such as integrating technology, improving essay exams, and motivating students to read.

CONFERENCES. The importance of making professional contacts and building networks cannot be overemphasized. Conferences help developers to build a network of colleagues that can ward off isolation and help sustain the lone developer, a strategy described in greater detail in Chapter Five. Conferences allow for identifying new developments in the field that can be applied on any campus and a greater sense of future directions. In addition to exposure to cutting-edge practices, data, and conceptual frameworks, conferences provide opportunities to gain presentation skills simply by watching experienced developers in action. For example, a session pertaining to providing faculty members with feedback will certainly build participants' knowledge in that area; and it will likely include a demonstration of appropriate ways to give feedback, which provides an opportunity for participants to practice skills learned in that same session.

FACULTY COLLEAGUES. Individuals at one's home institution are extremely valuable to an educational developer. These relationships are helpful when developing a skill set within a given discipline. An example might be getting assistance in sending out material to faculty about how to respond to students in class following a crisis. At that time, faculty with disciplinary knowledge in crisis management would be very helpful. Furthermore, there are times when a skilled instructor in a given department will simply hold more credibility than an educational developer with general knowledge. Amassing a list of faculty members willing to assist others takes organization and interpersonal skills, but it is worth the effort because it will enhance educational development efforts.

ELECTRONIC RESOURCES. Blogs, wikis, Twitter accounts, listservs, Facebook, RSS feeds, and a host of other online resources are quickly emerging and are likely to continue to increase in both importance and use. Electronic resources allow for open access to a wide range of materials that can be easily updated and expanded. These also provide wonderful educational tools for faculty, and therefore it is important for an educational developer to be aware of the teaching and learning potential of the most popular new delivery mechanisms. One very useful electronic resource is the "Tomorrow's Professor" listserv (http://ctl.stanford .edu/Tomprof). This listserv posts two resources weekly and has an extensive archive. With more than 30,000 subscribers, it is a frequently used resource by faculty and educational developers.

Getting Started

With the availability of conferences, workshops, books, journal articles, newsletters, electronic lists, blogs, online resources, and faculty colleagues, it is easy to become overwhelmed by the number of choices. Educational developers might best start with their own knowledge base and build from there. It is good advice to start small and build on successes. For example, if a developer has been teaching large classes for several years in the sciences, it would be relatively easy and beneficial for faculty members to start with a workshop or Web resource on teaching large classes. From that point, information and additional resources can be added using one's own expertise as the foundation, establishing friendships with other educational developers, and building collaborative relationships with faculty members from the campus and surrounding community.

Understanding Institutional Issues

As noted in Chapter Five, a solid understanding of one's home institution is very important in developing a sustainable educational development effort. Knowledge and skills in absence of institutional context have limited value. For example, an institution that is primarily focused on strong teaching and learning will have a different emphasis on tenure and promotion than one with a strong research emphasis. The institutional climate, politics, and policies may also determine to a large extent what a developer can and cannot do. In building knowledge and skills to become an effective educational developer, it is beneficial to know how the institution works, both formally and informally. In addition to the sage advice articulated in the previous chapter, building a strong foundation of knowledge and skills as an educational developer may well be served by specific attention to some of the systems, policies, and procedures already in place.

Unionized Institutions, Academic Senates, and Governance

Faculty unions and academic senate structures exist at many institutions. If an institution has one or both, it is valuable to spend some time finding out about these groups. Union regulations will often affect educational development efforts. For example, I worked on a campus at which the union did not allow for my educational development office to survey faculty about conditions of employment without explicit permission. Conducting a needs analysis with an item about how much time faculty members spent on research, teaching, and service without the union's permission would have quickly led to a grievance being filed against me on behalf of the faculty. In working *with* that same faculty union, we were able to accomplish many positive outcomes. Faculty senate organizations also make a powerful ally. Governance organizations such as unions and academic senates form campus committees, provide letters of support to the administration, and allow for an outlet to describe to campus representatives what services you offer. These same organizations, however, can be problematic if their procedures or protocols are not followed.

The committee chairs at an institution are a frequently overlooked resource. They are often influential individuals on campus, and the charges of the committees sometimes overlap with the charge of the educational development efforts. If there is no obvious place to go to for a list of committees and chairs, it is typically best to check with the office of the vice president for academic affairs or provost's office. Once the list has been secured, one can simply identify key committees that have specific ties to issues related to teaching and learning. From this point, it is possible to set up meetings with the chairs of those committees. These few steps may well pay huge dividends in a very short period of time. It allows for a quick determination about what is happening within the institution and lets key stakeholders know there is someone available to assist with those issues. Committees rarely turn down assistance, and this outreach could result in a seat at the table when important new policies are being developed or resources allocated.

Institutional Governance Documents

Although it was noted in Chapter Five, it is important enough to warrant repeating here: one should read the campus procedures and policies related to teaching and learning. In addition to knowing about organizational structures, it is helpful to determine how promotion and tenure guidelines function. Even at institutions with the highest level of research and grant activity, teaching is important; and many faculty members will desire assistance with teaching and learning issues. The value of assistance with respect to teaching and learning exists at every institution; it is how these issues are approached and how individuals are engaged that affects participation rates of faculty members. Overall, it will take a relatively short period of time to read all policies and procedures related to teaching and learning across campus. It is a little discussed fact that many individuals, even those who speak loudly on a variety of issues, are likely *not* to have read the relevant documents. An individual may well be able to read all documents pertaining to faculty governance and classroom instruction within a few days. One may then quickly become a resident expert on these matters, which, again, is helpful in establishing and building credibility. I experienced this when faculty at an academic senate meeting started to debate a university policy. Even high-level administrators were unsure of the policy. I explained that I had recently read the policy and became an instant expert on the topic, which carried forward in that I subsequently received several phone calls asking about other university policies.

Planning and Assessment

In addition to knowledge of pedagogical approaches, promotion and tenure, and faculty governance, educational developers must possess a fundamental understanding of planning and assessment. Planning allows the developer to use resources wisely and to show the largest return on the institutional investment in the center. Understanding the basics of assessment and evaluation will prove critical in demonstrating the impact of the center (for example, Banta, 2002). Three chapters in Part Two of this volume provide additional details on assessment and evaluation: "Program Assessment for Faculty Development" (Chapter Nine), "Assessing Teaching Practices and Effectiveness for Formative Purposes" (Chapter Ten), and "Assessment Practices Related to Student Learning" (Chapter Eleven).

Needs/Interest Survey, Focus Groups, and Individual Conversations

Getting involved at an institution is not a problem for any educational developer who shows initiative. The issue is how to handle the multitude of requests once the floodgates are opened. Planning is a skill needed for a center to be effective, or even to survive. Setting both short- and long-term goals requires knowledge of the field of educational development and also the skill to know how much can be accomplished in a period of time given the institutional climate, the available resources, and the time management skills of the developer.

One method of planning involves completing a needs/interest survey. Educational developers need only a basic understanding of survey construction to complete this kind of survey. The information gathered from individuals throughout the institution is helpful in workshop development and resource acquisition. Additional information regarding the best future directions of a center or focused effort can come from focus groups. This undertaking requires the developer to lead a small group discussion in a meaningful way and also illustrates how teaching experience can be used as an educational developer. The same deftness used to lead a discussion in a small seminar course will aid a developer well in leading a focus group discussion (Stewart, Shamdasani, & Rook, 2007).

In collecting this vital information, a few basic points on gathering it from others is helpful. First, it is necessary to identify who best can provide information on or about the institution. Respected faculty, strong administrators, and students should be included. Second, one should accept what they offer as nonjudgmental suggestions and resist the urge to get defensive by explaining how efforts are already in place or being developed to do what they suggest. As information is being amassed, actionable items are noted and a plan for implementation developed. Finally, one has to realize that there is a limit to how much can be accomplished; and one should identify, as a next step, those areas that can have the most impact with the fewest resources.

Regardless of how information is gathered, it is important to speak continually and informally with faculty members regarding current issues, teaching interests and concerns, and their interest in creating positive learning environments for their students. Strong interpersonal skills will facilitate engaging individual faculty members from a variety of disciplines in conversations about teaching and learning. This includes the ability to understand the faculty member's perspective on teaching and the concerns they have and to identify ways to provide assistance based on the literature in the field. The time spent cultivating these informal relationships is extremely valuable in developing both institutional support and resource networks.

Strategic Plan and Implementation Plan

A strategic plan is helpful for educational development efforts. This endeavor essentially consists of using information collected from the institution as noted in the needs/interest survey, prioritizing that information, adding knowledge from the field of educational development, and then developing an action plan that is realistically grounded by available resources. With this plan in place, the developer is charting the direction of the center or centralized effort. Implementing the plan will necessitate skills in both project management and in budgeting. In many ways, developing a strategic plan and delivering on the resulting initiatives utilizes many of the skills and much of the knowledge a director must have to run a center or oversee the institution's educational development effort.

Communication Skills

Effectiveness in educational development work is heavily affected by the communication skills needed to speak to individuals at many levels within the organization. Although most conversations are likely to be with faculty members, there will be conversations and meetings with students, teaching assistants, chairs, deans, provosts, vice presidents, and presidents. It is very important to be able to do this in a way that shows respect for and comfort with each person or group addressed. An educational developer should not speak "down" to a teaching assistant nor be intimidated by the institution's president. Others will look to the educational developer as a leader in teaching and learning, and an effective person in this role has tremendous influence at the institution. However, influence only comes with respect from the individuals with whom one works, and that emerges from respect given to others for their talents and experience.

Communicating with Individuals

Effective communicators keep the focus on the person with whom they are speaking. Faculty members will have issues related to teaching and learning about which they are greatly concerned. In most cases, the individual seeking assistance from the educational developer is expecting support and guidance, but in a way that respects the person making the request. It is "their" issue, not the developer's; and suggestions should be presented delicately. Some things that seem obvious to an outsider may provide a wonderful insight to the person doing the requesting. If the educational developer directly or indirectly indicates that a solution is "simple," then the person who requested assistance might feel foolish. It is also important to note that the individual who is requesting assistance may not be an expert in the area of teaching and learning but does have a great deal of expertise in some academic area. That is, he or she may not know anything about collaborative learning techniques and yet be a national leader within a specific area of physics. Faculty members, like anyone else, prefer not being talked to as though they were novices in an area in which they are respected for their knowledge.

Assisting a faculty member and maintaining respect is particularly relevant in the debriefing session after a classroom observation. This discussion will be a strong test of interpersonal skills. Almost everyone gets nervous when being observed and evaluated, as one's job performance is a reflection of oneself. After completing the classroom observation, feedback is typically provided regarding the observed class period. During this interaction it is important to balance suggestions for improvement with recognition of things done well. Determining how many and what types of "suggestions" the faculty member can handle at that session is a valuable skill. Even if ten things the faculty member could do to improve are noted in a single class period, it might well be best to speak of only a few in that first meeting to keep from overwhelming the individual. Feedback on teaching is a skill that is developed over time and requires more effort and expertise than most realize (for example, Svinicki & Lewis, 2008).

When speaking to a faculty member about teaching and learning, including a discussion following a classroom observation, it is essential to refrain from jumping to a quick conclusion regarding the quality of a faculty member's approach to teaching based on the pedagogical approach used. If a faculty member states that lecturing is the best method to teach students, it is not helpful to jump immediately to the conclusion that the instructor is out of date and using ineffective methods. Similarly, the use of newer technologies does not automatically indicate high-quality instruction. The incorporation of YouTube and Second Life into a service-learning project does not, by itself, guarantee a well-structured learning experience. The point here is to reserve judgment about the quality of the course or pedagogical approaches of the instructor until there has been an opportunity for an extended conversation with the person so that one can better understand the instructor's perspectives. This discussion will assist in getting a feel for the situation in which the person is teaching and enable identification of the individual's strengths and weaknesses.

Another important consideration for interpersonal work with faculty members is confidentiality. Knowing what is appropriate to share with whom, and when, is a critical skill. As mentioned elsewhere in this volume, recommendations for faculty consultation confidentiality can be found in the ethical guidelines established by the POD Network (http://www .podnetwork.org/faculty_development/ethicalguidelines.htm). A misspoken sentence by an educational developer could cost a trusting faculty member tenure or promotion, and any indication of information from consultations being shared with another will almost immediately result in a loss of the faculty member's confidence. For example, a faculty member may be uncertain about how to evaluate senior projects in a capstone course effectively. The faculty member may have asked for assistance out of fear that going to a department chairperson or colleague to explain the concern may call into question the faculty member's ability to teach the course. Regrettably there are those who might negatively interpret this kind of uncertainty when considering promotion and tenure.

Communication with Administrators

The skill necessary to communicate with administrators is similar to that required for establishing good relationships with faculty members, but some adjustments are needed. Similarities include appreciating the situation of the person in the conversation, recognizing he or she is an individual with unique issues and keeping the message positive. The biggest difference is that faculty members will primarily want to know what can be provided to help them as individuals, and administrators will primarily want to know what can be provided to help the institution. By the nature of their positions, administrators are responsible for entire areas or systems within the college or university. For example, a vice president for diversity is responsible for the way in which the entire faculty perceives and interacts with individuals from a variety of underrepresented groups. This vice president may want to know how to present information effectively to faculty members, but she or he is probably more interested in assistance in achieving the overall diversity goals of the institution. In such situations one must know when and to what extent to get involved. Large-scale projects can have a major impact on the institution, but they often take tremendous resources of time and perhaps funding. Knowing when to step in and at what level to commit is a skill that will develop across time and with experience.

Individual Versus Group Communications

You will most likely work with individual faculty members and also collaborate with groups from a variety of offices throughout the institution. Many developers find one situation more comfortable and perhaps rewarding than the other, but the ability to work with both individuals and groups is important. Collaboration requires a special skill set that is quite different from that used when working with individuals. Communication is particularly vital in collaborative efforts. Often, a good place to start a collaborative effort is with a discussion of how individuals will communicate. I typically include a discussion about miscommunication and what to do if that arises. That is, discuss up front what happens if a mistake happens or if something is not communicated well. How will angry or hurt feelings be addressed and how will things get "back on track"? An introductory conversation about those issues is rarely conducted prior to a collaborative effort, but it can be extremely helpful to the process when done effectively. It is also important to be sure to discuss how "credit" will be allocated for the project early in the project development. Not only does this reduce disagreements following the completion of the project, but it also allows for allocating an appropriate amount of work to the project. For example, if a person's office is to be listed first in terms of collaborating offices, that office will typically do most of the work and/or be responsible for leading the project.

Writing Skills

In addition to strong oral communication skills, effective writing communication skills are important to the educational developer in order to summarize pedagogical resource material for faculty members, write promotional material to promote workshops or institutes, draft institutional policies, construct letters of recommendation, and develop administrative reports. The ability to write to a variety of disciplines and different levels within the organization is a standard part of the job. For the most part, writing must be clear, concise, and supported well by evidence. Long papers and use of jargon of any kind are rarely appreciated. Citing what other institutions have done, finding related articles in the *Chronicle of Higher Education,* summarizing research studies, and identifying related reports is often very much appreciated by both faculty members and administrators. As with other areas, the skills of both knowing where to find supporting material and knowing who might be able to assist you in finding needed information will increase with time. The work produced serves as a model of excellence for others and is indicative of the excellence of one's program. To project the best image and professionalism, even less formal written communication such as e-mails and Web pages should be well written and free from grammatical and spelling errors.

Organization, Multi-Tasking, and Time Management

Keeping one's own life on track as an educational developer will be no small accomplishment. One of the difficulties with the field of educational development is that it is still being established and defined, and it is frequently not well understood by others. The result is a confusing array of expectations and demands accompanied by large variations among the different kinds of centers and centralized efforts at many hundreds of institutions. This is one reason a strategic plan can be essential to the success or even survival of an educational development center. In addition, a variety of skills is needed to keep educational development efforts moving in a positive direction.

Organizational skills will be tested daily. A day in the life of a educational developer can include visiting a faculty member's class, writing a summary of the observation, attending committee meetings, drafting support letters for external grants, reviewing policies for an upcoming committee meeting, and pulling together materials for a workshop (which includes remembering to order food and print name tags). With such varied activities, staying organized can be difficult. There are systems and techniques in both the business and academic world to assist one in organizational skills, and it is well worth the effort to invest time and energy into finding or creating systems that will work, building from expertise developed as a faculty member.

Another skill needed is the ability to say "No" when appropriate. Every educational developer I have ever known has had a full plate of activities. Given the central role played by anyone leading educational development efforts, many requests will arrive asking for assistance on a multitude of worthwhile and relevant committees and task force efforts. Some individuals are seeking needed expertise, others will do so for political reasons, and still others will simply want to be sure consideration is given where consideration is due. When establishing a center or educational development effort on campus, it is important to have relatively high institution-wide involvement as a way to become woven into the institutional fabric. In a very short period of time, however, such obligations may well become overwhelming. Learning to identify when and where an impact can be made is an essential skill to develop, and one must determine very quickly what is most important to accomplish and then establish priorities. It is very easy to have a long list of accomplishments at the end of the year that are by themselves very important, but perhaps were not intended when the effort or center was begun.

When deciding what responsibilities to accept and what to decline, one should keep in mind the recommendation that a balanced portfolio is best.

As an educational developer, there must be time to do classroom visits; but one must also stay involved with institution-wide planning and support of campus initiatives where appropriate. If a majority of one's time is spent in individual consultation or doing classroom observations, the faculty members are indeed directly assisted, but the overall impact of one's work is limited. If one spends a lot of time working with committees and planning groups, there will be less time for direct work with individual faculty members, but there may be greater impact at the institutional level. If one spends a great deal of time in the office developing teaching and learning materials, there is less time for building real connections within the institution. Skillfully done, a balanced involvement will seek to provide the greatest benefit to the institution at large.

Human and Financial Resource Management

Management and leadership skills are vital; a director of a large center with a staff may well result in supervision of five or more full-time employees. That not only means skills in running meetings and strategic planning but also managing teams, completing performance reviews, balancing budgets, designing collaboration systems within the center, and handling vacation time. Also, with large centers one often finds large budgets. The immediate reaction from most educational developers to having a large budget is the feeling that finally there is enough money to do a significant amount of good work. It is easy to see why an educational developer may get very excited when given a budget of more than $1 million. However, that excitement is likely to diminish quickly when it is discovered that 90 percent of the budget is salaries and that very little money exists for support and programming. For those with larger staffs, it is advisable to get to know the human resource specialists at the institution as they may well become some of your best resources. Also many resources are available within the business world for developing management, leadership, and budgeting skills.

Workshops

If there is one common element that exists among almost all educational development efforts, it is the offering of workshops. The development of presentation skills will assist in communicating the pertinent issues of the workshop topic to groups of faculty members and, at times, directors of centers and other administrators responsible for student learning. Critical aspects of conducting workshops include a solid knowledge of the material being presented, ability to present in an engaging manner, and inclusion of some form of collaborative or active learning on the part of the participants. Often, finding the right person to conduct the workshop is as important as the topic itself.

The educational developer is frequently the presenter, and all presenters can certainly become even better presenters. To enhance skills as a presenter, it is valuable to attend conferences dedicated to both educational development and teaching and learning. At these conferences, the developer should go to sessions of interest; but, in addition to learning about the content, one can learn a lot by noting specifically how the material is presented—watching the audience and paying particular attention to the reactions to the content delivered and the style of delivery. Presentations that appear ineffective may indeed be well received by others. Noting such occurrences will assist in developing metacognitive skills that help presenters to become more skilled in working with a variety of audiences. Aside from augmenting presenter skills by attending conferences, it is also beneficial to speak with a faculty member in the area of speech communication. One could even invite an instructor in the speech communication department to attend a workshop to provide feedback. Not only will the communication faculty member be able to provide valuable feedback about the educational developer's presentation skills, this experience will enhance the developer's ability to empathize when conducting classroom observations for faculty.

Although developers are often the presenters, there are other options. The expertise of faculty members at the institution may be helpful in developing and providing workshops and resources to the entire faculty. At times, even if a choice is available, workshops may be better facilitated by faculty members than by the educational developer. For example, a workshop on grading rubrics to assess writing might best be presented by someone who has disciplinary knowledge in English or education. Using others as the presenters of workshops also models collaboration, and faculty members learn that they can use each other as resources.

In addition to selecting the best and most appropriate presenters for the events, planning and implementing workshops require skills in marketing, ordering food and refreshments, finding space, and a host of other skills. Because workshops typically require much effort, it is usually best for new developers to set up only one or two at a time at first.

Conclusion

Educational development efforts vary widely, depending on the size of the institution, the extent to which teaching and learning is valued, the size and scope of the center or centralized effort, and the personality and skills of the developer. As a result, the skills and knowledge of the successful educational developer are also varied; where one chooses to expend energies will depend heavily on what is needed at one's home institution and available resources. To assist in the development of skills and knowledge in educational development, there is a strong and growing body of published work in the educational development literature and a continually increasing collection of online resources. Often overlooked institutional resources are the talents and knowledge of the individuals throughout the organization. Getting to know institutional policies and campus-based entities is helpful in determining how best to move development efforts forward. The developer will find that resources of time and funding are limited, and as a result planning and assessment are critical. Collaborations will greatly augment what can be accomplished, and effective communication is important to any collaborative effort. A good communication structure informs individuals throughout the institution about the educational development program and increases their understanding of the benefits to be gained through this activity. Finally, one needs to be mindful of the importance of establishing procedures and protocols and of understanding the budget and related processes even though such tasks may seem trivial at first. This is the first venture into the world of administration for many new educational developers. It brings new responsibilities, such as accountability for institutional funds and for the livelihoods of those persons who work for you.

The field of educational development is not an exact science, and there is no single formula that can be applied to ensure your success. Effectiveness as a developer will grow as skill sets increase and as relevant professional knowledge is developed. One's skills and knowledge will indeed grow and increase over time, and each individual educational developer will have areas of natural strength as well as areas of weakness. All successful developers started as novices; and, like them, persons new to the field of educational development will come to have a positive impact on the lives of many faculty members and others within their institutions.

REFERENCES

Banta, T. W., & Associates. (2002). *Building a scholarship of assessment.* San Francisco: Jossey-Bass.

Boyer, E. L. (1990). *Scholarship reconsidered: Priorities of the professoriate.* Princeton, NJ: Carnegie Foundation for the Advancement of Teaching.

Bransford, J. D., Brown, A. L., & Cocking, R. R. (1999). *How people learn: Brain, mind, experience, and school.* Washington, DC: National Academy Press.

Hatch, T. (2005). *Into the classroom: Developing the scholarship of teaching and learning.* San Francisco: Jossey-Bass.

IDEA Center. (2008). Retrieved December 1, 2008, from http://www.theideacenter.org/

Jossey-Bass Publishers. (2007). *Jossey-Bass reader on the brain and learning.* San Francisco: Jossey-Bass.

Jossey-Bass Publishers. (2008). Retrieved December 1, 2008, from http://www.josseybass.com/WileyCDA/

Naylor, S. (2006, March 14). *Scholarship of teaching and learning (SoTL) potential publishing outlets.* Retrieved December 1, 2008, from http://www.ilstu.edu/~sknaylor/sotl.htm

Stewart, D. W., Shamdasani, P. N., & Rook, D. W. (2007). *Focus groups: Theory and practice* (2nd ed.). Thousand Oaks, CA: Sage.

Stylus Publishing. (2008). Retrieved December 1, 2008, from http://www.styluspub.com/Books/Features.aspx

Svinicki, M., & Lewis, K. (2008). *Preparing for peer observation: A guidebook.* Retrieved December 1, 2008, from http://www.utexas.edu/academic/cte/PeerObserve.html

7

PROMOTING YOUR PROGRAM
AND GROUNDING IT IN THE
INSTITUTION

Ed Neal and Iola Peed-Neal

PROGRAM PROMOTION IS A COMPLICATED PROCESS, one that requires careful planning and deft execution. In this chapter we outline important considerations for gaining and sustaining institutional commitment and creating effective promotional strategies.

Successful faculty development programs need competent practitioners, adequate resources, and above all the support of the institution. However, "support" should be understood as a quality that goes far beyond the endorsement of the administration; it means that the program is integrated into the cultural fabric of the institution. Administrators come and go, but institutional culture abides.

People are not usually conscious of the culture of the institution in which they work; like fish in water, they are immersed in the element itself. Starting a program or taking over an existing one requires that one study the culture for clues about the values, assumptions, beliefs, and ideologies that shape the institutional environment and the power structure.

Understanding Institutional Culture

If you move from one institution to another, you will quickly find that the new organizational culture is different from your former one. Not only are rules and regulations different, but the social structure and "ambience" of the place will feel strange. Of course, some generalizations are possible. For example, small liberal arts colleges usually share values related to their commitment to effective teaching and the development of the "whole student." However, an institution's culture is shaped by many factors: its mission, governance, leadership, curriculum, institutional history, outside affiliations, geographic location, influence of alumni, and the relationship between students and faculty (Austin, 1990). Cultural differences arise from variance in these institutional features.

Tierney, in a classic article on the culture of higher education (1988), suggested that studying an institution's culture is similar to the task of an anthropologist studying a clan or a village; it is an ethnographic exercise. Although few faculty developers are trained as ethnographers, anyone can practice systematic observation of the institutional environment and learn how to use it to promote a development program.

Surveys and needs assessment instruments can provide useful data about faculty members and their preferences, but they do not provide much information about the ambient culture. *Talk* to people—individually and in groups—at all levels of the institution; observe their interactions in public and private meetings; read memos, policy statements, and news items to develop an in-depth picture of the culture. Learn the stories and sagas that inform institutional memory and shape its values and beliefs. The goal is to learn about how the institution operates as a *social organism* so that you can design a program that harmonizes with its rules and customs. Obviously, you cannot postpone your program until you have had time to completely investigate the culture; but, as a citizen of the academic world, you already know many things about the general culture of higher education that will enable you to start building a program while you learn more about the institution. The discussion below addresses selected concepts from the research literature that will be useful for understanding the culture of your institution. Suggestions for systematically collecting this kind of information appear under the section of this chapter titled "Market Research."

How would you characterize the general institutional environment? Is it open and supportive? Informal? Impersonal? Highly competitive and entrepreneurial? One cannot make assumptions about the environment based on size or type of school; large institutions can be open and supportive, and small institutions can be autocratic and impersonal.

In a competitive, entrepreneurial environment (for example, in some large, private research universities), a faculty developer needs to operate as an independent contractor, gathering resources wherever they can be found and negotiating "trades" for goods and services with schools and departments. The same behavior could be perceived as inappropriate or overly aggressive in a different environment.

In some land-grant universities, each school operates almost as an independent entity, making it difficult to develop a centralized program across competing fiefdoms. The strategy for program development in this environment requires diplomacy and skillful negotiation. On the other hand, land-grant institutions often have a very strong commitment to teaching and faculty support since they are by nature service-oriented institutions and may therefore provide more fertile ground for faculty development activities.

How much does the institutional mission influence curriculum, administration, and day-to-day work of the faculty, staff, and decision makers? How often do people refer to the mission statement or its relevance? If the mission does play a significant role in the institution's affairs, linking your program to the mission will help establish its value and credibility. Individual programs and services should also be tied explicitly to the mission in your promotional materials.

How does information circulate within the institution? How is *important* information disseminated, and by whom? Large institutions present enormous challenges to promoting a program since they are highly fragmented and rarely have efficient communication between or among different constituencies. Moreover, the sheer amount of information circulating in a large university creates a serious problem of "information overload" among faculty members. Small institutions do not usually have this problem, but they may have informal communication channels not obvious to a newcomer and therefore difficult to identify and use.

Who are the leaders? Leadership is both positional and nonpositional; some individuals may be very influential even though they are not in formal leadership roles, and some who hold leadership positions may have little real influence. Opinion leaders often wield power beyond their nominal status in the organization, and they can make or break a new faculty development program by giving or withholding their support. Obviously, getting the endorsement of important administrators is essential for a faculty development program, but winning the support of opinion leaders is equally and sometimes more important.

Subcultures exist within educational institutions, based on institutional structure (schools and departments), disciplinary affiliation (for example, humanities, social sciences), and organizational role (for example, student affairs, libraries, administration). The culture of a given academic unit may differ dramatically from that of the institution at large; these subunits often develop "spheres of ownership" regarding curriculum, teaching practices, and even (or especially) physical space (Kashner, 1990). In smaller institutions one can quickly identify the sub-cultures and learn their peculiarities, but it may take years to do so in a university with many schools, departments, curricula, institutes, and centers. Promotional activities will be more effective if you can target specific constituencies within the institution, and to the extent possible your strategies should take into account the characteristics of the subcultures to which they belong.

Marketing: Creating and Sustaining Relationships

In academia the words *marketing* and *promotion* often have distasteful connotations; we associate them with exaggerated claims about products advertised in the mass media. However, applying marketing principles to faculty development can yield highly successful results, as many nonprofit organizations have learned. Since most faculty developers are unfamiliar with the formal discipline of marketing, they tend to rely on a trial-and-error approach in promoting their programs. Although marketing concepts are important for designing promotional strategies, remember that faculty members are *not* customers; they are allies, supporters, and friends—and, ultimately, one's marketing strategy should help develop *partnerships* with them.

The term *marketing* has no standard definition in the business literature. However, the following definition captures the essence of the concept and is particularly relevant to marketing faculty development programs: "Marketing is the process of planning and executing the conception, pricing, promotion, and distribution of ideas, goods, services, organizations, and events to create and maintain relationships that will satisfy individual and organizational objectives" (Boone & Kurtz, 2005, p. 7). In other words, *every* activity and service of a teaching center is part of its marketing strategy, not just its newsletters, brochures, and Web pages.

Every interaction between a staff member and a faculty member is an opportunity to make a good or bad impression on the client. If the individual who answers the telephone is a student assistant who knows little about the mission, values, and purposes of the program or does not really care about the job, he or she could leave a very bad impression on callers. When your product is service, *every* member of your staff is a salesperson.

Obviously, one needs to know what faculty members *want,* as well as what they *need,* so the first step is to perform a market analysis.

As Thoreau once wrote, "The greatest compliment that was ever paid me was when someone asked me what I thought, and attended to my answer."

Market Research

There are many ways that information can be collected, and one should use as many of them as possible to develop an accurate picture of the needs and interests of the college community. Program decisions must be based on reliable data, and acquiring information from many sources will help ensure success.

SURVEYS. In faculty development, the most widely used (and often the only) method of market research is the "needs assessment" or "interest assessment" survey. However, these surveys are often poorly constructed and are usually much too long. Since faculty members are oversurveyed and always busy, return rates can be dismally low and therefore unreliable. A short instrument (two to five questions), mailed or online, is more likely to have a good response rate than a long questionnaire. Follow four simple rules for questionnaires:

○ Ask only for information that is essential for goal setting and program planning.
○ Keep the language simple and clear.
○ Avoid tendentious phraseology.
○ Always provide opportunities for open-ended responses.

EVENT EVALUATIONS. Workshop evaluations are very popular as a means of collecting data about faculty preferences. However, participants are usually in a hurry to leave after an event and therefore do not spend much time filling out the forms. Again, the longer the form, the less likely it is to yield usable information. Distributing the evaluation form at the *beginning* of the event and encouraging participants to make notes on it during the presentation can yield more detailed and thoughtful responses.

FOCUS GROUPS. Although conducting focus groups is more labor and time intensive than administering questionnaires, focus groups provide in-depth information about the needs, wants, and perspectives of faculty members. Facilitating short, well-designed group meetings (no more than one hour) with target groups of faculty members is therefore well worth the effort. Short focus groups can be conducted as part of other events at which faculty members are already gathered. For example, one can ask participants in a workshop if any of them would be willing to stay after the event and answer a few questions. School or department faculty meetings might serve as venues for brief focus group activities. Conducting focus groups is not as simple as it might seem; an excellent handbook for this activity is *Focus Groups: A Practical Guide for Applied Research* (Krueger & Casey, 2009).

ADVISORY COMMITTEES. Most faculty development programs have a faculty advisory body, and one should rely on this group as an important source of marketing information. In a sense, the advisory committee is a long-term focus group; and their meetings can be facilitated in the same way as the focus groups you assemble in other contexts.

INDIVIDUAL INTERVIEWS. The richest kind of marketing information is only available through one-on-one interviews. Of course, it is necessary to conduct many interviews to ensure that the responses of the interviewees reflect the ideas and opinions of the larger community. Individual consultations with faculty members provide opportunities to collect in-depth information about important issues.

OBSERVATIONS. Each time you conduct a workshop or attend a faculty meeting provides an opportunity to collect information about marketing issues. Recording your observations about what faculty members and administrators say at meetings and other events is a "low-impact" market research method, and you should train other members of your staff to be observant in the same circumstances.

The "Four Ps"

Traditionally, marketing consists of four basic elements: product, price, place, and promotion. These elements are important to the marketing of teaching centers, but they mean different things in the context of higher education than they do in business and industry.

PRODUCT. Libraries, hospitals, colleges, and teaching centers provide *services* far more frequently than physical *products*, but for marketing purposes there is no real difference. You need to know what your clientele wants from the services you provide and how likely they are to use them, given the "cost" to clients. Of course, it is often necessary to "sell" a service that they may not want to buy, at least until they can understand its value.

Price. In selling products like computers or potatoes, *price* is a very important element of marketing strategy, but, since we typically give away our services for free, it seems to be irrelevant to marketing faculty development. However, it is a universal principle in higher education that *time* is the most valuable commodity to faculty members; and there are very real costs to our clients in the time they spend on our services. Attending a workshop or even reading a newsletter takes time that could be spent on other things. In research universities, the "time cost" for nearly any faculty development activity is high since the institution's reward system is skewed toward scholarship and sponsored research rather than teaching. In teaching-focused institutions, the cost to clients is lower and may even be perceived as a good investment by faculty members, but faculty development is still not "free." It takes time that might otherwise be used for lesson planning, course development, or advising students. Faculty members have a right to expect value for the price they pay, and one needs to be sensitive to their "price schedule." Offering fewer workshops and programs of uniformly high quality is better than scheduling a plethora of services of uneven quality.

A good example of sensitivity to this price schedule is the "Five-Minute Workshop," originated by Todd Zakrajsek at Central Michigan University. These workshops are literally only five minutes in length, designed to teach a few basic concepts very quickly, and can be presented in department meetings or other faculty gatherings at minimal cost. Afterward, faculty members often seek more information from the presenter since their interest has been piqued and they are prepared to "spend" more on pursuing the topic (Zakrajsek, 2003, sec. 10).

PLACE. The physical location where products are sold or services offered is an important consideration in the marketing "mix." A program's location, layout, and even its interior decoration will affect how faculty members feel about it and whether they are comfortable using its services. The physical appearance should convey the impression that important academic work occurs there, but it should also be warm and welcoming. Faculty members should *want* to spend time there, and they need to be able to reach it quickly. Placement of program offices in a central location sends the message that the institutional administration values its investment in faculty development. The same factors also affect how members of the college or university community at large perceive the center's importance, and these perceptions are important to marketing the program.

PROMOTION. This term refers to the means you use to reach your target audience. Just as you need to have to have a strategic plan for program development, you need to create a plan for program promotion that takes the institutional culture into account. The following questions are useful for developing such a plan.

Who is the target audience? If you are establishing a new program, your first impulse might be to try and reach as many faculty members as you can, as fast as you can, using every available means. However, the scattershot approach may not provide a good return on the resource investment and may overload (and annoy) the recipients of your message. Initially, you may wish to focus on target groups already favorably disposed to the goals of your program. For example, new faculty members and graduate students are often enthusiastic about learning how to teach effectively (and to avoid the disasters that they fear might occur). However, an exclusive focus on one or two target populations should be a short-term strategy since a program with a broad mandate could risk being narrowly stereotyped ("They only work with teaching assistants"). A sophisticated marketing plan will identify several different target populations and develop different kinds of communication strategies for each of them.

Which features of the program and its benefits do you want to convey to these audiences? If you are targeting new faculty members for a program of teaching circles, for example, your promotional messages must not only describe the program but also enumerate the expected benefits to the participants: "Participants will learn how to organize and run effective student learning groups." On a larger scale, the benefits provided by the faculty development program itself should be clearly communicated in all materials, but especially in its mission statement. Marketers emphasize the importance of the "value proposition" of an organization, referring to what it does and why that is important to clients. The value proposition should be clearly presented in your mission statement. If the mission statement is high sounding but vague, it is useless as a promotional tool.

To which communications media or methods are individuals most likely to respond? To answer this question, you will need to investigate the target groups' characteristics and understand the cultural factors that govern communication in your institution. Some institutions remain "print" cultures in which letters, memos, or announcements communicate the most important information. Others have moved almost completely into Internet communications, but a given department may still operate primarily in print.

When will different strategies be employed? The distribution of materials and the posting of online resources and announcements must be timed to match the rhythm of the semester and the school year. Workshops and events need to be scheduled at times when they are likely to draw maximum participation. These are simple, common-sense considerations; but they require long-range planning.

Who will manage the promotional program? Someone must oversee the design and delivery of promotional materials and activities to ensure that they match the overall plan. In smaller faculty development programs the director is usually responsible; but in larger centers other staff members can often manage promotion once the director has set the standards for design, tone, and delivery methods.

How will you evaluate the effectiveness of your strategies? A faculty developer at a large university once toured the mail rooms of nineteen departments after sending an announcement to the entire faculty about an upcoming event. To his dismay, he found the majority of the announcements discarded in the mail room trash cans. Every promotional plan must include provisions for evaluation of its components; otherwise you risk wasting resources on strategies that have little impact. To assess the effectiveness of your strategies, you should examine each strategy with respect to three elements: the target audience for the promotion, the quality of the offering itself, and the cost relative to the return on your investment.

How many of the instructors targeted for an activity actually participate? Of course, low response rates do not necessarily mean that the target group failed to receive the invitation. The activity may not have been relevant to them, they may have had scheduling conflicts, or previous interactions with your center may have been disappointing. Ascertaining the cause, or causes, is important for refining your promotional strategies and for the success of your entire program. In addition to questions about quality and utility, the evaluation form for any activity should include a question about how the participants learned about it.

Could the same constituency have been reached by using a less costly strategy? If one sends individual invitations to all instructors for an event or activity, resource costs are significant, so this strategy should be carefully examined with respect to its success in increasing attendance.

Principles of Persuasion

In his seminal work, *Influence: The Psychology of Persuasion* (1993), Cialdini presented examples of normative behaviors that advertisers and marketers use to influence consumer behavior. These principles are to some extent interrelated, and they work well for promoting faculty development programs.

RECIPROCATION. Humans are "programmed" to return favors; that trait helped us survive as a species. Reciprocation is also the reason that charities send free address stickers and greeting cards in their appeal letters; they have discovered that free gifts, no matter how small, increase the likelihood that people will send a contribution. In faculty development we often provide food at events, and we know that participants appreciate these "gifts" and often mention the quality of the food in their evaluations. Distributing free custom-labeled flash drives or canvas totes to workshop participants can foster a sense of obligation to reciprocate the favor and support your program. In addition, labeled gifts also advertise the name of the program to other members of the faculty.

COMMITMENT AND CONSISTENCY. Written or verbal commitments wield a powerful influence on behavior; people tend to honor their commitments. Moreover, once we have made a commitment, we are more likely to see that commitment as "correct behavior" and continue to pursue it. In faculty development, we use a number of techniques that flow from this principle. Preregistration for workshops and other faculty development events usually ensures that individuals will show up, especially if there is follow-up (such as e-mail reminders of the "commitment" to attend). Once individuals have begun to use the services of your center, chances are that they will continue to do so.

SOCIAL PROOF. Humans tend to view a given behavior as "correct" if they see others doing it. If you stand on the sidewalk and stare fixedly upward, soon everyone who passes you will do the same. In the same way, faculty members will be more likely to attend an event if they know that their peers are attending or have attended in the past. Two strategies that exploit this principle are publishing testimonials from program participants or uploading short video interviews with them onto your Web site.

LIKING. We are more likely to do something if someone we like asks us to do it. Cialdini (1993) explained the enormous success of the

Tupperware company in terms of the "liking" principle. If a friend asks you to attend a Tupperware party, the impulse to go is very strong. Note also that these parties provide free gifts for the participants. We tend to like people who are similar to ourselves, which is a good reason for faculty developers to emphasize their similarity to "regular" faculty members by remarking on elements of faculty life that you share. This technique is much easier if you teach courses or conduct research and publish; but, if this is not the case, you can talk about your prior teaching or research experience.

AUTHORITY. An extreme example of this principle is the well-known "Milgram Study" (Milgram, 1974), in which subjects continued to give what appeared to be severe electric shocks to others simply because a white-coated authority figure told them to do so. A few years ago, when the dean of arts and sciences at a major research university simply suggested that "teaching effectiveness should be taken into account" in promotion and tenure decisions, the statement immediately affected the practices of all department-based tenure committees. If an authority figure of that stature endorses your program and encourages participation, you will soon see a beneficial effect.

SCARCITY. "Opportunities seem more valuable to us when their availability is limited" (Cialdini, 1993, p. 228). This principle is related to the human fear of potential loss; if we miss an opportunity, we "lose out." In faculty development, we can use this principle in a variety of ways. For example, closing registration for an event when preregistrations have reached a set number and announcing, "Registration for this workshop is closed. Please contact us if you wish to be placed on the waiting list." In advertising any event, it is a good idea to include the warning, "Space for this event is limited. Please register early to reserve your seat." When announcing small grants for faculty development activities, emphasize that only a few grants are available. This strategy will help ensure that you will receive many applications and that you can select only the strongest proposals.

Promotional Methods

GENERAL PRINCIPLES. David Ogilvy, the "father of modern advertising" once said, "If you're trying to persuade people to do something, or buy something, it seems to me you should use their language, the language in which they think" (Higgins, 1990, p. 83). Always use language that the faculty will understand and recognize as a "scholarly" communication. Avoid jargon and neologisms at all cost. For example, terms such as "virtual learning space," "content provider," and "learning objects" are still not widespread in the vocabulary of higher education faculty. If you *must* use specialized terms, define them so faculty members will know what they mean.

Monitor the quality of all communications issued by your program or center. Faculty members are highly critical of poor writing wherever they find it; clumsy phraseology, misspellings, and typographical errors will damage the program's credibility. Double- and triple-check written materials for style, clarity, and other types of errors.

Spending time and money to develop a special logo for your program is probably not necessary, but you do need to make sure that the look and style of your materials are distinctive, coordinated, and consistent. A consistent color palette should be used across all electronic and print communication so that it will be easier for your audience to distinguish between your valuable materials and junk mail. Many institutions have design departments that will perform these services at low cost.

Make sure that any collaborative initiative you support (with financial or developmental assistance) credits your office for its contributions in its promotional material, flyers, and handouts. Perhaps they will include a link on their Web site to your program's Web site. Get all the recognition you can, unless you have a good reason to remain anonymous.

ONLINE TOOLS. Web sites, e-mails, and electronic mailing lists are critical tools for promotion today; you need to consider how to use them strategically and tactically in your promotional program. Most large institutions have technical offices that provide Web design services, but these services work best when they know exactly what you want.

Your program Web site. First, make the site as simple, uncluttered, and functional as possible. Make it easy for faculty members to find information quickly. Navigation bars and buttons should allow for quick return to the homepage or main menu; this feature will also facilitate browsing. Avoid complicated drop-down menus; instead provide menus as lists on the pages themselves. Users of your site should be able to see clearly exactly where they are when they are deep into the site. Label the pages clearly, and provide tracking information at the top, for example:

Home→Workshops→Fall Schedule.

Ensuring quick downloads of all your Web pages is essential. PDFs (portable document formats) should only be used for content that you expect users to download and print, *not* for content that you expect people to read online. Check the accessibility and readability of your site on browsers and operating systems that your readers might use. Make sure the site is compliant with the Americans With Disabilities Act (ADA) guidelines. For example, provide alternative text for graphical elements for the visually impaired, and choose darker colors for text so that it will be readable on a lighter background for readers with colorblindness.

Avoid long sections of text without paragraph breaks, subheadings, or other kinds of reading aids; and make sure that blocks of text are narrower than the page width. Avoid extremely large fonts that make it appear you are shouting and extremely small font sizes that are unreadable without adjusting the browser settings.

The design will probably have to conform to your institution's Web design specifications, but within these constraints you should always strive for a site that is warm and welcoming. If you have color choices, pastel colors are friendlier and more pleasing to the eye than saturated colors. Fancy graphics, animations, and moving images (or shuffling pictures) are distractions and often make the site load very slowly. Pop-ups and audio loops should also be avoided since they annoy many people and distract your readers. Users should be able to choose to launch video testimonials and should not be forced to turn such messages off or wait until the video ends.

After creating a template for your homepage, make a color printout and tack it on the wall upside down. Close your eyes for a moment and then open them on the printout. The images that you see first are the same ones that users will see first; if these are not the ones you intend users to focus on, change the design. If nothing on the page stands out, then you have failed to cue your users to the organization and navigation of the site. In either case, redesign the site, and repeat the experiment until you get satisfactory results.

The content of your Web site is the most important factor in its value to the faculty; it must contain resources and tools that faculty will actually use. Until you can develop your own resources, provide links to materials posted online by other faculty development programs at institutions like yours. Keep track of faculty members' requests for information in workshops and consultations. Compile a list of those mentioned most frequently; create materials to fill these needs, and post them on the Web site. Ask faculty members with whom you work for permission to post their syllabi and descriptions of teaching practices (such as group exercises, grading schemes, paper assignments, and grading rubrics). Review print resources that you distribute (monographs, newsletters, workshop handouts) to see if they can be adapted for posting on the Web site, saving printing costs.

Update the site as often as possible, and post the date that each page was last updated. If the site has links to other sites, check weekly to ensure that they are still functioning. Software is available that will perform this task automatically.

Provide a way for users to give you feedback on your site, such as a hotlinked e-mail address. If they are having difficulties with any aspect of the site, you need to know that. Consider providing two links, one to your Webmaster for reporting technical problems and one to you for program and service inquiries.

Try to secure the best place for a link to your program on the institution's homepage. If new teachers want to find your program's Web site, they will probably start their search there. Typically, the homepage contains a drop-down menu labeled "For faculty and staff" or "Academic support" that has links to various support resources for faculty members. Your program needs to appear on each list that instructors visit frequently.

Links to Web sites of allied support units (for example, the writing center, a leadership program, the graduate student center, the postdoctoral affairs office) are useful to the faculty. They also establish your program's reputation as a gateway to faculty development in the broadest sense.

Tracking user data is very important for assessing the effectiveness of your site. The number of hits and the length of time users remained logged on provide rough measures of your site's utility for the faculty. Hits from users outside your institution are an important measure of the impact of your program beyond the campus.

Electronic mailing lists. Become familiar with the capabilities of your institution's e-mail list tools, and set up your list to support the kind of communication you wish to promote. Starting an electronic mailing list for teachers who are interested in your program is a good idea, but do not create automatic lists from your workshop participants without asking their permission. Make it easy for recipients to drop out if they want to. Most electronic mailing list software provides a line at the bottom of the message template that informs the recipients of the name of the list to which they are subscribed and a link to enable them to unsubscribe. Do not abuse the list by using it for purposes beyond its original intent, or you will annoy subscribers.

Targeted e-mails. Do not flood e-mail channels with messages targeted at a subset of your audience. If you want to promote a program for graduate student instructors, send promotional material directly to them, to the departmental directors of graduate studies, and graduate student associations.

PRINT MATERIALS. Brochures, leaflets, newsletters, and monographs are staple promotional tools in most faculty development programs. However, printing is expensive; and you need to ensure that the impact of the materials justifies their cost. Never send a document to a department and ask them to print and distribute it. If you do not have the funds to print the materials, chances are good that the department does not have them either.

Brochures. In a simple and clear way, brochures should describe your center, your mission statement, contact information, policies, and basic faculty development opportunities. You should create brochures based on the assumption that faculty members who find your programs of interest will keep them for a long time. Using heavy-weight paper stock and colors coordinated with your Web site or other promotional materials helps reinforce the message that the information in your brochure has lasting value. Omit time-specific and time-limited offerings because you do not want to receive inquiries about them years after the brochure was published.

Newsletters. The appeal and utility of newsletters vary across institutions. On a small campus where your program provides the only opportunity for faculty development, newsletters can be effective tools to announce new programs, services, or workshops that you offer alone or in collaboration with an allied organization (the faculty senate, student government, student support services, and so on). On a large campus where your program may be only one of many faculty development initiatives, newsletters may be more effective as tools to promote campus cohesion and knowledge of the range of support available to the faculty. In this case, the newsletter can inform faculty of resources provided by other campus services, but be sure to check with these units before you include information about their offerings. Regardless of institutional size, newsletters are a good way to inform faculty of local, regional, and national conferences, especially if funding is available to subsidize faculty travel or registration fees.

Monographs. The distribution of *short* monographs on effective teaching techniques is an ideal way to introduce these ideas to faculty members who may not have the time or inclination to attend faculty development events. Research-based monographs are particularly effective for persuading faculty members that they should take the results seriously. Practice-based monographs are most valuable when they are coauthored by a well-known and highly respected faculty member.

PERSONAL CONTACTS (WORD OF MOUTH). Social relationships are the glue that holds organizations together, and personal contacts are one of the best ways you can promote your faculty development program. Establishing social relationships with faculty members and administrators enables you to learn what appeals to them and what does not. In your initial meetings, try to learn something about individuals that will help you remember them. Ideally, learn something distinctive about their professional activities, their concerns, and their interests or service assignments. Share something similar about yourself, but try to maintain the conversational distance set by the person you have met. As you talk to people, always keep in mind how well their information fits or contrasts with what you are learning about the culture of the institution and its subgroups.

Hosting a "meet and greet" reception for faculty members (especially newly hired people) is useful in acquainting them with the staff of the center. Staff members have an opportunity to establish relationships with faculty members, learn more about their individual needs, and show how the center can help them. Such an event also helps new faculty members meet their peers and begin to establish social relationships of potentially long-term value.

Word of mouth promotion is perhaps the best strategy of all, but it is not one that you can control very well. Providing high-quality programs and services ensures that the campus "buzz" will be positive, but quality control can never be relaxed since bad news travels faster than good news.

Conclusion

Promoting a faculty development program is a much more complex and difficult activity than many practitioners realize; even the most energetic promotional efforts will fail if they are not in tune with the culture of the institution. Although the time and energy required to research and understand this culture (and its subcultures) are considerable, the knowledge gained is indispensable for the success of your program. You must be able to represent your program to faculty members and the administration in ways that they understand and accept, communicate with them with appropriate language through established channels, and demonstrate that your program is in tune with institutional goals, values, and expectations. Promoting your program successfully and grounding it in the institution are essentially the same process.

REFERENCES

Austin, A. E. (1990). Faculty cultures, faculty values. In W. G. Tierney (Ed.), *New directions for institutional research, no 68. Assessing academic climates and cultures* (pp. 61–86). San Francisco: Jossey-Bass.

Boone, L. E., & Kurtz, D. L. (2005). *Contemporary marketing.* Mason, OH: Thompson South-Western.

Cialdini, R. (1993). *Influence: The psychology of persuasion.* New York: William Morrow.

Higgins, D. (1990). *The art of writing advertising: Conversations with masters of the craft.* Lincolnwood, IL: NTC Business Books.

Kashner, J. B. (1990). Changing the corporate culture. In D. W. Steeples (Ed.), *New directions for higher education, no. 71. Managing change in higher education* (pp. 19–28). San Francisco: Jossey-Bass.

Krueger, R. A., & Casey, M. A. (2009). *Focus groups: A practical guide for applied research.* (4th ed.). Thousand Oaks, CA: Sage.

Milgram, S. (1974). *Obedience to authority: An experimental view.* New York: Harper & Row.

Tierney, W. (1988). Organizational culture in higher education. *Journal of Higher Education, 59*(1), 2–21.

Zakrajsek, T. (2003). The five-minute workshop. *Innovation ideas from POD participants.* Retrieved October 20, 2008, from http://www.wku.edu/teaching/db/podbi/main.php

8

PRACTICAL SUGGESTIONS FOR PROGRAMS AND ACTIVITIES

Donna E. Ellis and Leslie Ortquist-Ahrens

WHETHER YOUR INSTITUTION LOCATES SUPPORT for faculty development in a teaching center, as the responsibility of a standing committee, or positions it as the province of a single individual with a course release, you can create effective programming for faculty members, part-time instructors, and graduate teaching assistants by drawing from a slate of options. At first the possibilities may seem overwhelming; however, you can prioritize by considering your mandate and the available resources. Consider, too, that, regardless of your circumstances, you have more potential human resources than yourself, your committee, or your teaching center's staff. A recent study of faculty development over time has, in fact, dubbed the current era the "Age of the Network"; it will be possible to meet needs and expectations only through collaborations and partnerships (Sorcinelli, Austin, Eddy, & Beach, 2006, p. 4). Your potential clients can assist in designing and implementing whatever programs and activities you choose to offer (Wilhite, Lunde, & Latta, 2000). In addition, other departments such as educational technology, the library, student services, service learning, and disability services can help. These valuable resources bring additional expertise and can help to increase the reach of your programming and participant buy-in.

In this chapter, we offer ideas that we have found useful at our home institutions, which are quite different: the University of Waterloo and Otterbein College. The University of Waterloo is a large, research-intensive, comprehensive university with a center of twenty staff members and an advisory council that works through the associate vice president, academic. Otterbein College is a small, private, comprehensive, liberal arts institution, which was long well-served by an active faculty development committee and a single faculty member with a course release; it now has a young teaching center and a full-time director. Like Waterloo, Otterbein College's center also has an advisory committee and reports to the vice president for academic affairs. The suggestions we outline have been implemented at our institutions as well as at numerous others in North America.

Options for Programs and Activities

Instead of creating an exhaustive list of programming possibilities, we have chosen to categorize options as either one-time events or ongoing programming; we provide steps to follow when preparing and offering these programs. The categories are not entirely discrete since some options could fall into both. As you review the descriptions, consider what could best serve your institutional needs and culture and meet the mandate of your center or program. Offering variety in your programming helps to respect the differing needs of your client base; however, we recommend that you avoid trying to do too much too quickly, just as others have advised in this volume. Instead, the aim should be to make purposeful programming decisions.

One-Time Events

The options outlined here could be open to the entire institutional community, although many could be scaled back for individual departments or a small group of related departments. Many are stand-alone events rather than part of larger, ongoing programs. However, some one-time events, such as annual conferences or teaching academies, may be offered regularly.

WORKSHOPS. These events are a mainstay offering for faculty development. Workshops may run from thirty minutes or less to a full day and sometimes even longer; they may also be offered online. At many institutions, sixty to ninety minutes is the typical time frame for most general, face-to-face workshops; often they are held over lunch or late in the day. At other institutions, workshops are held before the academic year or at a time set aside in the calendar specifically devoted to faculty development. Generic topics, such as designing assessments of student learning, teaching large classes, providing constructive feedback to students, designing courses, understanding learning styles, or facilitating discussions, typically have broad appeal and are useful to instructors institution-wide. It can be powerful to bring instructors from different departments together to learn from one another. Center staff or faculty members with expertise in the topic area may serve as facilitators. In any case, effective workshops are generally interactive (Chambers, 2002; Fleming, 1997). More details on running such events are presented in the next major section of this chapter titled "Mechanics."

INSTITUTES AND ACADEMIES. Sometimes a topic warrants more time than a one-day workshop. In this case, multiday events can provide the time required to engage more deeply with a complex topic such as course or curriculum design. At the University of Waterloo, we hold an annual Teaching Excellence Academy, which runs for four days and targets midcareer faculty members who would like time to redesign a course in a community environment. In small groups, the participants work through a course design process and finish with a revised course outline that they display and present to other participants and their department chairpersons and deans.

SYMPOSIA AND CONFERENCES. Another large-scale option is a teaching symposium or conference. Such events might focus, for example, on teaching and learning issues; or they could revolve around the scholarship of teaching and learning. The target audience and presenters are often instructors from your own institution, allowing you to showcase and celebrate local expertise. However, these events can also, depending on your circumstances, include participants and presenters from a larger radius. This wider outreach may be particularly important if your institution is small as was the case when Otterbein hosted a statewide conference on the scholarship of teaching and learning. Outside keynote speakers may be included in these events, which, of course, is likely to increase costs. One caution: organizing a symposium or conference takes a lot of time and resources, so be sure that you have enough assistance before agreeing to plan and host one.

OPEN CLASSROOM EVENTS. At Waterloo, award-winning faculty members are asked to "open" their classroom to colleagues. The observers receive details in advance about the class they will observe, including the context, topic, teaching methods, and goals for that class. Then they attend the open class (the number of observers depends on the available seats) and are encouraged to note ideas to use in their courses and questions for the instructor. A debriefing discussion occurs immediately afterward, and focused discussions often ensue. This type of event provides not only examples but also a wonderful way for outstanding faculty members to give back to their community. Both new and experienced faculty members have benefited from attending these events.

Ongoing Programming

You may sometimes decide to design and support programming that spans a longer time period. When you want to create extended conversations or provide in-depth professional development opportunities, one-time events are not likely to suffice (Easton, 2005; Gaudelli, 2001). Moreover, some professional development groups, such as book clubs or faculty learning communities, can be relatively self-sufficient and self-sustaining, which helps when your resources are limited. You might design a structure for cross-disciplinary groups to come together based on a common interest, career phase, or gender; or you could have department-specific programs that address a common interest or concern.

BOOK CLUBS OR DISCUSSION GROUPS. Many institutions sponsor book discussion groups. Such opportunities represent a relatively simple and inexpensive programming option as well as a way for participants to explore important topics in some depth. If your institution does not have a teaching center or if you are launching a new center, you may find these to be good starting points. Faculty members can recommend topics or suggest particular books, or those responsible for faculty development can advertise a series of titles with brief descriptions and invite applications. Where funding permits, it is an incentive to provide a book for each participant in exchange for the commitment to read it, meet regularly, and discuss it actively in the group. Typically, such groups meet several times during a term, perhaps once a week for an hour over the course of four weeks; and participants agree to read a certain amount for each meeting.

TEACHING CIRCLES, COMMUNITIES OF PRACTICE, AND FACULTY LEARNING COMMUNITIES. These terms are used somewhat interchangeably to represent group structures that support in-depth development over time. When successful, such groups can help faculty members to make teaching "common property" (Huber & Hutchings, 2005; Hutchings, 1996), overcome "pedagogical solitude" (Shulman, 1993), and redress what many experience as "hollowed collegiality" (Massy, Wilger, & Colbeck, 1994). Common characteristics of such groups generally include a shared focus or topic, regular meetings over an extended period of time (just one term or a full academic year or more), and a stable membership of five to twelve persons. These groups are inquiry based and collaboratively organized and facilitated rather than led by an expert. Collegiality and community are important values and outcomes; frequently the agenda includes producing a tangible product such as a redesigned unit for a course, a presentation for a local or national conference, or the beginnings of a manuscript. Such groups rest on the conviction that faculty members have much to learn together and from each other within the local context.

Teaching circles, made popular through an American Association for Higher Education (AAHE) volume about collaboration and peer review (Hutchings, 1996), are often the most informal of the three types of groups. In some institutions, teaching circles involve collegial discussion of a series of readings, thus constituting a kind of extended book club. Communities of practice are more complex and can involve various components such as workshops, microteaching, class visits, and regular meetings (Holmgren, 2005). Some institutions, including Minnesota State University Mankato, Northern Essex Community College, The Ohio State University, and the University of British Columbia, offer communities of practice around the scholarship of teaching and learning. In some community of practice models, membership remains fluid as people join and leave over time. The lifespan of groups is indefinite and can extend as long as interest remains, sometimes over many years. In other models, for example, in the faculty learning communities that Cox and Richlin (2004) have developed, refined, and broadly disseminated over the past three decades, membership is fixed for an academic year to target the growth of trust and community as well as the study of one's own teaching.

One crucial note: such groups should not aim to function as committees or advisory councils. They should focus on learning rather than on institutional policy making or decision making.

PROGRAMS FOR NEW FACULTY. Many faculty development programs dedicate significant time and resources to support new faculty members' development and extended orientation. Boice (1991) has demonstrated that career success is more likely when new faculty members display behaviors and attitudes that characterize "quick starters"; such behaviors and attitudes can be cultivated in long-term programming that targets new faculty. Increasingly, institutions offer one-time orientation programs that deal with both logistical concerns, such as human resource topics, and teaching and learning issues. These orientations may include workshops, resource fairs, scavenger hunts, progressive meals where new faculty receive different courses of a meal at different campus locations, and other social events. For example, at Waterloo's new faculty orientation, we have a family-oriented barbecue at our president's farm to enable faculty members to make some social connections the evening before our one-day orientation. The orientation day begins with two teaching-based workshops, followed by a resource fair and a faculty panel on how to be successful at the university. Orientation activities may also extend beyond the beginning of the academic year to include workshops, social events, online handbooks and resources, learning communities, and mentoring groups specifically developed for new faculty members. This extended programming can help them make smoother transitions to a new institutional context. At Otterbein College, we are piloting a group mentoring program for new faculty members, adapted from a program at New Mexico State University (Gray & Birch, 2008), which combines topical meetings during the fall and winter quarters that address institutional mission, teaching effectiveness, scholarship and creative work, and service, with individual or small group mentoring in the spring quarter. New faculty participants nominate potential mentors from among faculty members who presented on panels in fall and winter. The goal for pairs or triads is to imagine a career trajectory for each participant's first five years at the institution.

CERTIFICATE PROGRAMS. A different type of ongoing programming involves bringing together cohorts of learners to achieve a certificate. For example, certificates for graduate teaching assistants represent another common type of program, particularly at centers at larger institutions. Often very keen to develop solid teaching skills, these learners are motivated participants. At the University of Waterloo, a comprehensive certificate program is available to graduate students. The program includes workshops; reflective, application-oriented response papers; a teaching dossier; a research-based project; and teaching observations. More details about such programs can be found in Chapter Twenty of this volume, "Graduate and Professional Student Development Programs."

Certificates for faculty members may also be of value; see, for example, the Instructional Skills Workshop (ISW), which was begun at the British Columbia Institute of Technology (http://www.bcit.ca/ltc/workshops/isw .shtml), or the Faculty Certificate Program at the University of British Columbia (http://www.tag.ubc.ca/programs/facultycertificate/).

DEPARTMENT-LEVEL CURRICULUM (RE)DESIGN. A growing area of activity at some centers involves assisting departments with curriculum design issues. As accreditation and external quality assurance movements continue to take hold in higher education, the need for accountability has never been greater. If you have the resources, one powerful way to affect an entire department is to assist with a curriculum development project. Possible activities can include stakeholder data collection and analysis, curriculum mapping exercises, and activities to solicit the attributes of an ideal graduate (Evers & Wolstenholme, 2007; Wolf, 2007). These activities can work for designing new curricula and for revising existing ones. However, such activities are often time intensive, typically requiring multiple meetings. Ongoing curriculum work can also result in follow-up workshops on topics such as writing learning outcomes or teaching with problem-based learning or the case method. Such workshops are often best designed and delivered in collaboration with a departmental representative.

MENTORING AND CONSULTATIONS. Some activities are best focused on the individual; these efforts often represent some of the most transformative, but also time-intensive, work that faculty developers do. These activities are ongoing, and they generally involve multiple meetings. One common mentoring model involves one-on-one relationships intended to help new faculty members with transition and career development. You can help establish appropriate pair relationships between an experienced faculty member and a junior faculty member, and you can support them with additional resources. Some institutions also use a peer-mentoring approach when experienced faculty members are struggling or want to work on teaching development. Sometimes mentoring activities are also undertaken in cooperation with a department.

Individual consultations are one of the most common faculty development programs offered to those interested in honing their teaching. Some faculty members prefer this individual focus to working in group settings; a series of individual consultations can be a powerful means to help faculty members reflect on and make adjustments to their teaching or course-related materials such as a syllabus (Piccinin, 1999). To learn more about effective consultation practices, see Chapter Ten, "Assessing Teaching Practices and Effectiveness for Formative Purposes."

WEB SITES. While not often thought of as programming, a faculty development program's Web site is of increasing importance. Most teaching centers have a Web site that, at minimum, outlines available services and resources. However, to maximize relevance and utility, you need to think about your Web site as virtual programming that needs regular, ongoing attention. For example, Web sites can feature Podcasts of workshops or speakers, provide synchronous or asynchronous online workshops, or include blogs or wikis to enable discussions about teaching and learning. These types of resources can provide "just-in-time" faculty development and can be on any topic but are often on technology-related topics (for example, use of personal response systems or clickers). More standard features are also worth considering, such as online registration for events which may be linked to an underlying participant database, links to external resources such as "Tomorrow's Professor" listserv (http://ctl.stanford.edu/Tomprof/subscribe.html), or links to your own resources such as teaching handbooks. At Waterloo, we have a collection of "Teaching Tip Sheets" that colleagues from around the world can also access. At Otterbein, our site showcases a series of faculty course portfolios that have emerged from learning communities. We need to keep the material fresh so that users will return again and again. More details about using this aspect of technology for faculty development can be found in Chapter Sixteen, "Issues in Technology and Faculty Development," and Chapter Seven, "Promoting Your Program and Grounding It in the Institution."

GRANTS. Many teaching centers also provide grants of varying sizes to support faculty and instructional development. Small grants—from a few hundred dollars to a few thousand—might be used, for example, to help faculty members with technological innovations, provide project assistance by supporting a graduate student, develop course materials, attend teaching-related conferences, or plan a teaching-based conference or symposium within a department or college. Some centers are also able to offer larger grants (for example, $10,000 to $20,000+) to support scholarship of teaching and learning projects. If a center has such funds, it is appropriate to have standardized application and review procedures; and generally a deliverable product, such as a summary report, a seminar given by the grant recipient, or a technological product, is expected at the conclusion of the grant. Programs such as faculty learning communities may also be supported by teaching center grant funding.

The Mechanics of Running an Event

Now that you have a variety of options from which to choose, you may want some guidance on implementation. This section covers steps in planning and running a one-time event; the next section highlights coordinating ongoing programming. In both sections we explain the steps sequentially; however, as with any process, the steps can be followed more flexibly and are often iterative.

Doing Your Homework

Events work best when they are planned for an intended audience. When you know the potential participant pool, you can brainstorm with these participants in mind or even ask the group what is most relevant. We may feel that we know what our instructors require, but often it is best just to ask. If you have an advisory committee, its members can be an excellent source of information. Alternatively, you may have working group committees to help you run an event; or you may be able to enlist past participants from workshops, academies, or institutes to serve as future planners and facilitators. At Waterloo, we draw on past participants from our Teaching Excellence Academy to serve as planners and cofacilitators for future offerings. A survey of your potential participant pool can identify their most salient needs. This needs assessment can be done independently or can be a regular question on the evaluation forms that you use for your events.

Planning the Event

Once you know your audience, you need to identify the intended learning outcomes. What should participants leave being able to do, know, or value? Just as we encourage instructors to consider learning objective taxonomies when writing learning goals or outcomes (Anderson & Krathwohl, 2001; Fink, 2003), we should do the same when planning events. As we identify outcomes, we should consider how we will know that our participants have reached them. What activities during or after the event might demonstrate their learning? If you are having someone else facilitate the event, the outcomes and the activities can be developed by that person alone or in conjunction with a member of your teaching center. If you are using a panel discussion in your session, bringing the panelists together before the event to discuss their ideas and approaches is advisable to clarify their areas of focus. To set reasonable outcomes, you need to know the duration of the event. Then, you can choose desired concepts to convey and plan appropriate activities. Consider using various instructional approaches in events to model active learning methods. One of Waterloo's most effective workshops uses various activities with 100+ participants in an active learning workshop to demonstrate how to facilitate this type of learning with large classes.

You must also take care of administrative tasks such as booking a location and arranging for refreshments. Not all events require refreshments; but, if you are holding events during lunch, late in the day, or for more than two hours, you may want to keep your participants fueled! Finally, you need to know your budget to cover costs for facilitators or speakers, room bookings (if applicable), refreshments, and the preparation and copying of materials.

EXECUTING THE PLAN. Now you need to consider how to make the event happen. The first element to consider is how to advertise, based on your target participant numbers and your available budget. Often multiple methods and repeated advertisements are necessary. When multiple methods are used, consider the timing of the advertisements. Spreading them out over a few weeks will prolong the exposure and help to build interest. Inviting participants to "bring a friend" with them is another good way to spread word-of-mouth advertising and increase the exposure of your events to a wider audience. When planning Waterloo's first few Learning About Teaching Symposia, we asked our advisory council members to bring three or four colleagues to help increase our attendance numbers and spread interest across the institution. (See Chapter Seven, "Promoting Your Program and Grounding It in the Institution.")

This last suggestion about bringing colleagues involves an interesting decision about whether your event will be open to all or require nominations to attend. Waterloo's Teaching Excellence Academy uses the nomination method, which enhances the prestige of the event. Limiting the number of spots can also increase the desire to attend since only a few people will have the opportunity to be there. Of course, spots may be limited due to the nature of the event. For example, it takes time to have individuals present mini-lectures in a workshop format and receive in-depth feedback; but participants can be encouraged by the slightly competitive nature of enrollment.

You also need to consider how you will handle registration. Many events require some type of preregistration so that you can secure an appropriately sized room, enough materials, and food. Online registrations make this process smooth and can even provide automatic reminders to registrants. Programs with databases behind their registration systems may be able to allow participants to cancel their own registrations and help keep your participant data more accurate for annual reporting. Other events may not require preregistration, but you should still collect a list of participants so that you have data about all events. Despite these efforts, most events experience "no shows."

Some programs choose to charge a fee for these situations while others may take 10 to 15 percent more registrations than stated to compensate for those who register but do not come. Tracking your registration and attendance patterns over time will enable you to decide how best to handle this situation.

With administrative steps taken care of, you can return your focus to the event itself. If participants need to complete work before the session—for example, readings or a worksheet—you need to distribute this a week or so beforehand. Participants can return completed documents online for the facilitator to review and use to tweak the event plan, if applicable. This presession work can also enable participants to secure their spots in the session, can be used to assign individuals to groups, and can serve as examples that a facilitator can incorporate into the event.

With any prework collected and reviewed, you are ready to stage your event. Remember to take whatever materials you will need (audiovisual equipment, handouts, markers, name tags, and so on), the attendance list, and evaluation forms. You may also want to have a backup plan in case your chosen technology does not work, and a handout can often serve this purpose. Remember, too, that you are working with adults who bring much experience and expertise to your events even though teaching and learning theory may be new to them. Draw on their strengths, be open to their ideas, and work on making connections with them that may lead to future follow-up departmental workshops or individual consultations.

Evaluating the Event

Many faculty development programs request that participants complete, at minimum, a satisfaction-based survey. Questions often focus on how useful or relevant the session material was and typically seek both quantitative and qualitative responses. For example, you could ask participants to rate how helpful the session was and then ask them to describe what made the session helpful, how the session could be changed, and what other session topics participants would like. One variation focuses more on the participants' learning. Questions that ask what motivated participants to attend the session, what they learned, and what they will try to apply in their own teaching put the focus more on the participants' learning instead of on the workshop facilitation. If you encourage participants to include questions for follow-up on these same forms, then you can begin a conversation that extends beyond the event.

Coordinating and Overseeing Ongoing Programming

Ongoing programming, such as faculty learning communities, can require special steps to work well; the role of the developer is often different yet integral to the overall effectiveness of such programs.

Doing Your Homework

Many guidelines for one-time events are relevant when you are planning and supporting ongoing programming, for example, considerations about audience, design, publicity, and evaluation. As with preparation for one-time events, doing your homework is an essential first step. This preparation consists of at least three components: assessing the topics of interest to stakeholders and participants, making decisions about the programming to offer and support (how complex, how long-term, departmental or cross-disciplinary), and determining how to train facilitators or how to structure and sustain programming over time. If, for example, you decide that a faculty learning community approach would work best, you will need to learn more about underlying principles and key components of this approach; a comprehensive and useful guide and bibliography can be found at Cox's Web site: http://www.units .muohio.edu/flc/index.php. You may wish to consult with colleagues experienced with such a program, or you might attend a Professional and Organizational Development (POD) Network conference session dedicated to helping participants launch a faculty learning community. Long-term programming can yield rich rewards; once a program is in place, it can be sustained largely by experienced participant facilitators. You should be aware, however, that it also represents a significant time commitment.

Developing an Overview of the Programming

Again, as in the case of one-time event planning, it is good practice to engage in backward design. While the expected outcomes of a book club or discussion group and its organizing principles may be quite modest—no more than completion and discussion of the book by the group—desired outcomes for communities of practice or faculty learning communities tend to be more numerous and complex. As mentioned previously, collegiality, collaboration, and community are as important as learning about the topic at hand and developing successful projects. Starting with an awareness of your multiple goals will help you determine what activities might engage participants, when you might set program milestones or project due dates, and possible formative and summative assessment activities. Administering a midyear anonymous survey, for example, can help you and the participants to gauge whether the group is on target toward its goals. Good practice also involves assessing programming at its conclusion and adjusting future iterations.

Launching and Supporting Programming over Time

You can begin with ideas that you know are attractive to potential participants, or you can invite faculty members to submit proposals for topics they would like to explore with colleagues. Once the focus of the group is identified, publicity can begin. While informal groups such as book clubs often operate on a first-come, first-served basis, more complex and longer-term structures are generally better served by requiring and carefully reviewing applications for membership. Without adequate participant commitment, groups such as faculty learning communities easily flounder.

As program director, your next task may be to consider and develop at least a loose set of policies, guidelines, and expectations for the group's work. For example, at Otterbein College, book club members receive a one-page set of general guidelines; facilitation, discussion leadership, note taking, and other responsibilities typically rotate among members. All participants commit to attending and actively participating in at least three of four sessions. Facilitators of faculty learning communities, on the other hand, generally receive extensive training, resources, and ongoing support to help them undertake the facilitation role in a way that will most likely foster the desired outcomes (Ortquist-Ahrens & Torosyan, in press). While you or another teaching center staff member may choose to facilitate a pilot teaching circle, community of practice, or faculty learning community, you will not be able to facilitate them all. Remember the value of engaging others in facilitative roles. Part of the power of collaborative group approaches to development comes from the opportunity to extend your reach and multiply your range of effectiveness. Be prepared to troubleshoot with facilitators as the term or year unfolds, and be proactive in approaching them regularly to check how things are going.

Responsibility for procuring reading materials, ordering refreshments, securing reimbursements, reserving spaces, and other logistics may rest with group members or the group's facilitator. If you have the staffing, it is helpful for you to provide this administrative support, which then allows participants to focus their time and energy on the task.

Finally, remember to provide closure for groups that have worked together over time. Year-end celebrations that recognize group members' accomplishments serve several purposes. An event such as a celebratory luncheon not only for program participants but also for their department chairpersons and other institutional leaders can celebrate accomplishments, further publicize teaching and learning activities, and garner recognition from leadership. Good ideas incubated in communities of practice may also contribute to thoughtful and well-researched institutional initiatives. At Otterbein College, many key components of the college's new strategic plan were incubated in faculty learning communities that investigated effective programming options for first-generation college students, teaching to support global learning outcomes, and undergraduate research. Meaningful closure for participants in groups may, in fact, involve inviting them to envision how their learning might become embodied not only in individual but also in institutional practice.

Conclusion

Running faculty development programs can be invigorating. Numerous options exist to help you with your work; you can find many variations on these ideas through articles, Web sites, conferences, and discussions with colleagues. No one right mix of programming and activities exists. The needs of your instructors, the institutional culture, and the mandate of your program should help to guide your decisions. One thing we have learned, however, is that what works in one type of institution may not work in another; and what works one year may not work the next. The contexts of higher education institutions are continually evolving, which means that the needs of our clients are also changing. We try to anticipate such changes, knowing that the most successful faculty development programs are flexible and responsive. So look for ways to adapt known practices to your own environment, and be ready to try new activities when the timing seems right.

REFERENCES

Anderson, L. W., & Krathwohl, D. R. (Eds.). (2001). *A taxonomy for learning, teaching, and assessing.* New York: Longman.

Boice, R. (1991). Quick starters: New faculty who succeed. In M. Theall & J. Franklin (Eds.), *New directions for teaching and learning, no. 48. Effective practices for improving teaching* (pp. 111–121). San Francisco: Jossey-Bass.

Chambers, R. (2002). *Participatory workshops: A sourcebook of twenty-one sets of ideas and activities.* London, UK: Earthscan.

Cox, M. D., & Richlin, L. (Eds.). (2004). *New directions for teaching and learning, no. 97. Building faculty learning communities.* San Francisco: Jossey-Bass.

Easton, L. B. (2005). Power plays: Proven methods of professional learning pack a force. *Journal of Staff Development, 26*(2), 54–57.

Evers, F., & Wolstenholme, J. (2007). Integrating knowledge, skills, and values into the curriculum development process at the University of Guelph-Humber. In J. Christensen Hughes & P. Wolf (Eds.), *New directions for teaching and learning, no. 112. Curriculum development in higher education* (pp. 83–91). San Francisco: Jossey-Bass.

Fink, L. D. (2003). *Creating significant learning experiences.* San Francisco: Jossey-Bass.

Fleming, J. A. (Ed.). (1997). *New directions for adult and continuing education, no. 76. New perspectives on designing and implementing effective workshops.* San Francisco: Jossey-Bass.

Gaudelli, W. (2001, November). *Professional development, global pedagogy, and potential: Examining an alternative approach to the episodic workshop.* Paper presented at the Annual Meeting of the National Council for the Social Studies, Washington, DC.

Gray, T., & Birch, J. (2008). Team mentoring: A participatory way to mentor new faculty. In D. R. Robertson & L. Nilson (Eds.), *To improve the academy: Vol. 26. Resources for faculty, instructional, and organizational development* (pp. 230–241). San Francisco: Jossey-Bass.

Holmgren, R. A. (2005). Teaching partners: Improving teaching and learning by cultivating a community of practice. In S. Chadwick-Blossey & D. R. Robertson (Eds.), *To improve the academy: Vol. 23. Resources for faculty, instructional, and organizational development* (pp. 211–219). Bolton, MA: Anker.

Huber, M. T., & Hutchings, P. (2005). *The advancement of learning: Building the teaching commons.* San Francisco: Jossey-Bass.

Hutchings, P. (1996). *Making teaching community property: A menu for peer collaboration and peer review.* Washington, DC: American Association for Higher Education.

Massy, W. F., Wilger, A. K., & Colbeck, C. (1994). Overcoming hollowed collegiality. *Change 26*(4), 10–20.

Ortquist-Ahrens, L., & Torosyan, R. (in press). The role of the facilitator in faculty learning communities: Paving the way for growth, productivity, and collegiality. *Learning Communities Journal, 1*(1), 29–62.

Piccinin, S. (1999). How individual consultation affects teaching. In C. Knapper & S. Piccinin (Eds.), *New directions for teaching and learning, no. 79.*

Using consultants to improve teaching (pp. 71–83). San Francisco: Jossey-Bass.

Shulman, L. S. (1993). Teaching as community property: Putting an end to pedagogical solitude. *Change, 25*(6), 6–7.

Sorcinelli, M. D., Austin, A. E., Eddy, P. L., & Beach, A. L. (2006). *Creating the future of faculty development: Learning from the past, understanding the present.* Bolton, MA: Anker.

Wilhite, M. S., Lunde, J. P., & Latta, G. F. (2000). Faculty teaching partners: Engaging faculty as leaders in instructional development. In M. Kaplan & D. Lieberman (Eds.), *To improve the academy: Vol. 18. Resources for faculty, instructional, and organizational development* (pp. 181–192). Bolton, MA: Anker.

Wolf, P. (2007). A model for facilitating curriculum development in higher education: A faculty-driven, data-informed, and educational developer-supported approach. In J. Christensen Hughes & P. Wolf (Eds.), *New directions for teaching and learning, no. 112. Curriculum development in higher education* (pp. 15–20). San Francisco: Jossey-Bass.

PART TWO

KEY PRIORITIES IN FACULTY DEVELOPMENT: ASSESSMENT, DIVERSITY, AND TECHNOLOGY

The eight chapters of Part Two address the assessment of programs, teaching, and student learning; explore what is critical for educational developers to become multiculturally and interculturally competent and how best to help faculty, students, and staff to do the same; and discuss how educational developers can help faculty to use technology effectively in their teaching as well as how educational developers can use technology effectively in their own work.

9

PROGRAM ASSESSMENT FOR FACULTY DEVELOPMENT

Kathryn M. Plank and Alan Kalish

PROGRAM ASSESSMENT IS A VITAL PART of faculty development. With increasing demands for accountability and fiscal responsibility in higher education, now more than ever members of the field need to document the impact of their work. The very existence of faculty development programs may depend on effective assessment, but program assessment is more than simply reporting to others. Just as assessment is central to quality teaching, program assessment is critical to effective faculty development. It informs decision making and improves practice.

While most faculty development professionals recognize the need for assessment, efforts to gather, organize, and make sense of the data can easily become overwhelming. This chapter provides a framework for thinking about program assessment and explores practical strategies for designing assessment that accurately measures the impact of educational development work, helps others understand and value the work, and provides useful data for improving it. This chapter discusses how best to measure, track, and report data; and we share ideas on how to use both summative and formative assessment to make the work of a faculty development unit easier and better.

Defining the Context

When discussing program assessment for faculty development, one must first examine what is meant by the words *program* and *assessment* in the context of faculty development. Faculty development is not a fixed discipline. It is something that rises repeatedly at different institutions to meet different needs and goals. Any assessment must take into account the range of variation in faculty development and look at specific individual and structural characteristics that will affect program assessment (for example, size, staffing, type of institution, budget, age of program, and reputation). One also needs to confront the challenges of assessment when a central goal of the field—student learning—may be at best a tertiary effect. That is, if a developer works with an instructor on a teaching strategy, then that instructor must adopt the strategy and use it in a class; and a student must learn from it in order to have achieved the desired outcome. Documenting that kind of indirect impact can be difficult.

In *Creating the Future of Faculty Development: Learning from the Past, Understanding the Present,* Sorcinelli, Austin, Eddy, and Beach (2006) provided both an historical review of the field and a snapshot of it at the time of their work. Their survey represents a broad picture of faculty development units across institution types in North America. Their largest group of respondents was from research and doctoral universities; somewhat fewer from comprehensives; and even fewer from liberal arts colleges, community colleges, and Canadian institutions (p. 31). Seventy percent of their respondents reported holding multiple titles. More than half had five or fewer years of experience in the field (pp. 32–33).

About half of the responding institutions (54 percent) reported having a central unit with a dedicated staff; 19 percent reported that educational development was the responsibility of an individual faculty member or administrator; 12 percent indicated that it was charged to a committee; 4 percent had a clearinghouse coordinating multiple programs and offerings; and 11 percent reported some other structure (Sorcinelli et al., 2006, pp. 37–38). The larger the institution, the more likely it was to have a central faculty development unit. A "program" may mean something as large as the Center for Research on Learning and Teaching at the University of Michigan, which in its forty-sixth year has a full professor as director and a full-time staff of twenty-six persons, to something as small as a single faculty member at a small comprehensive institution with one course release and the center located in the bottom drawer of a filing cabinet.

Programs differ by mission and range of services. Some work only with faculty members, while others work with graduate students, adjunct faculty, and staff. Moreover, there are different models for what services are provided under the umbrella of faculty development. At some institutions, it includes support for instructional technology, language testing for international teaching assistants (TAs), and testing services; on other campuses these are managed by parallel units.

Obviously, the specific data collected and the collection and reporting methods will vary according to these factors. This chapter offers suggestions for faculty development programs organized in all configurations and of all sizes. While the authors' own experience has been almost entirely in central units at research universities, the chapter also draws upon the experiences of persons at other types of institutions.

Assessment as Integration

Faculty developers come to the field from a variety of disciplinary backgrounds, often with no formal training in program assessment. Fortunately, the field has a rich collection of resources on the assessment of teaching and learning, much of which can be applied to assessing faculty development. For example, the American Association for Higher Education's (AAHE) "Principles of Good Practice for Assessing Student Learning" provide useful guidance for the process (AAHE Assessment Forum, 1997), as does the advice in Walvoord's book, *Assessment Clear and Simple: A Practical Guide for Institutions, Departments, and General Education* (2004). The AAHE principles are as follows:

1. The assessment of student learning begins with educational values.

2. Assessment is most effective when it reflects an understanding of learning as multidimensional, integrated, and revealed in performance over time.

3. Assessment works best when the programs it seeks to improve have clear, explicitly stated purposes.

4. Assessment requires attention to outcomes but also and equally to the experiences that lead to those outcomes.

5. Assessment works best when it is ongoing, not episodic.

6. Assessment fosters wider improvement when representatives from across the education community are involved.

7. Assessment makes a difference when it begins with issues of use and illuminates questions that people really care about.

8. Assessment is mostly likely to lead to improvement when it is part of a larger set of conditions that promote change.

9. Through assessment, educators meet responsibilities to students and to the public.

[AAHE Assessment Forum, 1997, pp. 11–12]

From these resources emerge a few core principles for assessing faculty development work, regardless of program size, type of institution, or range of services. Particularly important for faculty development is the principle of integration. In order for the outcomes of an assessment to tell a coherent story, it is important to treat one's practice as multidimensional and integrated and to be able to demonstrate the connections across seemingly disparate areas of service. One can look at integration in a number of different ways.

Integration with Institutional and Program Goals

A key principle for any assessment is to assess what matters. As Walvoord (2004) stated, "People don't want to 'do assessment'; they want to realize a dream, improve what they're doing, or be excited by a new initiative. So when you are asked to 'do assessment,' link it to institutional dreams, goals, and processes that are important to the campus" (p. 12).

In their 1997 survey of evaluation practices in teaching centers, Chism and Szabo concluded that "a substantial amount of evaluation activity occurs across programs" (p. 61). However, they also discovered that assessment activities were not equally distributed across the services provided and often focused primarily on satisfaction surveys. The goal should be to collect the data that are most important, not just those that are easiest to collect. In applying the AAHE's first principle, Banta, Lunde, Black, and Oblander (1996) stated that "institutional assessment efforts should not be concerned about valuing what can be measured but, instead, about measuring that which is valued" (p. 5). For example, if an institution has placed a high value on interdisciplinary collaboration, it is useful for a faculty development program to assess its support of such collaboration.

Integration as a Single Cohesive System

As Chism and Szabo (1997) discovered, many educational developers already collect a lot of data. However, it is often in different places and in different formats. For example, the office in which the authors of this chapter work used to collect attendance at events in one system and evaluations in another. Consultants kept their own paper files of consultations, while an annual database of client names was maintained by the office associate. Like many, this program had a lot of data, but it was not easy to access or use. To achieve integration, as suggested by AAHE Principles 2 and 5, it is useful to create a single data system that accomplishes as many record-keeping functions and administrative tasks as possible (see Plank, Kalish, Rohdieck, & Harper, 2005).

Integration into Daily Work Life

Perhaps the biggest obstacle to conducting program assessment is time. Just as some faculty members fear that assessing instruction may infringe on teaching time, educational developers are concerned "that the amount of time that would be needed to evaluate well would prevent staff members from serving their clients adequately" (Chism & Szabo, 1997, p. 60). In this case, it would be useful for educational developers to listen to their own advice. When developers talk with faculty members about assessment of learning, they often echo Walvoord and Anderson's (1998) argument that teachers must integrate assessment into the teaching process, not "shove it to the periphery" (p. 13). If assessment is an additional task in the lives of already overburdened faculty members, it will not receive the attention it needs to succeed. Likewise assessment of the work of educational developers must be integrated into their daily work lives in order to be feasible as well as useful and usable.

Integration with Strategic Planning

The most important element of the assessment process is its collaborative nature. "There is, perhaps, no more important principle in the assessment literature than this: successful assessment requires collaborative efforts" (Banta et al., 1996, p. 35). If a program has more than one staff member, all staff should be involved in the creation and daily use of the assessment system. If a solo practitioner uses faculty fellows or collaborates with colleagues in other units, including them in the assessment process can strengthen connections and promote consistency. Appropriate peers, constituents, and administrators should be invited into the process. Involving stakeholders and users throughout the process creates buy-in and makes closing the assessment loop much easier.

Efforts to develop categories for data, to generate consensus on what to count and how, and to discuss how to use the data can be central to staff codevelopment and strategic planning efforts. Active collaboration is crucial to aligning unit goals with the goals of the institution and assuring that the end product remains useful and intuitive.

The Cycle of Program Assessment

One fundamental principle in all of the assessment literature is that good assessment is cyclical. That is, ask a question, collect data, make changes, and ask more questions.

Setting Goals

The first stage of program assessment is to define goals. One may be eager to jump into collecting data before taking the time to plan what one wants to know and why. However, the goal is to be scholarly in faculty development, which requires thoughtful assessment. Preassessment planning is an important and productive part of the process, and there is much to gain before collecting even a single piece of data.

KNOWING THE CONSTITUENTS. Nobody works alone, not even solo practitioners. To be effective, educational developers must consider all of their stakeholders. It may be useful at this time to do some needs assessment (Milloy & Brooke, 2003), whether through a full-scale survey of all possible clients or speaking with a few; it is important to know their expectations and perceptions of what services are most effective. As part of this process, it is important to take ownership of these goals and make sure that one feels comfortable with what constituents are asking the program to do.

ALIGNMENT WITH INSTITUTIONAL GOALS. Also, faculty developers need to link their program goals to the institution's strategic plan, thereby demonstrating how the unit is assisting the institution in reaching its strategic goals. This process helps higher administration understand a program's worth. It is also a good check to make the connection between the work of a faculty development program and these larger goals.

One crucial goal of most institutions is to improve the education of their students. While faculty development programs may not be able to measure directly (or take credit for) the learning in the classroom, they can connect their work to that goal. One way to demonstrate indirect effects is to show a stepwise alignment along the process and provide evidence at all steps possible. In this case, useful measures might be the number of faculty members who have worked with the program to collect midterm student feedback or the number of students whose voices have been represented in Small Group Instructional Diagnoses (SGID) conducted by program staff. One can then add qualitative reports from faculty members of how they changed their teaching in response to student feedback and what results they saw. Aligning these measures to the larger goal gives the numbers meaning beyond simply a count of where faculty development staff members spend their time.

TARGETING SPECIFIC NEEDS. Instead of thinking of assessment as yet another responsibility, educational developers should try to think of it as something that can help them. What are the program's biggest challenges? How can an integrated program assessment system help? For example, if a program is new, assessment can help plan its growth and set priorities. Conversely, if a program is large and well established, assessment data can help determine which services are most effective and which should be reconsidered. Just as faculty developers often recommend that instructors take a scholarly approach to teaching by using feedback to guide their decision making, so too should their own practice be scholarly and informed by data.

PLANNING THE INTENDED USES OF ASSESSMENT. Other issues that should be explored before collecting data include how one plans to use the assessment, with whom it will be shared, and how the process of assessment fits into the unit culture. For example, performance evaluation of individual staff members may require different information than that which is needed to justify continuing or expanding a specific program or service. If one's only purpose is to provide data for administrative supervisors, that may look different from information intended to be published on a Web site or used in marketing efforts.

Determining Outcomes and Measures

Once goals have been defined and aligned, one can begin to determine how to measure achievement of those goals—what the outcomes will be. This in turn leads to deciding what sources of data will be used and what kind of evidence accurately reflects the work.

Although programs differ in mission and services, Sorcinelli et al. (2006) found that regardless of institutional type, certain services were similar. These included:

- Consultations for individual instructors
- Institution-wide orientations and workshops
- Intensive programs
- Grants and awards for individuals and departments
- Resources and publications (pp. 14–16)

These services provide logical areas of focus for gathering data. A good assessment plan documents the impact of each service as well as the relationships among them. Although "bean counting" is not sufficient by itself, it does have its place in an assessment plan. Tracking such measures as the number of people with whom the educational development unit interacts, how widespread within the institution these contacts are, the number of unique attendees and repeat attendees at events, and the cost of services in both money and staff time is important in measuring success. These data are usually easy to collect and record.

Most programs are already collecting some of these data. For example, many already collect evaluations at the end of events to assess participants' satisfaction. However, both the authors' own experience and Chism and Szabo's survey (1997) suggest that many faculty developers are likely less systematic in following up to find out whether participants tried anything new in their teaching as a result of the program and whether such attempts were successful. To collect information to document outcomes of educational development work, longitudinal measures such as follow-up surveys of those who have used services are necessary.

It is also important to think about the aspects of educational development work that may be less visible and less easily counted than workshops and consultations. For example, faculty developers are frequently called upon to provide expertise on campus committees. Such service can be an important contribution, but it is rarely documented.

Time is, in most cases, the biggest cost of faculty development. Although it is often not part of academic culture to track hours, doing so can provide useful data. Making cost/benefit decisions can be informed by knowing what a particular service or event costs in precious work hours, especially when integrated with other data about effectiveness. If a particular workshop requires many hours of preparation but did not attract a large attendance or strong evaluations, one might decide to change it or drop it all together. If another service that is aligned with a high-priority goal for the institution requires a large time investment, those data could be used to argue for more staff. (For more on analyzing return on investment, see Bothell & Henderson, 2003).

In addition to client feedback, there are many other crucial sources of data, starting with faculty developers themselves. Self-assessment is necessary. If developers do not reflect on what they are trying to accomplish, they will not be able to determine whether or not they have succeeded. Evaluations from colleagues within a center or persons with similar programs on other campuses and supervisor evaluations are also useful.

Collecting Data

Once one has decided what kind of data to collect, the next challenge is creating a process that makes collection regular, timely, accurate, and feasible. It does not matter how good the assessment system is if it is so cumbersome that no one uses it. Faculty developers—whether they work alone while also carrying a full load of classes or in a center with other persons to provide services to thousands of instructors at a large university—are already stretched thin, and no one has time for extra work.

BUILDING ON WHAT ALREADY EXISTS. Does the program already have processes in place that work? If so, it makes sense to start there. One can begin by looking at what is already collected, whether in paper folders, spreadsheets, or electronic databases, and then decide what is really used, what is collected but never used, and what gaps should be filled.

If a program has multiple staff members, it is important to get input from everyone and decide on who will do which parts of the work. In working with different centers, the authors have found that staff members in different positions make useful and complementary contributions to the process. While a center director may have good insight into what data would be convincing to central administration in an annual report, instructional consultants will have ideas on what information would be useful to them in planning events; clerical staff may have valuable suggestions on the best way to incorporate an event registration process into the system. Solo practitioners may find themselves partnering with other units to create a single shared system. They may also look at their system not just as a way to coordinate with other staff but with their successors in order to create institutional memory.

BUILDING AN INTEGRATED SYSTEM. To achieve this integration, it may be useful to create a single data system that accomplishes as many record-keeping functions and other administrative tasks as possible. The same system can manage work-time, schedule appointments, track event registration, collect evaluation feedback, maintain contact lists, generate mailings, and produce monthly and annual reports. The goal is to have each piece of data entered only once yet made readily available for a number of different outputs and purposes.

Creating a database system requires an investment of time, but in the long run it makes data collection and reporting more manageable. Some centers have staff members who have written their own database programs; but many use commercial software (such as Filemaker or Access) that can be easily learned by a novice. Whatever one uses, the key is to create a *relational* system that allows data to be stored separately in files but shared among the files for greater flexibility of use.

For example, a relational system can hold separate tables for clients, consultations, and events that will "talk" to each other. So when looking at a particular client's record, one will be able to see records of that person's attendance at events as well as any consultations. Likewise, the record for an event will show not only attendance but also evaluations, materials used, planning time, and whatever other information would be useful. A relational system can help to answer questions as they come up, whether it is finding out which departments make the most use of services or what percentage of consultations are with junior faculty members or whether morning or afternoon workshops have higher attendance. Because the system is integrated into daily work, data are entered as part of routine tasks like scheduling consultations and registering people for workshops; and these data are then readily available when questions arise. (An electronic tutorial for developing a relational database system is available from the authors of this chapter by request).

SEEKING OUT ADDITIONAL DATA. As discussed previously, it is necessary to go beyond collecting attendance figures and satisfaction surveys toward more longitudinal data about the impact of educational development work. At Ohio State, for example, a general survey was developed that asks about everything the University Center for the Advancement of Teaching (UCAT) does, including events, consultations, and institutional and professional service (for example, committee membership, grants support, professional and organizational development [POD] committees, and such). The survey asks clients to indicate in what ways they had interacted with UCAT within the past year. The list includes such things as workshops, individual consultations, and assistance on grant projects. Clients also select the topics addressed during the interaction, using the same list of topics as is in the database system. Next they are asked to describe in what ways, if any, they have modified their teaching as a result of the interaction. The survey provides a list but also provides ample space to add other actions.

This survey is distributed annually to one-fourth of that year's clients. The database system makes it easy to select a sample of the year's clients at random, print out mailing labels, and record which clients were surveyed within a particular year (to prevent the same person from getting surveyed every year). After a couple of cycles, UCAT decided that focused feedback on specific services was also needed. This led to the development of a second survey only for those clients with whom UCAT staff members had done individual teaching consultation. The combination of both the general survey and one focused on a specific service has proven useful. The center also conducts focus groups, both in person and electronically, to explore specific issues in greater depth.

Interpreting and Reporting Data

No matter how much data one collects, in order to be useful the data must be interpreted and presented succinctly to those who will use it. Audience is a crucial consideration when interpreting the data. Faculty developers will very likely have both internal and external users of their assessment results.

Internal uses of assessment include both the mundane and the strategic. Having good client histories can help when someone returns after a long hiatus. If the data are in the appropriate form, they can be used to generate attendance lists and nametags for events or to create address labels for mailings. On a larger scale, good data about the usage of various services can help to decide where to focus limited resources and time.

Descriptive statistics such as the mean scores of satisfaction ratings and frequency of attendance are often enough when analyzing and interpreting data. (If one has access to statistical expertise, these quantitative data can be explored through more sophisticated multivariate analyses.) However, sometimes it is useful to be able to link the costs in staff time and money to outcomes in order to do simple cost/benefit analyses. It is also important to put these numbers in the context of the institutional culture so as to know what they mean. For example, attendance figures for campuswide events are meaningless on their own. If a faculty developer at a small college with a strong tradition of faculty participation spends many hours planning a major event and enlists other faculty as facilitators, having twenty faculty attend could be seen as a huge disappointment. However, if a teaching center at a large institution in which faculty attending events outside their own departments goes against the cultural grain offers a brownbag lunch that requires very little preparation, center staff may consider twenty participants to be a great success.

There is also a value to doing qualitative assessment by collecting and interpreting discursive comments. Both of the surveys described previously include open-ended questions. While these data, as well as feedback from focus groups, may be less widely representative than quantitative survey results, they can offer a richer, deeper picture of how the work is being received. These data help "tell the story" of one's work. A selection of quotes can be incorporated into an annual report to illustrate the impact of a program. Written comments are also useful for self-reflection and improvement. Clients' descriptions of their experience of the consultation process and its impact on their work provide insight into the development of practice. Data from faculty members who do not use faculty development services may also provide insight.

It is sometimes useful to compare oneself with peers. This kind of benchmarking can be done by direct survey of other programs or by consulting the literature (Chism & Szabo, 1997; Sorcinelli et al., 2006). Benchmarking can help to set realistic goals for a program and help institutional stakeholders do the same.

Demonstrating to external audiences that a faculty development program meets the needs and standards of an institution is a critical use for assessment data. This pressure is usually why one starts the process in the first place. Therefore, it is important to pay attention to the alignment among the strategic goals of the institution, the specific mission assigned to the program, and the data that are collected. Doing so should make it possible to connect the outcomes of one's work to the objectives the program has been asked to meet.

However, not all the same data needs to be shared with all constituencies. The provost is probably interested in a different slice of information than the faculty advisory group, and yet a different piece may be better to use in marketing materials. Understanding the information needs of various constituencies helps one to create the most useful reports from the mass of data collected.

Summary reports of activities and feedback also make it easier to provide specific evidence for the claims made in self-assessments for individual performance reviews. Data can provide a richer and more detailed picture of the work and make annual staff performance reviews both more efficient and more accurate. It can also feed into personnel decisions such as promotions of existing staff members or the writing of new job descriptions.

An integrated data system can make generating the reports needed to document work to various stakeholders—deans and chairs, advisory committee, and central administration—almost automatic. It also means that budget requests can be supported by a wealth of evidence to show that the programming for which funding is requested meets actual needs and addresses published institutional goals. The bottom line, though, is that services should be effective in meeting the stated goals of the educational development effort, and the only way to know that is to gather data about it.

Finally, extending program assessment to the scholarship of educational development can allow one to use information gathered for internal review to inform others in the field. If one is collecting these data anyway, it can be interesting and useful to ask research questions about professional practice and share the results with the community of educational developers.

Closing the Loop

As with any complete system of evaluation, program assessment for faculty development should accurately describe practice and also shape it. Individually, staff members should have regular access to all the data on their activities and the feedback received from clients; as a unit, they should use these data to inform program planning and to improve individual efforts.

The assessment effort can become central to the planning processes. Discussions of what events to offer each term and what books to buy can be informed by data on which topics faculty most frequently make inquiries about or ask for consultation on. Decisions on new, major projects can be based on estimates of staff time and costs on data from prior activities.

Perhaps more interestingly, an unintended outcome can be that those involved in the assessment process will have spent time thinking about what everyone does. Staff members or faculty fellows can become more aware of each other's projects and spend time discussing the nature of their work. Discussions of how best to categorize a particular activity or when new categories need to be created may lead to a better understanding of what each member of the team does, how it fits into the fabric of the institution, and how to best describe its value to clients. Collaborative, integrated program assessment can create community and ongoing dialogue about the work among staff, advisory groups, and others.

Conclusion

No matter what a program of faculty development may look like, what services it offers, how many or how few instructors it serves, or in what kind of institution it is housed, the requirements of accountability and fiscal stewardship demand that it document the impact of its work. Faculty developers may know that their programs do outstanding work, but they need to build the structures that let them prove it.

However, if the process of collecting, interpreting, and using data is not made an integral part of daily work, it will likely be seen as a burden. The planning processes discussed in this chapter should assist in devising a system that fits local needs. Involving the entire team, and perhaps other stakeholders, in the design process in itself serves as professional development and strategic planning for the program. This practice also makes it much more likely that the evaluation will be used for formative purposes, both for improving individual performance and for connecting unit services to client and stakeholder needs.

As with all evaluation, collecting data on center activities and effectiveness should not be used only for summative purposes. One must "close the loop." Program assessment is more than reporting to others and justifying the existence of a program. A good program assessment system helps guide and improve one's work, inform decision making, and allow the program to demonstrate its effectiveness to others.

REFERENCES

AAHE Assessment Forum. (1997). *Learning through assessment: A resource guide for higher education.* L. F. Gardiner, C. Anderson, & B. L. Cambridge (Eds.). Washington, DC: American Association of Higher Education.

Banta, T. W., Lund, J. P., Black, K. E., & Oblander, F. W. (1996). *Assessment in practice: Putting principles to work on college campuses.* San Francisco: Jossey-Bass.

Bothell, T. W., & Henderson, T. (2003). Evaluating the return on investment of faculty development. In C. M. Wehlburg & S. Chadwick-Blossey (Eds.), *To improve the academy: Vol. 22. Resources for faculty, instructional, and organizational development* (pp. 52–70). Bolton, MA: Anker.

Chism, N.V.N., & Szabo, B. (1997). How faculty development programs evaluate their services. *Journal of Staff, Program, and Organizational Development, (15)2,* 55–62.

Milloy, P. M., & Brooke, C. (2003). Beyond bean counting: Making faculty development needs assessment more meaningful. In C. M. Wehlburg & S. Chadwick-Blossey (Eds.), *To improve the academy: Vol. 22. Resources for faculty, instructional, and organizational development* (pp. 71–92). Bolton, MA: Anker.

Plank, K. M., Kalish, A., Rohdieck, S. V., & Harper, K. A. (2005). A vision beyond measurement: Creating an integrated data system for teaching centers. In S. Chadwick-Blossey & D. R. Robertson (Eds.), *To improve the academy: Vol. 23. Resources for faculty, instructional, and organizational development* (pp. 173–190). Bolton, MA: Anker.

Sorcinelli, M. D., Austin, A. E., Eddy, P. L., & Beach, A. L. (2006). *Creating the future of faculty development: Learning from the past, understanding the present.* Bolton, MA: Anker.

Walvoord, B. E. (2004). *Assessment clear and simple: A practical guide for institutions, departments, and general education.* San Francisco: Jossey-Bass.

Walvoord, B. E., & Anderson, V. J. (1998). *Effective grading: A tool for learning and assessment.* San Francisco: Jossey-Bass.

ASSESSING TEACHING PRACTICES AND EFFECTIVENESS FOR FORMATIVE PURPOSES

Michael Theall and Jennifer L. Franklin

THIS CHAPTER EXAMINES COLLEGE TEACHING PROCESSES and outcomes in order to enhance teaching and learning; we discuss activities intended to inform thinking about teaching effectiveness and also to suggest revisions for improvement. Thus this chapter is about "formative" processes that can occur at any time and are most often confidential. We are not concerned in this chapter about "summative" assessment efforts that are normally terminal activities, the results of which are public and are intended to inform decisions about the continuation of courses or curricula. Nor do we discuss the evaluation of faculty teaching or overall performance for personnel decision making. Our focus is on identifying sources of data that may be useful for improving teaching and learning as part of ongoing programs that support professional development and student achievement.

Assessing teaching effectiveness involves exploring teacher and learner experiences inside and outside the classroom as well as the results of these experiences. This means gathering instrumental data about processes such as teaching methods and classroom activities and also gathering consequential data about outcomes such as student learning. Formative assessment inherently aims to improve processes and practices (that is, instructional strategies, teaching techniques, and measurement of learning) in order to improve the results (the teacher's skills and ability and the student's achievement of instructional objectives). Deciding what processes and which outcomes to assess is the first step in determining what kinds of data are needed.

Assessing how well a teaching practice is working may require assessing what the teacher is doing, or what students think the teacher is doing, and what impact it has on student learning. One basic recommendation is that faculty developers should use both instrumental and consequential data for formative purposes, but they should also be aware that this information can serve summative purposes. Most developers are not involved in summative decisions, but the work they do can have an impact on those decisions. Developers should know enough about measurement and evaluation to be able to recommend the kinds of data that are or are not useful for formative or summative purposes, and they should support the teacher's right to retain the confidentiality of data gathered for formative purposes.

To further clarify the differences, Table 10.1 provides examples of the kinds of instrumental and consequential data usable for formative and summative purposes. Specifics are provided later in this chapter.

In this chapter, we highlight important research findings for faculty developers to consider when assessing teaching effectiveness. The following topics provide the framework for the discussion:

○ What *is not* known and *is* known about college and university teaching

○ How teaching and learning are linked

Table 10.1. Data for Formative and Summative Uses.

Focus → Purposes ↓	Teaching Methods	Classroom Activities	Course Outcomes	Student Progress	Student Learning
Formative	Focus groups	Peer and other observations	Ongoing, informal assessments	Knowledge surveys	Ungraded quizzes
Summative	Multiple data types and sources	Media records, surveys, student ratings	Costs and benefits, student learning, content issues, curricular fit	Grades; performance in later courses	All kinds of assessments, longitudinal data
Data type →	Instrumental Data		Consequential Data		

- ○ What kinds of tools and strategies are available for the assessment of teaching
- ○ How assessment and evaluation data can be used formatively

What Is Not Known . . . Yet

What is clear from more than seventy years of research is that teaching and learning are complex, multidimensional, interdependent activities complicated by the fact that they require human communication and interaction. It is sobering to acknowledge that until very recently our knowledge of learning has been acquired indirectly by observation and inference about human behavior. Recent developments in cognitive science promise to lead us at last to the biological mechanisms of human cognition. As a result, many beliefs about effective teaching will likely require serious revision while other beliefs will not only prove valid but will be understood with greater clarity, thus leading to new and better instructional practices. We will have to compare and contrast extant knowledge with emerging knowledge and expand the range and depth of our pedagogical understanding. Developers should be aware of new research on the brain and learning; it can suggest how and why various pedagogies work. For example, Zull (2002) overlaid the cycle of brain activity in learning onto David Kolb's (1984) "experiential learning" model to show how similarly the two operate.

What is known is linked to the fact that, historically, the research about teaching and learning has primarily involved traditional students in traditional settings. This research offers a solid foundation for teaching in comparable contemporary settings. However, beginning in the 1960s teaching began to change, albeit slowly; what we do not know yet is how these changes have affected teaching and learning, that is, which practices are best used where and to what effect. Happily, acknowledging what is *not* known can be consistent with a spirit of inquiry and reflection that developers value in their own practices and aim to cultivate in clients. In a changing environment, assessing teaching effectiveness may offer the only window of opportunity for improving or enhancing that effectiveness.

Identifying reader-friendly summaries of current reviews of the literature is an essential part of getting the larger view needed to put research findings in perspective. Developers must come to understand research well enough to know when to suggest what might work and when to avoid the imposition of new ideas that might not work due to resistance, inadequate resources, or other factors. Many resources exist to help new developers, and perhaps the Professional and Organizational Development (POD) Network listserv and Web site are among the most accessible. There is a voluminous literature on college teaching and learning, but often developers need to respond quickly to a specific question from one teacher. When there is not time for a deep literature search, the POD listserv can put one in touch with scores of experienced practitioners. Accessing the POD Web site opens a host of possible connections to teaching and learning materials. Publications such as *The Teaching Professor* (http://www.teachingprofessor.com/) and *The National Teaching-Learning Forum* (http://www.ntlf.com/he) distill important findings from the literature in easy-to-use formats. The Individual Development and Educational Assessment (IDEA) Center provides resources created in collaboration with POD; these resources are specifically designed to support formative and summative use of the IDEA student ratings instrument (http://www.theideacenter.org). Of course, more formal literature is always available in educational and discipline-specific journals and the many books published every year.

So What Do We Know?

The skills, behaviors, motivations, and individual styles of teachers and learners in "traditional" instructional settings have been investigated in depth; and much is known about teacher knowledge (Shulman, 1986), the dimensions of college teaching (Feldman, 1997), effective teaching practices (McKeachie & Svinicki, 2006), the effects of college on students (Pascarella & Terenzini, 1991, 2005), promoting student success (Kuh et al., 2005), individual differences among teachers and learners (Grasha, 1996), motivational factors (Theall, 1999a; Wlodkowski, 1998, 1999), and emerging knowledge about brain functions and their connection to learning (Zull, 2002). Knowledge of foundational research and theory is important for developers and instructional consultants as a basis for their own decision making, but it is also important because they serve as a resource for faculty members unfamiliar with this literature.

Teacher Knowledge and the Faculty Developer

Shulman (1986) identified three kinds of knowledge important for teaching. "Content knowledge" is the deep understanding of the subject matter. "Pedagogical content knowledge" is an understanding of basic teaching and learning strategies applied to teaching the subject. "Curricular knowledge" is a refined combination of the first two, gained as the teacher develops a repertoire of specific understanding, skills, and strategies that relate to teaching the subject matter to a variety of students effectively. Curricular knowledge also involves the ability to identify important principles and to translate complex concepts and ideas into understandable and usable form. Curricular knowledge embodies instructional strategic thinking since teachers with curricular knowledge are able to assess student learning and to respond to and remedy issues and problems impeding learning. Assessing teaching involves examining the extent to which a teacher possesses these three kinds of knowledge, and assisting teachers involves helping them to move from being primarily content experts to enhancing the connections between content and effective pedagogy.

A parallel notion can be proposed for faculty developers. While the faculty member provides necessary content knowledge and perhaps some amount of pedagogical content knowledge, faculty development and related services providers must possess:

○ *Their own content knowledge* (theories and practices related to effective teaching and learning across the disciplines)

○ *Their own pedagogical content knowledge* (that is, consultative and instructional methods to help faculty members in a variety of instructional and disciplinary settings enhance or acquire teaching and instructional design skills and knowledge)

○ *Their own curricular knowledge* (application of deep knowledge, interpersonal, and consultative skills to specific situations)

These broad categories encompass diverse areas such as assessment and evaluation skills, knowledge of instructional technology applications, understanding of individual differences, and knowledge of other factors affecting teaching and learning.

Skilled developers can assess teaching and learning situations and suggest effective strategies or help their clients develop and apply them. They can integrate research and theory, and they use a variety of strategies for working with diverse clients (Brinko & Menges, 1997; Lewis & Lunde, 2001; Theall & Franklin, 1991a). New developers, like beginners in any field, move from novice to expert roles over time. Experienced practitioners have knowledge and skills similar to the "curricular knowledge" identified by Shulman (1986), but beginners may not yet have these skills. However, new developers can benefit from the experience of their clients and particularly by working with senior faculty. New developers may have pedagogical knowledge as a result of their graduate training or, if coming from faculty positions, pedagogical content knowledge in their disciplinary areas. Locating and working with experienced faculty is one way to broaden the base of pedagogical content knowledge and curricular knowledge while at the same time establishing a cadre of supportive colleagues.

Dimensions of College Teaching

Another way of looking at college teaching is to consider whether it has identifiable dimensions. Research in this area has been summarized by Feldman (1997, 2007), and his summaries provide a solid foundation of knowledge about college teaching and its relationship to learning. Seventeen major dimensions were identified and rank ordered according to the strength of correlation to student achievement and to students' ratings of teachers. The most important dimensions relating to student achievement include

- The teacher's organization and preparation
- The teacher's clarity and "understandableness" (Feldman's term)
- The teacher's ability to promote learning
- The teacher's ability to stimulate students' interest in the subject

The four dimensions most strongly related to student ratings were

- The teacher's ability to stimulate students' interest in the subject
- The teacher's clarity and "understandableness"
- The teacher's ability to promote learning
- The teacher's provision of intellectual challenge

There is clear evidence of the correlation of student ratings of teaching effectiveness with student achievement (Cohen, 1981) and the effectiveness of combining student ratings feedback with knowledgeable instructional consultation (Cohen, 1980).

Faculty developers need to be prepared to apply these findings in interpreting student ratings but also to appreciate the limits of student ratings. One generalization holds: while some aspects of teaching loom large in every setting, excellence can be achieved in different ways. Helping faculty members understand and appreciate the validity of student ratings in such terms is an art and challenge for faculty developers and requires a careful reading of reviews in the field and practice guides based on them (Marsh, 2007; Murray, 2007; Perry & Smart, 2007; Theall & Feldman, 2007).

Effects of College and the Importance of Student Engagement

Perhaps the broadest generalization one can make about the effects of a college education is that the entirety of the experience is what counts. Pascarella and Terenzini (1991, 2005) pointed out that classroom and subject learning are important; but the application of new learning, socialization, maturation, experimentation, the development of life skills, and exposure to new ideas and people are major elements in bringing about change. Kuh et al. (2005) have demonstrated the importance of students' engagement in their own learning. Faculty members may need to understand this broader perspective and the importance of methods promoting learning strategies that contribute to student engagement in order to help teachers incorporate strategies that capitalize on what we know about the effects of college on students.

Motivation and Related Factors

Student motivation is the central mechanism of engagement, and motivation and emotion are key elements in learning (Zull, 2002). Theall (1999b) reviewed fourteen motivational models and extracted six common components: (a) inclusion, (b) attitude, (c) relevance, (d) competence, (e) leadership, and (f) satisfaction. These factors connect logically with contemporary teaching methods involving activity, engagement, collaboration, and discovery; links to the dimensions of teaching are also apparent.

Motivational outcomes are also connected to students' perceptions of their own efficacy (Bandura, 1977) and to their attributions about their performance. Students who succeed are much more likely to internalize that success ("my ability and/or effort") and to anticipate future success. Perry (1991) and other researchers have demonstrated that students who are having academic difficulty can be helped to take a more proactive, positive approach. They learn to accept more responsibility for their learning, and they begin to understand that they can succeed through their own efforts. Learning is enhanced, which leads to satisfaction based on performance; more important, this enhancement has an impact on intrinsic motivation. In other words, students can say, "I learned something valuable through my own efforts, and I will be able to do it again."

Motivation and consulting effectiveness is also worth noting. The same principles and strategies used with students apply to working with faculty (Theall, 2001). Faculty developers must be familiar with motivational and related principles and techniques to help faculty and to help themselves be more effective in consultative roles. Like faculty members who get intrinsic motivation from the successes of their students, developers are motivated by the successes of their faculty clients; like students, faculty members and developers should be able to say, "I did it myself, and I can do it again."

Assessment: The Link to Learning

We often hear the question, "If there is no learning, can there have been any teaching?" Phrased another way, the question asks whether the essence of teaching is (a) the design of instruction, (b) the delivery of information and required activities, or (c) the result of that delivery (learning). The question is not trivial because proponents of all three choices hold strong beliefs, sometimes favoring one choice to the exclusion of the others. The best strategy for assessing either teaching or learning effectiveness is to gather different kinds of evidence, and the greatest danger is sole reliance on only one kind of data. When faculty developers are asked to help teachers gather evidence, knowledge of quantitative and qualitative methods, test construction, and survey methods is particularly useful. However, equally important are the skills needed to interpret, use, and translate the data for faculty members (Franklin & Theall, 1990; Menges & Brinko, 1986; Theall & Franklin, 1991b). The roles and efforts of instructional consultants and developers become much more important when we keep this issue in mind because the outcomes of our work affect not only teaching and learning but also faculty careers and future student success.

Systematic instructional development and assessment are means to many ends. The key to gauging the impact of any practice or innovation is a systematic approach that uses assessment to gather the relevant data. One of the most powerful tools for a faculty developer is cultivating a commitment to reflective practice on the part of faculty members, helping them to adopt a "scholarship of teaching and learning" strategy to assess systematically the effectiveness of their instructional design. Systematic assessment logically follows systematic design, and it is the action that leads to improvement.

For developers, this means exploring the teacher's goals and objectives; the course content issues and requirements; the students' predispositions, skills, and knowledge; the ways in which learning is assessed; and the overall environment in which the teaching and learning take place. Faculty developers cannot be wed to only one or two favorite instructional methods. They must help teachers to work through instructional problems using a systematic process that considers many aspects of a specific situation and to model an instructional planning and development process that is transferable to other situations. The process helps teachers to construct their own understanding of teaching and learning, thus enabling them to provide more learning opportunities for their students.

Faculty developers must possess clear personal definitions and positions relating to pedagogical matters. They must also be able to work with those who hold differing views about such matters and to facilitate discussions that lead to balanced emphases on teaching and learning, using reliable and valid data for decision making. Equally important, development professionals must be sufficiently skilled in psychometrics (measurement) to assist faculty in using test or assessment data and in constructing and validating their own classroom tests. Finally, developers must be sensitive to the political dynamics and realities within departments and be able to adjust their strategies so as to be most effective given existing contextual factors. Plentiful resources are available to help new educational developers become more knowledgeable in these areas.

Assessment Tools and Strategies

There are several useful sources of information about assessing teaching and learning (for example, Angelo & Cross, 1993; Arreola, 2007; Brinko & Menges, 1997; Chism, 2007; Lewis & Lunde, 2001). Specifically, Berk (2006) provided an array of thirteen strategies particularly useful to instructional developers and consultants who must translate a large body of literature for faculty and administrators in order to help them interpret and use assessment data independently.

We often hear that formative and summative processes must be kept absolutely separate, but we believe that this is a mistake. The two kinds of purposes and the data they generate can be mutually supportive. However, the focus of this chapter is on the application of many kinds of information for the purpose of helping teachers enhance their teaching. Faculty developers should not be involved in summative decision making, and they should be free from pressures to violate the necessary confidentiality of a formative relationship. (See "POD Network Ethical Guidelines" at http://podnetwork.org/faculty_development/ethicalguidelines.htm.)

Tools for Assessing Teaching

Students can provide critical information about teaching. Student ratings of courses may be gathered with the use of a nationally distributed instrument, and one can feel comfortable that the instrument has undergone extensive validation and testing. Many institutions, however, prefer to use instruments developed and analyzed locally. While many such instruments have been tested and validated over time, a far greater number of local instruments have not undergone sufficient investigation. The use of a nonvalidated instrument can pose a threat to the quality of the data, the ability of users to correctly interpret and use results, and the potential of the instrument and process to be beneficial. Indeed, these untested instruments, especially when improperly analyzed and reported, can pose dangers to faculty careers. Many of the complaints heard about student ratings stem from the use of poor instruments and the misuse and misinterpretation of the information they provide.

Most student ratings instruments allow students to make comments about the course and the teacher. These comments can be particularly valuable for formative purposes; they can provide the insights, reasoning, and affective issues that are not well represented in quantitative data from a survey. However, the danger in using students' comments is that strongly worded negative comments can have a disproportionately powerful effect. One harsh, unfair, or even inaccurate comment can diminish the importance of several positive notes from students; and it becomes important for consultants to provide a balance that allows the teacher to make best use of this information.

Other sources of information about teaching must be used to supplement data gathered from students. Small Group Instructional Diagnosis (SGID) (Clark & Bekey, 1979) is a technique that is simple, efficient, and useful for clarifying comments teachers receive; a newer process called Quick Course Diagnosis (Millis, 2004) offers advantages in the usefulness of the data generated and the ability to produce reports that can include specific examples of these data. Another useful strategy for cross-checking student ratings results is videotaping a class and reviewing the tapes with the teacher. Video documentation is unambiguous and can be illuminating, but some cautions must be kept in mind. First, the presence of the camera influences the teacher and the students; what is seen and heard on tape may not represent what happens on a regular basis. Moreover, many teachers do not react well to seeing themselves on tape for the first time and are overly self-critical. These cautions suggest that videotaping, if done at all, should be done frequently enough to provide a representative sample of classroom activity and dynamics and to reduce or remove the influence of the camera itself. More exposure to video documentation also reduces the tendency of teachers to overemphasize trivial issues related to appearance or verbal habits.

Additional information can also be provided by the teacher, peers, subject or pedagogy experts from beyond the home campus, the consultant-developer, and by administrators (with specific cautions and limitations). Portfolios prepared and provided by the individual are an accepted source of information (Seldin, 1991); formative review can include discussion of teaching philosophies, narratives about classroom and other teaching experiences, reactions to student work or student evaluations, and other kinds of information. Developers who establish connections with department chairs and other administrators and who work with senior faculty will have a solid base of knowledge about important issues and even criteria used to judge portfolio materials. Knowing about the technical issues and the procedures of the evaluation process can be very helpful as developers work with new and junior faculty.

Two issues must be kept in mind when administrators are involved in classroom or other observations: (a) the observer must be acceptable to, trusted by, and credible to the teacher; and (b) the process must be considered confidential. Even when it is possible for a department head to observe teaching, that administrator should not use information from the observation as evidence in summative processes. This situation is delicate, and sometimes institutional or department policy requires observation as part of the summative process. If that is the case, then it is best not to have an administrator observe for formative purposes. Peer review is less subject to concerns about a formative-summative conflict. However, it is important to ensure that both the teacher and the observer are comfortable with the process and each other and to follow established processes (Chism, 2007) that provide the greatest efficiency and most useful information. External expert reviewers can comment on course content, instructional design, syllabi, course readings or activities, and assessment strategies. Also, they can examine students' tests or other work. Such review is necessary when no local peer is available who is sufficiently knowledgeable of the content area or other aspects of the instruction.

It is particularly difficult for an instructional developer or consultant to assess and enhance teaching and learning without having observed the teacher and the class. Firsthand observation of several class meetings and review of videotapes always provides information that clarifies or corroborates information from student ratings, observations by others, portfolio materials, and data from other sources. Instructional consultants and developers must be well versed in the student ratings literature, in observation and assessment techniques, and in organizing and coordinating data gathering. Also, they should be skilled in interpreting the data so as to provide useful feedback to the teacher. Favoring only quantitative or qualitative data is a disservice to the client, so data from multiple sources must be used.

Tools for Assessing Learning

The most common assessment device of student learning is the classroom test. Classroom tests, however, are rarely validated; and consequently test results may be less reliable than those from standardized measures (for example, professional certification tests in many fields) or from validated instruments. Tests can be examined to determine their connection to teaching goals, instructional objectives, and teaching methods. Developers can help teachers construct classroom tests and conduct basic validation activities such as item analysis. Standardized tests, especially those used in professional licensure and certification, serve similar purposes and have the virtue of being usable for comparing individual performance or the performance of groups of students. These tests focus on content generally agreed to be important in the field, and thus they can also be used to validate the content of courses or programs.

Recent emphasis on the assessment of learning outcomes has provided an array of effective, efficient, and convenient tools. Angelo and Cross (1993) compiled a large number of Classroom Assessment Techniques (CATs), and Walvoord (2004) suggested simple ways of assessing learning outcomes at the department and program levels. These tools are important because faculty members must often contribute assessment data to program evaluation projects or to disciplinary and other accreditation teams. Nuhfer and Kipp (2003) described "knowledge surveys" that collect students' self-reports of their confidence about their subject knowledge. This information can help teachers adjust course content, put extra emphasis on areas of difficulty, and determine how successfully students have met the instructional objectives.

Classroom Research and the Scholarship of Teaching and Learning

The Scholarship of Teaching and Learning (SoTL) proposed by Boyer (1990) sought to reframe teaching as a kind of scholarship; by inference that meant to include as part of teaching the same kinds of questions and issues and processes as in assessment. Cross and Steadman (1996) offered guidelines for investigations of classroom process and outcomes as a way to implement the scholarship of teaching. They noted that classroom research does not always require the large samples and statistical procedures common to more traditional empirical research, but that classroom research can be focused, reflective, and useful without the need to achieve significant differences. These approaches present excellent opportunities for developers since helping teachers answer classroom questions often means helping the department and the institution as well. As the emphasis on pedagogical scholarship moved to The Scholarship of Teaching and Learning (Shulman & Hutchings, 1999) and making the research work more similar to reviewed, public scholarship in disciplinary fields, another important outcome became apparent: when faculty developers assist teachers with SoTL projects that result in professional presentations or publications, a major career development objective is achieved. In other words, *the value of development goes beyond enhancing teaching and learning and becomes a part of the faculty member's professional development agenda.*

Using Data to Enhance Teaching and Learning

A broad array of assessment possibilities exists, from simple dialogue with the teacher to formal investigation of teaching and learning issues. This array is critical to understanding both process and outcomes, and it provides a rich source of information for personal and professional growth. Faculty developers provide important service when they help teachers and departments to blend assessment, evaluation, and SoTL. These efforts work best as complementary activities, and none works as well in a vacuum. Faculty developers will succeed if they keep in mind some basic guidelines for effective consulting and if they attend to the unique aspects of working with faculty. The following list provides helpful guidelines.

GENERAL GUIDELINES FOR ENHANCING TEACHING AND
LEARNING

○ Establish your own credibility as a knowledgeable and skilled colleague and academic professional by as much involvement as possible in teaching, scholarship, and service.

○ Work to make your services central to the mission of your institution as well as the needs of your clients.

○ Establish a positive environment for the client (you are supporting professional growth and enhancing performance, not fixing a broken teacher).

○ Communicate regularly and in as many ways as possible (face to face as well as electronically).

○ Listen, listen, listen.

○ Follow up and keep in touch.

○ Help the client gather useful data.

○ Ensure confidentiality of the process and any information it generates.

○ Do not overextend, overcommit, or make promises you cannot keep.

○ When possible, create peer networks or other mechanisms for individuals to avoid isolation (especially for new faculty).

○ Work with administrators (especially department chairpersons) to establish yourself and your services and also to understand their perspectives and needs better.

○ Be a strong advocate for best practice and excellence.

○ Focus on success for the teacher and the students.

○ Listen, listen, listen.

SPECIFIC GUIDELINES FOR ENHANCING TEACHING AND LEARNING

○ Stress the need for useful data from many sources, and seek additional data whenever possible.

○ Help the teacher to separate teaching goals (what the teacher will do) from learning outcomes (what the students will acquire) and then to use a systematic process to design instruction that allows both to be achieved.

○ Begin with and build on strengths, but do not avoid problem issues.

○ Balance data from students with data from other sources.

○ Note the numbers of comments and quantitative responses from student ratings, and be sure there are representative samples of both.

○ Help the teacher integrate and interpret the data with specific purposes in mind (that is, have targets of opportunity and specific goals for the process).

○ Suggest practical, possible interventions or changes with the potential for short-term as well as long-term improvements.

○ Blend assessment and evaluation data along with SoTL results, other documentation, and direct observation whenever possible.

o View the assessment of teaching as having multiple objectives that culminate not only in enhanced teaching and learning but also in enhanced opportunities for professional growth and advancement.

Conclusion

Ultimately, instructional and faculty development are activities that require effective partnerships. The direct consultant-client relationship is supplemented by the participation of others, but the most effective consulting takes place in environments where all stakeholders actively support continuous efforts to enhance teaching and learning. Many kinds of assessment data must be used, and careful examination of context and other issues is as important as review of information such as test scores or student-provided data. Beyond the immediate assessment process is the extent to which institutional policy and practices provide credible and clear evidence of the valuing of teaching. Faculty developers can provide an important service to their clients and institutions by being actively involved in advocating for strong and sustained resources for personal and professional growth.

REFERENCES

Angelo, T. A., & Cross, K. P. (1993). *Classroom assessment techniques: A handbook for college teachers* (2nd ed.). San Francisco: Jossey Bass.

Arreola, R. A. (2007). *Developing a comprehensive faculty evaluation system* (3rd ed.). Bolton, MA: Anker.

Bandura, A. (1977). Self efficacy: Toward a unifying theory of behavioral change. *Psychological Review, 84*(2), 191–215.

Berk, R. A. (2006). *Thirteen strategies to measure college teaching.* Sterling, VA: Stylus.

Boyer, E. L. (1990). *Scholarship reconsidered.* Princeton, NJ: Carnegie Foundation for the Advancement of Teaching.

Brinko, K. T., & Menges, R. J. (1997). *Practically speaking: A sourcebook for instructional consultants in higher education.* Stillwater, OK: New Forums.

Chism, N.V.N. (2007). *Peer review of teaching* (2nd ed.). Bolton, MA: Anker.

Clark, D. J., & Bekey, J. (1979). Use of small groups in instructional evaluation. *Insight into teaching excellence, 7*(1), 2–5. Arlington: University of Texas at Arlington.

Cohen, P. A. (1980). Effectiveness of student-rating feedback for improving college instruction: A meta-analysis. *Research in Higher Education, 13*(4), 321–341.

Cohen, P. A. (1981). Student ratings of instruction and student achievement: A meta-analysis of multisection validity studies. *Review of Educational Research, 51*(3), 281–309.

Cross, K. P., & Steadman, M. H. (1996). *Classroom research: Implementing the scholarship of teaching.* San Francisco: Jossey Bass.

Feldman, K. A. (1997). Identifying exemplary teachers and teaching: Evidence from student ratings. In R. P. Perry & J. C. Smart (Eds.), *Effective teaching in higher education research and practice.* New York: Agathon Press.

Feldman, K. A. (2007). Identifying exemplary teachers and teaching: Evidence from student ratings. In R. P. Perry & J. C. Smart (Eds.), *The scholarship of teaching and learning in higher education: An evidence-based perspective* (pp. 93–129). Dordrecht, The Netherlands: Springer.

Franklin, J. L., & Theall, M. (1990). Communicating ratings results to decision makers: Design for good practice. In M. Theall & J. L. Franklin (Eds.), *New directions for teaching and learning, no. 43. Student ratings of instruction: Issues for improving practice* (pp. 75–96). San Francisco: Jossey-Bass.

Grasha, A. F. (1996). *Teaching with style.* Pittsburgh, PA: Alliance.

Kolb, D. A. (1984). *Experiential learning: Experience as the source of learning and development.* Englewood Cliffs, NJ: Prentice-Hall.

Kuh, G., Kinzie, J., Schuh, J. H., Whitt, E. J., & Associates (2005). *Student success in college.* San Francisco: Jossey-Bass.

Lewis, K. G., & Lunde, J. P. (Eds.). (2001). *Face to face: A sourcebook of individual consultation techniques for faculty/instructional developers.* Stillwater, OK: New Forums.

Marsh, H. W. (2007). Student evaluations of university teaching: Dimensionality, reliability, validity, potential biases, and usefulness. In R. P. Perry & J. C. Smart (Eds.), *The scholarship of teaching and learning in higher education: An evidence-based perspective* (pp. 319–384). Dordrecht, The Netherlands: Springer.

McKeachie, W. J., & Svnicki, M. (Eds.). (2006). *Teaching tips. Strategies, research, and theory for college and university teachers* (12th ed.). Boston: Houghton Mifflin.

Menges, R. J., & Brinko, K. T. (1986, April). *Effects of student evaluation feedback: A meta-analysis of higher education research.* Paper presented at the meeting of the American Educational Research Association. San Fracisco. (ERIC Document Reproduction Service No. ED 270 408)

Millis, B. J. (2004). A versatile interactive focus group protocol for qualitative assessments. In C. M. Wehlburg & S. Chadwick-Blossey (Eds.), *To improve the academy, Vol. 22. Resources for faculty, instructional, and organizational development* (pp. 125–141). Bolton, MA: Anker.

Murray, H. G. (2007). Research on low-inference behaviors: An update. In R. P. Perry & J. C. Smart (Eds.), *The scholarship of teaching and learning in higher education: An evidence-based perspective* (pp. 184–200). Dordrecht, The Netherlands: Springer.

Nuhfer, E., & Kipp, D. (2003). The knowledge survey: A tool for all reasons. In C. Wehlburg & S. Chadwick-Blossey (Eds.), *To improve the academy: Vol. 21. Resources for faculty, instructional, and organizational development* (pp. 59–74). Bolton, MA: Anker.

Pascarella, E. T., & Terenzini, P. T. (1991). *How college affects students.* San Francisco: Jossey-Bass.

Pascarella, E. T., & Terenzini, P. T. (2005). *How college affects students. Vol. 2: A third decade of research.* San Francisco: Jossey Bass.

Perry, R. P. (1991). Perceived control in the college classroom. In J. C. Smart (Ed.), *Higher education: Handbook of theory and research* (Vol. 7, pp. 1–56). New York: Agathon.

Perry, R. P., & Smart, J. C. (Eds.). (2007). *The scholarship of teaching and learning in higher education: An evidence-based perspective.* Dordrecht, The Netherlands: Springer.

Seldin, P. (1991). *The teaching portfolio: A practical guide to improved performance and promotion/tenure decisions.* Bolton, MA: Anker.

Shulman, L. S. (1986). Those who understand: Knowledge growth in teaching. *Educational Researcher, 15*(2), 4–14.

Shulman, L. S., & Hutchings, P. (1999). The scholarship of teaching: New elaborations, new developments. *Change, 31*(5), 11–15.

Theall, M. (Ed.). (1999a). *New directions for teaching and learning, no. 78. Motivation from within: Encouraging faculty and students to excel.* San Francisco: Jossey-Bass.

Theall, M. (1999b). What have we learned? A synthesis and some guidelines for effective motivation in higher education. In M. Theall (Ed.), *New directions for teaching and learning, no. 78. Motivation from within: Encouraging faculty and students to excel* (pp. 99–109). San Francisco: Jossey-Bass.

Theall, M. (2001). Thinking about motivation: Some issues for instructional consultants. In K. G. Lewis & J. P. Lunde (Eds.), *Face to face: A sourcebook of individual consultation techniques for faculty/instructional developers* (pp. 77–91). Stillwater, OK: New Forums.

Theall, M., & Feldman, K. A. (2007). Commentary and update on Feldman's (1997) "Identifying exemplary teachers and teaching: Evidence from student ratings." In R. P. Perry & J. C. Smart (Eds.), *The scholarship of teaching and learning in higher education: An evidence-based perspective* (pp. 130–143). Dordrecht, The Netherlands: Springer.

Theall, M., & Franklin, J. L. (Eds.). (1991a). *New directions for teaching and learning, no. 48. Effective practices for improving teaching.* San Francisco: Jossey-Bass.

Theall, M., & Franklin, J. L. (1991b). Using student ratings for teaching improvement. In M. Theall & J. L. Franklin (Eds.), *New directions for teaching and learning, no. 48. Effective practices for improving teaching* (pp. 83–96). San Francisco: Jossey-Bass.

Walvoord, B. E. (2004). *Assessment clear and simple: A practical guide for institutions, departments, and general education.* San Francisco: Jossey-Bass.

Wlodkowski, R. J. (1998). *Enhancing adult motivation to learn: A comprehensive guide for teaching all adults.* San Francisco: Jossey-Bass.

Wlodkowski, R. J. (1999). Motivation and diversity: A framework for teaching. In M. Theall (Ed.), *New directions for teaching and learning, no. 78. Motivation from within: Encouraging faculty and students to excel* (pp. 7–16). San Francisco: Jossey-Bass.

Zull, J. E. (2002). *The art of changing the brain.* Sterling, VA: Stylus.

ASSESSMENT PRACTICES RELATED TO STUDENT LEARNING

TRANSFORMATIVE ASSESSMENT

Catherine M. Wehlburg

ASSESSMENT PRACTICES IN HIGHER EDUCATION have been around for a long time. One can argue that assessment of student learning is so entwined with teaching that assessment and teaching are actually two sides of the same coin. However, in higher education, the term *assessment* has typically been understood as a method for identifying student learning goals and outcomes, gathering data to demonstrate learning, and then using the results to make improvements so that students' learning increases. In addition, assessment has also been tied to accountability in order to demonstrate performance to stakeholders—most notably, those in regional and specialized accreditation agencies. Assessment has, therefore, often been seen as a "top-down" requirement that must be done correctly—or else! Assessment of student learning, however, is something that all faculty members do as part of teaching. Individual students are assessed by the faculty on a regular basis to provide evidence that is later used to submit a course grade. With the background of the role of the faculty developer in the assessment process, in this chapter I provide an overview of assessment as a tool for gathering evidence of student learning in order to transform teaching and enhance the learning process.

Unfortunately, assessment has often been perceived and used as a tool for accountability, which has created the relatively widespread belief that assessment is primarily done to demonstrate performance to others rather than using the process to improve student learning. Accreditation needs are seen as reasons "why" assessment is occurring, but there are other areas to which an institution must be accountable. Institutional stakeholders such as boards of trustees, alumni, parents of current students, and even state legislative bodies can require information demonstrating that goals and outcomes are being met. Because of this focus on "doing" assessment for external mandates to demonstrate success, the process is often seen as a time-consuming and bureaucratic annoyance. This perception does nothing to improve student learning or faculty members' teaching. "If we ignore it, it will go away, and we can go back to doing things the way we have always done them!" is something that has probably been said by more than one faculty member, dean, or college president. Assessment of student learning is a topic that is coming up ever more frequently within higher education circles, and faculty members are often required to add this task to their "service" to the institution or the department. Faculty developers have a significant role in the assessment process in that they can help to ensure that it is done well and ultimately leads to the enhancement and improvement of student learning.

Walvoord (2004) has defined assessment of student learning as "the systematic collection of information about student learning, using the time, knowledge, expertise, and resources available, in order to inform decisions about how to improve learning" (p. 2). Faculty members work with students in order to know what they are learning; they are often some of the most creative and authentic assessors on campus. In turn, faculty developers can work with the faculty to use the results of assessment for learning improvement.

The Importance of Assessment Practices

In coming years, assessment processes within higher education will likely become increasingly widespread and complex. Regional and specialized accrediting agencies will continue their assessment requirements and, in all likelihood, increase the demands on assessing all aspects of institutional performance. Concern about the quality and cost of higher education has led to the creation of governmental committees, seemingly unending congressional debate, and the creation of new requirements, which, in turn, will require more and better assessment of student learning outcomes. In addition to external motivational factors, there are many reasons for faculty members (and therefore faculty developers) to participate fully in assessment. Assessment is a process that leads to the identification of areas in which students are not learning as much as is desired by the instructor, the department, or the institution. Clearly, the elements of this process are determined best by those with the responsibility for teaching.

Shulman (2007) described assessment as using data to tell the story of the department. In this metaphor, assessment is the process for gathering the information to build a narrative that can be shared with others. "The story told by an assessment is thus ultimately a function of the dimensions of measurement that determine the possible directions the narrative might take. So accountability requires that we take responsibility for the story we commit ourselves to telling. We must make public the rationale for choosing that story as opposed to alternative narratives . . . only then should we defend the adequacy of the forms of measurement and documentation we employ to warrant the narratives we offer" (Shulman, 2007, p. 22). Viewing assessment as a means of sharing information is vital, but the process should not be developed only for use by external agencies. Assessment must be the way that the faculty, departments, and the institution gather meaningful information about student learning within the context of the local institution. The faculty and those in faculty development must give voice to the "story" of learning in higher education because it is only with the participation by faculty in the development and use of the assessment process that the true story of student learning can be told.

Levels of Assessment Practice

Assessment occurs at every level of an institution. While the overall procedures used to assess learning are often similar across institutions, the implementation and the terminology used to describe assessment practices often lead faculty members and administrators to view these different levels quite differently. "Every good teacher continually examines student work not just to give a grade but to improve teaching. . . . This is assessment, but it has been confined to the individual classroom" (Walvoord, 2004, p. 6). The assessment that occurs within the classroom should be aligned with the program and the entire institution. Faculty members often do not consider that student learning data from the course level can and should inform the assessment practices of the department, program, and institution. Faculty developers can help with this reframing of how information on student learning can be used.

Course-Based Assessment

Assessment of student learning has always occurred at the course level in the teaching and learning process. Faculty members often modify their approaches for a particular part of a course or an individual class period based on student questions or patterns of classroom response. This type of assessment is generally not even recognized as "assessment of student learning" in the formal sense because it is viewed as part of the teaching process.

Course-based assessment can be implemented in a variety of ways. For example, a faculty member might ask a question in class and make a teaching decision based on the student response. If there is confusion, the instructor may go back over a particular concept. Another kind of course-based assessment occurs when a faculty member reads student papers or exams. If there is an area of difficulty, the faculty member will likely take some time in subsequent classes to ensure better understanding. Faculty members who work with faculty developers to improve teaching or revise a course are often using the results of course-based assessment.

Assessment activities within the course are used to find out what a student knows or can do within the context of that course. These assessment measures already exist in every course—exams, papers, projects, or presentations, for example. Additional instruments have been designed for faculty use and can be easily modified to fit into a particular course. These are often called Classroom Assessment Techniques (CATs) (Angelo & Cross, 1993). CATs are methods of assessing "what students are learning in the classroom and how well they are learning it" (Angelo & Cross, 1993, p. 4).

There are hundreds of examples of classroom assessment techniques (some sites to find examples include http://www.ntlf.com/html/lib/bib/assess.htm and http://pedagogy.merlot.org/Classroom_AssessmentTechniques.html). Some CATs take more time to administer than others; some work well in online environments; and some can be done with almost no preparation. Thus, faculty developers can and should encourage faculty members to integrate CATs into their courses (Wehlburg, 2006).

Walvoord (2004) encouraged faculty members to build on the grading process as they create and modify their departmental and course-level assessment plans. While most assessment offices and accreditation agencies have indicated that grades cannot be used for assessment, the information that goes into the grade can and should be used as a direct measure of student learning. "A letter grade by itself does not give enough information about the learning that was tested or the criteria that were used" (Walvoord, 2004, p. 13).

Department or Program Assessment

Department or program-level assessment focuses on student learning goals and outcomes. As a group, the faculty within a department often finds it difficult to articulate the elements of a student's educational journey in a few goals and outcomes; they may not even initially agree that there are specific outcomes that all students should reach. The task may seem overwhelming and frustrating when the faculty considers all of the courses and experiences that a student might encounter while pursuing a degree. The role of faculty developers in this process can be significant. They can work with departments to facilitate the discussion on what should be learned by students within the context of the degree program or department. Having a facilitator from outside the department can actually benefit the dialogue because the faculty developer may not come with the academic "baggage" that might exist within the department. While it can be difficult to gain entrée into a departmental meeting, many department chairs welcome another facilitator. Faculty developers can initiate the conversation with the department chair by offering to help facilitate a discussion within the department on learning outcomes and pedagogy, tactfully seeking an invitation to do so.

To begin the dialogue about assessing a department or program, it is first necessary for the faculty within the discipline to agree on the elements of an "ideal" graduating student. One way to get started is to ask the entire departmental faculty to describe briefly (in writing or any other method) the "ideal" graduating student. What abilities does this student have? What skills can she or he demonstrate? What ethical beliefs are held? What elements of the program have been influential on the development of this student? Asking these types of questions will have the faculty looking at outcomes that are meaningful, somewhat measurable, and philosophically relevant to the faculty.

Next the faculty members are asked to share their lists. It may be that not everyone agrees with the entire list. To build the list of learning outcomes, faculty developers can help move the dialogue forward by reminding the faculty that it is best to start with something that is small and acceptable to all. In a psychology department, for example, the faculty could agree only on one broad area at the beginning of the discussion—writing and referencing in an appropriate style. It took several discussions and some compromising to develop what finally came to be a meaningful set of outcomes acceptable to all.

If chairpersons (or others) try to push through a set of outcomes, the faculty rarely buys into it; and the information that is subsequently gathered will not be used to enhance teaching and learning. This is not a process that can be done in a single meeting or even a single semester. It takes time to discuss outcomes and measures. During such discussions, the faculty often wants to know how much is "enough" in terms of student learning. In other words, how high should the bar be set when measuring student learning outcomes? In general, if the standard is too low, most students will meet the outcome, but does this type of finding provide sufficient data to the department for making meaningful change? Probably not. While setting low standards might make a department look as if all or most of its students are doing well, the reality is that this measurement activity becomes a bureaucratic task rather than an opportunity to find out what students may *not* be learning. Knowing what students are not learning provides the data to make transformative changes.

Faculty developers must be sensitive to the individual departmental cultures and ensure that this process does not turn into one that merely blames the faculty members who are teaching introductory courses, which can happen frequently. Building on existing relationships between and among the faculty members and those in faculty development is essential (Wehlburg, 2008).

Institution-Level Assessment

Nearly every institution (and all institutions with regional accreditation) has a mission statement. The ways in which the institution acts on its mission may vary widely, however. An institutional mission is a broad statement that sounds wonderful. However, many institutions do not have measureable and meaningful ways to discover whether students are in fact meeting the learning goals stated in the mission.

At the institutional level, assessment of student learning is usually perceived as a task that must be done to demonstrate accountability in order to satisfy accrediting agencies or governmental requirements. This focus on demonstrating compliance can cause assessment to be seen as a mechanistic task instead of an ongoing effort to measure something multifaceted, complex, and transformative. To meet the specific needs of outside agencies, institutions often oversimplify the process so as to align their assessment plans and reports with the requirements of the outside agencies. Unfortunately, this oversimplification has led to a certain amount of disgust on the part of the faculty and the administration. As one author wrote, "No matter how much they [outcomes assessment practices] purport to be about 'standards' or student 'needs,' they are in fact scams run by bloodless bureaucrats who, steeped in jargon like 'mapping learning goals' and 'closing the loop,' do not understand the holistic nature of a good college education" (Fendrich, 2007, p. B6). It is truly unfortunate that some faculty view assessment as only a bureaucratic process rather than as something that can inform our discussions about teaching and learning.

Faculty developers can work within their institutions to ensure that assessment is not perceived in this negative way. While assessment data may initially be collected for accreditation, the process provides a wonderful opportunity to discuss teaching learning and pedagogy. Faculty developers can use the program-level data to encourage a department to align its curricula with the desired outcomes, which, in turn, affects institutional assessment.

Aligning Course-Based and Program-Level Assessment

Courses exist for a purpose: they are designed to ensure that students can learn and appropriately use the content about a particular subject and, as faculty members have mentioned, can "think" in the ways of the discipline. Courses also are created so that the sum of a set of courses leads into a major or a degree. Some of the elements that students gain within a course are more easily measured than others. Behaviors, skills, and tests of knowledge are relatively easy to transform into measurable outcomes. Other aspects of a course, however, are more difficult to measure. How does one measure critical thinking? Some aspects thereof are certainly measurable. It is possible, however, that certain areas are not easily measured; but, when faculty members state that they "know it when they see it," there are nonetheless measurable elements and a measurable outcome present.

As part of an ongoing faculty development program, many institutions encourage faculty to list outcomes for general education or for the major on the course syllabus. Faculty developers can help to create curriculum maps to determine how a specific course fits into the overall departmental or program learning (for more information, see Kallick & Colosimo, 2009). Clearly, student learning outcomes are measured at the course level. "We faculty have been doing assessment of student learning in our classrooms all along, but we have not seen the need to make it more visible or valued externally. It has been 'stealth' assessment" (Walvoord & Anderson, 1998, p. 5).

Learning outcomes at the course level should be intentionally aligned with overall program level outcomes. This practice has several benefits: faculty members know what students should have learned in prerequisite courses, and students know what they should be learning and how that learning is integrated with other courses.

Yet ensuring this alignment can be a difficult thing to do. Opening the discussion about alignment in a department or program is likely to bring up concerns about academic freedom and the overall "impossibility" of assessing something as complicated as learning. However, to assess the learning that occurs within a program, there must be discussion of overall learning outcomes and expectations for students who have completed the program; part of this discussion must focus on what students learn as they take the courses that are required for that particular degree. The important aspect to acknowledge, however, is that teaching and learning are the responsibility of the faculty members; and they have the right to create curriculum in ways that align with their disciplinary norms and the institutional culture. So, while an institution may require that the faculty within departments assess student learning, what the student learns is not changed by the assessing of that learning.

Student Learning, Assessment, and Accreditation

Faculty members know what their students have learned, and they use this information to make modifications to their courses and sometimes even to the sequencing of courses within a major or the general education program. Using data in this way has been called "transformative assessment," which is designed to enhance teaching and learning in an ongoing, meaningful, and appropriate way (Wehlburg, 2008). Regrettably, discussions of accreditation often do not begin with the concept of learning. Instead, as discussed earlier, the push only to meet external standards may arise, which returns the process to a focus on accountability to others rather than on the enhancement of student learning.

Banta (2007) asked, "Can assessment for accountability and assessment for improvement coexist? Can the current accountability focus actually strengthen assessment for improvement? Or will an accountability tidal wave roll across the fields, crushing the fragile green sprouts of assessment for improvement that have begun to appear?" (p. 9). These questions express the tension that exists between accountability and transformation as the result of assessment efforts. Often, faculty members are caught in the middle of this discussion. The institution desires that faculty demonstrate accountability to accrediting agencies, boards of trustees, parents, and others while faculty members generally want to focus on teaching and learning within their courses. Because the term *assessment* has so often been linked only to accountability purposes, it is not surprising that this tension exists and that many faculty members do not perceive or appreciate the potentially transformative nature of assessment.

Nonetheless, this accountability approach does have benefits. Without the requirement from accrediting agencies regarding the need for assessment, the movement would never have grown as it has over the past three decades; and it would not have the power to influence the use of resources within an institution. Decisions made by regional and specialized accrediting agencies have caused institutions to focus seriously on the need to identify outcomes, to measure them appropriately, and then to use the results for improvement. The top-down approach to mandating has led at times, unfortunately, to the institutional perspective that assessment is "a means to appease the accreditors, not necessarily as a way to learn about their own institutions, because the stakes have become so high" (Schilling, 2006, p. 2).

The primary purpose of any assessment plan at any level must be focused on student learning. Palomba and Banta (1999) defined assessment as "the systematic collection, review, and use of information about educational programs undertaken for the purpose of improving student learning and development" (p. 4). Another definition of assessment is that it is the "process of gathering and discussing information from multiple and diverse sources in order to develop a deep understanding of what students know, understand, and can do with their knowledge as a result of their educational experiences; the process culminates when assessment results are used to improve subsequent learning" (Huba & Freed, 2000, p. 8). Allen (2004) stated that "as a whole, assessment is a framework for focusing faculty attention on student learning and for provoking meaningful discussions of program objectives, curricular organization, pedagogy, and student development" (p. 4).

None of these well-accepted definitions of assessment includes reference to collecting information for accountability purposes. The focus is on improving and enhancing student learning, with accreditation as an important but secondary function. It has been said, "You can't steer the boat by watching the wake." This old saying is certainly pertinent to institutions of higher education. Faculty developers can help by broadening the focus of assessing student learning to more than is requested by the outside accrediting agency. By focusing too narrowly on just those outcomes to be reported to the external agency, institutions run the risk of measuring only those areas that will make the institution shine. True transformation can only happen by also looking closely at those areas that need improvement. Using the institutional mission as the motivating force behind the entire assessment process is vital if the focus is going to remain on enhancing teaching and learning within the classroom.

Using External Criteria to Improve Learning: Transformation

Accreditation requirements are not just some passing fad. They are here to stay and, most likely, will continue to become even more focused on assessment and the comparisons of assessment results among institutions. Regional accreditation agencies (including the Southern Association of Higher Education, the Higher Learning Commission of the North Central Association of Colleges and Schools, and the Middlestates Association of Colleges and Schools) incorporate a process of peer review to indicate that specific standards have been met. Regional accreditation agencies focus on a specific geographic location, and each regional accreditation body uses slightly different standards. However, all focus on accrediting the entire institution rather than individual departments or programs. Because of these expectations, assessment has become a part of almost all institutions of higher education in the United States. The case can be made that this mandate has pushed higher education institutions into more reflective practices that will improve education.

Regional accrediting agencies also play an important role by working with the U. S. government in the creation and enforcement of policies and in assuring the general public that higher education is doing what it says that it is doing. This should not be understood negatively. The regional accrediting agency acts as a buffer between individual institutions and the federal government, which allows individual institutions to maintain their unique identity without being subject to overly prescriptive requirements that would be the same for all types of institution. The standards, criteria, and principles set forth by the regional accrediting agencies are designed to ensure quality and encourage ongoing reflection on effectiveness; but they also allow for institutional differences.

In addition to regional accreditation agencies, numerous specialized accreditors exist that examine specific degree programs or areas within an institution. For example, the Association to Advance Collegiate Schools of Business accredits only schools of business, while the National League for Nursing Accrediting Commission focuses on nursing programs. Most such agencies require assessment of student learning outcomes. Therefore, regardless of the source of the requirement, accreditation has helped to push institutions to focus on assessment.

Faculty developers are in a position to translate the requirements of accreditation to faculty members in a way that will enable them to focus on the transformative approach to assessment. Because faculty development focuses on teaching and learning, faculty members may be more likely to develop transformative assessment plans when these plans are brought to them by someone who is also focused on student learning. In addition, because institutions consider reaccreditation to be such an important task, there are often significant resources tied to improving assessment. Faculty developers can work with the institution-level assessment office to highlight the need to have useful and important student learning outcomes that can be used at the course level to improve teaching and learning and at the departmental level to demonstrate that same student learning in the larger context. The importance of these connections cannot be overemphasized.

Regional accreditation agencies have been modifying their standards for more than a decade to include additional explicit requirements about measuring and improving student learning, and these changes benefit faculty development efforts. One of the comprehensive standards for the Commission on Colleges of the Southern Association of Colleges and Schools (SACS) illustrates these recent changes: "The institution identifies expected outcomes for its educational programs (including student learning outcomes for educational programs) and its administrative and educational support services, assesses whether it achieves these outcomes, and provides evidence of improvement based on analysis of those results" (Southern Association of Colleges and Schools, 2008, p. 14). This standard has now made it necessary for all institutions accredited by SACS, which covers eleven states, to have student learning outcomes for all educational programs, administrative programs, and support areas; they must measure those outcomes and use the resulting information for enhancing the entire institution. The Higher Learning Commission (HLC) of the North Central Association of Colleges and Schools states as one of its core components that "the organization's ongoing evaluation and assessment processes provide reliable evidence of institutional effectiveness that clearly informs strategies for continuous improvement" (Higher Learning Commission of the North Central Association of Colleges and Schools, 2003, p. 327). In addition, the HLC requires institutions to demonstrate that "the organization values and supports effective teaching" (Core Component 3b) and that "the organization's learning resources support student learning and effective teaching" (Core Component 3d). The Middlestates Commission on Higher Education (2006) states that institutions must have a "documented, organized, and sustained assessment process to evaluate and improve the total range of programs and services; achievement of institutional mission, goals, and plans; and compliance with accreditation standards" as part of Standard 7 (p. 28). Clearly, the requirements of the U.S. regional accrediting bodies are providing an external mandate that faculty developers can use internally to create an institutional need to focus on enhancing the quality of teaching and the resulting student learning. Faculty developers should be a part of this overall dialogue at all levels institutional, national, and even international.

However, accreditation standards are not the only outside influence on institutional practices. Other external demands are contributing to changes in internal practices. For example, the *U.S. News and World Report* rankings each year or the data requested by the Integrated Postsecondary Education Data System (IPEDS) can cause institutions to change what data are collected because of what the agencies request. Any change to the IPEDS reporting requirements will immediately cause individual institutional research offices to change what they measure and how they report it. Additional external mandates have arisen in efforts to meet the public need for information and accountability. For example, the Voluntary System of Accountability (VSA) is designed to collect specific information from public four-year universities and communicate that information to the public through a common Web portal. Not all reaction to the VSA has been positive, however. Hawthorne (2008) commented, "We'll generate scores for convenient (if not necessarily meaningful) comparison. But will education be any better as a result?" (p. 29). More information about the VSA is available at http://www.voluntarysystem.org.

Given national trends, it appears that higher education will be involved in assessment for many years to come. Therefore, it is vital that assessment data be used for transformation and not only for accountability. Since much of student learning occurs within the context of academic courses, the faculty must create an assessment process that will give them the information they need. Armed with this data, the faculty can make modifications in ways that will enhance student learning. Consequently, faculty developers are necessary change agents within the institutional culture. The focus, however, is not always on what faculty developers can do to support assessment activities. The collection of data about student learning can enhance the ways that faculty developers work with faculty to enhance teaching. Pedagogical discussions can be based on data from course- or program-level assessment to inform the eventual decisions that are made. Put simply, appropriate and meaningful use of assessment data from student learning outcomes can help faculty members improve their teaching.

Faculty Developers' Responsibilities

Faculty developers have access to faculty members and their pedagogy because they work with them on teaching practices, technology, and assessment. This partnership creates a perfect opportunity to bring these elements to wider institutional attention. If the staff at a faculty development center can work with faculty members to enhance teaching and learning and meet the institution's mission, the entire institution will be improved. With this opportunity comes responsibility. Faculty development staff must adapt and grow to meet the needs of their institution and higher education in general.

In accord with this responsibility, faculty developers serve as change agents. One of the first things that can be done is to become involved with the institutional assessment officer. There is often overlap between the goals of faculty development and assessment efforts, and this synergy should be used intentionally and explicitly. Faculty development centers want to enhance teaching to benefit student learning. Assessment offices typically want to measure student learning and create an action plan that will enhance student learning. Clearly, the entire institution will gain when there is increased partnership and teamwork. As faculty developers work with faculty members on creating meaningful student learning outcomes at the course level, discussions about aligning course outcomes with departmental outcomes only make sense. The faculty member can then clearly see how what is done at the individual course level can have an impact at the department level. At the same time, assessment staff can work with departments to create assessment plans and use the work that is being done at the course level to ensure authentic measures of student learning. A clear example of this partnership is in the development of a departmental curriculum matrix that demonstrates which outcomes are addressed in which courses.

Faculty developers also have a responsibility to stay informed about accrediting agencies' standards and policies. By knowing what is required for an accreditation report, faculty developers can help channel the work so that there is a greater level of preparedness at the time the report is due. A good way to understand accreditation requirements is to attend a regional accreditation conference. Not only will the faculty developer benefit from better understanding the standards, but the voice of faculty development is needed within the accreditation conversation. Faculty developers have knowledge about pedagogy, teaching practices, and methods for assessing student learning that need to be included in the overall picture of accreditation standards. Faculty developers have long appreciated the complexity of the teaching and learning process, and this awareness is an essential part of accreditation if it is going to be more than just an exercise in counting. There have been great strides in addressing the quality of student learning by accreditation standards; if this progress is going to continue, new and valid, reliable, and meaningful measures need to be created.

Faculty developers also have the ongoing responsibility to ask faculty members to discover more about their own course-level assessment practices. Faculty developers can assist faculty members in identifying areas within their own courses that do not meet the specific learning outcomes and to work with them to consider how to make appropriate course-level changes. This is one way to change the thinking about assessing student learning. When a faculty member comes to talk about course revisions, faculty developers can help the client focus on what students are learning and, more important, what they are not learning. Then the focus can be on enhancing the course by keeping what works and changing what is not working.

Conclusion

At this time, it seems clear that institutional accreditation needs and the assessment of student learning will remain important. What will grow and change are the methods used to measure learning: "While virtually all states currently report on collegiate learning using proxies, e.g. graduation rates, colleges and universities are now being asked to assess learning directly" (Shavelson, 2007, p. 26). The methods used must work within both the local institutional culture and the national educational system, with benefits to the institution, the students who are demonstrating their learning, and ultimately society as a whole.

Faculty developers hold one of the keys, a very important one, to ensuring that assessment is a transformative process that provides the information needed for growth and change. Assessment is not just a top-down mandate—it is embedded in the very process of teaching and learning. The faculty must be empowered to use the assessment process to improve teaching and learning rather than being forced to assess for others. Faculty development centers, workshops, and consultations can all work to help faculty regain ownership of the process and use it to transform higher education one course at a time.

REFERENCES

Allen, M. J. (2004). *Assessing academic programs in higher education.* Bolton, MA: Anker.

Angelo, T. A., & Cross, K. P. (1993). *Classroom assessment techniques: A handbook for college teachers.* San Francisco: Jossey-Bass.

Banta, T. W. (2007). Can assessment for accountability complement assessment for improvement? *Peer Review, 9*(2), 9–12.

Fendrich, L. (2007, June 8). A pedagogical straitjacket. *The Chronicle of Higher Education,* p. B6.

Hawthorne, J. (2008). Accountability and comparability: What's wrong with the VSA approach? *Liberal Education, 94*(2), 24–29.

Higher Learning Commission of the North Central Association of Colleges and Schools. (2003). *Handbook of accreditation* (3rd ed.). Chicago: Higher Learning Commission of the North Central Association of Colleges and Schools.

Huba, M., & Freed, J. E. (2000). *Learner-centered assessment on college campuses: Shifting the focus from teaching to learning.* Needham Heights, MA: Allyn & Bacon.

Kallick, B., & Colosimo, J. (2009). *Using curriculum mapping and assessment data to improve student learning.* Thousand Oaks, CA: Corwin.

Middlestates Commission on Higher Education. (2006). *Characteristics of excellence in higher education: Eligibility requirements and standards for accreditation.* Philadelphia: Middlestates Commission on Higher Education.

Palomba, C. A., & Banta, T. W. (1999). *Assessment essentials.* San Francisco: Jossey-Bass.

Schilling, K. (2006). Assessment methods should match institutional goals. *Academic Leader, 22*(6), 2–6.

Shavelson, R. (2007). Assessing student learning responsibly: From history to an audacious proposal. *Change, 39*(1), 26–33.

Shulman, L. S. (2007). Counting and recounting: Assessment and the quest for accountability. *Change, 39*(1), 20–25.

Southern Association of Colleges and Schools. (2008). *Principles of accreditation: Foundations for quality enhancement.* Atlanta: Southern Association of Colleges and Schools.

Walvoord, B. E. (2004). *Assessment clear and simple: A practical guide for institutions, departments, and general education.* San Francisco: Jossey-Bass.

Walvoord, B. E., & Anderson, V. J. (1998). *Effective grading: A tool for learning and assessment.* San Francisco: Jossey-Bass.

Wehlburg, C. (2006). *Meaningful course revision: Enhancing academic engagement using student learning data.* Bolton, MA: Anker.

Wehlburg, C. M. (2008). *Promoting integrated and transformative assessment: A deeper focus on student learning.* San Francisco: Jossey-Bass.

12

OVERVIEW OF DIVERSITY ISSUES RELATING TO FACULTY DEVELOPMENT

Mathew L. Ouellett

SINCE THE 1960S, INSTITUTIONS OF HIGHER EDUCATION have grappled with the social and political implications of doors opening to an increasingly diverse undergraduate student body (Anderson, 2002; Karen, 1991; Musil, Garcia, Moses, & Smith, 1995). In response, innovative teaching and learning environments have arisen to provide for the success of all students, support an increasingly diverse faculty, meet institutional aspirations of excellence, and prepare students to join an ever more complex society (Gurin, Dey, Hurtado, & Gurin, 2002; Hurtado, Milem, Clayton-Pederson, & Allen, 1999).

From the earliest conceptualization of educational development in the 1960s, practitioners have valued a multifaceted approach encompassing individual consultation and other faculty, instructional, and organizational development activities (Diamond, 1988; Lewis, 1996). Central to these endeavors has been respect and appreciation for the growth and development of the individual as well as the community, even as conflicts stimulated by differences in perspectives have emerged (Gillespie, 2000; Graff, 1993).

Sorcinelli, Austin, Eddy, and Beach (2006) have described educational development as currently experiencing pressure to collaborate across the institution and address a complex range of individual, departmental, and institutional challenges related to teaching. As we respond to these demands, a multicultural organizational development perspective offers a lens of analysis and models for action that account for and embrace the essential contributions of a diverse faculty and student body (Jackson, 2005). The call today is for expanded models of educational development practices that respond more completely to the complex issues that institutions of higher education will face into the future (Chesler, Lewis, & Crowfoot, 2005; Ouellett, 2005).

Looking to the future, the importance increases for educational developers to enhance and deepen their understanding and range of strategies related to diversity and multiculturalism on campus. As I explore in this chapter, this preparation is likely both professional *and* personal.

Systemic Approaches to Multicultural Change

As discussed in Chapter One, "Overview of Faculty Development: History and Choices," organizational development as a method of analysis and as a tool for change has been embedded in faculty development work since its inception in the 1960s (Diamond, 1988). Today, as faculty developers realize the importance of systemic change efforts that span the organization and link to central institutional and civic goals (Milem, Chang, & Antonio, 2005), they seek initiatives to align strategic efforts by students, instructors, campus leaders, and communities with multicultural and diversity-related goals (Hurtado et al., 1999; Marchesani & Jackson, 2005).

Over time, strategies for creating hospitable and welcoming classroom environments, often designed to help predominately white faculty members, have evolved from a focus on the social needs of students of color (Cones, Noonan, & Janha, 1983) to their academic needs. Instructors who were considering the teaching and learning processes holistically were often the driving force behind these changes (Banks, 1995; Roberts et al., 1994).

Efforts to recruit and retain diverse undergraduate populations were concurrent with similar efforts for faculty (Bach, Barnett, Fuentes, & Frey, 2006; Chesler et al., 2005; Gainene & Boice, 1993). These efforts have led to greater emphasis on understanding how changing demographics shape the experiences and perspectives of students and faculty of color in predominately white institutions (Chesler, Lewis, & Crowfoot, 2005; Stanley, 2006). Our understanding of how *all* students benefit in direct, important, and positive ways from a diverse student body and a diverse faculty has evolved, too (Astin, 1993; Burgsthaler & Cory, 2008; Gurin et al., 2002). From these findings have emerged efforts to support the growth and development of faculty and students of color within the disciplines and the institution, as well as a better understanding of the complexity of these issues (Hendrix, 2007; Moody, 2004; Tusmith & Reddy, 2002; Wijeyesinghe & Jackson, 2001). Another important example of these new frameworks for equity in higher education is the *Making Excellence Inclusive* series published by the American Association of Colleges and Universities (Bauman, Bustillos, Bensimon, Brown, & Bartee, 2005; Milem et al., 2005; Williams, Berger, & McClendon, 2005). New resources based on recent research on the multifaceted experiences of faculty are also now available (Chesler et al., 2005; Chesler & Young, 2007; Moody, 2004; Stanley, 2006). Chapter Fourteen, "Working with Underrepresented Faculty," in this volume addresses this subject further.

According to recent research, Historically Black Colleges and Universities (HBCUs) and predominately Hispanic Serving Institutions (HSIs) are also experiencing the evolution of multicultural organizational development priorities (Dawkins, Beach, & Rozman, 2006; Frederick & James, 2007). As HBCUs continue to attract and retain undergraduates and faculty members who are more diverse, some organizational development priorities are becoming similar to the social and cultural challenges seen in predominately white institutions, such as acquiring sufficient institutional support, addressing the changing roles and rewards for faculty, and balancing multiple faculty roles. However, this research also indicates that initiatives that support institutional priorities such as unit and program evaluation and assessment are of equal or more importance to educational developers in HBCUs (Dawkins et al., 2006).

Another recent innovation is the introduction of the position of chief diversity officer on many campuses (Williams & Wade-Golden, 2008). This position, often located on the provost's staff, is a senior academic administrative position with resources essential for success: budget and staffing; the "ear" of the senior academic leadership team; and, as a member of the provost's staff, the opportunity to work across disciplines and administrative units. However, unless this position is supported by a systemic multicultural organization development initiative, this innovation may unintentionally perpetuate some of the weaknesses in earlier organization change models by continuing to isolate diversity issues as the work of a particular person or office.

Inclusive Practices in Educational Development

Continuing complex interactions offer educational developers an opportunity to transform instructor responses to issues of diversity (Adams & Love, 2005; Chism, Lees, & Evenbeck, 2002; Diamond, 2005; Lindsey, Robins, & Terrell, 2003; Lockhart & Borland, 2001). While these unfolding issues are significant to our individual institutions, there are some common challenges that may prove worth prioritizing collectively. These include adequately defining our diversity-related concepts and terms, identifying both the stakes and stakeholders for these issues across our institutions, and research and assessment-driven methods for consistently modeling our aspirational values and behaviors.

Terms

The language and implications associated with multicultural initiatives continue to change in response to social, political, and economic changes and our evolving understanding and analyses of them. In education, the terms *multicultural* and *diversity* have often been substitutes for *race*, and the word *race* has often been reduced to mean black-white relationships (Anderson, 2002; Tusmith & Reddy, 2002). While the implications of race continue to be a compelling, pivotal aspect of these discussions locally, regionally, and nationally, such clean distinctions are impossible for many individuals; for example, race, gender, and economic class can be inextricably intertwined (Anderse & Collins, 2000; Hendrix, 2007; Kumashiro, 2001; Weber, 2004). I find it is essential to link together discussions of social identity dimensions, which have meaningful implications for access to power, privilege, and authority and thereby broaden diversity to include a systemic analysis of how such forces work together to hold systems of discrimination and oppression in place (Burgsthaler & Cory, 2008; Hardiman & Jackson, 1997; Johnson, 2001; Yeskel & Collins, 2005). As Audre Lorde so eloquently wrote, "There is no hierarchy of oppressions" (1983, p. 9).

Stakeholders

As in broader societies, there are few models of healthy, sustained intergroup discourse in the academy (Graff, 1993; Schoem, Frankel, Zúñiga, & Lewis, 1993). A climate of individualism, crisis intervention management strategies, and the traditionally dominant paradigms of learning and knowing continue to drive us (Hendrix, 2007; hooks, 2003). Too often, our students and instructors, faculty colleagues, and departmental and institutional leaders settle for what I refer to as "drive-by dialogues." In lieu of sustained, meaningful give-and-take of dialogue, participants, perhaps working under latent anxieties associated with talking across communities in conflict, can find themselves numbly lobbing the equivalent of sound bites at each other. The persisting emotions associated with prior negative experiences can be astonishing even when the experiences may have happened years ago, been isolated events, or be the result of one's perception about another person's lived experience. Such prior events unskillfully handled or resolved harmfully may leave participants swearing to avoid any such further encounters at all costs.

At the other end of the spectrum, I sometimes encounter students and colleagues, especially those of a certain age, who assume that they have no inherent role in or derive no benefit from participating in such multicultural education development initiatives; they have already "been there, done that" social diversity "thing." This attitude can be due to any number of assumptions on their part, but two concerns emerge from it. The first is that just as our social identities evolve, so too do social justice issues in education and in our local communities. The second is that new research and better models for practice are continually enhancing and extending diversity and education issues. Therefore, educational developers can offer expertise in convening and facilitating dialogues between and among groups and individuals and, by doing so, bring new resources and better practices in teaching and learning to our communities. We have an opportunity to help our students, colleagues, and leaders understand their stake in these issues (regardless of rank, identity, or discipline) and to implement innovative practices that address their priorities.

Modeling

Much as it is often true in broader society, colleges and universities continue to struggle to find appropriate strategies for balancing the affective and experiential with the cognitive aspects of learning, both for instructors and students. However, if one's engagement is strictly in the cognitive domain, it is difficult to imagine any sort of sustained growth or development, much less success in addressing issues of inclusion, diversity, and difference. Colleagues, despite being well meaning, may still have few venues within which to explore issues such as how access to status, power, and authority in the institutional environment can be regulated by perceptions of one's social identities (for example, one's race, gender, sexual orientation, religious affiliation, economic status, or physical ability) (Adams, Bell, & Griffin, 2007).

Educational developers have rich experiences in convening and sustaining dialogues via faculty learning communities with positive results for both course-based and systemic innovations related to diversity (Cox, 2003; Ouellett & Sorcinelli, 1995). Faculty learning communities facilitate ongoing interaction with instructors from across disciplines and cultures. Petrone (2004) found that participants in such communities who focused on diversity issues benefited by contrasting an increased awareness of individualistic and collective needs. This participation led to opportunities to reflect on the interpersonal and intrapersonal knowledge helpful in integrating diversity into the curriculum, teaching approaches, and classroom settings of participants. Such endeavors can be essential in sustaining these initiatives as priorities when the individual, department, or institution is not in crisis.

Faculty development units have opportunities to model such responses by making interracial and interdisciplinary collaborations a central motif of our work. We can do this by cultivating the entrance of underrepresented populations into our field, for example, as staff members of our centers (Cook & Sorcinelli, 2005; Stanley, 2001). In addition, we can model it in our professional growth and development as teachers and educational developers. Over the past decade I have had the opportunity to coteach a course at a local college with a colleague who also happens to be an educational developer. Our class, "Racism in the United States: Implications for Social Work Practice," is a required second-year course in a master of social work program. Since 1993, the school has offered about six sections of this course every summer. Instructors teach the course in teams, and members represent tenure system faculty and summer adjunct appointments about equally. What makes this teaming unique, however, is that pairs are deliberately interracial and, when possible cross gender, sexual orientation, or religion. When describing my social identity, I usually include being white, male, gay, able-bodied, and a nonpracticing Catholic. My coteacher is African American, female, heterosexual, able-bodied, and a practicing Christian. My primary position is in faculty development at a large public university, and hers is in faculty development at a small HBCU. Based on a research study we conducted with instructors from across the program, we identified five levels of simultaneous interaction (Ouellett & Fraser, 2005). These included:

1. The individual teacher's internal processes of self-reflection and meaning-making
2. The team members' relationship with each other
3. The team's relationship with students
4. Relationships between the individual instructors and students
5. Relationships among students

Additionally, from the beginning we have collected both formative and summative feedback on our teaching. Across our sections and over years, we found several themes emerged consistently. An unanticipated outcome was students' regular feedback that the most important attribute of the course for them was the opportunity to watch us work together as an interracial teaching team. Our relationship became the most powerful learning resource. Upon reflection, this made sense to me because I am deeply aware of how much I have learned from my coteacher over the years as well as from our students. In many respects, our friendship, collegiality, and ongoing teaching partnership created for students a model of sustained dialogue on diversity, multiculturalism, and, of course, race in the United States. The second unexpected outcome was that we became mutual mentors in a collegial relationship that became supportive across our professional and personal lives (Beach, Henderson, & Famiano, 2008; de Janasz & Sullivan, 2004; Yun & Sorcinelli, 2008).

Course-Based Multicultural Change

Longitudinal research studies on what matters most in the undergraduate experiences of successful college students have helped educational developers to understand changes in campus climates and student expectations (Astin, 1993). Using such research and data from experiential applications, educational developers have offered a number of multicultural course development models (Adams, Bell, & Griffin, 2007; Morey & Kitano, 1997) as well as programs that support the acquisition of the knowledge, values, and skills necessary in becoming multiculturally competent instructors (Bach et al., 2006; Chesler, 1998).

Instructional development models at the collegiate level shifted to value goals such as developing teacher self-reflection, assisting students in acquiring knowledge that reflects accurate contributions of all involved, presenting material from multiple perspectives, helping students to value diversity, and supporting different learning styles and student-to-student learning (Kitano, 1997; Miller & Garran, 2008). The elegance of such models is that they offer instructors multiple points of entry into the multicultural course development process. For example, Marchesani and Adams (1992) deconstructed the process into four key dimensions: instructor self-awareness, pedagogical decisions, course content, and understanding who our students are individually and collectively. Educational developers can support the course innovation process at any one of these points, depending on the developmental readiness and the curiosity of the instructor and his or her disciplinary priorities. In my experience, this flexibility has been essential in springing over the "ditches" into which one can fall into when encouraging faculty members to consider such innovations—for example, dissuading cautious instructors of the misconception that multicultural course design is a covert exercise in political correctness or that one must be a "diversity expert" to address diversity-related topics in the classroom.

In Chapter Thirteen, "Conceptualizing, Designing, and Implementing Multicultural Faculty Development Activities," Stanley further explores the conceptualization, implementation, and assessment of multicultural faculty development activities at the course, program, and institutional levels. I suggest that it is as essential to learn about these frameworks as it is to learn about active learning, student motivation, and assessment.

Transformation

While multicultural course planning and development is important, systemic change is nevertheless inextricable from personal and social transformation. Educational development practices have long benefited from social science research such as studies on racial identity development (Hardiman & Jackson, 1997; Wijeyesinghe & Jackson, 2001) and models of student motivation and intellectual growth (Svinicki, 2004). Particularly promising has been the investigation of intergroup dialogues (Hurtado et al., 1999). A racially diverse student and faculty profile at an institution impacts the likelihood that students will engage in formal and informal learning and other diversity-related activities while in school and, consequently, in other diversity-related civic engagements postgraduation (Gurin et al., 2002; Hurtado et al., 1999). More recently, Denson and Chang (2009) have suggested that at institutions that consistently place high priority on positive race relations there may also be generalized diversity-related benefits for students beyond one's individual engagement in crossracial interactions and knowledge seeking.

More recently, discipline-based work is emerging from natural sciences and mathematics with direct implications for inclusive teaching and learning. An applied example of this recent work is Project Kaleidoscope (PKAL) (Megginson, 2006). The hallmark of this work is the integration of research on learning and best practices in teaching into language and frameworks that resonate well with many scientists. It has been especially important in contributing to the discipline-based discourses on implications of students' diversity in learning styles, cultural backgrounds, and preparation for academic success in the sciences.

Increasingly, the interests of researchers and practitioners have turned also to the teaching experiences of international faculty and graduate students in classrooms in the United States. Fox (1994) postulated that instructors should be aware of three fundamental differences between Eastern and Western approaches to oral and written communication. These include a different appreciation of the disinclination to directness and a preference for subtlety over straightforwardness so as to avoid offending the other person, priority given to the collective versus the individual, and the preference for ancient wisdom versus what is novel or new. Issues such as establishing authority when speaking with an accent (McLean, 2007), responding to student expectations (Muhtaseb, 2007), and the increasing internationalization of classrooms (McCalman, 2007) have begun to be explored.

In addition to such international diversity on campuses in the United States, it is evident that educational development efforts are thriving around the globe. Schneider (2008) suggested that educators in the United States may glean much from a careful look at the emerging international body of literature and practices on educational development and multicultural inclusion efforts abroad. In Chapter Fifteen, "International Faculty Development," Chism, Gosling, and Sorcinelli address this global perspective on educational development.

Reflections on Personal Preparation

I close this chapter with a story about an element of my childhood that I believe contributed a defining attribute in my development as a teacher and educational developer (Bell, Love, Washington, & Weinstein, 2007). I grew up in a military family, following my Air Force father all over the world as well as from one end to the other within the United States. My first classroom experience was in a foreign language. Cultural norms, preferences, standards, and expectations different from those of my family mediated my social life during this period. When we did live "stateside," we often moved within two years of arriving anywhere. Wherever we landed, my parents often chose to live in the surrounding nonmilitary communities. Consequently, my siblings and I were usually the "new kids"; and we were a novel kind of "foreigner," even at home. Much later I was to find out that our experiences as "third-culture kids" mirrored those of other children of parents serving with government and nongovernmental organizations around the world (Wertsch, 1991).

Similar to any other circumstance, there were both positive and negative aspects to this life. The rewards of a multicultural childhood were the joy of discovery; the excitement of new places, new experiences, and new people; and the self-reliance that came from knowing I could find the best in any situation. I think now it is where I gained my resiliency and penchant for loyalty and idealism. The challenges I associate with it are mostly associated with the frequent changes necessary. Generally, I have an ability to feel at ease anywhere, but I also live with a free-floating sense of rootlessness. Clearly, both aspects left a stamp on my identity in that part of my orientation today is toward looking for others who may share that sensibility of not yet being "home."

In retrospect, this intercultural upbringing was superb preparation for working on issues of diversity and social justice issues in higher education. Much like the military, higher education institutions are replete with hierarchies. The community is both highly stable and transitory, and the missions of these institutions produce tensions between individual goals and accomplishments and the desire to work for the good of the whole of our society. Unlike the military, though, members of the academy do not usually wear their rank on their shoulders (with the notable exceptions of special occasions like commencement when the regalia come out of the closet). In general, in higher education power and authority are decentralized. However, in my experience, members of academic communities are highly sensitive to rank and where we each stand in relation to each other in terms of status and perceived authority. When meeting a new colleague on campus, the conversation or progression of our thoughts often goes something like this: "What department are you with? Are you faculty or staff? If you are an instructor, do you have tenure? If you have tenure, what discipline is it in? Do you have a grant? If you have a grant, how big is it?" I am confident that readers can take the example from here.

I share this brief story as a way to model the self-reflection and disclosure that can help our faculty members and students to identify and work developmentally with their own experiences, values, and beliefs. There are a number of important benefits for instructional consultants who use reflective practice for their own growth and development (Kardia, 1998; Smith, 1997; Bell et al., 1997). Additionally, this better prepares us to help facilitate transformational learning for our students (Fox, 2001). Telling our stories and reflecting on our experiences more transparently— by including the heart and hands as well as the brain—is essential to understanding what we bring to the teaching and leaning endeavor.

Conclusion

The good news is that we know much more than ever before about what matters most and what works when developing, implementing, sustaining, and assessing multicultural initiatives in higher education. The next three chapters in this volume address key questions. As we become more multiculturally and interculturally competent education developers, what is essential to know? How can we better meet the needs of instructors, students, and staff members in our complex and fast-changing climates? What matters and works in creating and sustaining inclusive higher education environments? Educational developers, with thoughtful exploration of these questions and related issues, can support the multifaceted goals of our complex higher education environment.

REFERENCES

Adams, M. A., Bell, L. A., & Griffin, P. (Eds.). (2007). *Teaching for diversity and social justice* (2nd ed.). New York: Routledge.

Adams, M. A., & Love, B. J. (2005). Teaching with a social justice perspective: A model for faculty seminars across academic disciplines. In M. L. Ouellett (Ed.), *Teaching inclusively: Resources for course, department & institutional change in higher education* (pp. 587–619). Stillwater, OK: New Forums.

Anderse, M., & Collins, P. H. (2000). Introduction. In M. Anderse & P. H. Collins (Eds.), *Race, class, and gender: An anthology* (4th ed., pp. 1–11). Belmont, CA: Wadsworth.

Anderson, J. A. (2002). Race in American higher education: Historical perspectives on current conditions. In W. Smith, P. Altback, & K. Lomotey (Eds.), *The racial crisis in American higher education* (rev. ed., pp. 3–22). Albany: State University of New York Press.

Astin, A. W. (1993). *What matters in college? Four critical years revisited.* San Francisco: Jossey-Bass.

Bach, D. J., Barnett, M. A., Fuentes, J. D., & Frey, S. C. (2006). Promoting intellectual community and professional growth for a diverse faculty. In S. Chadwick-Blossey & D. R. Robertson (Eds.), *To improve the academy: Vol. 24. Resources for faculty, instructional, and organizational development* (pp. 166–182). Bolton, MA: Anker.

Banks, J. A. (1995). Multicultural education: Historical development, dimensions, and practice. In J. A. Banks & C.A.M. Banks (Eds.), *Handbook of research on multicultural education* (pp. 3–24). New York: Macmillan.

Bauman, G. L., Bustillos, L. T., Bensimon, E. M., Brown III, M. C., & Bartee, R. D. (2005). *Achieving equitable educational outcomes with all students: The institution's roles and responsibilities.* Washington, DC: American Association of Colleges and Universities.

Beach, A. L., Henderson, C., & Famiano, M. (2008). Co-teaching as a faculty development model. In L. B. Nilson & J. E. Miller (Eds.), *To improve the academy: Vol. 27. Resources for faculty, instructional, and organizational development* (pp. 32–71). San Francisco, CA: Jossey-Bass.

Bell, L. A., Love, B. J., Washington, S., & Weinstein, G. (1997). Knowing ourselves as social justice educators. In M. Adams, L. A. Bell, & P. Griffin (Eds.), *Teaching for diversity and social justice* (2nd ed., pp. 381–394). New York: Routledge.

Burgsthaler, S. E., & Cory, R. C. (2008). *Universal design in higher education: From principles to practice.* Cambridge, MA: Harvard Education Press.

Chesler, M. (1998). Planning multicultural organizational audits in higher education. In M. Kaplan & D. Lieberman (Eds.), *To improve the academy: Vol. 17. Resources for faculty, instructional, and organizational development (*pp. 171–202). Stillwater, OK: New Forums.

Chesler, M. A., Lewis, A., & Crowfoot, J. (2005). *Challenging racism in higher education: Promoting justice.* Lanham, MD: Rowman & Littlefield.

Chesler, M. A., & Young Jr., A. A. (2007, Fall). Faculty members' social identities and classroom authority. In M. Kaplan & T. T. Miller (Eds.), *New directions for teaching and learning, no. 111. Scholarship of multicultural teaching and learning* (pp. 11–19). San Francisco: Jossey-Bass.

Chism, N. V. N., Lees, N. D., & Evenbeck, S. (2002). Faculty development for teaching innovation. *Liberal Education, 88*(3), 34–41.

Cones III, H. H., Noonan, J. F., & Janha, D. (Eds.). (1983). *New directions for teaching and learning, no. 16. Teaching minority students.* San Francisco: Jossey-Bass.

Cook, C., & Sorcinelli, M. D. (2005). Building multiculturalism into teaching development programs. In M. L. Ouellett (Ed.), *Teaching inclusively: Resources for course, department and institutional change in higher education* (pp. 3–20). Stillwater, OK: New Forums.

Cox, M. D. (2003). Proven faculty development tools that foster the scholarship of teaching in faculty learning communities. In C. M. Wehlburg & S. Chadwick-Blossey (Eds.), *To improve the academy: Vol. 21. Resources for faculty, instructional, and organizational development* (pp. 109–142). Bolton, MA: Anker.

Dawkins, P. W., Beach, A. L., & Rozman, S. (2006). Perceptions of faculty developers about the present and future of faculty development at historically black colleges and universities. In S. Chadwick-Blossey & D. R. Robertson (Eds.), *To improve the academy: Vol. 24. Resources for faculty, instructional, and organizational development* (pp. 104–120). Bolton, MA: Anker.

de Janasz, S. C., & Sullivan, S. E. (2004). Multiple mentoring in academe: Developing the professional network. *Journal of Vocational Behavior, 64,* 263–283.

Diamond, R. M. (1988). Faculty development, instructional development, and organizational development: Options and choices. In E. C. Wadsworth

(Ed.), *POD: A handbook for new practitioners* (pp. 9–11). Stillwater, OK: New Forums.

Diamond, R. M. (2005). The institutional change agency: The expanding role of academic support centers. In S. M. Chadwick-Blossey & D. Robertson (Eds.), *To improve the academy: Vol. 23. Resources for faculty, instructional, and organizational development* (pp. 24–37). Bolton, MA: Anker.

Denson, N., & Chang, M. J. (2009). Racial diversity matters: The impact of diversity-related student engagement and institutional context. *American Educational Research Journal, 46*(2), 322–353.

Fox, H. (1994). *Listening to the world: Cultural issues in academic writing.* Urbana, IL: National Council of Teachers of English.

Fox, H. (2001). *When race breaks out: Conversations about race and racism in college classrooms.* New York: Peter Lang.

Frederick, P., & James, M. (2007). "Heritage Rocks": Principles and best practices of effective intercultural teaching and learning. In D. R. Robertson & L. B. Nilson (Eds.), *To improve the academy: Vol. 25. Resources for faculty, instructional, and organizational development* (pp. 172–188). Bolton, MA: Anker.

Gainene, J., & Boice, R. (Eds.). (1993, Spring). *New directions for teaching and learning, no. 49. Building a diverse faculty.* San Francisco: Jossey-Bass.

Gillespie, K. H. (2000). The challenge and test of our values: An essay of collective experience. In M. Kaplan & D. Lieberman (Eds.), *To improve the academy: Vol 18. Resources for faculty, instructional, and organizational development* (pp. 27–37). Bolton, MA: Anker.

Graff, G. (1993). *Beyond the culture war: How teaching the conflicts can revitalize American education.* New York: Norton.

Gurin, P., Dey, E. L., Hurtado, S., & Gurin, G. (2002). Diversity in higher education: Theory and impact on educational outcomes. *Harvard Educational Review, 72*(3), 330–366.

Hardiman, R., & Jackson, B. W. (1997). Conceptual foundations for social justice courses. In M. Adams, L. Bell, & P. Griffin (Eds.), *Teaching for diversity and social justice* (pp. 16–29). New York: Routledge.

Hendrix, K. G. (Ed.). (2007). *New directions for teaching and learning, no. 110. Neither white nor male: Female faculty of color.* San Francisco: Jossey-Bass.

hooks, b. (2003). *Teaching community: A pedagogy of hope.* New York: Routledge.

Hurtado, S., Milem, J., Clayton-Pederson, A., & Allen, W. (1999). *Enacting diverse learning environments: Improving the climate for racial/ ethnic diversity in higher education.* ASHE-ERIC Higher Education Report, vol. 26, no. 8. Washington, DC: George Washington University, Graduate School of Education and Human Development.

Jackson, B. (2005). The theory and practice of multicultural organization development in education. In M. L. Ouellett (Ed.), *Teaching inclusively: Resources for course, department & institutional change in higher education* (pp. 3–20). Stillwater, OK: New Forums.

Johnson, A. G. (2001). *Privilege, power, and difference.* New York: McGraw-Hill.

Kardia, D. (1998). Becoming a multicultural faculty developer: Reflections from the field. In M. Kaplan & D. Lieberman (Eds.), *To improve the academy: Vol. 17. Resources for faculty, instructional, and organizational development* (pp. 15–34). Stillwater, OK: New Forums.

Karen, D. (1991). The politics of class, race and gender: Access to higher education in the United States, 1960–1986. *American Journal of Education, 99*(2), 208–237.

Kitano, M. K. (1997). What a course will look like after multicultural change. In A. Morey & M. Kitano (Eds.), *Multicultural course transformation in higher education: A broader truth* (pp. 18–34). Needham Heights, MA: Allyn & Bacon.

Kumashiro, K. (2001). Queer students of color and antiracist, anti-heterosexist education: Paradoxes of identity and activism. In K. Kumashiro (Ed.), *Troubling intersections of race and sexuality: Queer students of color and anti-oppressive education* (pp. 1–25). New York: Rowman & Littlefield.

Lewis, K. G. (1996). A brief history and overview of faculty development in the United States. *International Journal for Academic Development, 1*(2), 26–33.

Lindsey, R. B., Robins, K. N., & Terrell, R. D. (2003). *Cultural proficiency: A manual for school leaders* (2nd ed.). Thousand Oaks, CA: Corwin.

Lockhart, M., & Borland Jr., K. (2001). Incorporating diversity in *all* faculty/staff development programs . . . Regardless of the content. *Journal of Faculty Development, 18*(2), 57–64.

Lorde, A. (1983). There is no hierarchy of oppressions. *Interracial Books for Children Bulletin, 14*(3–4), 9.

Marchesani, L. S., & Adams, M. (1992). Dynamics of diversity in the teaching-learning process: A faculty development model for analysis and action. In M. Adams (Ed.), *New directions for teaching and learning, no. 52. Promoting diversity in college classrooms: Innovative responses for the curriculum, faculty, and institutions* (pp. 9–19). San Francisco: Jossey-Bass.

Marchesani, L. S., & Jackson, B. (2005). Transforming higher education institutions using multicultural organizational development: A case study of a large northeastern university. In M. L. Ouellett (Ed.), *Teaching inclusively: Resources for course, department & institutional change in higher education* (pp. 3–20). Stillwater, OK: New Forums.

McCalman, C. L. (2007, Summer). Being an interculturally competent instructor in the United States: Issues of classroom dynamics and appropriateness, and recommendations for international instructors. In K. G. Hendrix (Ed.), *New directions for teaching and learning, no. 110. Neither white nor male: Female faculty of color* (pp. 65–74). San Francisco: Jossey-Bass.

McLean, C. A. (2007, Summer). Establishing credibility in the multicultural classroom: When the instructor speaks with an accent. In K. G. Hendrix (Ed.), *New directions for teaching and learning, no. 110. Neither white nor male: Female faculty of color* (pp. 15–24). San Francisco: Jossey-Bass.

Megginson, R. E. (2006). What works, A PKAL F21 Essay: Why change? *What works, what matters, what lasts, 4.* Washington, DC: Project Kaleidoscope (PKAL).

Milem, J. F., Chang, M. J., & Antonio, A. L. (2005). *Making diversity work on campus: A research-based perspective.* Washington, DC: Association of American Colleges and Universities.

Miller, J., & Garran, A. M. (2008). *Racism in the United States: Implications for the helping professions.* Belmont, CA: Thompson Brooks/Cole.

Moody, J. (2004). *Faculty diversity: Problems and solutions.* New York: Routledge.

Morey, A., & Kitano, M. (1997). *Multicultural course transformation in higher education: A broader truth.* Boston: Allyn & Bacon.

Muhtaseb, A. (2007). From behind the veil: Students' resistance from different directions. In K. G. Hendrix (Ed.), *New directions for teaching and learning, no. 110. Neither white nor male: Female faculty of color* (pp. 25–34). San Francisco: Jossey-Bass.

Musil, C. M., Garcia, M., Moses, Y. T., & Smith, D. G. (1995). *Diversity in higher education: A work in progress.* Washington, DC: AAC&U Publications.

Ouellett, M. L. (Ed.). (2005). *Teaching inclusively: Resources for course, department & institutional change in higher education.* Stillwater, OK: New Forums.

Ouellett, M. L., & Fraser, E. (2005). Teaching together: Interracial teams. In M. L. Ouellett (Ed.), *Teaching inclusively: Resources for course, department and institutional change in higher education* (pp. 189–210). Stillwater, OK: New Forums.

Ouellett, M., & Sorcinelli, M. D. (1995). Teaching and learning in the diverse classroom: A faculty and TA partnership program. In E. Neal (Ed.), *To improve the academy: Vol. 14. Resources for faculty, instructional, and organizational development* (pp. 205–217). Stillwater, OK: New Forums.

Petrone, M. C. (2004). Supporting diversity with faculty learning communities: Teaching and learning across boundaries. In M. D. Cox & L. Richlin

(Eds.), *New directions for teaching and learning, no. 97. Building faculty learning communities* (pp. 111–125). San Francisco: Jossey-Bass.

Roberts, H., Gonzales, J. C., Harris, O. D., Huff, D. J., Johns, A. M., Lou, R., et al. (1994). *Teaching from a multicultural perspective: Vol. 12. Survival skills for teaching.* Thousand Oaks, CA: Sage.

Schneider, C. G. (2008). Globalization and U. S. higher education. *Liberal Education, 94*(4), 1–2.

Schoem, D., Frankel, L., Zúñiga, X., & Lewis, E. (1993). *Multicultural teaching in the university.* Westport, CT: Praeger.

Smith, R. (1997). Instructional consultants as reflective practitioners. In K. T. Brinko & R. J. Menges (Eds.), *Practically speaking: A sourcebook for instructional consultants in higher education* (pp. 255–259). Stillwater, OK: New Forums.

Sorcinelli, M. D., Austin, A. E., Eddy, P. L., & Beach, A. L. (2006). *Creating the future of faculty development: Learning from the past, understanding the present.* Bolton, MA: Anker.

Stanley, C. A. (2001). A review of the pipeline: The value of diversity in staffing teaching and learning centers in the new millennium. *Journal of Faculty Development, 18*(2), 75–86.

Stanley, C. A. (Ed.) (2006). *Faculty of color: Teaching in predominantly white colleges and universities.* Bolton, MA: Anker.

Svinicki, M. (2004). *Learning and motivation in the postsecondary classroom.* Bolton, MA: Anker.

Tusmith, B., & Reddy, M. (2002). *Race in the college classroom: Pedagogy and politics.* New Brunswick, NJ: Rutgers University Press.

Weber, L. (2004). A conceptual framework for understanding race, class, gender, and sexuality. In S. N. Hesse-Biber & M. L. Yaiser (Eds.), *Feminist perspectives on social research* (pp. 121–139). Cambridge, UK: Oxford University Press.

Wertsch, M. E. (1991). *Military brats: Legacies of childhood inside the fortress.* St. Louis, MO: Brightwell.

Wijeyesinghe, C. L., & Jackson III, B. W. (Eds.) (2001). *New perspectives on racial identity development: A theoretical and practical anthology.* New York: New York University Press.

Williams, D. A., Berger, J. B., & McClendon, S. A. (2005). *Toward a model of inclusive excellence and change in postsecondary institutions.* Washington, DC: American Association of Colleges and Universities.

Williams, D. A., & Wade-Golden, K. C. (2008, September 26). The complex mandate of a chief diversity officer. *The Chronicle of Higher Education, 55*(5), B44. Retrieved on November 10, 2008, from http://chronicle.com/weekly/v55/i05/05b04401.htm

Yeskel, F., & Collins, C. (2005). *Economic apartheid in America: A primer on economic inequality and insecurity* (2nd ed.). New York: New Press.

Yun, J., & Sorcinelli, M. D. (2008). When mentoring is the medium: Lessons learned from a faculty development initiative. In L. B. Nilson & J. E. Miller (Eds.), *To improve the academy: Vol. 27. Resources for faculty, instructional, and organizational development* (pp. 365–384). San Francisco: Jossey-Bass.

13

CONCEPTUALIZING, DESIGNING, AND IMPLEMENTING MULTICULTURAL FACULTY DEVELOPMENT ACTIVITIES

Christine A. Stanley

AS COLLEGES AND UNIVERSITIES become increasingly diverse, and as we respond to calls from internal and external constituencies to prepare students to be global citizens (Krutky, 2008), instructors no longer see the traditionally dominant representation of white middle- and upper-class students. Rather, we are seeing more students of color; women; nontraditional students; gay, lesbian, bisexual, and transgender students; students with disabilities; and others whose unique characteristics such as culture, nationality, religion, and class may be visible or invisible.

This increase in diversity challenges faculty members to take a critical look at teaching, moving them from traditional modes to ways of designing teaching and learning activities that meet the needs of diverse learners (Marchesani & Adams, 1992; Ouellett, 2005). A multicultural classroom embodies a teaching and learning environment in which interdependence is valued, racism is confronted, differences are affirmed, communities are strengthened, knowledge is presented from multiple perspectives, and equity and social justice are maintained (Anderson, 1995; Wlodkowski & Ginsberg, 1995). To help meet these instructional challenges and support the institution's teaching and learning mission, many institutions rely on faculty development units.

In order to respond to the multicultural development needs of faculty, it is imperative that faculty developers be knowledgeable about diversity. This requires faculty developers "to reflect on our socialization and its relevance to this work, examine assumptions and stereotyped beliefs . . . , and regularly examine our attitudes, values, and behaviors, thinking, points of view, and reactions in and outside of educational contexts" (Stanley, Saunders, & Hart, 2005, p. 567). Working with faculty in this arena requires careful thought as to how we conceptualize, design, and implement multicultural faculty development initiatives in the faculty, instructional, and organizational development process so as to enhance the quality of teaching and learning. The literature in this area is replete with faculty development models that call for our understanding of how we conceptualize multicultural teaching (Adams, Bell, & Griffin, 1997; Adams, Blumenfeld, Castañeda, Hackman, & Anderson, 2000; Jackson & Holvino, 1988; Marchesani & Adams, 1992; Ouellett, 2005; Wlodkowski & Ginsberg, 1995). These models share several threads that provide faculty developers with a practical framework from which to assist faculty in the following:

○ The design of an inclusive curriculum

○ The development and exploration of their own multicultural awareness

○ The development of a variety of instructional approaches

○ The development and understanding of students' multicultural awareness

Based on these models and my own experience as a faculty developer, this chapter offers a practical guide for new and experienced faculty developers on how to approach multicultural faculty development initiatives.

Getting Started: Factors to Consider

If institutions and faculty developers want to begin a purposeful, multicultural faculty development effort or seek to enhance an existing program, several factors need to be considered.

Institutional Commitment

A multicultural faculty development program cannot be effective in accomplishing its goals without institutional commitment. Without commitment firmly established at the heart of the program, the faculty will see these activities as not making a difference. Institutional commitment, resources, and verbal support must come from senior-level administrators such as chancellors, presidents, provosts, and deans. Program activities should complement existing efforts that enhance the diversity mission of the institution. Working in collaboration with other appropriate and involved units on a college campus can strengthen the content of multicultural faculty development activities. Examples include such offices as the following:

- Diversity and/or multicultural affairs
- Student life, disability services
- International student services
- Gay, lesbian, bisexual, or transgender student services
- Women student services

A multicultural faculty development program should provide for faculty ownership of program activities that undergird the institutional commitment. Program goals should be established with the guidance of a faculty advisory committee, the membership of which should reflect not only diversity within its members and across disciplines but also expertise in the area of multicultural teaching.

Program Rationale

Articulating the rationale for a multicultural faculty development program is critical for the support, implementation, and evaluation of activities. It is not unusual for faculty development units to take charge of coordinating multicultural faculty development activities after the need has been identified. For example, at The Ohio State University, the justification for a multicultural faculty development program was born out of data gathered in the late 1980s that revealed low retention rates for black students. These data led to the development of the Teaching for Black Student Retention program, which was subsequently expanded to the Multicultural Teaching Program and later the Commitment to Success Program. At the center of these kinds of initiatives is the rationale that the classroom is a critical variable that contributes to students' success.

A multicultural faculty development program should articulate the meaning of diversity and multicultural teaching. The goal of such programs in preparing faculty to teach in a diverse environment is to provide an understanding of how diversity affects teaching and learning so that changes can be made to improve the classroom environment for all students (Chism & Whitney, 2005; Cook & Sorcinelli, 2005; Schmitz, Paul, & Greenberg, 1992).

Theoretical and Pedagogical Rationale

Once institutional commitment and a program rationale are articulated, it is imperative to develop a theoretical and pedagogical framework upon which multicultural faculty development activities will be grounded (Adams et al., 1997; Jackson, 2005; Schmitz et al., 1992; Smikle, 1994). If the goal of the program is to provide faculty members with an understanding of how diversity affects the teaching and learning process, the framework should reflect this goal. The theoretical frameworks that have proven most useful for multicultural faculty development activities are those espoused by pluralists (Kallen, Bayor, & Whitfield, 1997). Such authors have argued that interdependence is supported and valued in a diverse classroom and that students are able to explore their differences and to appreciate cultural experiences. Cultural pluralism emphasizes common features between and among groups.

The pedagogical frameworks that I have used are drawn from social justice education practice, which utilizes principles of cognitive development theory, learning styles, intergroup relations, human relations, experiential education, interactive learning and teaching, and feminist pedagogy (Adams et al., 1997; Adams, Bell, & Griffin, 2007). Social justice education argues that instructors pay attention to these principles as we examine the classroom environment, particularly the teaching and learning process, whereby knowledge is explored and instructional approaches are planned to include all participants.

Domains of Multicultural Teaching

I have found that it is essential to have a conceptual framework to help faculty members understand the domains of multicultural teaching. The dynamics of the multicultural teaching and learning model developed by Jackson and Holvino (1988) and later adapted by Marchesani and Adams (1992) suggest a framework for faculty members in any classroom to encounter the complex task of understanding four dimensions of the teaching and learning process that are operative within a diverse classroom. These four dimensions—faculty, teaching method, course content, and students—are summarized in Exhibit 13.1. Other frameworks include those offered by Chism and Whitney (2005), Cook and Sorcinelli (2005), Jackson (2005), and Tomkinson (2005).

○

EXHIBIT 13.1. FOUR DIMENSIONS OF MULTICULTURAL TEACHING.

1. Faculty

- Know oneself.
- Develop monocultural/multicultural socialization.
- Examine assumptions and stereotyped beliefs.
- Mentor students.

2. Teaching Method (implicit messages)

- Examine the culture of the classroom.
- Broaden repertoire of teaching methods to address multiple learning styles.
- Establish classroom norms that emphasize respect, fairness, and equity.

3. Course Content (explicit messages)

- Use a curriculum of inclusion.
- Represent diverse perspectives.
- Draw examples and illustrations from diverse life experiences.

4. Students

- Know your students.
- Develop monocultural/multicultural socialization.
- Examine assumptions and stereotyped beliefs.

Source: Adapted from Jackson and Holvino (1988) and Marchesani and Adams (1992).

○

Roles and Responsibilities of the Faculty Developer

Clearly, faculty developers themselves are a significant factor in the implementation or enhancement of the multicultural development effort; and there are several aspects to consider.

KNOWLEDGE OF SELF. Working in the area of multicultural teaching requires that the faculty developer have a high level of self-awareness and sensitivity (Coleman, 1990; Kardia, 1998; Nakayama & Martin, 1999; Smikle, 1994; Wijeyesinghe & Jackson, 2001) and must know how to recognize and manage conflict (Algert & Stanley, 2007).

If we are going to encourage faculty members to reflect upon their own multicultural awareness, it is only natural to look critically at our own biases and assumptions. We have to know who we are, where we are, what we are about, and why we are doing this work. For example, knowing who we are requires that we examine our identity and socialization and consider what we bring to our charge. As Kardia (1998) appropriately stated, "As a faculty developer working on multicultural issues, I need to be able to reflect on a variety of issues including what I know from experience versus what I need to learn from the experiences of others; my own cultural biases and blind spots that may interfere with my interactions with faculty; and how I might be perceived by faculty whose experiences are significantly different from my own" (p. 26).

Knowing where we are takes into account the faculty development unit and institutional commitment and vision relating to diversity issues. Knowing what we are about requires that we develop program goals congruent with the unit's mission; and knowing why we do this work demands that we empower individuals to share the dialogue around multicultural issues such as teaching and learning, philosophy, social justice, and institutional transformation. It is also important to understand that one's identity, whether it be along racial, cultural, or other social diversity lines, will have an impact on how we conceptualize and deliver training in this area. For example, experts generally advise that delivering workshops and seminars as a biracial team rather than solely as a member of the dominant or target group makes a considerable difference in how a predominantly white audience receives the information.

KNOWLEDGE OF SCHOLARSHIP. Faculty developers should read materials that address social and cultural aspects of teaching for the diverse classroom. They must have a working definition of multicultural teaching but, more important, must also know how diversity and oppression are defined in academia (Anderson, 1995; Asante, 1991; Banks, 1995; Feagin, 2006; Nieto, 1992; Ouellett, 2005). Diversity, in some instances, is defined in terms of and associated with multiculturalism, culture, democracy, learning, curriculum change, the learning environment, demographics, instruction, assimilation, and pluralism. One should take a critical look at these definitions, their breadth, and the implications behind them. One must also be able to conceptualize how these ideas fit within the institution's culture and mission and the faculty development unit.

AUDIENCE AWARENESS. It is important that faculty developers give careful thought to the audience in planning activities such as workshops, orientations, and consultations. Careful research of the audience enables us to meet participants' needs and engages interest and increases motivation for change. For example, we must take into account identity characteristics such as race, ethnicity, age, culture, religion, nationality, class, gender, disability, and sexual orientation. Obviously, some of these characteristics are not visible, but seeking to know to the extent possible the makeup of the audience is critical to the success of any workshop. The materials, media, and exercises selected for multicultural faculty development activities should reflect faculty awareness, needs, and ease of implementation (Smikle, 1994).

MANAGING CONFLICT. Faculty developers should be effective conflict managers. Facilitating a conversation about multicultural issues is, in essence, about managing change in teaching and learning. Frequently, when individuals are faced with change, there is resistance, fear, a tendency to revert to one's natural behavior styles, and conflict. Conflict, by definition, is a struggle or contest between or among individuals with opposing needs, values, beliefs, ideas, or goals (Algert & Stanley, 2007). It is not always negative, however. Productive conflict management enhances productivity, awareness, respect, and dialogue. I have worked to assess and learn about my own conflict management style, including its limitations, and found the information to be useful in facilitating difficult dialogues around diversity with administrators, faculty, staff, and students. The Thomas-Kilmann Conflict Mode Instrument (Thomas & Kilmann, 1974) is a widely used assessment tool for determining conflict modes. It takes less than fifteen minutes to complete and yields conflict scores for five modes: competing, avoiding, accommodating, compromising, and collaborating. Understanding these modes is essential to facilitate difficult dialogues and enhance relationships between and among groups.

PROFESSIONAL ALLIES. Faculty developers can learn from effective allies—those who have experience in multicultural teaching and education and who are not afraid of "walking the talk." Allies have worked to develop an understanding of social and cultural issues, have taken risks, are able to examine their own biases and assumptions, share experiences and resources, and are positive change agents. They might be faculty members, professional colleagues, or staff members. According to Ferren and Geller (1993), faculty members already doing work in this area can serve as resource persons, providing information about multicultural issues in their disciplines. Faculty developers can also learn from other faculty developers. Talking with and making site visits to faculty development centers coordinating multicultural faculty development programs can contribute significantly to one's own professional development, the sharing of ideas, and garnering resources for program enhancement.

CONTRIBUTING TO CAMPUS POLICIES. Faculty developers should be included in the dialogue concerning multicultural teaching and learning issues in order to influence institutional transformation so that students, staff, faculty, and administrators identify and understand issues surrounding the social and cultural aspects of the institutional environment and take action for change. By serving on key campus committees that address multicultural initiatives, we begin to develop campus partnerships to affect attitudes and behaviors inside as well as outside the classroom.

Designing Multicultural Faculty Development Activities

For the design of multicultural faculty development programs, it is essential that the content be relevant and practical for the appropriate academic unit. Content should raise awareness about multicultural issues and identify institutional resources for supporting multicultural teaching, thus creating avenues for follow-up.

Workshops

Many faculty members grapple with the idea of incorporating multicultural issues into their courses and curricula. Lack of awareness and insensitivity varies among disciplines (Cook & Sorcinelli, 2005; Cooper & Chattergy, 1993), and many espouse the concept that their discipline is culturally neutral. In preparing workshops, faculty developers should first articulate a set of attainable goals. While workshop goals should reflect participants' needs and size of the group, some general guidelines might include:

- To provide a definition and conceptual framework for multicultural teaching
- To heighten participants' self-awareness about teaching for diversity and social justice
- To have participants examine how social and cultural diversity issues are manifested in the classroom

○ To identify a range of strategies for teaching for the success of all students

○ To make instructors aware of institutional resources for teaching in a diverse classroom

It is necessary to develop a framework for the format and content. I ask participants to reflect on Marchesani & Adams's (1992) four dimensions of multicultural teaching from the perspective of "what we teach—course content," "how we teach—teaching methods," "whom we teach—students," and "who we are—as instructors" (Borton, 1970). A general format for a multicultural faculty development workshop might follow the outline shown in Exhibit 13.2.

○

EXHIBIT 13.2. WORKSHOP OUTLINE

Introduction and Goals

Purpose: Provides a conceptual framework for multicultural teaching and raises assumptions about what constitutes a diverse classroom

Activity: Facilitator and participants introduce themselves and explain what they hope to gain from the workshop; establishes tone and enables facilitators to get a sense of how to meet participants' needs

Principles of Teaching for the Diverse Classroom

Purpose: Provides an overview of these underlying principles

Topics: Examples of topics covered when addressing diversity issues in the classroom

- Changing nature of teaching, learning, and scholarship (Sorcinelli, 2007)
- Changing student demographics
- Changing faculty demographics
- Changing roles and expectations for faculty
- A conceptual framework for defining the problem such as Marchesani and Adams's (1992) four dimensions of multicultural teaching
- Ground rules for participation and
- Research that relates the issues to the discipline such as recruitment and retention, workforce, and demographic data

The Changing Classroom Climate for Teaching and Learning

Purpose: Establishes the rationale that the teaching and learning process is complementary, provides examples of how these two relationships operate in the classroom and of behaviors that enhance and impede learning, and focuses on what will help participants to care and realize ways in which they can make a difference or worsen the problem

Activity: Common classroom concerns as reported from the research on diverse student groups (may use video vignettes, self-assessment exercises, case studies on teaching and learning behaviors to facilitate discussion). Consider the following case scenarios and self-assessment exercise as examples of activities that could be used to raise participant awareness as well as spark deeper dialogues on the issues raised in this chapter or the workshop outline.

Case Scenario Directions

Read the following case scenarios that portray some common issues arising in the college classroom. View the situation from the perspectives of the students, then from the instructors' perspectives. What might each be thinking? What suggestions for action do you have for each situation or for avoiding the situation in the first place?

Scenario 1: A department faculty wonders how to be more inclusive in its curriculum.

David Wong is chairperson of his department. The Hispanic student association has sent him a letter urging the department to include the accomplishments of Hispanic scholars and significant issues pertaining to Hispanics in its curriculum. At a department meeting, Wong brings the letter to the attention of faculty and graduate teaching associates. The instructors feel that the students' suggestions are unreasonable; instructors say that they don't generally speak of the source of the scholarship, that their course is "culturally neutral," and that they don't see how they can accommodate these concerns.

Scenario 2: What is the instructor's responsibility?

Clarice Golden is having a classroom discussion on the changing profile of the American family. A student in the class raises the point of gay and lesbian couples having children. Immediately after saying this, another student, Patrick Williams, says, half-humorously, "Oh, God, that's sick!" The class laughs. Golden quiets the class, quickly passing over the suggestion as potentially too disruptive, and continues facilitating the discussion on "safer" grounds. After class, Ann, a student in the class, comes to her office and identifies herself as lesbian. She is angry and offended, accuses Golden of homophobia, and asks that she reprimand Williams.

Scenario 3: To intervene or not to intervene?
Jim Burton, an African American senior student, has done poorly on the first two exams in Barbara Ross's course. Jim doesn't participate in class and has not come to see Barbara outside of class. Even if he does exceptionally well on his final two exams, he will not get a good grade. Ross fears that Burton will not do well and will most likely fail, given his performance to date. She generally leaves it up to students to come see her when they are in trouble, but in this case she thinks that Burton might be shy and makes a point of asking him to see her. In talking with him, she determines that he is not very realistic about his performance and the prospects of reversing his grade. She suggests that he might consider dropping this course and taking a lower-level one so that he will not damage his grade point average. She feels that she has gone out of her way to help Burton and is puzzled when he resents being singled out and thinks that her suggestion is insulting.

Scenario 4: An instructor expresses his concern to you that a student has accused a colleague of patronizing the disabled.
John Green approaches his colleague, Gordon Wexner, and says that Leslie Bicknell, a student in Wexner's class, stopped by the office to express concern over an issue in his class. She explained that she is uncomfortable with his insensitivity toward the disabled. She said that throughout the semester Wexner has consistently pointed out how wonderful it is that Bill Hudson has overcome his disability. He also tends to speak loudly to Bill, which is offensive, since Bill's disability is visual. Wexner gets angry, saying that he is only trying to make Hudson feel welcomed in class and teachers these days are just "damned if they do and damned if they don't." Leslie Bicknell left feeling that Wexner just doesn't get it.

Sample Self-Assessment Exercise on Teaching Underrepresented Student Populations

Instructions: Circle the response that best describes your behavior. This inventory will not be "scored." It merely serves as a starting point for discussion.

In teaching, advising, or interacting with students, do you find yourself . . .

Usually   Sometimes   Rarely   Never

1. Wondering if a student of color plagiarized when he or she turns in a well-written paper

    a   b   c   d

2. Thinking that gay, lesbian, bisexual and transgender students are identifiable by certain mannerisms or physical characteristics

    a   b   c   d

3. Requesting verification from students who tell you that they have a learning disability

    a   b   c   d

4. Treating all students the same

    a   b   c   d

5. Having lower expectations for students of color

    a   b   c   d

6. Trying to relate course work and research to a student's life situation

    a   b   c   d

7. Transforming course content by using examples and material that are inclusive so as to represent diverse perspectives

    a   b   c   d

8. Calling on male students more than female students

    a   b   c   d

9. Consciously or unconsciously choosing males to be team or lab leaders

    a   b   c   d

10. Wondering why all students of color sit together in class

    a   b   c   d

11. Being sensitive to the needs of adult learners

    a   b   c   d

12. Finding yourself surprised when a student of color performs well in your class

    a   b   c   d

13. Expecting more from Asian American students than from other minority students

    a   b   c   d

14. Wishing that older students wouldn't talk about their life experiences so much

    a   b   c   d

15. Feeling uncomfortable talking about sensitive issues in class

    a   b   c   d

16. Trying to find out what special needs and abilities your students have

    a   b   c   d

17. Nominating students of color for awards and fellowships

    a   b   c   d

18. Interrupting or calling on women and students of color

    a   b   c   d

19. Getting irritated when a student of color shows up at your office without an appointment

    a   b   c   d

20. Expecting women to have math anxiety

    a   b   c   d

21. Being insensitive to the fact that students labeled "Hispanic" frequently prefer a more specific designation (i.e., Puerto Rican, Mexican) based on their family origins

    a   b   c

22. Making an extra effort to include reticent students in class discussions

    a   b   c   d

23. Relying on past test scores as sole predictors on how a student will perform

    a   b   c   d

24. Varying your teaching strategies to meet students' learning styles

    a   b   c   d

25. Challenging your assumptions about the performance and expectations of your students

    a   b   c   d

Source: The scenarios and self-assessment have been adapted with permission from The Ohio State University's Teaching for Black Student Retention and Multicultural Teaching Programs.

The Need for Changes in Teaching and Learning

Purpose: Provides concrete teaching and learning strategies once areas in need of change have been identified

Activity: Examples of activities and strategies to recommend when addressing changes in teaching and learning
- Teaching and learning strategies that facilitate change
- Self-assessment exercises

- Personal contracts
- Multicultural course and curriculum change
- Classroom observations with feedback and
- Classroom assessment techniques

Teaching Support Services

Purpose: Provides follow-up information to participants who wish to explore and learn further about the activities and topics explored and leaves them feeling that they are not in this endeavor alone

Activity: Covers the following topics:
- Additional resources and opportunities for follow-up such as periodic recommitment seminars
- Further readings on the topic and
- Supporting service units on campus

Evaluation

Purpose: Gathers formative feedback in order to improve the structure and facilitation of future

Activity: An instrument allowing participants to provide feedback on the organization, content, facilitation, and benefits of the workshop and ideas for follow-up

---

○

This workshop is designed for a two-hour time period. Obviously, individual faculty developers will need to make adjustments for length, content, and audience. For example, faculty members in a sociology department might appreciate the use of qualitative data in presenting the "what," as opposed to faculty members in a mathematics department, who might appreciate the use of quantitative data. In a workshop specifically designed for the mathematics department, and as part of establishing the "what," I worked with a staff member to gather and present recruitment and retention data of underrepresented student populations in that department. These data were integral to setting the tone of the workshop and making the participants more receptive to owning the problem. I have found that copresenting with a faculty liaison from the department requesting the workshop helps the faculty developer establish credibility with participants.

Whatever the method chosen for the presentation, the content should be tailored to the discipline or be generic in its content so that it is applicable to most. For example, in using case studies, it is often helpful to work with the faculty liaison in developing scenarios that have occurred in the classroom or department. When they consider the scenario from the perspectives both of the student and instructor, faculty members find case studies productive and meaningful as they think through ways to develop appropriate actions for change.

Individual Consultation

Individual consultation can involve review of course and curriculum design as well as syllabi. This process is challenging. For many faculty members, integrating multicultural course content is often relegated to inclusion of a book or article addressing an aspect of diversity. Even more challenging is working with a faculty member who feels that the course does not lend itself well to incorporating issues of diversity. Consultations should start by helping instructors to realize how diversity permeates all that we do; faculty members might begin by examining themselves and their behaviors.

Based on a survey of twenty-five faculty members conducted by Weinstein and O'Bear (1992), Adams, Bell, and Griffin (1997) suggested that knowing ourselves as instructors should take into account issues such as the following:

- Being aware of one's own social identity
- Confronting one's own biases
- Responding to biased comments in the classroom
- Acknowledging one's doubts and ambivalence about multicultural issues
- Realizing that students may feel uncomfortable talking about multicultural issues
- Dealing with emotional intensity and fear of losing control
- Negotiating authority
- Disclosing our knowledge and experiences about diversity, and
- Identifying institutional risks and behaviors

Course and Curriculum Design

There are several approaches to integrating multicultural perspectives into the curriculum. The approach discussed here is adapted from Banks (1995) and consists of four levels: the contributions approach, the additive approach, the transformation approach, and the action approach. These levels of modification are explained in Exhibit 13.3.

○

EXHIBIT 13.3. APPROACHES TO MULTICULTURAL CURRICULUM REFORM.

Level 1: The Contributions Approach

Heroes, heroines, holidays, food, and discrete cultural elements are celebrated occasionally. For example, the contributions of Black Americans to history are celebrated only in February, Black History Month, or an introductory physics course might mention contributions made by the late African American physicist and astronaut Ron McNair.

Level 2: The Additive Approach

Content, concepts, lessons, and units are added to the curriculum without changing the structure. For example, an instructor adds Alice Walker's book, *The Color Purple,* or Shakespeare's *Othello* to a literature course without changing its structure.

Level 3: The Transformation Approach

The structure of the curriculum is changed to enable students to view concepts, issues, events, and themes from the perspectives of diverse ethnic and cultural groups. For instance, a lecture on World War II might describe the contributions and meaning of the war to African Americans and the role played by the Tuskegee Airmen. A twentieth-century literature course might include scholarship on the writings of James Baldwin, Maxine Hong Kingston, Maya Angelou, Rudolpho A. Anaya, and Leslie Marmon Silko. A general biology or zoology course might address AIDS and discuss the impact and effect of the disease on various communities such as gay, lesbian, and bisexual individuals, women, African Americans, and other populations.

Level 4: The Action Approach

Students make decisions on important personal, social, and civic problems and take action to help solve them. To illustrate, a class studies the effects of institutional discrimination practices in higher education and develops an action plan to improve these practices at their own institution.

Source: Adapted from Banks (1995).

○

The ease of implementation decreases from the lowest to the highest level. Many researchers agree that levels 3 and 4—transformation and action—are what instructors should strive for in course and curricular reform (Banks, 1995; Ginsberg & Wlodkowski, 1997; Green, 1989; Jackson & Holvino, 1988; Ognibene, 1989; Ouellett, 2005; Schoem, Frankel, Zúñiga, & Lewis, 1993). These two levels also demand a deliberate institutional approach. It is important to remember that the contributions and additive approaches, though easier to implement, have their disadvantages, one of which is that they are easily eliminated if instructors are pressed for time in covering content. Another is that students often view contributions or additives as outside the realm of course content if they are not well integrated so as to promote several perspectives on the content.

Working with multicultural course content and curriculum change requires that instructors take a close look at these approaches and then reflect on how they might incorporate them. Kitano (1997) argued that reforming each level requires considerable planning, experimentation, and revision and that each activity should be a continuous process over time.

Syllabi

It is essential to articulate multicultural goals for the course. Kitano (1997) offered a working model for course and syllabus change and defined a multicultural course as one that appropriately incorporates multicultural content, perspectives, and strategies. In developing such goals, faculty should ask themselves the following questions:

- Is it a goal of this course to assist students in acquiring knowledge that reflects the accurate contributions of all individuals?
- Is it a goal of this course to present content from multiple perspectives?
- Is it a goal of this course to help students value the richness of diversity?
- Is it a goal of this course to prepare students to function in a global society?
- Is it a goal of this course to support different learning styles?

The overall course and multicultural goals articulated on the syllabus should be consistent with how the course is organized, implemented, and assessed and how the teaching methods are chosen. In addition to the usual information, an effective syllabus that is created from a multicultural perspective should pay attention to the checked items presented in Exhibit 13.4.

○

EXHIBIT 13.4. SYLLABUS.

Course Information
Includes course title, course number, credit hours, location of the classroom, days and hours of class/lab/studio, and so on

Instructor Information
Includes name, title, office location, office phone number, office hours, teaching associates (TAs).

Textbooks, Readings, and Materials
Includes title, author, date, publisher, and why it or they were chosen. Texts should be chosen for representation and treatment of course content and goals. Authors should be chosen for their treatment of multiple perspectives. Readings and materials should be chosen for their representation of diverse perspectives.

Course Description and Goals
Includes course and multicultural goals and why these goals are important for teaching and learning. Might include a rationale for instructional methods. Instructional methods should capitalize on students' experiences, learning, and cognitive styles. Course objectives for multicultural teaching and learning should address cognitive, affective, and behavioral domains (Kitano, 1997).

Course Calendar and Schedule
Includes a daily or weekly schedule of class activities such as readings, assignments and due dates, lecture topics, quizzes, and exams. Assessment strategies should provide students with a variety of ways for mastering course content.

Course Policies
Includes attendance, lateness, class participation, missed assignments and exams, lab safety, academic misconduct, and grading. Communicates a tone of high expectations for all students and knowledge of the research on differential interaction patterns of underrepresented groups.

Available Support Services and Resources
Includes a statement for students who may require support services from offices such as disability services, academic learning center, tutoring center, library, and computer center. Resources should accommodate the social and cultural characteristics and experiences of the students.

Source: Adapted from Altman and Cashin (1992).

○

Conclusion

Conceptualizing, designing, and implementing multicultural faculty development activities is challenging work. These activities require strong institutional commitment, solid grounding in theoretical and pedagogical rationales, in-depth exploration around who we are as faculty developers doing this work, excellent facilitation skills, and continuous professional development. Multicultural faculty development work is highly rewarding. It encourages us to expand our repertoire of social and cultural experiences as we work with the faculty and institutions in higher education to meet the teaching and learning needs of an increasingly diverse college student and faculty population. Finally, conceptualizing, designing, and implementing multicultural faculty development activities is ultimately of value to everyone. When faculty developers embrace any such call to action, we not only enrich the pool of educational resources at our institutions, but the entire academy as well.

REFERENCES

Adams, M., Bell, L., & Griffin, P. (Eds.). (1997). *Teaching for diversity and social justice*. New York: Routledge.

Adams, M., Bell, L., & Griffin, P. (Eds.). (2007). *Teaching for diversity and social justice* (2nd ed.). New York: Routledge.

Adams, M., Blumenfeld, M. J., Castañeda, R., Hackman, H. W., Peters, M. L., & Zúñiga, X. (Eds.). (2000). *Readings for diversity and social justice: An anthology on racism, anti-Semitism, sexism, heterosexism, ableism, and classism.* New York: Routledge.

Algert, N. E., & Stanley, C. A. (2007). Conflict management. *Effective Practices for Academic Leaders, 2(9),* 1–16.

Altman, H. B., & Cashin, W. E. (1992). *Writing a syllabus.* Idea Paper no. 27. Manhattan: Kansas State University, Center for Faculty Evaluation and Development.

Anderson, J. A. (1995). *Merging effective models of diversity with teaching and learning in the curriculum.* Raleigh: North Carolina State University.

Asante, M. (1991). Multiculturalism: An exchange. *The American Scholar, 60(2),* 267–276.

Banks, J. A. (1995). Multicultural education: Historical development, dimensions, and practice. In J. A. Banks & C.A.M. Banks (Eds.), *Handbook of research on multicultural education* (pp. 3–24). New York: Macmillan.

Borton, T. (1970). *Reach, touch, and teach.* New York: McGraw-Hill.

Chism, N.V.N., & Whitney, K. (2005). It takes a campus: Situating professional development efforts within a campus diversity program. In M. Ouellett

(Ed.), *Teaching inclusively: Resources for course, department and institutional change in higher education* (pp. 34–45). Stillwater, OK: New Forums.

Coleman, T. (1990). Managing diversity at work: The new American dilemma. *Public Management, 70*(10), 2–5.

Cook, C. E., & Sorcinelli, M. D. (2005). Building multiculturalism into teaching development programs. In M. L. Ouellett (Ed.), *Teaching inclusively: Resources for course, department and institutional change in higher education* (pp. 74–83). Stillwater, OK: New Forums.

Cooper, J. E., & Chattergy, V. (1993). Developing faculty multicultural awareness. An examination of life roles and their cultural components. In D. Wright & J. Povlacs Lunde (Eds.), *To improve the academy: Vol. 12. Resources for faculty, instructional, and organizational development* (pp. 81–95). Stillwater, OK: New Forums.

Feagin, J. R. (2006). *Systemic racism: A theory of oppression.* New York: Routledge.

Ferren, A. S., & Geller, W. W. (1993). The faculty developer's role in promoting an inclusive community: Addressing sexual orientation. In D. L. Wright & J. Povlacs Lunde (Eds.), *To improve the academy: Vol. 12. Resources for faculty, instructional, and organizational development* (pp. 97–108). Stillwater, OK: New Forums.

Ginsberg, M. B., & Wlodkowski, R. J. (1997, May). *Developing culturally responsive teaching among faculty: Methods, content, and skills.* A session presented at the 10th Annual Conference on Race and Ethnicity in American Higher Education, Orlando, FL.

Green, M. F. (Ed.). (1989). *Minorities on campus: A handbook for enhancing diversity.* Washington, DC: American Council on Education.

Jackson, B. W. (2005). The theory and practice of multicultural organization development in education. In M. L. Ouellett (Ed.), *Teaching inclusively: Resources for course, department and institutional change in higher education* (pp. 3–33). Stillwater, OK: New Forums.

Jackson, B. W., & Holvino, E. (1988). Developing multicultural organizations. *Journal of Religion and the Applied Behavioral Sciences, 9*(2), 14–19.

Kallen, H., Bayor, R., & Whitfield, S. (1997). *Culture and democracy in the United States.* Edison, NJ: Transaction.

Kardia, D. (1998). Becoming a multicultural faculty developer: Reflections from the field. In M. Kaplan & D. Lieberman (Eds.), *To improve the academy: Vol. 17. Resources for faculty, instructional, and organizational development* (pp. 15–33). Stillwater, OK: New Forums.

Kitano, M. K. (1997). What a course will look like after multicultural change. In A. Morey & K. Kitano (Eds.), *Multicultural course transformation in higher education: A broader truth* (pp. 18–34). Needham Heights, MA: Allyn & Bacon.

Krutky, J. B. (2008). Intercultural competency—preparing students to be global citizens. The Baldwin-Wallace Experience. *Effective Practices for Academic Leaders, 3*(1), 1–16.

Marchesani, L. S., & Adams, M. (1992). Dynamics of diversity in the teaching learning process: A faculty development model for analysis and action. In M. Adams (Ed.), *New directions for teaching and learning, no. 52. Promoting diversity in college classrooms: Innovative responses for the curriculum, faculty, and institutions* (pp. 9–19). San Francisco: Jossey-Bass.

Nakayama, T. K., & Martin, J. N. (Eds.). (1999). *Whiteness: The communication of social identity.* Thousand Oaks, CA: Sage.

Nieto, S. (1992). *Affirming diversity: The sociopolitical context of multicultural education.* New York: Longman.

Ognibene, E. R. (1989). Integrating the curriculum: From impossible to possible. *College Teaching, 37*(3), 105–110.

Ouellett, M. L. (Ed.). (2005). *Teaching inclusively: Resources for course, department and institutional change in higher education.* Stillwater, OK: New Forums.

Schmitz, B., Paul, S. P., & Greenberg, J. D. (1992). Creating multicultural classrooms: An experience-derived faculty development program. In L. Border & N.V.N. Chism (Eds.), *New directions for teaching and learning, no. 49. Teaching for diversity* (pp. 75–87). San Francisco: Jossey-Bass.

Schoem, D., Frankel, L., Zúñiga, X., & Lewis, E. A. (1993). The meaning of multicultural teaching: An introduction. In D. Schoem, L. Frankel, X. Zúñiga, & E. A. Lewis (Eds.), *Multicultural teaching in the university* (pp. 1–12). Westport, CT: Praeger.

Smikle, J. L. (1994). Practical guide to developing and implementing cultural awareness training for faculty and staff development. *Journal of Staff, Program and Organizational Development, 12*(2), 69–80.

Sorcinelli, M. D. (2007, Fall). Faculty development: The challenge going forward. *Peer Review, 9*(4), 4–9.

Stanley, C. A., Saunders, S., & Hart, J. (2005). Multicultural course transformation. In M. L. Ouellett (Ed.), *Teaching inclusively: Resources for course, department and institutional change in higher education* (pp. 566–585). Stillwater, OK: New Forums.

Thomas, K. W., & Kilmann, R. H. (1974). *The Thomas-Kilmann conflict mode instrument.* Palo Alto, CA: Consulting Psychology.

Tomkinson, B. (2005). Transcultural issues in teaching and learning. In M. L. Ouellett (Ed.), *Teaching inclusively: Resources for course, department and institutional change in higher education* (pp. 58–73). Stillwater, OK: New Forums.

Weinstein, G., & O'Bear, K. (1992). Bias issues in the classroom: Encounters with the teaching self. In M. Adams (Ed.), *New directions for teaching and learning, no. 52. Promoting diversity in college classrooms: Innovative responses for the curriculum, faculty, and institutions* (pp. 39–50). San Francisco: Jossey-Bass.

Wijeyesinghe, C. L., & Jackson III, B. W. (Eds.). (2001). *New perspectives on racial identity: A theoretical and practical anthology.* New York: New York University Press.

Wlodkowski, R. J., & Ginsberg, M. B. (1995). *Diversity and motivation.* San Francisco: Jossey-Bass.

14

WORKING WITH
UNDERREPRESENTED FACULTY

Franklin Tuitt

IN RECENT YEARS, EMERGING SCHOLARSHIP has focused on experiences of underrepresented faculty (women, faculty of color, and faculty with visible and invisible disabilities) in areas such as recruitment and retention (Tuitt, Sagaria, & Turner, 2007), promotion and tenure (Trower & Chait, 2002), work environment and climate (Turner & Myers, 2000), mentoring (Tillman, 2002), and wage disparities (Trower & Chait, 2002). One area in the faculty development literature that has not received a great deal of attention is the implications of underrepresented faculty as they relate to considerations, strategies, and best practices for working with underrepresented individuals and groups. Accordingly, the purpose of this chapter is to explore the experiences of underrepresented faculty in the academy and the implications these experiences have for faculty developers. This discussion is framed through the lens of inclusive excellence (Milem, Chang, & Antonio, 2005). The chapter concludes with a discussion of how faculty developers can promote inclusive excellence in their work with underrepresented individuals and groups.

Inclusive Excellence

In 2005, the AAC&U released a series of three articles that called for higher education institutions to move away from a fragmented focus on diversity and begin to think about how to promote inclusive excellence in predominantly white institutions. Specifically, they challenged leaders to move from rhetoric to action by involving the entire campus community in the work of infusing diversity and excellence (Milem et al., 2005). The introduction to this article series defines inclusive excellence as a purposeful embodiment of inclusive practices relating to multiple student identity groups. This involves:

○ Focusing on intellectual and social development

○ Developing and utilizing organizational resources purposefully to enhance organizational effectiveness by establishing an environment that challenges and supports each individual to achieve at the highest level

○ Paying attention to the cultural differences diverse individuals bring to the organizational setting and to how those cultural differences enhance the enterprise

○ Creating a welcoming community that engages all of its diversity in the service of individual and organizational learning (Milem et al., 2005)

Accordingly, the concept of inclusive excellence provides an appropriate and compelling framework for understanding the important work in which faculty developers engage with underrepresented faculty. To help institutions guide and assess their efforts to promote and achieve inclusive excellence, Williams, Berger, and McClendon (2005) proposed the *Inclusive Excellence Scorecard,* which consists of four dimensions: access and equity, diversity in the curriculum, campus climate, and learning and development. In the area of faculty development, *access and equity* refers to the compositional representation and success of underrepresented faculty; *campus climate* considers the development of a supportive organizational climate; *diversity and teaching* encompasses the experiences of underrepresented faculty in a teaching context; and *growth and development* concerns the professional development of underrepresented faculty in research, scholarship, promotion, and tenure (see Table 14.1).

Access and Equity

In recent times, higher education has experienced a significant increase in the number of underrepresented faculty members. For example, as outlined in Table 14.2, Snyder, Dillow, & Hoffman (2008) reported that the total number of women working as full-time faculty members in degree-granting institutions has increased by nearly 86,000 (48.9 percent) from 1992 to 2003. Likewise, faculty members of color increased by nearly

Table 14.1. Framing Inclusive Excellence Scorecard for Faculty Development.

Inclusive Excellence Scorecard (Students)	Inclusive Excellence in Faculty Development (Underrepresented individuals and groups)
Access and equity	Access and equity (current demographics of underrepresented faculty)
Diversity and teaching	Diversity and teaching (experiences of underrepresented faculty as it relates to teaching)
Campus climate	Campus climate (sense of belongingness and respect for diversity in the academia)
Learning and development	Growth and development (opportunity to engage and develop a community of scholars; support for research areas; promotion, and tenure)

Source: Adapted from Williams et al. (2005).

Table 14.2. Full-Time Instructional Faculty in Degree-Granting Institutions (by Gender, Race/Ethnicity).

Gender	1992	2003	Absolute Increase	Percentage Increase
Male	353	420	68	19.2
Female	176	261	86	48.9
Race/Ethnicity				
White	457	548	91	19.9
Black	27	38	11	38.9
Hispanic	14	24	10	71.8
Asian/Pacific Islander	28	62	35	124.8
American Indian/Alaska Native	3	10	7	289.1
Total Faculty of Color	72	134	62	86.1

Note: Number in thousands.
Source: Snyder et al. (2008).

62,000 (86.1 percent) during the same period. Moreover, from 1992 to 2003, representation of faculty of color improved from 13.6 percent to 19.6 percent of the total full-time instructional faculty. Although on the face of it these statistics suggest that there is indeed something to celebrate, upon a closer examination the outlook may not be as bright.

One of the realities of this increased access for underrepresented individuals is that the doors have been opened in some but not in all degrees and disciplines. For example, in fall 2003, only 2.6 percent of the total faculty was Hispanic as compared to 20.1 percent Asian/Pacific Islander (see Table 14.3). Among the various disciplines, the percentage of black faculty was the highest in education (7.8 percent). Not surprisingly, engineering and natural sciences accounted for the smallest percentages of faculty of color (Snyder et al., 2008). These disciplinary differences were also noted in gender; women were overrepresented in education disciplines but were underrepresented in the engineering, natural sciences, and business disciplines. In fact, gender disparity was acute in the engineering disciplines; women represent only 8.5 percent of the full-time instructional faculty.

We do not see significant growth in the numbers of underrepresented faculty members when institutional type and employment status are taken into consideration. Compared to private four-year colleges, public four-year institutions seem to be more accessible to faculty of color; they employ 5,763 more Hispanics and 12,302 more Asian/Pacific Islanders than do private institutions. Interestingly, there is no apparent difference of representation by institutional type among blacks (see Table 14.4). In academic rank, Asian/Pacific Islander faculty members tend to occupy more full-time positions than do colleagues who identify as black, who are overrepresented in part-time positions (Snyder et al., 2008).

Moreover, there are differences in advancement opportunities for faculty of color and women. For example, black (5.2 percent), Hispanic (3.4 percent), Asian/Pacific Islander (7.2 percent), and American Indian/ Alaska Native (0.5 percent) comprise 16.3 percent of total full-time instructional faculty; however, they form only 12.3 percent of the total full professors (see Table 14.5). This disparity is particularly accentuated for black instructors; they represent 6.2 percent of assistant professors but only 3.2 percent of the full professor rank. Of the women faculty, 15.4 percent and 26.8 percent are at the ranks of assistant professor and full professor respectively, compared to 21.4 percent and 31.5 percent for men. When we consider gender and race together, the representation of female faculty is higher among blacks and lower among all other races, including whites. This disparity is most evident among Asian/Pacific Islanders (9,180 male compared to 1,880 female full professors).

Table 14.3. Full-Time Instructional Faculty in Degree-Granting Institutions (by Sex, Race/Ethnicity, and Discipline, Fall 2003).

	All Fields		Business		Education		Engineering		Natural Sciences	
Sex										
Male	61.7%	420,402	68.5%	29,550	39.3%	19,980	91.5%	30,880	74.5%	94,810
Female	38.3%	261,424	31.5%	13,610	60.7%	30,910	8.5%	2,850	25.5%	32,390
Race/Ethnicity										
White	80.3%	547,719	79.5%	34,300	80.59%	40,970	70.9%	23,700	77.8%	99,000
Black	5.6%	38,061	4.5%	1,930	7.8%	3,910	5.4%	1,810	4.1%	5,260
Hispanic	3.5%	23,796	2.3%	990	4.7%	2,390	2.6%	870	2.9%	3.69
Asian/Pacific Islander	9.1%	62,297	12.2%	5,250	4.8%	2,430	20.1%	6,730	14.3%	18,240
American Indian/Alaska Native	1.5%	9,954	1.6%	700	2.2%	1,710	1.0%	330	0.8%	1,010

Source: Snyder et al. (2008).

Note: Faculty of color as a percentage of total faculty, excluding race/ethnicity unknown.

Table 14.4. Full-time Instructional Faculty in Degree-Granting Institutions (by Employment Status and Institutional Type, Fall 2005).

Race/Ethnicity	Public Four-Year		Private Four-Year		Full-Time		Part-Time	
	Percentage	Total	Percentage	Total	Percentage	Total	Percent	Total
White	82.0%	372,215	84.0%	325,283	83.00%	527,900	84.0%	459,878
Black	5.5%	24,875	6.3%	24,431	5.5%	35,458	7.0%	40,987
Hispanic	4.0%	17,953	3.2%	12,190	3.5%	22,818	4.3%	23,842
Asian/Pacific Islander	8.0%	35,952	6.1%	23,650	7.5%	48,457	4.1%	22,542
American Indian/ Alaska Native	0.5%	2,565	0.4%	1,384	0.5%	3,231	0.5%	3,112
Total		453,560		386,938		637,864		550,361

Source: Snyder et al. (2008).

Note: Faculty of color as a percentage of total faculty, excluding race/ethnicity unknown.

Table 14.5. Full-Time Instructional Faculty in Degree-Granting Institutions (by Sex, Race/Ethnicity, and Academic Rank, Fall 2005).

	Total	White	Black	Hispanic	Asian/ Pacific Islander	American Indian/ Alaska Native	Race/ Ethnicity Unknown	Non-resident Alien\2\
Total	675,624	527,900	35,458	22,818	48,457	3,231	9,703	28,057
Professors	169,192	145,936	5,484	3,793	11,060	519	1,014	1,386
Associate professors	138,444	112,507	7,402	4,319	10,144	564	1,296	2,212
Assistant professors	159,689	114,470	9,897	5,728	14,922	706	2,809	11,157
Instructors	98,555	76,359	7,462	5,261	4,740	905	1,853	1,975
Lecturers	27,215	20,982	1,286	1,233	1,714	109	480	1,411
Other faculty	82,529	57,646	3,927	2,484	5,877	428	2,251	9,916
Males	401,507	313,685	17,029	12,486	31,711	1,697	5,668	19,231
Professors	126,788	109,128	3,498	2,680	9,180	348	764	1,190
Associate professors	84,783	68,303	3,947	2,551	7,099	296	835	1,672
Assistant professors	86,182	60,244	4,459	3,003	8,903	306	1,601	7,666
Instructors	46,481	36,034	2,987	2,581	2,320	472	978	1,109
Lecturers	12,976	9,898	595	495	839	51	264	834
Other faculty	44,297	29,998	1,543	1,176	3,370	224	1,226	6,760
Females	274,117	214,215	18,429	10,332	16,746	1,534	4,035	8,826
Professors	42,404	36,808	1,986	1,113	1,880	171	250	196
Associate professors	53,661	44,124	3,455	1,768	3,045	268	461	540
Assistant professors	73,507	54,226	5,438	2,725	6,019	400	1,208	3,491
Instructors	52,074	40,325	4,475	2,680	2,420	433	875	866
Lecturers	14,239	11,084	691	738	875	58	216	577
Other faculty	38,232	27,648	2,384	1,308	2,507	204	1,025	3,156

Source: Snyder et al. (2008).

Notes: [1]Minority faculty as a percentage of total faculty, excluding race/ethnicity unknown.
[2]Race/ethnicity not collected.

Overall, the figures presented suggest that, while there has been increased access for underrepresented faculty in the academy, these gains do not appear to cross all disciplines.

Furthermore, the numbers indicate that, when underrepresented faculty gain access to the academy, opportunities for advancement—from part-time to full-time and for promotion and tenure—are limited for faculty of color and women. In addition, while various reports indicate a steady increase in the number of women and faculty of color, as of 2009 there were no national data sources that provide accurate numbers on faculty with disabilities (Knapp, 2008); and opportunities to examine the inclusion of gay, lesbian, bisexual, and transgendered (GLBT) faculty members in the academy are very limited and complicated (Steward, 2003).

Despite these gaps, compositional diversity is one of the critical components of promoting inclusive excellence in higher education (Milem et al., 2005; Williams et al., 2005). However, it is important to keep in mind that faculty developers must move beyond a sole focus on numbers and toward a comprehensive application of diversity that is embedded throughout every aspect of the organization (Milem et al., 2005). In particular, an open and welcoming environment is critical to ensuring that underrepresented faculty members feel authentically included as part of the community (Milem et al., 2005).

Climate and Culture

While in general the overall number of underrepresented faculty has increased, depending on the discipline and type of institution many women and faculty of color still find themselves as one of only few in their program or department (Turner & Myers, 2000). Accordingly, this isolation can create a chilly campus climate that leaves some underrepresented faculty members feeling marginalized, alienated, and invisible (Stanley, 2006). According to Trower (2003), existing research provides evidence that underrepresented faculty:

- o Experience overt and/or covert racism, including being stereotyped and pigeonholed
- o Experience isolation and exclusion and the resultant lack of colleagueship, networks, and mentors, leaving them less attuned to the rules that affect academic work life, including promotion and tenure
- o Are marginalized and find that their research is discredited, especially if it concerns minority issues

○ Bear a tremendous burden of tokenism, including feeling like they must be an exemplar of their entire race and gender and feeling they have to work twice as hard to get half as far

○ Are more "culturally taxed," that is, feel more obligated to show good citizenship by representing their race and ethnicity on multiple committees that help the institution but not necessarily the individual, and to mentor and advise many same-race students—a huge hidden workload that goes unrewarded in the promotion and tenure system

○ Place greater emphasis than whites on the affective, moral, and civic development of students and are much more likely to enter the academy because they draw a connection between the professoriate and the ability to effect social change

○ Suffer from negative, unintended consequences of being perceived as an affirmative action or target-of-opportunity hire

Experiences such as those described by Trower (2003) have significant implications for how underrepresented faculty members encounter the work environment, in that their perception of that environment further affects their work satisfaction (Saddler & Creamer, 2007). The notion that institutional climate and culture can influence satisfaction, advancement, and retention rates of underrepresented faculty is not surprising. Barnes, Agago, and Coombs (1998) found that one of the most important predictors of a faculty member's intent to leave an institution is a lack of a sense of community. This sentiment was supported by Cora-Bramble (2006), who reported that academic minority physicians seem to have less satisfaction with their jobs, are more likely to report experiencing racial harassment, have lower promotion rates, and more frequently report that they are considering leaving academic medicine.

Research conducted by Saddler and Creamer (2007) suggests that there may be more significant differences in the perception of campus climate by race at the institutional level as compared to the department level. For example, black faculty members perceive the university climate as less hospitable in comparison to white and Asian faculty members (Saddler & Creamer, 2007). This results in differential job satisfaction levels being highest for Asian and Pacific Islander faculty members and lowest for Hispanic and black faculty members (Saddler & Creamer, 2007). This research provides a subtle reminder that not all underrepresented faculty experience institutional climate in the same way.

While some scholars have argued that there is a difference between perception and reality, several researchers have demonstrated that the existence of a chilly climate is more than a figment of imagination for underrepresented faculty. Research on the experiences of faculty of color indicates that racial and/or ethnic minority members experience severe marginalization on campuses and perceive that their contributions are devalued (Aguirre, Hernandez, & Martinez, 1994; Astin, 1997; Turner & Myers, 2000). Correspondingly, Stanley (2006) argued that "the wounds of covert and overt racism, sexism, xenophobia, and homophobia run deep for many faculty of color" (p. 705). She found that many faculty members of color describe their campus climate as living in "two worlds," reflecting a continual tension of being pulled between their ethnic culture and the institutional culture. This also puts them in situations of constant stress and higher workloads as compared to their white counterparts (Stanley, 2006).

Similarly to faculty of color, research suggests that women who find themselves in academic departments are more likely to experience tokenism and discrimination (Trower, 2003). Trower (2003) contended that women experience bias in hiring, promotion, pay, and other rewards; are more adversely affected by dual-career decisions; and have to navigate institutional climates that ignore family responsibilities and childbearing commitments, which can affect scholarly productivity and conflict with the tenure clock (Trower, 2003). Trower (2003) stated, "Academic women of color have an especially difficult time because they face both racism and sexism, although most say racism is the more salient" (p. 6). Overall, the research on underrepresented faculty members declares that faculty of color and women feel acute personal isolation and need for support (Sorcinelli, 1994). This need for support also has significant implications for faculty developers who intend to help underrepresented faculty improve their teaching and overall work performance and satisfaction level.

Teaching and Diversity

Research suggests that the experiences of the underrepresented faculty both within and outside the classroom are quite different in comparison with white faculty members (Meyers, Bender, Hill, & Thomas, 2006; Stanley, 2006). Apparently, demographic characteristics such as race, age, and gender matter in how underrepresented faculty members experience the classroom environment (McGowan, 2000; Meyers et al., 2006). Stanley (2006) found that faculty of color faced challenges such as problematic student attitudes and behaviors as well as questioning of their authority and credibility in the classroom. Likewise, the results of McGowan's study (2000) indicated that black faculty perceived that some white students were more ready to (a) critique their classroom effective-ness, (b) challenge their authority, (c) have a lower level of respect, and (d) report their concerns and critiques to department chairpersons than they would for white faculty.

In addition to the various challenges underrepresented faculty members face in the classroom, several studies have shown that they share the per-ception of being negatively affected by student evaluations of their teaching (McGowan, 2000; Vargas, 2002). In particular, these studies indicate that underrepresented faculty who use inclusive pedagogical practices are more likely than others to receive negative comments from students (McGowan, 2000; Vargas, 2002). For instance, Milem (2003) reported that diversifying the faculty can result in more (a) student-centered approaches to teaching and learning, (b) utilization of diverse curricular offerings, and (c) focus on issues of race/ethnicity and gender. In this context, underrepresented faculty who teach multicultural courses or work to incorporate a multicultural perspective into their courses may experience resistance from white students (Stanley, 2006, Vargas, 2002). Additionally, Umbach (2006) established that faculty of color were "more likely to interact with students, to employ active learning and collaborative learning techniques, to create environments that increase diverse interactions, and to emphasize higher-order thinking activities in the classroom" (p. 337). Thus, the propensity to use more inclusive teaching practices coupled with demographic characteristics may com-plicate how underrepresented faculty negotiate the classroom and may have significant implications for their teaching evaluations (Meyers et al., 2006). Overall, the notion that underrepresented faculty members are more likely to be scrutinized and held to higher standards extends beyond the boundaries of the classroom and has significant implications for the overall growth and development of the underrepresented faculty.

Growth and Development

Research suggests that the academy's poor track record in promoting and advancing underrepresented faculty stems in part from (a) the limited access that they have to role models and networks that support their overall growth and development (Blackwell, 1996; Hagedorn & Laden, 2000; Turner & Myers, 2000), (b) the failure of the academy to understand the unique demands and pressures placed upon women and faculty of color (Adams, 2002; Stanley, 2006; Gregory, 2001), and (c) the invalidation of the academic legitimacy of underrepresented faculty (Garza, 1988; Blackwell, 1996).

ROLE MODELS AND MENTORS. According to Tillman (2002), the lack of success for some underrepresented faculty members can be attributed to professional and social isolation. She argued that the ability to establish mentoring and networking relationships with other faculty members who can relate to the range of psychosocial and cultural isolation is vital (Tillman, 2002). These relationships are especially important to underrepresented faculty members who are likely to find themselves isolated as the only or one of few women or faculty of color in their department (Blackwell, 1996; Hagedorn & Laden, 2000; Turner & Myers, 2000). Tillman (2002) suggested that faculty developers and mentors who are cognizant of the range of psychosocial demands that underrepresented faculty members face in the academy can provide these individuals and groups with a sense of competence, identity, and work-role effectiveness by (a) serving as an appropriate role model regarding attitudes, values, and behaviors; (b) conveying unconditionally positive regard for the underrepresented faculty; and (c) encouraging underrepresented individuals to talk openly about anxieties and concerns and giving the faculty member support that facilitates socialization and helps in coping with job stress and work demands of the new faculty role.

UNIQUE DEMANDS AND PRESSURES. Adams (2002) suggested that the new faculty in general, and underrepresented faculty in particular, may be unsure about how to judge the importance of multiple requests for service that are usually made upon them. She contended that underrepresented faculty may be especially vulnerable to such requests, given their additional responsibilities of serving as role models for underrepresented students and as institutional representatives for issues related to gender and race ethnicity. Similarly she maintained that "extra" expectations occur for new female faculty in disciplines that are nontraditional for women. "They also often find themselves carrying extra service commitments in part because of stereotypes about their 'innate' abilities to counsel students and organize departmental social events" (Adams, 2002, pp. 7–8).

A related factor concerning the growth and development of underrepresented faculty is the extent to which their choice to engage in service to the institution and community will be recognized and rewarded rather than punished during the tenure process (Blackburn & Lawrence, 1995; Springer, 2002). This in turn creates a service conundrum for underrepresented faculty members who want to honor their desire and commitment to give back to their community (Stanley, 2006).

ACADEMIC LEGITIMACY. In addition to the classroom context, under-represented faculty members experience multiple threats when their skin color, gender, research focus, and research methods are overly scrutinized and their scholarly credentials are devalued or largely ignored by their majority colleagues and host institutions (Hagedorn & Laden, 2000; Turner & Myers, 2000). The unfortunate reality is that, for many under-represented faculty members, race and gender, together and separately, are factors that determine whether or not a faculty member is granted tenure (Ards & Woodard, 1997). Research suggests that the majority faculty often view underrepresented faculty members narrowly as "diver-sity or gender and ethnicity specialists" because of their interest in researching diversity related issues. Consequently, they face the risk of being pigeonholed, stigmatized, dismissed, and not regarded as credible experts in their disciplines (Blackwell, 1996; Garza, 1988). In theory, this invalidation of the academic legitimacy of underrepresented faculty only serves to reinforce a sense of isolation, resulting in scholarship segregation and stagnation (Alger, 1999; Gregory, 2001).

Implications

Overall, the experiences of underrepresented faculty discussed in this chapter have several implications for faculty developers seeking to work with underrepresented individuals and groups. In this final section, we return to the areas of access and equity, campus climate, teaching and diversity, and growth and development to frame our discussion of how faculty developers can promote inclusive excellence in their work.

To begin, in order to promote inclusive excellence, faculty developers must enhance their understanding of the experiences of underrepresented faculty. While access has increased for underrepresented individuals and groups in general, faculty developers want to consider how the experi-ences of underrepresented individuals and groups may vary based on their location within the academy as it relates to discipline, academic department, and institutional type. The reality is that many underrepre-sented faculty members still find themselves isolated as the only one or one of a few women, GLBT faculty, faculty members with disabilities, or faculty of color in their academic departments or programs. In such cases, underrepresented faculty members may be vulnerable to psycho-logical conditions such as solo status (Kanter, 1977). Kanter's seminal work suggests that a faculty member who is the single representative or one of few representatives of an underrepresented group may experience extreme work pressures and stress. Faculty developers can better assist underrepresented professors by participating in programs that help to expand their own knowledge base of the issues that underrepresented faculty face in the academy (Stanley, 2006). Faculty developers may want to attend conferences like the biannual "Keeping Our Faculties" symposium, which invites research and evidence-based scholarship related to developing, recruiting, retaining, and advancing underrepresented faculty (http://www.cce.umn.edu/conferences/kof/). The annual Professional and Organizational Development (POD) Network conference also always includes sessions relating to diversity and multicultural issues.

Recognizing that some underrepresented individuals and groups feel marginalized, alienated, and invisible (Stanley, 2006), faculty developers should keep in mind that not all underrepresented faculty members experience an environment in the same way. It is important for faculty developers *not* to assume that an individual identifies strongly with a particular group just because the individual is a member of that group. While experiences of marginalization, isolation, and discrimination cut across all groups, faculty developers will want to consider that underrepresented individuals have multiple complex identities where race, gender, and sexual orientation intersect with other social identities, both visible and invisible, to provide unique experiences worthy of individual attention. Therefore, promoting inclusive excellence requires that faculty developers learn about and examine the experiences of underrepresented faculty collectively and individually and design programs that address their specific needs and unique experiences. To that end, faculty developers must be careful that the programming content and activities they choose do not further marginalize the underrepresented individuals and groups they are trying to serve. Finally, faculty developers should design programs that help majority faculty better understand the unique experiences of underrepresented faculty and how their actions (intentional and unintentional) can contribute to a chilly climate. One such program was recently developed at the University of Denver, where an entire issue of a faculty publication was dedicated to inclusive excellence and the experiences of underrepresented faculty on campus (http://www.du.edu/facsen/papers.html). This publication was distributed to the entire faculty by the faculty senate president, who in turn encouraged department chairs to discuss the publication's content with their faculty.

Another area in which faculty developers can help promote inclusive excellence in their work with underrepresented faculty is by designing programs that address the various challenges these individuals and groups experience in the classroom. Since research suggests that demographic characteristics such as race, age, sexual orientation, physical ability, and gender matter in underrepresented faculty members' experience of the classroom environment (McGowan, 2000; Meyers et al., 2006), faculty developers need to familiarize themselves with the range of best practices related to creating inclusive learning environments (Tuitt et al., 2007) and develop programs that enhance the overall effectiveness of under-represented faculty in the classroom. In particular, faculty developers want to keep in mind the reality that multicultural courses might require additional efforts from the faculty members who teach these courses (Stanley, 2006). Faculty developers also want to consider how they can support underrepresented faculty members in their efforts to address acts of intolerance and resistance in the classroom. The Derek Bok Center for Teaching and Learning at Harvard University provides such support by listing on its Web site a range of resources related to managing "hot moments" and addressing race in the classroom (http://isites.harvard.edu/icb/icb.do?keyword=k1985&pageid=icb.page29721).

Last, in order for underrepresented faculty to experience the growth and development that will ensure their success in the academy, faculty developers must be prepared to provide professional support and guidance to these individuals and groups as needed (Sorcinelli, 1994). According to Springer (2002), the criteria for promotion and tenure sometimes have a built-in albeit subtle discriminatory impact. In order to help minimize this potential bias, faculty developers should have an understanding of the need of underrepresented individuals and groups to have additional time to build professional networks in research and teaching and be accommodating of their additional commitments to serve their families and/or respective communities (Alger, 1999; Sorcinelli, 1994). Moreover, faculty developers can assist underrepresented individuals and groups by connecting them to role models and mentors who can build a meaningful professional relationship with thoughtful attention to identity affirmation, professional development, and practical training. In addition to working directly with underrepresented faculty members, faculty developers should also work with key administrators to ensure that deans and program chairpersons are aware of and promote policies and practices that build inclusive organizational environments.

Conclusion

It is imperative that faculty developers concerned with ensuring the success of underrepresented faculty discern how to promote inclusive excellence in their institutions through their work with these individuals and groups. Promoting inclusive excellence in faculty development requires that we identify new models for creating institutional change and working with underrepresented individuals and groups. This can be accomplished by engaging in inclusive measures that signal the following to all members of the organization in general and specifically to under-represented individuals and groups (Tuitt et al., 2007):

○ Their unique and individualized cultural characteristics, and not only their gender and/or skin color, will be an asset to the institution. They will be appreciated and respected as intellectually competent.

○ Faculty developers are aware of the unique experiences and challenges underrepresented individuals and groups face in the academy.

○ Faculty developers are invested in their growth, development, and success by doing all possible to ensure that support and resources will be made available to underrepresented individuals and groups.

○ Faculty developers are committed to diversity and excellence.

○ Faculty developers pay attention to the climate and conditions under which underrepresented individuals and groups work.

○ Faculty developers can serve as potential allies—those in the institution who will work as change agents.

Faculty developers who are able to meet the challenge of achieving inclusive excellence will be in the best position to ensure that underrepresented individuals and groups thrive and succeed in the academy.

REFERENCES

Adams, K. (2002). *What colleges and universities want in new faculty.* Washington, DC: Association of American Colleges and Universities.

Aguirre Jr., A., Hernandez, A., & Martinez, R. O. (1994). Perceptions of the workplace: Focus on minority women faculty. *Initiatives, 56*(3), 41–50.

Alger, R. J. (1999). When color-blind is color-bland: Ensuring diversity in higher education. *Stanford Law and Policy Review, 10*(2), 191–204.

Ards, S. B., & Woodard, M. (1997). The road to tenure and beyond for African American political scientists. *Journal of Negro Education, 66*(2), 159–171.

Astin, H. (1997). *Race and ethnicity in the American professoriate, 1995–96.* Los Angeles: University of California, Los Angeles (UCLA), Higher Education Research Institute.

Barnes, L. B., Agago, M. O., & Coombs, W. T. (1998). Effects of job-related stress on faculty intention to leave academia. *Research in Higher Education, 39*(4), 457–469.

Blackburn, R. T., & Lawrence, J. H. (1995). *Faculty at work: Motivation, expectation, and satisfaction.* Baltimore, MD: Johns Hopkins University Press.

Blackwell, J. E. (1996). Faculty issues: Impact on minorities. In C. Turner, M. Garcia, A. Nora, & L. Rendon (Eds.), *Racial and ethnic diversity in higher education* (pp. 315–326). Needham Heights, MA: Allyn & Bacon

Cora-Bramble, D. (2006). Minority faculty recruitment, retention and advancement: Applications of a resilience-based theoretical framework. *Journal of Health Care for the Poor and Underserved, 17*(2), 251–255.

Garza, H. (1988). The "barrioization" of Hispanic faculty. *Educational Record, 68*(4), 122–124.

Gregory, S. (2001). Black faculty women in the academy: History, status and future. *Journal of Negro Education, 70*(3), 124–134.

Hagedorn, L. S., & Laden, B. V. (2000). Job satisfaction among faculty of color in academe: Individual survivors or institutional transformers? In L. S. Hagedorn (Ed.), *What contributes to job satisfaction among faculty and staff* (pp. 57–66). San Francisco: Jossey-Bass.

Kanter, R. M. (1977). *Men and women of the corporation.* New York: Basic Books.

Knapp, S. D. (2008). Why "diversity" should include "disability" with practical suggestions for academic unions. *American Academic, 4*(1), 103–130.

McGowan, J. (2000). Multicultural teaching: African-American faculty classroom teaching experiences in predominantly white colleges and universities. *Multicultural Education, 8*(2), 19–22.

Meyers, S. A., Bender, J., Hill, E. K., & Thomas, S. Y. (2006). How do faculty experience and respond to classroom conflict? *International Journal of Teaching and Learning in Higher Education, 18*(3), 180–187.

Milem, J. F. (2003). The educational benefits of diversity: Evidence from multiple sectors. In M. Chang, D. Witt, J. Jones, & K. Hakuta (Eds.), *Compelling interest: Examining the evidence on racial dynamics in higher education* (pp. 126–169). Palo Alto, CA: Stanford University Press.

Milem, J. F., Chang, M. J., & Antonio, A. L. (2005). *Making diversity work on campus: A research-based perspective.* Washington, DC: Association of American Colleges and Universities.

Saddler, T. N., & Creamer, E. G. (2007). *Faculty perceptions of climate and job satisfaction by race/ethnicity: Findings from 2005 AdvanceVT Work-Life Survey.* Retrieved July 27, 2008, from http:www.advance.vt.edu/Measuring_Progress/Faculty_Survey_2005/Minority_Survey_Report_Final.pdf

Snyder, T. D., Dillow, S. A., & Hoffman, C. M. (2008). *Digest of Education Statistics 2007* (NCES 2008–022). Washington, DC: U.S. Department of Education, National Center for Education Statistics, Institute of Education Sciences.

Sorcinelli, M. D. (1994). Effective approaches to new faculty development. *Journal of Counseling & Development, 72*(5), 474–479.

Springer, A. (2002). *How to diversify faculty: The current legal landscape.* Washington, DC: American Association of University Professors.

Stanley, C. A. (2006). Coloring the academic landscape: Faculty of color breaking the silence in predominantly white colleges and universities. *American Educational Research Journal, 43*(4), 701–736.

Steward, D. (2003). Working toward equality. *Academe, 89*(4), 29–33.

Tillman, L. (2002). Culturally sensitive research approaches: An African-American perspective. *Educational Researcher, 31*(9), 3–12.

Trower, C. A. (2003). Leveling the field. *The Academic Workplace, 14*(2), 1, 3, 6–7, 14–15.

Trower, C. A., & Chait, R. P. (2002, March–April). Faculty diversity: Too little for too long. *Harvard, 104*(4), 33–37.

Tuitt, F. A., Sagaria, M.A.D., & Turner, C.S.V. (2007). Signals and strategies: The hiring of faculty of color. In J. C. Smart (Ed.), *Higher education: Handbook of theory and research* (Vol. 22, pp. 497–535). New York: Agathon.

Turner, S. T., & Myers, S. L. (2000). *Faculty of color in the academy: Bittersweet success.* Boston: Allyn & Bacon.

Umbach, P. D. (2006). The contribution of faculty of color to undergraduate education. *Research in Higher Education, 47*(3), 317–345.

Vargas, L. (Ed.). (2002). *Women faculty of color in the White classroom.* New York: Peter Lang.

Williams, D. A., Berger, J. B., & McClendon, S. A. (2005). *Towards a model of inclusive excellence and change in postsecondary institutions.* Washington, DC: Association of American Colleges and Universities.

15

INTERNATIONAL FACULTY DEVELOPMENT

PURSUING OUR WORK WITH COLLEAGUES AROUND THE WORLD

Nancy Van Note Chism, David Gosling,
and Mary Deane Sorcinelli

ALTHOUGH FACULTY DEVELOPMENT has become a recognized field of activity only within the last fifty years, structures organized to support educators can now be found in many countries across the world. In English-speaking countries such as Australia, Ireland, New Zealand, South Africa, and the United Kingdom, faculty development is well established and generally known as "educational" or "academic" development. Faculty development thrives in many European countries: networks of developers are in place in India; Sri Lanka; Thailand; the Middle East, particularly the Persian Gulf states; Japan; and China.

Higher education, the context for development work, is becoming increasingly a global and international enterprise. In the United States, institutions have multinational faculty, students, and administrators; U.S. faculty members, administrators, and students also commonly visit countries across the globe. Global institutions that educate students, conduct research, and generate revenue in locations across multiple countries are also becoming common (Newman, Couturier, & Scurry, 2004).

Faculty development must therefore keep pace with the internationalization and emerging globalization of colleges and universities. Efforts to

243

support and enrich faculty work—particularly in a changing context—are critically important to faculty members, institutional leaders, and higher education throughout the world. Attention to diversity and multiculturalism is high on the agenda of many U.S. colleges and universities; helping faculty members develop more inclusive course materials and teaching methods to prepare students for a globalized world is now an important goal for many institutions, both here and abroad. Given rapid technological advances, faculty members are already called on to develop educational delivery in new formats that encourage international participation—through Web sites, short modules, and certificate programs. Many faculty members have not been trained to teach in these new contexts; and, while their specific needs may vary, they will require support and training to function optimally in this rapidly changing technological and global environment.

An advantage to the burgeoning global academic environment is the increase in opportunities for communication and collaboration between and among international faculty development colleagues, which can stimulate the creation and sharing of new knowledge and fresh perspectives. The concept of development for new faculty members, for example, has been enriched by European colleagues, who often are on the cutting edge of developing and evaluating the value of compulsory teaching certificate and portfolio programs. Globalization is also opening up new consulting opportunities for developers.

At the same time, the globalization of faculty development brings challenges. North American faculty developers, for instance, need to become more knowledgeable about curricular internationalization, the needs of international visiting faculty members at their institutions, constructing study abroad experiences, and a variety of other teaching and learning issues. For their work at home and for their international consulting work, developers need to acquire new skills and sensitivities in order to understand the faculty members' needs, which may be quite different from those of faculty members in the United States.

Fortunately, as is detailed further in this chapter, formal structures for faculty development have been moving to the top of institutional, national, and government agendas throughout the world. A number of international faculty development organizations have arisen to share expertise through journals and conferences. The future of the field will depend, in part, on its continuing capacity to fashion effective strategies for enhancing professional knowledge and skills as developers, stimulating and carrying out research into teaching and learning across the boundaries of nation states, and partnering to support the improvement of teaching and learning in the increasingly global world of higher education.

This chapter provides background information on the status of faculty development around the world. It also offers ideas on ways in which North American educational developers can work with and benefit from the scholarship and practice of their colleagues in other countries through travel abroad as a visiting faculty member or consultant, involvement in collaborative development or research projects, and hosting visiting international developers.

International Overview of the Profession

Information on the role of faculty development across the world is constrained by the lack of comparative data. However, some data are available on similarities and differences among the countries with the largest educational development networks, namely the United States, Canada, the United Kingdom, and Australia, based on research undertaken by the authors. The overview that follows also contains references to some smaller networks where data are available.

The central characteristics of educational or academic development in English-speaking countries across the world have much in common with the following goals identified by most North American faculty developers:

○ Create or sustain a culture of teaching excellence

○ Respond to individual faculty members' needs (for example, one-to-one consultation)

○ Advance new initiatives in teaching and learning

○ Foster collegiality within and among faculty members and departments

○ Act as a change agent within the institution (Sorcinelli, Austin, Eddy, & Beach, 2006)

In a study of U.K. educational development (Gosling, 2008), the most cited responsibilities of educational development centers (EDCs) were identified as:

○ Encourage innovation in teaching and learning

○ Implement the institution's own teaching and learning strategy

○ Improve teaching and learning quality

○ Provide professional development in teaching and learning

○ Promote scholarship of teaching and learning

It is worth noting that the U.S. emphasis on providing consultation and fostering collegiality is less strong in the United Kingdom and Australia, where greater weight is placed on developing a strategic approach to enhancing teaching and learning at the institutional level. However, across the globe there is "recognition of the proactive organizational role that faculty development can play in creating an institutional environment supportive of teaching and learning" (Sorcinelli et al., 2006, p. 43).

Many if not all EDCs across the globe have responsibility for academic programs designed to increase the scholarly base for teaching. In Sweden, for example, all faculty members are required to undertake a ten-week course in pedagogy. In the United Kingdom, all universities are expected to have a mandatory course of professional development for newly appointed faculty members. Typically these courses are formally examined at the master's level and require faculty members to produce a portfolio of evidence demonstrating that they have met the specified outcomes of the course. Applications for tenure often require successful completion of such courses. Similar academic courses in pedagogy have become increasingly common in Australia, South Africa, New Zealand, and Sri Lanka; but the extent to which such courses are compulsory for new faculty members varies. It is also common now to offer training to graduate students who undertake some teaching, not only in the United States and Canada, but in other countries as well.

Across the globe, faculty development centers face some common structural issues. Many centers were begun by a pioneering individual who had an enthusiasm for student learning and a concern for supporting teachers. Institutions tend to create EDCs when they are under pressure to improve student ratings, increase their student completion rates, or respond to changes in the student market and technology. The first step is often to create a small unit as a subsection of a larger administrative unit, which is likely to be within the central administration though in some cases it is within a school of education.

A second step is to create a stand-alone unit reporting directly to a senior manager and to adopt a wider, more strategic role. Increasingly, central units have also been experimenting with distributed structures—for example, appointing learning and teaching leaders or coordinators within each school, awarding teaching fellowships to academics who become champions within their own disciplines, and establishing learning groups or communities among interested faculty members. Some institutions have an associate dean for learning and teaching with a responsibility to improve teaching quality. All of these measures reflect the realization that educational development is a responsibility for the whole institution (D'Andrea & Gosling, 2005).

Although there are wide variations in the size, location, and responsibilities of EDCs worldwide, some broad types can be described. First is the small unit, comprised of very few academic developers who are often teaching and learning enthusiasts recruited from teaching departments to fulfill a cross-institutional role. Second, there are many medium-sized units, with perhaps three academic positions—a director, a small number of technical staff members who focus on developing and supporting e-learning, and some administrative support. Third, there are large EDCs with multiple roles. These larger units, often with a total staff of twenty or more faculty members and administrative staff, may be supplemented by other staff on short-term or fractional contracts funded for fixed periods to support specific projects. Units tend to be larger in Australia and the United Kingdom than in the United States.

Compared to those in the United States, university systems abroad are relatively small and more homogeneous, although they also reflect differences in size, status, wealth, and research orientation. While the number of universities in countries such as China and India is increasing rapidly and private universities are springing up throughout the developing world, the tremendous variety of institutional types and financial support structures that exists in the United States is unique. Educational development units across the world thus vary greatly in the context of their work and in the number of units within each country.

Because many universities outside the United States tend to be predominantly dependent on government funding, they are more directly influenced by national policy, which in turn influences educational development practice. In the United Kingdom, for example, the government has ordered universities to address certain priorities such as "widening participation" and enterprise. In Japan, the government has required all universities to establish EDCs. Similarly, in Sweden "the individual teacher, the department and the institution" have been informed that they should "take initiatives that will develop learning and teaching" (Roxa & Martensson, 2008). In South Africa, the declared intention of government policy to redress historical injustices in higher education has strongly influenced the way in which educational development units provide student support.

Government-funded reward schemes can very directly affect educational development activity in some countries. For example, in Australia a "Learning and Teaching Performance Fund" rewards excellence and improvement in undergraduate education. In the United

Kingdom, seventy-four well-funded Centers for Excellence in Teaching and Learning were established in 2005. There is a National Teachers Fellowship award for individual teachers who have demonstrated excellent practice. In both the United Kingdom and Australia, governments have funded national academies that are intended to support improvements in teaching and learning: the Australian Learning and Teaching Council (formerly the Carrick Institute [see http://altc.edu.au/carrick/go] and the Higher Education Academy in the United Kingdom [see http://heacademy.ac.uk]).

A key difference between faculty development in the United States and in other English-speaking countries lies in the literature that has been most influential. Works such as McKeachie's classic text *Teaching Tips* (McKeachie & Svinicki, 2005), Angelo and Cross's *Classroom Assessment Techniques* (1993), Tinto's theories on student retention (1993), Barr and Tagg's paradigm shift from teacher-centered to student-centered practice (1995), and Boyer's (1990) and subsequently Shulman's, Hutchings's, and Huber's ideas on the scholarship of teaching and learning (Huber, 2006; Hutchings, 2000; Shulman, 1993, 1999) by U.S. authors are well known. Also influential are programs such as the First Year Experience, Carnegie Academy, and National Survey of Student Engagement.

However, significant literature that is less well known to U.S. faculty developers has been very influential abroad. One seminal line starts with Marton and Saljo's paper (1976) on differences in students' approaches to study, which was followed up by Entwistle and Ramsden (1983) and Gibbs (1992). The ethnographic methodology for studying educational settings proposed by Marton and subsequently promoted by Prosser and Trigwell (1999) became dominant and is still very influential, for example, in their work on approaches to teaching. A key text used in many courses for new faculty is Ramsden's *Learning to Teach* (2003). Another influential figure has been John Biggs, whose concept of "constructive alignment" (Biggs, 2003) has been very important. Authors such as Barnett (1997, 2000), Rowland (2000), and Knight and Trowler (2001) are more influential outside than inside the United States.

Challenges for Educational Development Centers

A characteristic of academic development internationally, as well as in North America, is that centers are continually subject to organizational change. EDCs continue to be reorganized or restructured at regular intervals. A recent study in the United Kingdom found that the rate at which EDCs are being formed or reformed has not lessened to any extent over the past fifteen years (Gosling, 2008). Reorganization is often associated with a change of the senior manager responsible for the EDC. Restructuring is normally concerned with aggregating or disaggregating functions such as e-learning, student support, general faculty development, and quality assurance functions. The continuing threat of reorganization tends to create a sense of marginalization and demoralization among EDC staff, but such changes can also bring new opportunities to expand the work of developers.

In recent years, the role and identity of faculty developers has emerged as a source of some uncertainty. A key issue here is whether educational developers are seen as part of the central administration or whether they are identified with academic faculty members. Increasingly, educational development has come to be seen as closely linked to the achievement of institutional goals and is used by senior administrators to support cross-institutional initiatives—for example, widening access to the university for disadvantaged groups, promoting internationalization of the curriculum, or encouraging entrepreneurship among students.

One reason for the international concern about the status and identity of educational developers is that there is currently no consensus on professional preparation for persons appointed to these roles, nor is there any common pathway to the profession. A Canadian-led international project researching "Pathways to the Profession" confirmed that educational developers come from all academic disciplines and that what led them to become involved has often been serendipitous events and key influential people who have supported them early in their careers (Gosling, McDonald, & Stockley, 2007). Chism (2008) found in a recent study that the proportion of educational developers who assumed their first development position with prior experience in educational development was highest in Australia and Canada (70 percent) and lowest in the United Kingdom and the United States (44 percent). She found that it is not uncommon for some individuals to be appointed to educational development positions from outside of higher education—particularly from precollegiate settings. The practice of hiring a sole practitioner as a director of faculty development without that person's ever having served as a staff member of an EDC seems to be much more common in North America than elsewhere.

International Professional Associations

Educational development abroad has generated a wealth of resources for exchange of scholarship and practices. Many of these activities are led by professional associations. The main organization that brings together members of professional associations for faculty developers around the world is the International Consortium for Educational Development (ICED). Presently, more than twenty associations are represented on the ICED Council, which meets yearly. These include organizations from Australasia, Belgium, Canada, Croatia, Denmark, Ethiopia, Finland, Germany, India, Ireland, Israel, the Netherlands, Norway, Russia, Slovenia, South Africa, Spain, Sri Lanka, Sweden, Switzerland, Thailand, the United Kingdom, and the United States. ICED also sponsors an international conference for developers every other year and is the home of the *International Journal for Academic Development*. Francophone countries have a separate tradition and are represented by the Association Internationale de Pédagogie Universitaire through three "zones," L'Europe, L'Ameriques, and L'Afrique.

The largest national professional associations are in the English-speaking countries of Australia, Canada, the United Kingdom, and the United States. A recent comparison of the work of these organizations (Seubka, Luksaneeyanawin, Tongroach, & Thipakorn, 2008) categorized their main activities as advocacy, publications, networking, member professional development, promotion of the scholarship of educational development, and awards.

The associations differ in their relationship with policymakers in their respective countries; those in countries with strong central control of higher education tend to work with governmental agencies, while those in countries where universities are more autonomous do not have these links. The associations frequently sponsor conferences, workshops, and institutes as key networking venues; some use electronic means, such as electronic lists, as well. They sponsor newsletters, journals, papers, and guides to practice or college teaching such as the *Guides* of the Higher Education Research and Development Society of Australasia (HERDSA), the Staff and Educational Development Association's Papers in the United Kingdom (SEDA), the *Green Guides* of the Society for Teaching and Learning in Higher Education (STLHE) in Canada, and the *Essays on Teaching Excellence* and the annual monograph *To Improve the Academy* published by the Professional and Organizational Development (POD) Network in the United States.

In addition to conferences and print or electronic approaches to the professional development of their members, some organizations have developed credentialing schemes, such as the fellowships program originated by the Staff and Educational Development Association (SEDA) in the United Kingdom. As part of this program, members submit portfolios documenting their work in order to apply for certification. This model is being emulated in Sweden. The scholarship of educational development is supported by several associations in the form of small grants for research as well as through dialogue and dissemination at conferences and in journals. Collaboration with the International Society for the Scholarship of Teaching and Learning (ISSoTL) supports this work. Finally, to highlight and recognize the work of developers, associations maintain awards programs.

International Conferences for Developers

Major conferences for developers are sponsored by the professional associations. As mentioned earlier, ICED sponsors international meetings every other year. These have been held in the United Kingdom, the United States, Finland, Canada, Australia, and Germany. Parallel offerings to the annual meeting of the U.S.-based POD Network are several large conferences from associations outside the United States, such as those sponsored by AIPU (May), STLHE (June), HERDSA (July), and SEDA (November). In addition to conferences specifically for developers, there are many international conferences on teaching and learning, such as the Improving University Teaching Conference sponsored by the University of West Florida and Pace University, the International Lilly Teaching Conference sponsored by Miami University of Ohio, and the Improving Student Learning Conference sponsored by Oxford Brookes University. These conferences address teaching and learning issues while an impressive array of other conferences take a discipline-specific view. A helpful posting of these events, called Teaching and Learning Conferences Worldwide, can be found at http://www.conferencealerts.com/school.htm.

International Journals for Developers

The publication of the first issue of the *International Journal for Academic Development (IJAD)* in 1995 was a milestone for cross-country dialogue on development issues. It has been joined by the *International Journal of Educational Development*. Several of the associations in countries outside North America have strong journals. Within the broader area of college teaching and learning, there are many more journals of international scope. Several come from faculty development associations; others are issued by institutions or commercial publishers. These journals are listed in the Appendix to this chapter.

Although the structures, approaches, and literature related to faculty development and postsecondary institutions vary considerably around the world, the number of common issues, conditions, and areas of inquiry that exist suggest that collaboration and increased interaction show exceptional promise for mutual benefit across national lines. The following section of this chapter discusses opportunities for professional exchange and practice.

Engaging in Faculty Development on an International Scale

North American educational developers can take advantage of working with colleagues in other countries through either traveling abroad as a visiting consultant or becoming involved in collaborative projects beyond the boundaries of North America. Without even traveling, developers can host visiting international developers or invite them to participate in projects initiated by their own institutions by using distance communication.

Working with Colleagues in International Settings

Conducting an effective international consultation or presentation consists of three steps: (1) careful planning and preparation, (2) on-site practices, and (3) postconsultation review and follow-up. Each consultation requires a good knowledge base about the host country prior to a visit. Consulting Web sites, travel guides, and colleagues who have worked abroad are helpful ways for learning what to anticipate and how to prepare. Most important, developers planning visits should communicate with hosts by phone and e-mail beforehand with the goal of adapting the presentation, handouts, or other materials so that they are appropriate and meet local needs. While North American developers are bringing experience and ideas to an international faculty, they also need to appreciate the knowledge, skills, and attitudes that international colleagues bring to the table.

While in the host country, the essential task for developers is to remain flexible and adaptable to local needs rather than assume that U.S. faculty development models or practices will transfer seamlessly. Short-term consultations are challenging in terms of long-term sustainability. It is helpful to frame the visit as one that will begin a longer-term conversation and the building of local capacity rather than one in which the developer simply presents materials and departs.

Hosting International Colleagues

In addition to traveling to other countries or participating in projects organized by international colleagues, North American developers can invite them to visit, be in residence, or collaborate from a distance on development or research projects. Networks such as ICED can help to link needs with the names of experts; reading international journals and attending conferences can also help to establish contact with colleagues who might be invited.

Hosting an international visit usually takes significantly more preparation than making arrangements for national colleagues. It may involve lags in communication due to language difficulties, time zone differences, or lack of similar technology. Preparations involve looking into travel documents; working with foreign agencies; and making arrangements for transportation, housing, medical care, and other essentials when long-term visits are being planned.

Once on campus, international visitors will need work space (particularly for long-term stays), clerical support, and connection to the campus computing and library systems. Hosts will need to work with visitors to outline expectations for what they will accomplish and how they will contribute to the work of the development unit. Although it takes some energy to make these arrangements, the presence of an international developer can be extremely enriching, generating ideas for projects and fresh insights on the work of development.

Collaborating on Development or Research Projects

Faculty developers may gain much by collaborating with international colleagues on development or research projects. Joint development is quite likely to add richness to the final product but also is more efficient than separate undertakings. Engaging in international research has several special advantages. Such research is usually regarded as prestigious and provides an opportunity to demonstrate the consistency of findings in diverse contexts. Comparative studies may also increase the potential audience for a research project and achieve diverse perspectives through the inclusion of a study-respondent pool of faculty members or developers from more than one country. Having international research collaborators may enhance the research by bringing multiple theoretical perspectives to the design and analysis tasks.

A first step in conducting international projects or scholarship is to locate collaborators. North American developers may find partners through preliminary literature reviews that identify scholars interested in the topic at hand as well as through attending conferences, browsing Web sites, or reviewing electronic lists of professional associations. Once developers have identified international colleagues with similar interests, they can write to these colleagues directly but must keep in mind the reality that project work requires sensitivity and tact, a sense of common purpose, and openness to alternative approaches. It is helpful to prepare a brief description of the proposed project or research study, identifying the problem and anticipated methods broadly to allow for later modification. Ideas for funding agencies or publication outlets for the proposed work will enhance interest.

National professional associations can help to add an international dimension to study populations. While the size and quality of membership lists vary across organizations, most have e-mail distribution lists of members or can forward a request for participants through their member communications networks. Several challenges may arise. One of these is the ability to calculate response rates for survey research since open invitations to participate reach unknown numbers of people. Another is language difference, which may preclude people with limited English proficiency from participation unless survey instruments or interview protocols are available in translation. Special terminology may be misunderstood or may prevent respondents from continuing to participate in a research project. International collaborators may also find that people may be unwilling or reluctant to take part in research being conducted from an institution outside their own country. It is therefore valuable, and sometimes essential, to have the support or endorsement of an individual or organization within the country where the research is taking place. A third challenge is navigating the human subjects agencies in multiple environments, particularly when coresearchers are from institutions in countries where conventions might differ. Additionally, interpreting data across contexts can pose challenges, especially when respondents use terms or refer to people or agencies that are unfamiliar to the researchers.

The Internet can serve as an important resource for conducting cross-country research. The use of commercial survey tools such as SurveyMonkey or Zoomerang enables fast and reliable collection of opinions from around the world. In addition, Web-based communication tools, such as Skype and Adobe Connect, can be used for interviews and focus groups involving populations around the globe. These tools reduce cost and extend the range of communication quite conveniently.

Funding International Development or Scholarship

The current interest in the reconceptualization and expansion of higher education around the world makes this an ideal time to seek funding for international projects. International agencies such as the World

Bank and several agencies within the United Nations frequently fund projects toward the improvement of higher education around the world. International foundations have established programs aimed at the advancement of education, particularly for collaborations with colleagues in developing countries. The Partnership for Higher Education in Africa, for example, combines the resources of such prominent foundations as the Ford Foundation, Carnegie Corporation of New York, and the Rockefeller Foundation to fund promising efforts in Africa. The U.S. Fulbright Scholars program provides grants for research and teaching in countries throughout the world. U.S. agencies such as USAID and the Department of Education fund large collaborations between U.S. researchers and developers and their international colleagues. Large Washington, D.C., consulting firms, such as the Academy for Educational Development, Center for Academic Partnerships, and World Learning for International Development, often seek consultants to assist with their projects or subcontract with individuals and agencies to accomplish pieces of larger projects. The Consortium of North American Higher Education Collaboration funds programs for North American mobility in higher education, assisting with collaborations between and among Mexico, Canada, and the United States. In the United States, resources that are used routinely to identify funding sources such as the Community of Science and Grants.gov also allow one to specify international research and development efforts in funding searches. Since the university systems in many countries are highly controlled by the central government, government agencies in each country, or partnerships across countries, such as SEAMEO (Southeast Asian Ministers of Education Organization), can be good resources for research and development efforts, although a clear connection with lead colleagues in the country or region would have to be evident in any proposal. Not to be overlooked are grants from one's own institution, such as those issued by an internal grants competition for international scholarship. Establishment of a funding partnership between two institutions, one in North America and the other abroad, is a way of obtaining resources needed for a research or development project. Resources may be in-kind, such as faculty exchanges, or use of equipment or support staff as well as special funds.

Funding agencies usually request a letter of inquiry describing the proposed project, its significance, and the funding level sought. It is important in any fundraising activity to provide assurance of true collaboration with specific international colleagues who have local knowledge of the country or region involved. A record of previous international work and spirit of respect for the reciprocal nature of the work involved are very important assets to communicate. Although agencies are inundated with letters of inquiry, their staff members usually follow up within a reasonable amount of time. Scholars and developers proposing projects that have some appeal are asked to submit a more detailed proposal according to the parameters and procedures of the organization.

It is important when proposing a research or development project that the support services needed to accomplish the project are in place at one's own institution. Making complicated travel arrangements, communicating between countries, and keeping detailed fiscal records all take significant amounts of time that detract from the researchers' focus on the project itself if a good support system is not in place.

Conclusion

Fortunately, increased communication and collaboration among faculty developers is happening at a time when the need for faculty development is escalating and the globalization of postsecondary education is advancing. Developers are learning more about the similarities and differences across their institutions and practice, undertaking joint work, arranging reciprocal visits, and expanding the range of literature they read. This energy and these insights will help to shape higher education in the future.

Appendix

SELECTED LIST OF INTERNATIONAL JOURNALS ON FACULTY DEVELOPMENT OR POSTSECONDARY TEACHING AND LEARNING

Brookes Ejournal of Learning and Teaching (http://bejlt.brookes .ac.uk/)

College Teaching (Heldref)

Higher Education (Springer)

Higher Education Research and Development (HERDSA)

The Innovations in Education and Teaching International Journal (SEDA)

Innovative Higher Education (Springer; http://www.uga.edu/ihe/ihe.html)

International Journal for the Scholarship of Teaching and Learning (Georgia Southern University)

All Ireland Journal of Teaching and Learning in Higher Education (All Ireland Society for Higher Education, or AISHE)

The Journal of Faculty Development

Journal of University Teaching and Learning Practice (University of Woolongong)

The Journal on Excellence in College Teaching and Learning (Miami University)

Studies in Graduate Teaching Assistant Development

Studies in Higher Education (Routledge)

Teaching in Higher Education (Routledge)

ThaiPOD journal (Thailand Professional and Organizational Development Network)

REFERENCES

Angelo, T. A., & Cross, P. K. (1993). *Classroom assessment techniques: A handbook for college teachers.* San Francisco: Jossey-Bass.

Barnett, R. (1997). *Higher education: A critical business.* Buckingham, UK: SRHE/Open University.

Barnett, R. (2000). *Realizing the university in an age of supercomplexity.* Buckingham, UK: SRHE/Open University.

Barr, R. B., & Tagg, J. (1995). From teaching to learning: A new paradigm for undergraduate education. *Change, 27*(6), 13–25.

Biggs, J. (2003). *Teaching for quality learning at university: What the student does* (2nd ed.). Buckingham, UK: SRHE/Open University Press.

Boyer, E. (1990). *Scholarship reconsidered: Priorities of the professoriate.* Princeton, NJ: Carnegie Foundation for the Advancement of Teaching.

Chism, N.V.N. (2008, April). *A professional priority: Preparing educational developers.* Paper presented at the annual meeting of the American Educational Research Association, New York, NY.

D'Andrea, V-M., & Gosling, D. (2005), *Improving teaching and learning in higher education: A whole institution approach.* London: McGraw-Hill.

Entwistle, N., & Ramsden, P. (1983). *Understanding student learning.* London: Croom Helm.

Gibbs, G. (1992). *Improving the quality of student learning.* Bristol, UK: Technical and Educational Services.

Gosling, D. (2008). *Educational development in the UK.* London: Heads of Educational Development Group.

Gosling, D., McDonald, J., & Stockley, D. (2007). We did it our way! Narratives of pathways to the profession of educational development. *Educational Developments, 8*(4), 1–6.

Huber, M. (2006). Disciplines, pedagogy, and inquiry-based learning about teaching. In C. Kreber (Ed.), *New directions for teaching and learning, no. 107. Exploring research-based teaching* (pp. 69–78). San Francisco: Jossey-Bass.

Hutchings, P. (Ed.). (2000). *Opening lines: Approaches to the scholarship of teaching and learning.* Palo Alto, CA: Carnegie Foundation for the Advancement of Teaching.

Knight, P., & Trowler, P. R. (2001). *Departmental leadership in higher education.* Buckingham, UK: SRHE/Open University.

Marton, F., & Saljo, R. (1976). On qualitative differences in learning: Outcome and process. *British Journal of Educational Psychology, 46*(1), 4–11.

McKeachie, W. J., & Svinicki, M. D. (2005). *Teaching tips* (12th ed.). New York: Houghton Mifflin.

Newman, F., Couturier, L., & Scurry, J. (2004). *The future of higher education: Rhetoric, reality, and the risks of the market.* San Francisco: Jossey-Bass.

Prosser, M., & Trigwell, K. (1999). *Understanding learning and teaching: The experience in higher education.* Buckingham, UK: SRHE/Open University Press.

Ramsden, P. (2003). *Learning to teach in higher education* (2nd ed.). London: Routledge Falmer.

Rowland, S. (2000). *The enquiring university teacher.* Buckingham, UK: SRHE/ Open University Press.

Roxa, T., & Martensson, K. (2008). Strategic educational development: A national Swedish initiative to support change in higher education. *Higher Education Research and Development, 27*(2), 155–68.

Seubka, P., Luksaneeyanawin, S., Tongroach, C., & Thipakorn, B. (2008, June). *Professional development associations around the world: How can they support their members and the global scholarship of practice?* Paper presented at the annual meeting of the International Consortium for Educational Development, Salt Lake City, UT.

Shulman, L. S. (1993). Teaching as community property: Putting an end to pedagogical solitude. *Change, 25*(6), 6–7.

Shulman, L. S. (1999). Taking learning seriously. *Change, 31*(4), 11–17.

Sorcinelli, M. D., Austin, A. E., Eddy, P. L., & Beach, A. L. (2006). *Creating the future of faculty development: Learning from the past, understanding the present.* Bolton, MA: Anker.

Tinto, V. (1993). *Leaving college: Rethinking the causes and cures of student attrition* (2nd ed.). Chicago: University of Chicago Press.

16

ISSUES IN TECHNOLOGY AND FACULTY DEVELOPMENT

Sally Kuhlenschmidt

THOUGHTFUL APPLICATION OF TECHNOLOGY tools is essential to surviving and prospering in higher education today. According to a survey of faculty developers (Sorcinelli, Austin, Eddy, & Beach, 2006, p. 189), one of the top three challenges that faculty members encounter is the integration of technology into traditional teaching and learning. Thus, issues in technology are a priority for those working in faculty development. Technology falls into categories ranging from simple document preparation to collaboration tools, from equipment used in a classroom to software that enables Internet-based education. Although the tools are new, the criteria for success are familiar. The type of technology that is best for teaching and learning depends on the population affected and the objectives of the task, just as the selection of a teaching approach depends on the types of students and the learning objectives. The primary goal is to fulfill the learning objectives, calling upon technology when and if it provides more benefit than cost in achieving those objectives.

Faculty developers face four tasks in effectively using technology in their work. The first task is understanding faculty members' attitudes toward technology. The second is choosing appropriate technology. The third is using knowledge of clients and objectives to help faculty members integrate technology with teaching. The fourth is implementing appropriate technology for the various programs and goals of faculty development centers.

Faculty Members' Response to Technology

Understanding the attitudes of faculty members toward technology aids the developer in formulating advice, choosing an appropriate technology, and selecting faculty members to lead development activities. The general framework of Rogers's (1962, 2003) model of response to innovation is helpful in conceptualizing an instructor's values regarding technology. The model suggests four responses to technology from the most open attitude to the least: explorer, pioneer, settler, and "those who stay back East." The terms used here (*explorer, pioneer, settler,* and *those who stay back East*) are not Rogers's but are variously attributed to R. Clemmons (personal communication, February 13, 1999) or T. Rocklin (personal communication, March 8, 1999). The terms are less pejorative and more memorable than Rogers's language, but Rogers's terms (*innovator, early adopter, late adopter,* and *laggard*) are included for those familiar with his model. All of these labels are exaggerations and do not fit any given individual perfectly. Indeed, individuals may move across the categories for different types of innovations over the course of their careers.

Explorers, also known as "innovators," in Rogers's terminology, are interested in technology for the sake of technology and the pleasure of risk. They happily suffer the difficulties in adopting a tool, especially if it means they know something others do not. Because they prefer to learn on their own, they rarely attend development seminars. The major challenge in working with explorers is helping them to communicate with others without being intimidating and to connect technology to instructionally meaningful objectives. Explorers may make poor seminar leaders for other faculty members because of their strong personal investment in technology, their failure to communicate their critical reflection on technology, and their use of highly technical language. Although they are less likely to seek training on technology, if in a training situation, explorers will be impatient with instruction and will choose to follow their own paths.

Pioneers, or "early adopters" using Rogers's (2003) term, are typically second in adopting a technology because they wait until they understand and can make good decisions about the tool. They are generally opinion leaders, and they can either encourage or block dissemination. The pioneer is able to integrate new technology into preexisting knowledge easily and independently but will also attend seminars. Pioneers are generally the easiest persons with whom to work, and they usually make good seminar leaders because they will explain when and why a technology might be used as well as address its limitations.

Settlers (late adopters), about 60 or 70 percent of the faculty (Rogers, 2003), are only interested in a technology to the extent it helps students learn or achieves a particular disciplinary goal, such as increasing majors. They derive little pleasure from experimenting and want a technology that works with minimum effort. Settlers generally prefer learning with and from others, at least initially; but they will also want time alone to consider a tool for their particular goals. They can make very good seminar leaders as they are most similar to the typical audience, just wanting a technology support person available. When working individually with settlers, the developer needs to break a technology task into steps, preferably with a handout. Often settlers will want to explain their worries and what is important to them in teaching. The settler may need to be encouraged to manipulate the technology directly rather than passively watch the developer using the tool.

Finally, the ones who "stay back East," known as "laggards" in Rogers's (2003) model, fall into two groups: one successful and the other in crisis. The successful, or comfortable, ones genuinely have no need for a new technology because they feel successful in their current approaches. They value what has worked in the past and often consider themselves guardians of that which time has demonstrated to be of value. Convincing them to use a tool minimally requires explaining how the technology upholds a traditional value. For this group, making a technology look similar to something else they have done may be helpful. Examples include substituting icons for technical words, beginning a training session in a room other than a computer lab, moving to the computers only when necessary, or emphasizing a similarity to a software program with which they are familiar. This population is one for which it is difficult to predict outcomes. If they come to a development event, they may never revisit the tool; or they may become an expert because the technology meshed with a need they have. They learn best in groups from settlers, who share values with them, or in one-on-one sessions with the developer for time efficiency.

The other subset of the ones who "stay back East" are persons in the midst of a major crisis, such as a health problem, and have no energy or time to devote to the implementation of technology. Obviously, the developer should find the simplest, quickest solution for this group, one not necessarily involving technology.

Developers will also fit these categories. Developers who are explorers may need to verbalize their critical reflections, monitor their level of language, or find an intermediary to work directly with faculty members. The pioneer is probably best suited to development activities. Both of these groups naturally acquire technology skills because of personal interest. Developers who are settlers will favor enabling faculty members to share technology skills rather than doing the instruction themselves. Their challenge is to acquire an understanding and confidence in technology even if they do not have the inclination to develop the skills. This can be accomplished by learning key vocabulary and briefly testing a few new tools (for more ideas, see Kuhlenschmidt, 1997). The settler needs to have the courage to advocate for learning-friendly technologies in the face of explorer dominance. They should remember that they represent the mainstream and that the technology is serving their needs. Returning conversation to the basic goals is a powerful tool. Developers who "stay back East" out of respect for traditional values need to guard against becoming irrelevant as the majority gradually adopts technologies. Rogers's (2003) work on the adoption of innovation found that this group tended to become the most impoverished because they resisted change for too long. They need to realize that one can accept new tools and integrate them with old values. It is better to be driving the technology conversation than to be left out of it. They also can acquire the vocabulary of technology by listening, reading, and devoting a short time each week to try a new tool enough to understand the highlights. Developers who are "staying back East" for reasons of personal crisis should delegate technology issues to someone who has the resources to investigate issues. This developer can still use facilitation skills to enable others to discuss technologies analytically.

How to Evaluate Technologies

The number of technological tools can be overwhelming; yet often developers must make recommendations, or even choices on purchasing, for faculty members and for their own centers. Fortunately, when viewed from the perspective of familiar tools, the task is not overwhelming. For example, evaluating the effectiveness of a pen is accomplished easily. The bottom line is the pen has to produce a readable mark, be easy to use, be comfortable when held, require little effort to learn to use it, work reliably, and be adaptable to different goals. Sometimes that instrument may just be enjoyable to have.

When faced with a new technology, the developer should ask questions such as the following.

- ○ What is the purpose of the task for which the technology is being considered? Often a technology is seen as a solution before the problem is clearly understood. Ask faculty members what they want to accomplish, independently of the tool, and what learning will result from using the tool. Will a technology encourage active learning?
- ○ How well does the tool fit into the learning or strategic goals for the person or unit? Does the technology invite avoidance of tasks that must be done for instruction or promotion and tenure?

○ Is this tool part of a set of skills that will serve the user for years? Because much of work depends on relationships with others, key technologies are ones that connect people to people (for example, cell phones and e-mail).

○ Relative to the amount of time and effort the technology will take to learn and use, what is the return on that investment? Will it encourage more learning than do current methods? Will the novelty of the tool improve student motivation for at least a while?

○ Does the technology require maintenance? Is there a support staff or the time to manage maintenance? How soon will the tool become unusable due to typical rates of change?

○ Can a simpler technology provide a reasonable substitute? Will a pencil work?

○ Does the technology impede learning for any group? Persons with disabilities cannot access some delivery modalities. Can accommodations for those with disabilities be made easily or built in from the start?

Even though answers to the above questions may suggest the technology is not an optimal strategy, is there still interest in learning the tool? Learning a technology for pleasure or because it is popular is fine as long as time and energy are available and the tool does not interfere with the main goals.

Integrating Technology into Teaching

Faculty members face four challenges in effectively integrating technology into their teaching. They need to (1) remain current in their instructional content, (2) have knowledge of instructional design, (3) understand the technology—its strengths and weaknesses, and also (4) have the perspective necessary to integrate the three areas. The role of the faculty developer is to provide guidance in the instructional design process and knowledge of the technology, including recognizing when a tool is not likely to contribute to the faculty member's goals. The developer must be able to guide the faculty member in connecting the use of technology to learning principles (Chickering & Ehrmann, 1996).

Consultation on technology follows the same principles as consultation about nontechnological approaches for enhancement of teaching. The developer starts with the learning objectives and an assessment of the instructional strategies the faculty member uses, the instructor's values, and the types of students involved. All subsequent decisions follow from these factors. Ideally the developer defines the learning problem and suggests solutions, which may or may not include technology. Common errors of those involved include assuming a technology is necessary, reconstructing the teaching problem to fit a favored technology, or avoiding appropriate technology.

During the consultation process, the developer should evaluate the instructor's comfort level and skill with technology. The developer may ask how the instructor has used technology or what is the most complex task done with any sort of technology. Specific suggestions should be offered only after the instructor's learning objectives, types of students, and approach to technology are clarified. If the developer accepts the instructor's expectation that a particular technology is the answer, then, unfortunately, problem solving ends. The developer should determine how and why that tool was selected.

Examples of Technologies for Key Learning Goals

In the study by Sorcinelli et al. (2006), faculty developers identified four areas of focus with regard to technology: (1) use of technology to develop content knowledge, (2) digital information literacy, (3) using technology to develop problem-solving skills, and (4) using it to build connections between students via learning communities. I believe that a fifth area—the ethical and legal use of technology—is also critical in the successful use of technologies.

USING TECHNOLOGY TO DEVELOP CONTENT KNOWLEDGE AND DIGITAL INFORMATION LITERACY. Apart from ubiquitous searching of the Internet, technology is now a component of nearly all academic disciplines. Faculty developers cannot be conversant in all uses, but they can listen carefully to special concerns and advocate for faculty members with those who do technology support, explaining how a particular tool may be important for teaching in a discipline. Another key developer role is helping faculty members connect new tools to learning objectives so that students derive the intended benefit. Developers can also assist with enhancement of content knowledge by being willing to seek out resources for a discipline, for example, TeacherTube videos (TeacherTube, 2008) or other rich Web sites, such as MERLOT (2009), that offer videos, games, templates, and demonstrations.

The first focus area, developing content knowledge, is intimately tied to the second, information literacy. In an era when anyone can access information via search engines, the most important skill is sifting the good from the bad. A common instructional technique for enhancing students' digital information literacy is critical reflection on Web sites. Faculty members may have students review YouTube videos (2005) that illustrate content and evaluate posted reviewer comments to build analytical thinking. Global newspapers are easily accessible online, and comparing points of view builds international awareness. (Visit Kuhlenschmidt, 2007b, for a list of English-language newspapers.) Developers can help faculty members share their discipline-specific strategies through seminars, newsletter articles, or special events focusing on a cluster of disciplines.

USING TECHNOLOGY TO DEVELOP PROBLEM-SOLVING SKILLS. Specific problem-solving skills vary by discipline, but technology for general skills can serve as a model for discipline skills. Digital literacy training provides some support for critical thinking, but dialogue and method of instruction are most important. Technology tools such as e-mail and electronic mailing lists, discussion boards, chat rooms, blogs, wikis, instant messaging, and cell phones are possible venues for educational dialogue. For example, cell phones may be used to replace the clickers in personal response systems; instructors may deliver course content and discussion via Internet connections over cell phones. PowerPoint (Active Learning with Power-Point, 2008) or Quandary (Arneil, Holmes, & the University of Victoria, 2008b) can be used to encourage critical thinking. With these tools the instructor creates branching stories with a choice of actions. Students can then explore options to deepen their understanding of issues. Instructor- or student-created stories can be uploaded to Blackboard or an instructor Web site. Another option for developing scenarios that illustrate complex processes is to use interactive spreadsheets (Sinex, 2008). Students can alter different values to see the effect on outcomes. Faculty developers can identify and promote tools to encourage active learning and provide training and help faculty members share their innovative ideas.

Simulations offer real-world practice; and, although they can be done without technology, the use of real-world technology and multimedia can make them richer and more motivating for students if time and resources are available (Aldrich, 2005). Minimally, instructors can give students access to widely used software tools, such as MSOffice, to tackle professional tasks such as document creation, data collection and analysis, or collaboration. Developers can help faculty members conceptualize simulations and consider issues such as incorporating the accommodations that must be made for students with disabilities. For more complex tools, such as Second Life (Linden Research, 2008), a developer can build a learning community for faculty members who are using the tool.

USING TECHNOLOGY TO BUILD CONNECTIONS AMONG STUDENTS. Too often technology separates students, but it can be used to make connections. To encourage collaboration, student groups can share a computer and use wikis and Google Documents to exchange materials they are creating together. Del.icio.us (del.icio.us: social bookmarking, n.d.) is a social bookmarking site on which students can pool annotations on Web sites. Course management software, such as Blackboard or Moodle, provides rooms for group discussion. Facebook and MySpace could be adapted to building connections among learners in a discipline or course. Of course, these same tools can be used for faculty-student interactions and for faculty-developer interactions. As for other technologies, the developer can provide evaluation and training on the appropriate use of the tools in instruction, particularly with regard to legal and privacy issues.

ETHICAL AND LEGAL USE OF TECHNOLOGY. Faculty developers can and should have a strong impact in the area of ethical and legal issues in technology. We have a responsibility to keep abreast of concerns, infuse them into training, and encourage faculty members by organizing discussions around key issues. The major areas to monitor are academic integrity, intellectual property (including records management), accessibility for persons with disabilities, and privacy of student information. The developer unacquainted with these topics may solicit faculty members who have such knowledge to serve on panels and initiate the institutional discussion. The Custom Search Engine of the Professional and Organizational Development Network in Higher Education (POD; Professional and Organizational Development Network in Higher Education, 2007a) can be a source of reliable information on these as well as other development topics. This is a tool that searches only POD member Web sites. Consequently, each search will produce information immediately pertinent to development in higher education.

Teaching and Assessment

ASSESSMENT OF LEARNING. Technology is ideally suited to assessment. Within the classroom, the use of personal response systems, or clickers, provides students with immediate feedback. Instructors can use these devices in active ways that increase student engagement (Kuhlenschmidt, 2007a). Software such as StudyMate (StudyMate Author 2.0, 2000) or HotPotatoes (Arneil, Holmes, & the University of Victoria, 2008a) can easily create online quizzes. Although the immediate feedback can be a powerful tool to help students learn basic vocabulary, training is needed to help instructors create quizzes that are more than drills on lower levels of learning. Quandary can be used (Arneil et al., 2008b) to devise higher-level learning challenges.

With the course management system Blackboard, instructors can use the adaptive release feature to reveal extra lessons to students who perform below a cutoff standard or not to release advanced material until students learn the earlier material. These tools enable offering self-paced, mastery learning courses. Some student-centered learning assessment tools are available online, such as the Student Assessment of Their Learning Gains (Carroll, Seymour, & Weston, 2007).

EVALUATION OF INSTRUCTORS. A few online tools can aid in self-assessment of teaching. The Teaching Goals Inventory (Angelo & Cross, 1993) is available and can assist faculty members in identifying their goals prior to selecting a teaching method. The Teaching Perspectives Inventory is another online self-evaluation tool (Pratt & Collins, 2001). Teaching portfolios are a popular method of development, and a natural outgrowth has been electronic portfolios used for formative purposes (Cambridge, Kahn, Tompkins, & Yancey, 2001).

Student ratings are an ongoing issue for assessing teaching. In the past few years tremendous interest has developed in moving them online to save money and processing time. The challenge is motivating students to complete the ratings. As of fall 2009, no universal, successful approach for doing so has yet emerged. Another issue for developers is whether to use in consultations information about instructors that is available via the Internet, such as student-run ratings Web sites (Profeval, 2007) or social networking sites. Developers need to consider and discuss how to address these alternative sources of information about clients and the ethics of using them.

An important consideration when determining what level of technology to use is how that use will be viewed by the faculty member's chain of command for the purposes of promotion and tenure. Sometimes a faculty member can satisfy research requirements by publishing on technological applications to teaching, but some disciplines do not find that acceptable. The faculty developer should advise the faculty person to consult with senior faculty members in their department on how technology use for teaching is viewed in the promotion and tenure review process.

For instructors teaching online, a significant development is the creation of Quality Matters (QM), a national course-design peer-review system (Maryland Online, 2006). QM was started in 2003 by Maryland Online with a grant from the Fund for the Improvement of Postsecondary Education. The program provides peer review of the design (not delivery) of online courses for purposes of recognition, promotion, and tenure. The system is analogous to peer review of journal articles.

Technology for Faculty Developers

There are two broad areas in which a faculty development unit may use technology for its own goals: (a) for development activities and (b) for the administrative work of faculty development and faculty developers.

Faculty Development Activities

Developers should first consider their target populations and the objectives of their programs and then decide if a technology will advance their mission. Any center will have several populations to serve, with conflicting needs. A technological innovation may lead the institution in a desired direction but intimidate a target group. A Web site that is rarely used by faculty members may still be an important tool for staff or for establishing a reputation. The center can choose only a best, not a perfect, direction. Developers should assess their goals and make data-based decisions for any technology requiring time, resources, and maintenance. The evaluation criteria mentioned earlier also apply to center technology. At a minimum, to avoid embarrassment, center staff members need to be conversant in the basic technology tools used by most faculty members.

Technology does not have to be complex to be used effectively. Keeping an e-mail list of special interest groups and periodically sending a note to them is effective. An e-mail message may be the best option for reaching overwhelmed, new faculty members. Another simple action is to use an e-mail signature line that markets the center; adding a teaching quote is a subtle outreach. Developers can visit http://www.wku.edu/teaching/db/quotes/ for a large collection of quotes pertinent to college instruction (Kuhlenschmidt, 2008).

Any delivery system used for instruction can also be used for development and provides an opportunity to model thoughtful use of technologies such as Blackboard, electronic mailing lists, and Web pages. If an objective is to reach out to all instructors, developers can offer seminars via a variety of channels such as interactive television, e-mail, or the Web. These modalities may be favored by part-time faculty members and others with full schedules who cannot attend a face-to-face seminar. They also offer the option of partnering with other centers, nationally and internationally, to broaden the teaching perspectives of local faculty members. It is best to keep first attempts simple—text posted to a Web site following a template (for example, Teaching Issues Online Workshop Series, 2007). Discussion can be conducted using an electronic mailing list. A course management system may be available for seminars.

The center Web site can be an important source of just-in-time information for busy professionals if it is organized using faculty rather than developer language. One of the best sources for Web usability information is http://www.useit.com/ (Nielsen, 2008). For example, to help search engines locate information on a site, each Web page needs a title specific to its particular content.

Newsletters, a common center product, sent via e-mail can save money and provide a way of tracking recipients. However, an e-mail newsletter can be easily deleted or automatically filtered and never viewed. A few centers have experimented with providing Podcasting (for example, Center for Teaching, 2008), or streaming video seminars (for example, Zakrajsek, 2007). Online videos should be only a few minutes long and model good teaching practices, incorporating active learning. A video combined with a blog will be more interactive and provide assessment information.

If a center has the budget, some development activities could be outsourced. Several organizations and businesses, such as Atomic Learning, offer prepackaged online development (Atomic Learning, 2008). However, one must consider how well the activity fits the local situation. Outsourcing may be best suited for generic skills like MS Office.

Finally, a center may be able to loan equipment to faculty members. Having the center purchase a cutting-edge tool and loan it to faculty members is more cost efficient than each department funding a tool that only a few use. As the tool is being loaned, a developer has an opportunity to offer tips on appropriate use of the equipment for instruction. One ongoing challenge for developers is interfacing with information technology units that may also be engaging in development activities. Ideally the developer builds a working relationship with such units.

Administrative Activities

Apart from development activities, a center has administrative tasks to accomplish. Marketing is a critical component of a successful center. Some institutions allow e-mail to all faculty members. A scheduled day and time for announcements is less likely to be annoying than posting announcements at any time. If an institution does not allow free access to an institution-wide announcement, then a center e-mail list is helpful. (See also Chapter Seven, "Promoting Your Program and Grounding It in the Institution.")

The center Web site is an important representation of the center and should reflect the center's values. If scholarship is valued, staff scholarly products should be listed. If collaboration is valued, a page describing collaboration with other units is important. The Web site should provide timely information about events and resources. One can link faculty member reviews of center books to a list of center books. A Web site can provide instructions on making donations following institutional policies. Some centers hesitate to produce a Web site, hoping for the perfect document; but by their very nature Web sites are never complete. Having a minimal Web site is better than none. One solution for centers lacking technology skills is a content management system (CMS) such as Plone (2000), which allows units to create pages by filling in an online form. Some enable interaction, such as blogs or event registration. Offering Web registration for center events is ideal if a center has access to technology support or a CMS with registration tools. A simpler approach is an e-mail link in announcements for a return message requesting registration.

Local news media may lend their technology for publicity. Develop a center program for airing on local television or radio or for streaming via the Internet. Be aware that it takes a high level of skill to compete with other video and radio sources. A center can expend great energy to produce a video only to have it look amateurish and become dated quickly. As with most new technology, it is advisable to keep the first efforts very simple.

Other administrative goals, such as staff communication, can be technologically facilitated. A relatively simple tool often available is a shared drive for the center. An information technology unit can create computer space for documents on a central server. The space may be open for anyone to visit or may be only accessible by center staff. Common center documents (such as consultation templates or seminar planning materials) placed in shared space can be accessed by all members of a unit from their computers. Because technology personnel may have access to the space, it may not be appropriate for confidential materials. Another tool helpful in arranging appointments and meetings is scheduling software. If your institution lacks such software, try Doodle (2008).

The POD Web site has valuable resources for developers (Professional and Organizational Development Network in Higher Education, 2007b). The POD Listserv (Professional and Organizational Development Network in Higher Education, 2007c), with more than 1,200 subscribers, is a source of ideas and networking, and it provides a way of tracking trends. When posting to this list, the convention is to use a specific subject line, such as "PBL ideas" rather than a generic "Help." Regular readers will learn of topics likely to be raised at their institutions.

For graduate student developer needs, the electronic mailing list CTAD@lists.uwaterloo.ca (Holmes, T., & Taraban-Gordon, S., n.d.) has more than 150 members discussing teaching assistant (TA) training issues. The listserv of the Canadian Society for Teaching and Learning in Higher Education (STLHE) (Society for Teaching and Learning in Higher Education, 2008) is for both faculty developers and instructors.

Developers must often present on short notice data about their effectiveness, for tasks from accreditation to justifying existence during budget cuts. A database such as Microsoft Access or FileMakerPro provides continuous access to center data that can be analyzed in a variety of ways to answer changing questions. (See also Chapter Nine, "Program Assessment for Faculty Development.")

Another tool for center assessment is an online survey tool, such as SurveyMonkey (1999), Doodle (2008), or Zoomerang (MarketTools, 1999). These survey tools offer an easy way to solicit information on center programs. Once the data is collected, the Statistical Package for the Social Sciences (SPSS) can be used for quantitative analysis. Atlas.ti or other similar programs may be useful for qualitative analysis. Such tools can also be used to examine the data gathered about or by an individual instructor. However, Excel or a log book and paper and pencil may be satisfactory as well.

Conclusion

The key when working with technologies is starting with the problem to be solved or objective of the task and knowing the capacities of the target audience. Developers are familiar with this key principle from instructional consultations and need only integrate those skills with a working knowledge of technology. Because technology changes rapidly and because those aware of the latest tools generally favor technologies, finding objective reviews of technologies can be challenging. However, judging technologies is within the capacity of any person who uses the evaluation criteria mentioned previously. Whether the technology is hardware, software, or something not yet conceived, developers can approach technology with thoughtfulness, using critical analysis as they would with any teaching tool. No single person can stay current in all technologies, but developers can leverage the people of their institution to analyze new tools. We can guide faculty members to think critically about technology.

Developers can create teams of faculty members to learn together with the expectation that they will report to the rest of campus; encourage scholarly technology reviews, just like book reviews; and build expert evaluators at all levels of innovation adopters. Above all, faculty developers should keep the objective and the population to be served as an uppermost factor in making technology decisions, reflect on the key evaluation questions, and let these considerations drive the technology rather than being driven by the technology.

REFERENCES

Active Learning with PowerPoint™. (2008). Retrieved June 19, 2008, from University of Minnesota, Center for Teaching and Learning Web site at http://www1.umn.edu/ohr/teachlearn/tutorials/powerpoint/

Aldrich, C. (2005). *Learning by doing: A comprehensive guide to simulations, computer games, and pedagogy in e-learning and other educational experiences*. San Francisco: Wiley.

Angelo, T., & Cross, P. (1993). *The Teaching Goals Inventory*. Retrieved June 19, 2008, from University of Iowa, Center for Teaching Web site at http://fm.iowa.uiowa.edu/fmi/xsl/tgi/data_entry.xsl?-db=tgi_data&-lay=Layout01&-view

Arneil, S., Holmes, M., & the University of Victoria. (2008a). HotPotatoes [Computer software]. Victoria, BC, Canada: Half-baked Software, Inc. Retrieved August 3, 2008, from http://www.halfbakedsoftware.com/

Arneil, S., Holmes, M., & the University of Victoria (2008b). Quandary [Computer software]. Victoria, BC, Canada: Half-baked Software, Inc. Retrieved September 14, 2008, from http://www.halfbakedsoftware.com/quandary.php

Atomic Learning, Inc. (2008). *Atomic learning*. Retrieved August 3, 2008, from http://movies.atomiclearning.com/k12/home

Cambridge, B., Kahn, S., Tompkins, D., & Yancey, K. (Eds.). (2001). *Electronic portfolios: Emerging practices in student, faculty, and institutional learning*. Washington, DC: American Association for Higher Education.

Carroll, S., Seymour, E., & Weston, T. (2007). *The student assessment of their learning gains*. Retrieved June 19, 2008, from University of Wisconsin-Madison, Wisconsin Center for Educational Research Web site at http://www.salgsite.org/

Center for Teaching. (2008, July 17). *Vanderbilt Center for Teaching Podcast*. Retrieved August 3, 2008, from Vanderbilt University Web site at http://blogs.vanderbilt.edu/cftpodcast/

Chickering, A., & Ehrmann, S. (1996, October). Implementing the seven principles: Technology as lever. *AAHE Bulletin*, 3–6.

del.icio.us: social bookmarking [Computer software]. (n.d.). Retrieved June 19, 2008, from http://del.icio.us/

Doodle [Computer software]. (2008). Retrieved October 8, 2008, from http://www.doodle.ch/main.html

Holmes, T., & Taraban-Gordon, S. (n.d.). *CTAD—Consortium of TA Developers*. Retrieved August 3, 2008, from University of Waterloo Web site at https://lists.uwaterloo.ca/mailman/listinfo/ctad

Kuhlenschmidt, S. (1997). *Learning how to learn computers: General principles for the novice*. Retrieved October 10, 2008, from Western Kentucky University, Faculty Center for Excellence in Teaching Web site at http://www.wku.edu/teaching/tnt/lrncom.htm

Kuhlenschmidt, S. (2007a). *Clicking with clickers: Questioning effectively*. Retrieved June 19, 2008, from Western Kentucky University, Faculty Center for Excellence in Teaching Web site at http://www.wku.edu/teaching/booklets/clickers.html

Kuhlenschmidt, S. (2007b). *International English-language media for comparison to USA media*. Retrieved June 19, 2008, from Western Kentucky University, Faculty Center for Excellence in Teaching Web site at http://www.wku.edu/teaching/media/reading.html

Kuhlenschmidt, S. (Ed.). (2008). *Quotations for college faculty*. Retrieved June 19, 2008, from Western Kentucky University, Faculty Center for Excellence in Teaching Web site at http://www.wku.edu/teaching/db/quotes/

Linden Research, Inc. (2008). *Second Life*. Retrieved June 19, 2008, from http://secondlife.com/

Maryland Online, Inc. (2006). *Quality Matters*. Retrieved June 29, 2008, from http://www.qualitymatters.org/

MarketTools, Inc. [Computer software]. (1999). Zoomerang. Retrieved January 8, 2009, from Zoomerang Web site at http://www.zoomerang.com/

MERLOT. (2009). *Multimedia Educational Resource for Learning and Online Teaching*. Retrieved June 30, 2009, from MERLOT Web site at www.merlot.org/merlot/

Nielsen, J. (2008). *Useit.com: Jakob Nielsen's Web site*. Retrieved June 19, 2008, from http://www.useit.com/

Plone [Computer software]. (2000). Retrieved August 3, 2008, from http://plone.org/

Pratt, D., & Collins, J. (2001). *Teaching Perspectives Inventory*. Retrieved June 20, 2008, from http://www.teachingperspectives.com/

Professional and Organizational Development Network in Higher Education. (2007a). *POD custom search engine for POD Network faculty development centers*. Retrieved June 19, 2008, from http://www.podnetwork.org/search.htm#faculty

Professional and Organizational Development Network in Higher Education. (2007b). Retrieved June 19, 2008, from http://www.podnetwork.org/

Professional and Organizational Development Network in Higher Education. (2007c). *POD listserv*. Retrieved June 19, 2008, from http://www .podnetwork.org/listserve.htm

Profeval [Computer software]. (2007). Retrieved August 3, 2008, from http:// www.profeval.com/home/chooseschool.asp

Rogers, E. (1962). *Diffusion of innovations* (1st ed.). New York: Free Press.

Rogers, E. (2003). *Diffusion of innovations* (5th ed.). New York: Free Press.

Sinex, S. (2008). *Developers' guide to Excelets*. Retrieved August 3, 2008, from http://academic.pgcc.edu/~ssinex/excelets/

Society for Teaching and Learning in Higher Education. (2008). *STLHE-L@ LISTSERV.UNB.CA: Forum for teaching & learning in higher education*. Retrieved June 19, 2008, from University of New Brunswick, New Brunswick, Canada Web site at http://www.lsoft.com/scripts/wl .exe?SL1=STLHE-L&H=LISTSERV.UNB.CA

Sorcinelli, M. D., Austin, A. E., Eddy, P. L., & Beach, A. L. (2006). *Creating the future of faculty development: Learning from the past, understanding the present*. Bolton, MA: Anker.

StudyMate Author 2.0 [Computer software]. (2000). Redmond, WA: Respondus, Inc. Retrieved October 8, 2008, from http://www.respondus. com/products/studymate.shtml

SurveyMonkey [Computer software]. (1999). Portland, OR: SurveyMonkey .com. Retrieved October 8, 2008, from http://www.surveymonkey.com/

TeacherTube, LLC. (2008). *TeacherTube: Teach the world*. Retrieved June 19, 2008, from http://www.teachertube.com/

Teaching Issues Online Workshop Series. (2007). Retrieved June 19, 2008, from Western Kentucky University, Faculty Center for Excellence in Teaching Web site at http://www.wku.edu/teaching/teachingissues/

YouTube, Inc. (2005). *YouTube*. Retrieved October 8, 2008, from http://www .youtube.com/

Zakrajsek, T. (2007). *Interpreting written feedback from student ratings of instruction*. Retrieved August 3, 2008, from http://www.youtube.com/ watch?v=OTc0WcE8Ab4&feature=user

PART THREE

FACULTY DEVELOPMENT ACROSS INSTITUTIONAL TYPES, CAREER STAGES, AND ORGANIZATIONS

This part of the volume consists of seven chapters that explore educational development in various institutional types, for example, research universities, small colleges, and community colleges; examine ways in which educational developers can support faculty at various stages across their careers; and discuss the vital role that educational developers can play in organizational development at their institutions.

EFFECTIVE PRACTICES AT RESEARCH UNIVERSITIES

THE PRODUCTIVE PAIRING OF RESEARCH
AND TEACHING

Constance Ewing Cook and Michele Marincovich

RESEARCH UNIVERSITIES PRIORITIZE RESEARCH, of course, but teaching excellence is also a priority. Educational development centers often thrive at these institutions. In fact, the proportion of doctoral and research universities (as defined by the 2005 Carnegie Foundation classifications) that have educational development centers is greater than the proportion at other types of higher education institutions. A pilot study found that 65 to 70 percent of doctoral and research universities have a center that offers the faculty support for their teaching (Kuhlenschmidt, 2009).

Besides being the higher education institutions with the largest proportion of centers, research universities were the first to establish them. Founded in 1962, the Center for Research on Learning and Teaching (CRLT) at the University of Michigan was the first educational development center in the United States; Stanford's Center for Teaching and Learning (CTL), established in 1975, was also one of the earliest. Both centers have grown over time and become integral to their universities' support for faculty members, graduate student instructors (GSIs), and curricular reform. The authors' centers have benefited from enlightened university leadership and unusually large resources, but it is clear that certain principles for faculty development at a research institution have also contributed to the success of these centers and those of research university center colleagues at other institutions. What follows is an articulation of these principles that shape what research university teaching center directors do to create and sustain a shift in institutional culture. The strategies are divided into three sections: teaching center mission, leadership guidelines, and faculty development activities. To illustrate these principles, examples are included from a variety of research universities.

Teaching Center Mission

Highlighting Innovation, Not Remediation

The teaching center's mission should be about innovation, not remediation. Prominent faculty members do not think of themselves as deficient in their professional roles, nor should they. Nationwide, nearly 90 percent of faculty members consider their teaching to be above average in effectiveness (Blackburn & Lawrence, 1995; Bok, 2006), and the typical Michigan and Stanford teaching evaluation scores confirm this perception. Especially for research-oriented faculty, talking about special achievement or novel approaches has proven the most effective way of motivating them to improve their teaching.

At the University of Pennsylvania, for example, the Center for Teaching and Learning hosts Faculty-to-Faculty Lunches, during which faculty members lead discussions and teach peers about innovative pedagogical approaches they are using in their own classes. At Harvard University, as part of the new General Education program, the Bok Center for Teaching and Learning has been a central player in assembling and coordinating "SWAT Teams" of support services, with members drawn from instructional computing, student writing programs, and the libraries as well as from the center. The goal of these teams is to help faculty members plan new courses with a full awareness of the pedagogical and institutional resources available for nontraditional teaching methods (for example, approaches other than lectures, labs, and discussion sections) at an early stage of course development.

It is also wise to highlight programs that fit the research culture. Therefore, programs should be focused on cutting-edge research insights, innovative approaches, and emerging issues such as teaching ethics in the professions rather than focusing on more general teaching techniques, a topic that experience has shown tends to have less intellectual appeal for research-oriented faculty members. Studies show that faculty development centers at research universities are more likely than centers at other types of institutions to provide support for faculty members having difficulty, that is, 27 percent of research university respondents versus 17 percent at all types of institutions (Sorcinelli, Austin, Eddy, & Beach, 2006, p. 48). The Michigan and Stanford centers do so as well, but their improvement services are not the ones highlighted in their literature and communications.

Emphasizing the Complementarity of Teaching and Research

In an early classic of the faculty development literature, Ken Eble (1972) noted that teaching and research were pitted against each other on many college campuses, with teaching the inevitable loser. To put teaching in a competition that it cannot win is especially destructive at a research university. Therefore, the close and productive relationship between teaching and research should be emphasized in center programs and literature, along with the recognition of faculty members who use imaginative ways to make these two professional responsibilities mutually reinforcing. The development of undergraduate research opportunities has been especially effective in helping faculty members combine teaching and research. The Teaching and Learning Lab at the Massachusetts Institute of Technology (MIT) is one of the teaching centers that provides pedagogical support to faculty members who oversee undergraduates in their research projects.

Helping Implement the Agenda of the Institution's Leadership

At a research university, resources are more likely to flow to teaching improvement projects if they are associated with research priorities. Because many research university centers are part of the office of the provost or vice president for academic affairs, perhaps reporting to a vice provost, centers can learn early of new initiatives of the provost, president, or trustees and can then align their activities with these initiatives. If center staff members serve on key university committees, they can be prominent campus advocates for the teaching and learning aspects of new initiatives (Sorcinelli, 2002; Wright, 2000). Involvement in university decision-making processes also allows the faculty development center to be proactive, not just reactive (Chism, 1998). For example, when the provost seeks to promote interdisciplinarity, the center can include interdisciplinary teaching as a key component of its programs, publications, and grants.

Over the past decade, to help promote the provost's agenda, Michigan's CRLT has organized semiannual Provost's Seminars on Teaching for invited faculty, hosted by the provost on a topic chosen by her (http://www.crlt .umich.edu/faculty/psot.php). At Harvard, to help implement the institutional commitment to increasing the low rate of internal promotion and tenure, the Bok Center offers a three-day program for new junior faculty. Called the Junior Faculty Institute and held just before the fall semester begins, the program introduces participants to key members of the Harvard teaching community, gives them practice teaching, and offers a syllabus workshop. At Vanderbilt University, in preparation for the reaccreditation process, the Center for Teaching partnered with the provost's office to offer a workshop for department chairs and deans on learning outcomes assessment plans. Center consultants then met with chairs individually on the design of these plans and strategies for implementing them.

Surprisingly, many centers do not effectively align their priorities with those of the institution's academic leadership (Sorcinelli et al., 2006), especially in their early years. A new center may bring faculty members in the door by accepting almost any request for assistance; but, as centers mature, they may find it more strategic to prioritize requests by their relationship to the center's mission and the initiatives of the institution's leadership.

Leadership Guidelines for a Research University Center

Ensuring That the Center Has Faculty-Credible Developers

While the credentials of effective faculty developers vary widely, those on a research campus are likely to find it easier to earn credibility if they have not only faculty development experience but also university teaching experience and doctorates, just like the faculty they serve. Research university centers often have staff whose degrees are in a variety of disciplines, from biology to engineering to German Studies, so that the centers are better positioned to serve the many colleges and departments at their institutions. Faculty in some disciplines, especially science and engineering, seem to respond best to faculty developers with backgrounds in their own fields. Some of the Michigan consultants have responsibilities around specific functions (for example, instructional technology, multicultural teaching and learning, and evaluation research), while others are responsible for disciplinary groupings (for example, the humanities, interdisciplinary programs, or engineering). To ensure high-quality work in the profession of faculty development, as in all professions, it is important to train new staff members and then engage them in regular professional development activities.

Providing Discipline-Based Approaches and Working with Departments

Disciplines and departments dominate higher education. However, at a research university they have even more power than at other institutional types (Becher & Trowler, 2001). For this reason, the allegiance of research university faculty is often focused more on the discipline than on the institution (Hativa & Marincovich, 1995). It makes sense, therefore, for a teaching center to work within the departments and programs at the institution. Discipline-based work usually begins with needs assessment in the department and then responds to departmental priorities. It is often the teaching center's most effective work because it responds to specific concerns, is tailored to disciplinary cultures, and involves collaborating with local faculty to design customized programs and services.

Surprisingly, most centers do not prioritize their work within the departments (Sorcinelli et al., 2006). The teaching centers at Michigan and Stanford, however, do emphasize discipline-specific services. The range of these services varies widely each year based on the requests the centers receive; but it usually includes retreats, workshops, and research projects that support curricular and pedagogical reform. The Stanford CTL signals to new faculty its appreciation of the importance of their disciplinary perspective by giving them not only an institution-specific introductory teaching handbook (Marincovich, 2007) but also a handbook more tailored to their fields, such as Showalter's (2002) *Teaching Literature* for humanists or Davidson and Ambrose's (1994) *The New Professor's Handbook* for engineering faculty. CRLT at Michigan recently created the university's first department chairperson training program, which gives staff members more frequent contact with chairpersons and the ability to work more closely with them on teaching and learning improvements. It is important to realize that the chairperson is the key to creating a culture of teaching in a department (Wright, 2008).

Using Faculty Development to Promote Diversity and Inclusivity on Campus

A center is well positioned to focus campus attention on issues of diversity, a topic of considerable concern to research universities where the faculty and graduate student body may not be truly diverse. To stimulate excellent teaching, the center can provide programs addressing multicultural issues in specific academic contexts, classroom differences (for example, issues of student identity, preparation level, and styles of learning), transformation of course content, and management of instructor identity and authority in the classroom (Cook & Sorcinelli, 2005; Kaplan & Miller, 2007). These issues are discussed in more detail in Chapter Thirteen, entitled "Conceptualizing, Designing, and Implementing Multicultural Faculty Development Activities."

The Web sites of the teaching centers at both the University of Michigan and Indiana University-Purdue University Indianapolis (IUPUI) provide online resources for faculty interested in issues of multicultural education. At IUPUI, the Center for Teaching and Learning sponsors a Multicultural Teaching and Learning Institute organized in association with several other campus units. The institute focuses on promoting student voices in the classroom, improving intercultural communication, cultivating global competencies, fostering inclusive teaching pedagogy, using innovative technology to foster student learning, and exploring grants and partnership opportunities.

Involving Faculty Opinion Leaders in All Aspects of the Center's Work

Faculty development structures work best when they are created and owned by the faculty. Faculty buy-in is essential to a center's success (Cook & Sorcinelli, 2002; Eble & McKeachie, 1985; Sorcinelli, 2002; Sorcinelli et al., 2006); no lasting changes, including improvements in teaching, occur on a campus without a sense of faculty ownership.

The University of Michigan's CRLT was originally created by the faculty and makes good use of a faculty advisory board composed of opinion leaders. Since a teaching center should not be guided solely by the usual suspects (that is, faculty members who are known primarily for teaching excellence), it is important that those board members also be prominent researchers. Board members and other faculty members participate in the design of CRLT programs and then facilitate the programs or serve as speakers or panelists. At Stanford's CTL, faculty members who have won major university teaching awards and who, in most cases, are also prominent researchers are showcased in the award-winning "Teachers on Teaching" lecture series (http://ctl.stanford.edu/AWT/). These talks highlight excellent teaching on campus as well as discipline-specific pedagogical content knowledge.

Collaborating with Other University Offices

At a research university, a faculty development center is only one of multiple offices serving faculty needs, so centers can enhance their impact by regularly collaborating with other offices and programs

(Albright, 1988; Sorcinelli, 2002). Collaboration can involve joint and complementary programming, funding assistance, and publicity through the Web site and other communications with faculty. A center can take a new university initiative and build in a component on pedagogy such as, for example, helping a service learning office assist faculty members in designing their courses. At The Ohio State University, the University Center for the Advancement of Teaching partners with the Graduate School and the department of Education Policy and Leadership on a Graduate Interdisciplinary Specialization (minor) in College and University Teaching.

Making Good Teaching Highly Visible

Many faculty members on a research university campus will never make use of the faculty development center. Nonetheless, its visibility signals that the university leadership cares about good teaching, and the literature shows that faculty members respond positively to institutional priorities (Blackburn & Lawrence, 1995). To create and sustain a culture of teaching, campus leaders must make teaching and learning excellence a priority (Seldin, 1995). One way to do so is for university leaders to mention it frequently in their communications with the faculty. For example, at Michigan, CRLT organizes and hosts the annual new faculty orientation. By doing so, the faculty's first contact with the university features sessions on good teaching; the president and provost always emphasize teaching excellence in their welcoming remarks. They also recommend that faculty members utilize CRLT services, thereby giving them permission to ask for teaching support and implying that attention to teaching is normative behavior. Similarly, at Stanford's orientation program, faculty members hear that teaching is a major component of a successful faculty career. They learn that, at tenure time, the appointment papers will ask for evidence that they are "capable of sustaining a first-rate teaching program" (Stanford University Faculty Handbook, 2007, Appendix B, Form B3, p. 15).

It is important for a center to maintain high visibility by communicating regularly with the faculty and graduate student instructors. Communications may include brochures and e-mails about upcoming programs and grant deadlines, letters to campus leaders publicizing services, papers about the literature and research on good teaching, and Web sites with links to relevant literature and best practices (see http://www.crlt.umich.edu/tstrategies/teachings.php and also http://ctl .stanford.edu/).

Evaluating the Work of the Center

Regardless of institutional type, strong competition for resources exists. To gain support, a center must demonstrate good management and accountability. Many faculty developers enjoy informal, nonhierarchical approaches. For example, the Professional and Organizational Development (POD) Network in Higher Education, the North American professional organization for faculty developers, is called a network; and its governing body is called a core committee. As a center grows, however, it should be run with clear lines of responsibility and with data collection that leads to feedback and improvement of services. Both the Michigan and Stanford centers use productivity-tracking software to compile a list of programs and services, and their data show the large number of units and individuals they serve. Budget requests fare better when the director can demonstrate the center's value with annual data reports. (See also Chapter Nine, "Program Assessment for Faculty Development.")

Center directors typically encourage careful evaluation of campus curriculum and pedagogy. So they, too, need to evaluate and improve their own work continuously. In addition to gathering feedback on programs at the time they are given, the McGraw Center at Princeton University sometimes sends e-mails several months later to participants, asking, "What idea from our workshop(s) have you used (or are you likely to use) in your teaching?" They also send follow-up messages to those who have used their consultation services.

Faculty Development Activities at a Research University

Rewarding Good Teaching with Resources and Prestige

University leaders often create teaching awards in order to signal the value of teaching (Chism & Szabo, 1997; Menges, 1996). At research universities, the growing importance of good teaching is evident in the growing number of teaching awards. Centers help to improve publicity for the competitions, oversee selection processes and make them more transparent, and then celebrate the winners. As a result, the prestige associated with the awards has increased, as has the number of applicants or nominees.

At The Ohio State University, the teaching center provides staff support for the Academy of Teaching, which consists of those faculty who have won the university's Alumni Award for Distinguished Teaching. The Academy sponsors annual one-day conferences on teaching and learning, as well as the publication *Talking About Teaching at The Ohio State University* (http://ftad.osu.edu/read/teaching_showcase/talkingaboutteaching.html).

Supporting Curricular Reform

At all colleges and universities, curricular reform is a topic that the faculty considers important. By playing a role in the reform process at the department, college, and sometimes even institutional level, centers can contribute to better decision making and also demonstrate the expertise and value of center staff members. Center staff can use focus groups, interviews, and surveys to gather data about the current curricula so that faculty decisions about improvements are based on empirical evidence. Center staff can also organize and facilitate meetings and retreats at which the faculty makes curricular decisions. They can provide pedagogical expertise to help with course design and enhancements, as well as generating ongoing data for formative evaluation of new curricula (Cook, 2001). They also make connections among faculty members with similar objectives: for example, the University of Iowa's Center for Teaching has worked with multiple colleges (Engineering, Pharmacy, Liberal Arts & Sciences, Business, Education, Nursing, and Medicine) to create a service-learning course in Mexico in partnership with the local Rotary Club.

Using Instructional Technology to Engage Faculty

For research universities, like other institutions, instructional technology (IT) is a hook that brings faculty members to a center for pedagogical innovation, not remediation; but surprisingly few teaching centers have staff with IT expertise (Sorcinelli et al., 2006). At many research universities, the responsibility for IT is decentralized, and the faculty development center serves as only one of many campus players. IT should not, however, be the primary focus of a center, because new technologies (that is, the required financial resources and the expertise required to keep current with technological developments) can easily swamp a center and prevent it from discharging its other responsibilities. Nonetheless, centers should have staff who are knowledgeable about IT and who can focus faculty attention on pedagogy and course goals as well as on the hardware and software (Zhu, 2008).

The Teaching and Learning Laboratory at MIT was part of a particularly ambitious institutional collaboration between MIT faculty and Microsoft Research through iCampus (http://icampus.mit.edu/), a multidisciplinary initiative to create educational technologies that would have an impact both within and outside the classroom. Hundreds of faculty and research staff members have participated in iCampus projects, which include, for example, visualization and simulation software, remote laboratories, and experimentation with pen-based computing.

Providing Efficient Support to New Instructors

Research university faculty members typically work more hours than faculty at other types of institutions (National Center for Education Statistics, 1992). Given the workloads, it makes sense to use faculty members' time spent on professional development as efficiently as possible by having the faculty development center provide just-in-time instruction. For example, if a faculty member decides to try group work for the first time in an upcoming course, he or she should be able to find immediate help on this topic. To do so, a center needs a very broad range of programs targeted to all stages of a faculty career (Seldin, 2006), that is, junior (Austin, 2003), midcareer (Baldwin & Chang, 2006), and senior faculty members (Wheeler & Schuster, 1990).

It is wise to focus special attention on new instructors. Junior faculty members are especially receptive to teaching advice in their pretenure years, so center staff should let them know that an early investment in their pedagogical knowledge will save them time in the long run. Staff can also emphasize strategies that allow them to combine their teaching and research responsibilities and make these responsibilities mutually reinforcing.

Many research universities are involved in the Preparing Future Faculty effort and offer conferences, seminars, and internships (for example, Cook, Kaplan, Nidiffer, & Wright, 2001) for this group. Graduate student instructors are future faculty members, and the training they get in graduate school may be the most in-depth training they will ever have as instructors. This development effort is important not only in its own right; it also contributes significantly to faculty development efforts (Marincovich, Prostko, & Stout, 1998) because often it is the graduate student instructors who first use center services and then recommend them to faculty members. (See Chapter Twenty, "Graduate and Professional Student Development Programs.")

Offering Funding for Teaching Innovations

At a research university, the coin of the realm is grant money. By definition, institutions have large research budgets, and those funds will always outpace funds available for innovative teaching projects. Nonetheless, it is helpful to offer multiple teaching grants with differing levels of funding and for multiple purposes and to publicize the grants well. Some of the grants should be large enough to fund substantial projects and offer prestige to their recipients. The Michigan and Stanford centers help organize the proposal review process; they also help faculty members develop proposals and assist them with project implementation and evaluation. Grants competitions bring in faculty members who may not have had previous contact with the center.

IUPUI's Center for Teaching and Learning has an interesting approach that combines technology and grant support. Called "Jump Start into Online Course Development," the program assists participants to envision new ways of facilitating learning and to redesign courses for improved student learning and more efficient use of their own time and resources. Faculty members participate in an intensive orientation to online learning; work with instructional design and technology consultants to redesign their courses; and are given a stipend that is matched by their department or school.

Using Faculty Development Resources for Community Building

On a large research university campus, it is easy for faculty members to be so immersed in their own discipline (both on campus and at conferences elsewhere) that they have little contact with campus colleagues in other fields. While many faculty development programs should be department or school/college based, centralized programs can provide a chance for faculty members with similar interests to come together across disciplines. Cross-disciplinary programs may draw faculty with an interest in new pedagogy or with expertise in the same topic—teaching statistics for example. Regardless of topic, faculty development centers provide an opportunity to network and create a critical mass of faculty members who are committed to teaching excellence (Sorcinelli, 2002).

Faculty development centers may also host festive events as a way to honor the best teachers and contribute to a sense of community. For example, the CTL at Stanford hosts an end-of-year "Celebration of Teaching," featuring a panel of committed and effective scholar-teachers of various ranks who discuss a theme such as keeping teaching fresh. Some centers also provide programs that are largely social in nature, such as Michigan's CRLT's dinner for international faculty, because networking leads to comfort in a new location and comfort is often an important ingredient in good teaching. Studies have shown that the community-building work of a teaching center is important to faculty (Sorcinelli et al., 2006). Since the provision of food can help facilitate the creation of community, catering is often a key budget item for centers.

Using Research to Inform Teaching Center Work

Faculty development centers should engage in action research, a research-oriented way to effect change. Action research usually involves several steps: identifying a problem and possible solutions, developing options for action plans, choosing and implementing a plan, reflecting on the data collected, evaluating the plan, and then using the data to inform an improvement process (St. John, McKinney, & Tuttle, 2006).

Action research can be used for curricular reform or improvements in faculty development practices. For example, CRLT recently studied the role of GSIs in undergraduate retention in the sciences. Through analysis of science student survey data, CRLT was able to recommend and then provide the staffing for curricular changes and improvements in GSI training (Cook et al., 2007; O'Neal, Cook, Wright, Perorazio, & Purkiss, 2007; Wright, Purkiss, O'Neal, & Cook, 2008); preliminary data indicate that retention has improved as a result.

To the extent possible, all faculty development center work should be data-driven for better needs assessment and better results—and also to establish the professionalism of the center's work. In 2007, for example, the Stanford CTL was able to present a very well-received report to the campus faculty senate because it could share hard data showing that the average end-quarter evaluation scores of TAs in the institution's largest school were going up steadily during the same years in which Stanford was stepping up its investment in training programs for graduate instructors. Data carry a lot of persuasive power at a research university.

Assisting Faculty with Research on Their Own Teaching

Faculty at a research university may be interested in doing research on their own teaching. The Carnegie Foundation for the Advancement of Teaching under the leadership of President Emeritus Lee Shulman has long promoted the Scholarship of Teaching and Learning (SoTL), a kind of action research in which faculty members test hypotheses about their own teaching, reflect on the results, share them with peers, and then make teaching improvements (Cambridge, 2004). Centers at research universities typically support SoTL through consultations that provide referrals to the relevant literature, funding to pay for the staff needed to do the research, programs to bring SoTL researchers together so they can share ideas, and publicity through local Web sites and newsletters or through referrals to faculty development journals. Indiana University offers a Scholarship of Teaching and Learning Leadership Award of up to $35,000. The winning teams propose a SoTL research initiative that promises to have a sustained impact upon instructional development and/or education and could serve as a model for others on and off campus.

Connecting to Others and External Resources

Research universities typically engage in collaborative efforts with peer institutions. Thus, what happens at a peer institution often matters at home. It is especially useful, therefore, for centers to refer to peer institutions' activities as a catalyst for local adoption. Development of a consortium of center directors has proven to be a good way to learn about peer institutions' practices and help university administrators remember that centers are integral to most institutions and are not just a local phenomenon.

As faculty development has become common in other countries, so, too, has the importance of international connections for centers. It is common for centers at research universities to work with counterparts at institutions around the world, just as faculty members work with their counterparts elsewhere. (See also Chapter Fifteen, "International Faculty Development.")

External grants are the bread and butter of a research university. It may not be a wise use of resources for a service-oriented teaching center to expend its energy writing proposals and prioritizing external initiatives, but attracting some external funding from federal agencies or foundations (for example, the National Science Foundation) certainly adds to a center's prestige on campus. The Michigan and Stanford centers, as well as centers at other research universities, also often serve as university liaisons to national projects, thereby acquainting faculty with trends and innovations and bringing more attention and expertise to teaching and learning on campus. Additionally, center staff members provide assistance on proposal writing and evaluation to faculty members working on their own research-related educational proposals.

Conclusion

Most centers across the country share certain goals, but there are differences among institutional types in the prioritization of those goals (Sorcinelli et al., 2006). The commonalities among research universities and the differences between them and other types of institutions give research university centers both opportunities and constraints. The fact that the vast majority of research universities have educational development centers indicates the extent of interest in teaching excellence on these campuses. When the mission, management, and programming of the centers reflect the realities of research university life, they serve an important role in creating a strong culture of teaching excellence.

REFERENCES

Albright, M. J. (1988). Cooperation among campus agencies involved in instructional improvement. In E. C. Wadsworth (Ed.), *A handbook for new practitioners* (pp. 3–8). Stillwater, OK: New Forums.

Austin, A. E. (2003). Creating a bridge to the future: Preparing new faculty to face changing expectations in a shifting context. *Review of Higher Education, 26*(2), 119–144.

Baldwin, R. G., & Chang, D. A. (2006). Reinforcing our "keystone" faculty. *Liberal Education, 92*(4), 28–35.

Becher, T., & Trowler, P. R. (2001). *Academic tribes and territories: Intellectual enquiry and the cultures of disciplines* (2nd ed.). Buckingham, UK: Society for Research into Higher Education and Open University Press.

Blackburn, R. T., & Lawrence, J. H. (1995). *Faculty at work*. Baltimore, MD: Johns Hopkins University Press.

Bok, D. (2006). *Our underachieving colleges: A candid look at how much students learn and why they should be learning more*. Princeton, NJ: Princeton University Press.

Cambridge, B. (Ed.). (2004). *Campus progress: Supporting the scholarship of teaching and learning*. Washington, DC: American Association for Higher Education.

Chism, N.V.N. (1998). The role of educational developers in institutional change: From the basement office to the front office. In M. Kaplan (Ed.), *To improve the academy: Vol. 17. Resources for faculty, instructional and organizational development* (pp. 141–153). Stillwater, OK: New Forums.

Chism, N.V.N., & Szabo, B. (1997). Teaching awards: The problem of assessing their impact. In D. DeZure & M. Kaplan (Eds.), *To improve the academy: Vol. 16. Resources for faculty, instructional and organizational development* (pp. 181–199). Stillwater, OK: New Forums.

Cook, C. E. (2001). The role of a teaching center in curricular reform. In D. Lieberman & C. Wehlburg (Eds.), *To improve the academy: Vol. 19. Resources for faculty, instructional and organizational development* (pp. 217–231). Bolton, MA: Anker.

Cook, C. E., Kaplan, M., Nidiffer, J., & Wright, M. (2001, November). Preparing future faculty—faster. *AAHE Bulletin, 54*(3), 3–7.

Cook, C. E., & Sorcinelli, M. D. (2002, June). *The value of a teaching center*. Retrieved November 21, 2008, from http://www.podnetwork.org/faculty_development/values.htm

Cook, C. E., & Sorcinelli, M. D. (2005). Building multiculturalism into teaching development programs. In M. Ouellett (Ed.), *Teaching inclusively: Resources for course, department and institutional change in higher education* (pp. 74–83). Stillwater, OK: New Forums.

Cook, C. E., Wright, M. C., & O'Neal, C. (2007). Action research for instructional improvement: Using data to enhance student learning at your institution. In D. R. Robertson and L.B. Nilson (Eds.), *To improve the academy: Vol. 25. Resources for faculty, instructional and organizational development* (pp. 123–138). Bolton, MA: Anker.

Davidson, C. I., & Ambrose, S. A. (1994). *The new professor's handbook.* Bolton, MA: Anker.

Eble, K. (1972). *Professors as teachers.* San Francisco: Jossey-Bass.

Eble, K., & McKeachie, W. J. (1985). *Improving undergraduate education through faculty development.* San Francisco: Jossey-Bass.

Hativa, N., & Marincovich, M. (Eds.) (1995). Editors' notes. In M. Marincovich & N. Hativa (Eds.), *New directions for teaching and learning, no. 64. Disciplinary differences in teaching and learning: Implications for practice* (pp. 1–4). San Francisco: Jossey-Bass.

Kaplan, M. L., & Miller, A. T. (Eds.). (2007). *New directions for teaching and learning, no. 111. Scholarship of multicultural teaching and learning.* San Francisco: Jossey-Bass.

Kuhlenschmidt, S. (2009, March). *Who are we? Where are we? Descriptive data about centers.* Paper presented at the Southern Regional Faculty Development Consortium, Louisville, KY.

Marincovich, M. (2007). *Teaching at Stanford: An introductory handbook for faculty, academic staff, and teaching assistants.* Stanford: Stanford University, Center for Teaching and Learning.

Marincovich, M., Prostko, J., & Stout, F. (Eds.). (1998). *The professional development of graduate teaching assistants.* Bolton, MA: Anker.

Menges, R. J. (1996). Awards to individuals. In M. D. Svinicki & R. J. Menges (Eds.), *New directions for teaching and learning: Vol. 65. Honoring exemplary teaching* (pp. 3–10). San Francisco: Jossey-Bass.

National Center for Education Statistics. (1992). *Full-time instructional faculty and staff, in institutions of higher education, by instruction activities and type and control of institution.* Retrieved August 18, 2008, from http://nces.ed.gov/programs/digest/d99/d99t232.asp

O'Neal, C., Cook, C. E., Wright, M., Perorazio, T., & Purkiss, J. (2007). The impact of teaching assistants on student retention in the sciences: Lessons for TA training. *Journal of College Science Teaching, 36(5),* 24–29.

Seldin, P. (1995). *Improving college teaching.* Bolton, MA: Anker.

Seldin, P. (2006). Tailoring faculty development programs to faculty career stages. In S. Chadwick-Blossey (Ed.), *To improve the academy: Vol. 24.*

Resources for faculty, instructional and organizational development (pp. 137–144). Bolton, MA: Anker.

Showalter, E. (2002). *Teaching literature*. Malden, MA: Blackwell.

Sorcinelli, M. D. (2002). Ten principles of good practice in creating and sustaining teaching and learning centers. In K. H. Gillespie (Ed.), *A guide to faculty development: Practical advice, examples, and resources* (pp. 9–23). Bolton, MA: Anker.

Sorcinelli, M. D., Austin, A. E., Eddy, P. L., & Beach, A. L. (2006). *Creating the future of faculty development: Learning from the past, understanding the present*. Bolton, MA: Anker.

Stanford University Faculty Handbook. (2007). Retrieved August 18, 2008, from http://facultyhandbook.stanford.edu/

St. John, E. P., McKinney, J. S., & Tuttle, T. (2006). Using action inquiry to address critical challenges. In E. P. St. John & M. Wilkerson (Eds.), *Reframing persistence research to improve academic success* (pp. 63–76). San Francisco: Jossey-Bass.

Wheeler, D. W., & Schuster, J. H. (1990). Building comprehensive programs to enhance faculty development. In J. H. Schuster, D. W. Wheeler, & Associates (Eds.), *Enhancing faculty careers* (pp. 275–297). San Francisco: Jossey-Bass.

Wright, D. L. (2000). Faculty development centers in research universities: A study of resources and programs. In M. Kaplan & D. Lieberman (Eds.), *To improve the academy: Vol. 18. Resources for faculty, instructional and organizational development* (pp. 291–301). Bolton, MA: Anker.

Wright, M. C. (2008). *Always at odds? Creating alignment between faculty and administrative values*. Albany: State University of New York Press.

Wright, M. C., Purkiss, P., O'Neal, C., & Cook, C. E. (2008). International teaching assistants and student retention in the sciences. *Studies in Graduate and Professional Student Development, 11*(1), 109–120.

Zhu, E. (2008). Breaking down barriers to the use of technology for teaching in higher education. In D. R. Robertson & L. B. Nilson (Eds.), *To improve the academy: Vol. 26. Resources for faculty, instructional and organizational development* (pp. 305–318). Bolton, MA: Anker.

18

EFFECTIVE PRACTICES IN THE CONTEXT OF SMALL COLLEGES

Michael Reder

THE PAST DECADE HAS WITNESSED tremendous growth in formalized faculty development programs and centers at small colleges (Mooney & Reder, 2008). A variety of internal and external forces, including pressure for accountability from accreditation agencies and funding sources, may in part account for this increase. Perhaps most signifi-cant, small, teaching-focused institutions are coming to understand that merely claiming to *value* good teaching is qualitatively different from *actively* supporting effective teaching (Reder & Gallagher, 2007). Increasingly, colleges are realizing that faculty members need to make their craft of teaching public, just as they do with scholarship and creative work, in order to improve their teaching practices (Reder, 2007). To use Shulman's term, faculty need to overcome their "pedagogical solitude" and make their teaching "community property" (1993). Small colleges across the country are starting faculty programs for teaching and learning or formalizing the faculty development work already taking place on campuses. From the handful of small college faculty developers who attended the Professional and Organizational Development (POD) Network Conference in 1999, the POD Network Small College Committee, formed in 2004, has seen its membership more than quadruple and now has almost 250 members. With the resources of the POD Network, this committee offers support to faculty developers in small colleges, including the Small College POD listserv, which serves as the primary means of communication for the membership of POD's

Small College Committee. (Visit http://oak.conncoll.edu/mailman/ listinfo/sc-pod.) While the range of activities that can come under the heading of "faculty development" are detailed elsewhere in this volume (see Chapter Eight, "Practical Suggestions for Programs and Activities"), this chapter assumes that working with faculty members on their teaching is the major, if not the single, focus of such work at small colleges.

Defining a Small College and the Faculty Development Work

What makes a small college "small" and what makes small college faculty development work distinctive? Kim Mooney and I (2008) have noted that, within the work of the POD Network's small college group, there is "no litmus test for 'small'"; and faculty developers have traditionally self-identified themselves as such according to their own needs and contexts (p. 159). We (Mooney & Reder, 2008) identified several general characteristics of such schools:

- Predominantly undergraduate (few, if any, graduate students)
- Centrality of teaching in the school's mission
- Fewer than 250 full-time faculty
- Relatively small classes ranging from, in general, fifteen to thirty students
- A large amount of interdisciplinary teaching and research.

Of these traits, it is the intimate, undergraduate-focused culture that is key, especially "the value placed on teaching" (Mooney & Reder, 2008, p. 160).

This distinctive faculty-run, student-centered culture shapes the nature of the educational development work at small colleges. Both the size of the institution and the nature of the administrative position of the person charged with leading faculty development within that institution create the context in which faculty development work takes place and determine effective strategies for creating successful programming.

Size does *matter.* Size influences the characteristics of the teaching culture, the economies of scale for undertaking and funding faculty development work, and the ways in which teaching is valued on campus. The teaching and learning culture of small institutions—whether residential liberal arts colleges, faith-based colleges, or independent professional schools (for example, health, art, music, science)—can be strikingly different from large universities. The nature of teaching and research at a small college contrasts with that of most large universities; at small colleges there are no graduate teaching or research assistants, meaning that undergraduates are taught mostly by full-time, tenure-track faculty members, who frequently work with undergraduate students on research projects. Thus, faculty research often becomes closely aligned with their undergraduate teaching. Additionally, because the cultures of small colleges differ markedly from the research universities where most new faculty members have been trained (Gibson, 1992), it is vital for small institutions to help their incoming faculty members successfully make the transition to the distinctive demands of faculty life and teaching in the new environment (Mooney & Reder, 2008; Reder & Gallagher, 2007).

Size also influences the role of the faculty developer. At a residential liberal arts college, for example, the number of faculty members is small; and faculty members generally know each other well. Unlike a large university with different colleges and a faculty that may number in the thousands, at the small college it is common for the person responsible for faculty development programming to know every faculty member by name and even to have an ongoing professional relationship with each of them, having served on committees together or engaged in collaborative projects. The chapters in this volume reveal the wide range of expertise faculty developers may be called to bring to their work on any campus; when that expertise resides in a single individual, as it often does in a small institution, the task can be both daunting and demanding. It can also be very rewarding.

Position matters, too. The nature of the administrative position of the director further influences the characteristics of faculty development work at small institutions. For the vast majority of small college developers, running programs for faculty is only a part of the larger set of responsibilities, which usually includes teaching. Faculty development directors often fill multiple roles within their institutions: administrator (dean, campuswide program director, department chair), faculty member (teacher, researcher, committee member), evaluator (tenure, decisions about resources), and mentor (as a senior colleague, as administrator), to name but a few. These multiple roles present distinctive challenges to running a successful program.

These two factors—institutional culture and the nature of the position of the person responsible for running faculty development—mean that the "small" in small college faculty development work is not exclusively about the size of the institution but about creating as effective a faculty development program as possible within a distinctive institutional and administrative context, especially given the usually limited amount of resources—almost always time, usually money, often both. Small colleges vary greatly in their missions, types of students, faculty-to-student ratios, teaching loads, and curricula. There are, however, certain characteristics that allow them to be clustered together and conceptualized as a diverse but characteristically cohesive group, especially when contrasted to larger, research-oriented universities. The specific set of skills and strategies that faculty developers employ to create an effective program within this distinctive institutional context defines "small college" faculty development.

Guiding Principles

There are three common misconceptions about faculty development programs, that, while not limited to small college cultures, play themselves out in distinctive ways on small college campuses where teaching is central (Reder, 2007): (1) that such programs are about remediation; (2) that they advocate "one right way" to teach; and (3) that such programs force faculty members to choose between teaching and scholarship. Faculty developers can address these fallacies by deliberately framing their work in a manner that directly challenges such beliefs, emphasizing that faculty development programs (1) foster teaching intentionally in order to create reflective, critical practitioners; (2) value a diversity of teaching styles and disciplinary approaches; and (3) attempt to create a culture in which teaching and scholarship are mutually supportive.

Cultivating Intentional Teaching and Critical Practice

At a small college that values teaching and promotes itself as a teaching institution, there is an assumption that good teaching happens "naturally" and that those who are hired to teach at such institutions do it well because they "care about teaching" (Reder, 2007; Reder & Gallagher, 2007). Therefore, in an environment in which teaching is the sine qua non, it is easy to view faculty work on the enhancement of teaching effectiveness as remedial. It is particularly important for any small college faculty development program to address such misconceptions quickly and clearly by making faculty programming about intentional and effective teaching. Faculty can and should see their teaching in a light similar to that of their scholarship and creative work, that is, as an intellectual act that they can improve by undertaking it in a purposeful manner and then making it public and subject to peer review (Shulman, 1999).

Just as faculty members are asked to be critical practitioners in their scholarly and creative endeavors, faculty development focused on teaching asks them to do the same with their teaching. By discussing teaching and thinking about it critically, the improvement of teaching becomes a public act that makes much of the good teaching already happening on small college campuses visible.

Valuing a Diversity of Teaching Styles and Approaches

Even on a small college campus where the student-to-faculty ratio is low and classes might average fewer than twenty students, there is still no one right—that is, *effective*—way to teach. Although campus cultures, expectations, and class size may dictate a classroom that is more interactive than the stereotypical large lecture class found at most larger institutions, an effective small college faculty development program must recognize that teaching styles and approaches vary according to a faculty member's experience, personality, and identity. Additionally, how a course is taught can be influenced by disciplinary or departmental norms and by the nature of the course itself—its goals, the subject matter, and the level at which it is taught. Quite simply, not all small courses, or even seminars, have the same goals; the teaching needs to reflect those differing goals. Even on a small college campus, an introductory first-year seminar may be taught differently from discipline to discipline, as might two introductory seminars within the same discipline. Thus, faculty development activities should embrace this diversity, bringing to light the large variety of effective teaching practices and approaches to course design.

The Relationship Between Teaching and Scholarship

The idea of the teacher-scholar resonates on many small college campuses where faculty members do both, often in equal measure. Effective teaching and scholarly research require similar habits of mind: intentionality, curiosity, questioning, self-reflection, and discipline, as well as critical skills such as analysis, synthesis, and creativity (Reder, 2007). The liberal arts ideal of the teacher-scholar extends not only into the classroom but also into the library or the lab. At many small colleges, faculty research is not only a source of inspiration for faculty members' teaching, it has also *become* their teaching. Faculty members teaching students through their research is becoming the norm in science departments at many small colleges; and the boundaries between teaching and research in other disciplines, including the humanities, are becoming more permeable

(Marx, 2005; Zimmer, 2005). In science and psychology labs, undergraduate students and faculty members often work side by side on experiments; and they regularly present work together at conferences or coauthor papers for professional journals. In the fine and performing arts, faculty members and students not only share physical spaces but engage in creative collaborations and public performances beyond the mere showcasing of "student" work. In the social sciences and humanities, growing numbers of undergraduate students and faculty members are collaborating on research and scholarly work. Thus, for many faculty members scholarship not only informs their teaching, it also becomes the vehicle for their teaching, which in turn allows their teaching to inform their research (Reder, Mooney, Holmgren, & Kuerbis, 2009; Zimmer, 2007).

Models for Small College Faculty Development

Large institutions with multifaceted faculty development programs usually employ full-time directors and have additional administrative positions such as associate directors, specialists who work with graduate students or within certain disciplines, and instructional designers or consultants. They have structures that are stable, self-supporting, and self-sustaining. These programs have their own budgets, physical space, and personnel lines. The administrative models of programs at small schools may be much less complex, but they present challenges not faced at most larger institutions.

The Challenge of Administrative Structure

Two critical issues for the administration of faculty development at small institutions are cultivating faculty ownership and ensuring continuity in leadership.

FACULTY OWNERSHIP. Faculty ownership is important because small college faculty members are accustomed not only to self-governance but also to administering much of the institution. More so than at most large universities, faculty members are involved in all aspects of running the college, from student advising to technology, from budgets and administration to planning and fundraising. In such institutions there is less of a division between the administration and the faculty. Faculty members are used to working with one another as peers, and often they are uncomfortable taking directions from "outside" (nonfaculty) specialists. For example, they may resent the idea of taking advice from an instructional designer who is not actually teaching students. Therefore, it is rare for a nonfaculty member to lead faculty programming at a small college.

CONTINUITY IN LEADERSHIP. Faculty ownership and faculty leadership create the challenge of continuity. The faculty member chosen to lead faculty development initiatives soon learns that teaching and learning is a discipline in itself, and there is a steep learning curve for creating and leading effective programming. The challenge around continuity stems not only from faculty sabbatical schedules and the natural rhythms of faculty careers, but also from the somewhat ironic move of taking an acknowledged faculty leader and effective teacher out of the classroom in order to run such programming. Because faculty ownership and continuity in leadership can be at odds with each other, the administrative structure of faculty development at a small college is a key challenge.

Types of Administrative Models

How a school chooses to design the administrative structures and programming of its faculty development effort depends largely upon the mission and goals of its programming (Reder et al., 2009). Nonetheless, the distinctive challenges of small institutions suggest specific administrative models and strategies for effective faculty development work. There are four common administrative models for running faculty development programming at small colleges: (1) a faculty committee; (2) as part of the portfolio of an academic dean; (3) a rotating faculty director who is often part-time; and (4) a center or program with a full-time, continuing director. Each of these models offers distinct advantages and poses specific challenges.

FACULTY COMMITTEE. Creating a faculty development program where none existed before can most easily be done by assigning this responsibility to a committee. The advantages to such a model are clear faculty ownership, regular input from a variety of faculty members in determining goals and priorities, and minimal to no start-up costs. Another advantage is that the administration is likely to support the work of a faculty committee working within the existing governance structures, which can make the committee a more effective advocate for funding and recognition than a program run by a single director. (See Chapter Four, "Working with a Faculty Development Committee.")

Relying solely on a regular faculty committee with a rotating membership and without any continuing leadership, however, has disadvantages. First and foremost, it is unlikely that a rotating committee chairperson, even with previous faculty development committee experience, can garner the required knowledge and experience to run a comprehensive and effective faculty development program. Even an enthusiastic chairperson will have other primary commitments (teaching, research, other service).

Time presents the biggest challenge—not only the time and energy it takes to run a successful program, but also the time it takes to learn about faculty development as a discipline, including issues such as understanding course design, leading effective workshops, consulting with faculty members, and offering comprehensive programming.

Even if the chairperson and committee members are granted reduced teaching loads, there is a steep learning curve to understanding the growing body of research and literature addressing effective teaching, student learning, and educational development. The rotating nature of committee assignments makes learning these things all the more challenging. In more than a decade of working with faculty developers at other institutions, I have often heard a faculty member who is serving a rotating term running faculty programming lament, "I am just getting the hang of doing this work, and now my term is over." This is not to say that a fledgling faculty development program cannot make headway with committee leadership. Rather, one must recognize the inherent limits to what a committee can accomplish. If a college is going to take teaching seriously, it has to dedicate real resources—beyond the time faculty are expected to devote to routine work on a committee—to that enterprise (Reder & Gallagher, 2007).

DEAN'S PORTFOLIO. At some small institutions, the responsibility for faculty development programming is part of the portfolio of a dean or associate dean. The advantage of this model is that there is clear and direct administrative support, and faculty development can become an immediate and visible institutional priority if such work is pursued vigorously through the office responsible for the overall academic leadership of the college. Additionally, a dean with good connections to the faculty can create a strong sense of faculty ownership, especially in conjunction with a faculty advisory board or committee.

There are also, however, disadvantages to running a faculty development program from a dean's office. The first is that a dean's portfolio of responsibilities is often wide and varying, and daily exigencies can overwhelm long-term priorities. Building and sustaining a strong faculty development program may then take second place to dealing with current personnel and staffing issues, short-term initiatives, and seemingly more pressing matters. The second disadvantage is that, even with a committed dean who has developed the skills to administer a successful program, deans rotate in and out of their positions. Changes within a dean's office can present a problem not just in terms of personnel, but in terms of priorities. For example, at one small liberal arts college with a well-established faculty development program run by their associate dean, a new dean of the faculty not only brought in his own new associate dean, replacing the person who had run faculty development, but also switched the office's priorities from teaching to research, virtually eliminating all faculty development programming overnight. Finally, much of the programming focused on improving teaching requires a "safe space" in which faculty can talk about their classroom successes and failures; if the programming is run by the office responsible for evaluation, promotion, and tenure, the creation of such a space is challenging, particularly when pretenure faculty are involved.

ROTATING FACULTY DIRECTOR. Another model for the administration of faculty development programming is that of a faculty director who, for a given period of time, assumes the primary responsibility for this effort. A term as faculty development director generally lasts anywhere from one to three years, and the faculty member usually receives course reductions in addition to an extra stipend. Because such rotating directors come from and return to the ranks of full-time faculty, they often maintain many of their other responsibilities, such as advising students, committee assignments, and other leadership positions. They also may need to keep their discipline-focused research agenda. Thus, most rotating directors are de facto part-time. The faculty member selected to fill the position of director needs to learn to balance the new responsibilities of the position with the continuing responsibilities of a faculty member.

This model has an advantage over a committee because faculty development becomes a primary responsibility of a single individual. However, there is still a disadvantage, as mentioned previously, in that one must learn the discipline of faculty development during this limited period of service. In addition, there is the risk of faculty development becoming associated with one single, sometimes charismatic personality, so that "faculty development" becomes synonymous with that faculty leader; hence, when this director rotates off, there is no clear successor and a program can languish.

FULL-TIME, CONTINUING DIRECTOR. A full-time, continuing director is the final model for running faculty development at small colleges. While once rare, this option is growing in popularity as small colleges realize the rewards of having a strong faculty development program and therefore allocate appropriate resources toward such programming. This model provides continuity and stability and allows the director to get to know faculty members' needs and to become familiar with the research on teaching and learning and the field of faculty development. This model requires dedicating significant resources to faculty development and sends the signal to the faculty, students, alumni, and other stakeholders that the institution takes teaching seriously.

Such directors might be drawn from the ranks of the tenured faculty or be hired into the position from nontenured faculty, either from within or outside of the institution. Directors who are known and respected by the faculty and who have teaching experience bring to the position a strong base of knowledge and credibility. For many years, small colleges rarely searched beyond their own campus for faculty development leaders; however, in recent years, with the professionalization of the field of faculty development, small colleges have increasingly undertaken national searches for directors. Regardless of where they are found, it is essential that the directors have classroom experience and teach at least one course a year (Reder et al., 2009).

Another advantage of a continuing, full-time director is that improving teaching and learning is the individual's primary focus, making that person an advocate for teaching on campus. It is that person's job to think about supporting faculty teaching that leads to improved student learning—issues that transcend departmental interests and go to the heart of the mission of the college. Because there is one person who may be thought of as the "face" of faculty development at an institution, maintaining faculty ownership can be a challenge with this model, as can keeping the program current and relevant. A program can address these challenges by using rotating "faculty fellows" who affiliate themselves with the program, by having a strong faculty advisory board, and by garnering ground-level support for specific programming by seeking input and participation from diverse faculty (Reder & Gallagher, 2007; Reder et al., 2009).

Space and Budget

Does space matter? Does budget matter? The questions of physical space and adequate budget always arise when discussing a new faculty development program or teaching and learning center. The standard answer for both questions is, "It depends." Space can matter, but at a small college it does not matter as much as having a strong program. Peter Fredrick, a mentor to many small college program directors, has often said that faculty development programs serve as a "metaphorical center" for faculty activities focused on teaching and learning, activities that may already happen at a variety of locations—both physically and programmatically—on a small college campus, for example as part of a first-year seminar program, an information literacy initiative, or a writing center (Frederick, 2007; Mooney & Reder, 2008; Reder et al., 2009). Having physical space can be a boon (a lovely space at the center of the campus) or a bust (an ill-maintained house at the edge of the campus); what matters most is that such a space enhances programming and increases the presence of the effort on campus (Reder et al., 2009).

Having a director who is able to commit time to creating and leading faculty teaching and learning programs with a healthy budget is one clear sign of a college's commitment to improving teaching. A large budget, while nice, is not as important as a college's dedicated time—faculty time—to teaching and learning. A budget should be large enough to provide good food for events, buy the books and supplies necessary to run a program, and allow the director to develop professionally by attending conferences. Most of all, it takes time to develop, plan, and execute effective faculty development opportunities and to spend money strategically. In other words, a faculty development program with a large budget and a leader who has only one course release is likely to be less vital and effective than a program with a smaller budget and a director with more time to put into planning. As the demand for events increases, both the budget for programming and the time needed to run the events should increase accordingly.

Local Culture

While local culture is an important consideration for all institutions, it is particularly so on a small college campus, where local norms may be more apparent because of the intimate nature of the academic enterprise and the small size of the faculty. What may work at one small college may not work at a similar peer school. Yet, I have found that the ideas and strategies that I mention in this chapter generally hold true, even when they are adapted to fit specific institutional traditions, needs, and priorities. (See Chapter Seven, "Promoting Your Program and Grounding It in the Institution.")

Practical Strategies for Successful Faculty Development

Previously, my colleagues and I (Reder et al., 2009) have enumerated thirteen specific principles for starting, building, and sustaining successful faculty development programming in a small institutional setting (see also Sorcinelli, 2002, and Chapter Three, "Establishing an Educational Development Program"). While each one of these principles informs and supports the others, I have combined them into three main strategies or goals for successful faculty development work: (a) building a program, (b) ensuring faculty ownership, and (c) creating a program that cultivates excellence and effectiveness. Finally, I offer a quick word on assessment strategies that are particularly relevant at small colleges.

Building the Program

The key to building a vital and effective program is to start small and grow carefully. It is best to start with one program and do it well and then the faculty demand for additional programming will naturally increase. When working with fledging centers or programs, we usually recommend starting with a year-long program for incoming faculty (Mooney & Reder, 2008; Reder et al., 2009; D'Avanzo, 2009). Such a program sends the clear message that teaching is supported and valued at the institution; additionally, over the course of several years, the program can transform a college's teaching culture (Reder & Gallagher, 2007). Programming for early-career faculty also creates a user base for a successful center's other programming.

When expanding the programming, be careful and deliberate, and do not overextend offerings beyond the program's resources or capabilities. A good second program will appeal to a wide range of faculty members who want to participate in a discussion or workshop focused on teaching. Such an offering could take the form of "occasional programming" that participants can choose to attend when a topic interests them, or longer-term seminars, in which a selected group of faculty may meet over the course of a semester or year. Good examples of such programs include St. Lawrence University's "Oral Communication Institute" (Mooney, Fordham, & Lehr, 2005), Allegheny College's "Teaching Partners" (Holmgren, 2005), St. Olaf College's initiative on the Scholarship of Teaching and Learning (Peters, Schodt, & Walczak, 2008), Connecticut College's "Talking Teaching" lunchtime series (http://ctl.conncoll.edu/programs.html#talking), Macalester College's midcareer faculty seminar (http://www.macalester.edu/cst/Mid%20Career%20Seminar/Index.htm), and Furman University's "Nexia" concept of linking courses (Love, 2008). Two successful and diverse programs—one for incoming faculty and one that appeals to a diversity of users—can form the basis for a successful and comprehensive faculty development program.

Ensuring Faculty Ownership

One way in which to ensure faculty ownership is to seek guidance from stakeholders, particularly from the faculty members. You may want to create an advisory board that can act as a sounding board for programming and advocate for your program or center. Choose advisory board members from a variety of disciplines and career stages and seek out the most respected faculty members. For programming it is advisable to try to use and highlight the local talent pool. So much great teaching takes place on small college campuses, and one of your jobs is to make that exemplary teaching visible. Your own faculty members best know the students on your campus, making your colleagues' insights into intentional and effective teaching both relevant and invaluable. They also know each other and are probably curious about what others do in their classrooms. By carefully assessing the faculty's needs and priorities and by allowing faculty members to shape and contribute to programming, they will feel as if the teaching and learning program belongs to them and will support it with their continued participation.

Cultivating Excellence and Effectiveness

Your programming should provide the opportunity for faculty members to talk about effective and intentional teaching. You should make every-effort to get the most respected faculty members involved—not just the "good teachers" but the best faculty members who are known for their teaching, scholarship, and leadership and service. One way to generate interest and participation in your programs is by sharing your plans with a select group of faculty members and getting their feedback before you officially announce them. You can also invite specific faculty members to serve as "discussants" or "featured faculty" for discussions and events. Advertising the wide range of faculty—and sometimes administrators or staff—already participating in an upcoming program increases its appeal; a diverse group of advertised participants (discipline, gender, approaches to teaching, stage of career) is likely to attract a larger, more diverse audience.

Wide and diverse offerings is one key to making your program relevant and useful. It is important to collaborate with other entities on campus that are already offering faculty development opportunities, making your programs the "center" of faculty conversations about teaching (Frederick, 2007; Reder et al., 2009). The details of your programming do matter: the quality of the food and the setting can all send the message that the conversations taking place and the work being done are important and that faculty participation is valued.

Assessing the Work

Assessment of your program's activities is an essential part of building a program, cultivating faculty excellence, and ensuring your program's effectiveness. While undertaking large-scale assessment projects or research-based scholarship of teaching and learning activities may be beyond the ability of a one-person shop, keeping accurate records of programming and gathering information from participants is key to the success and growth of a small college faculty development program. (For further information on basic assessment strategies for small-college faculty development programs, see Reder, 2009.)

While record keeping is important, remember that statistics do not tell the entire story. Especially when the size of a faculty is limited, numbers tend to be small and unimpressive—although not necessarily in terms of percentages. "Live by the numbers, die by the numbers" is a phrase to keep in mind. A 30 percent increase in faculty participation in your faculty book discussions is wonderful, but is it sustainable? The average attendance at lunchtime pedagogical discussions is eighteen people? That's great, but what if the numbers go down the following semester? What does that mean? The answers to these questions based on purely quantitative data are unclear. Yet, although quantitative data has its limits, faculty participation is key; if faculty members are not attending events, such events are not enhancing their teaching, making it difficult for the program to fulfill its objectives.

Additionally, in my experience numbers do not garner as much attention as the stories that faculty members have to tell about their experiences with faculty development activities and the program's impact on their lives as teachers. Gathering this type of evidence is especially important during the first years of the program or center. Always keep in mind that assessment is both imperfect and essential. (See Chapter Nine, "Program Assessment for Faculty Development.")

Conclusion

Sorcinelli, Austin, Eddy, and Beach (2006) identified a variety of issues facing faculty development as a whole. Two of these issues are central to faculty development programs at small colleges: the distinctive role that technology will play in the teaching and learning at such institutions and the changing nature of the professoriate (Mooney & Reder, 2008). In addition, small liberal arts colleges in particular are being asked to take the immense amount of data we gather about student learning—assessment data—and translate it into action that directly improves student learning. Improving student learning should be central to the mission of any small college faculty development program. Preliminary results from the Wabash National Study of Liberal Arts Education (n.d.) suggest that faculty teaching practices have a direct impact on the goals of a liberal arts education. The results indicate that the overall quality of teaching—including faculty interest in student development and a high level of challenge—correlates positively with student growth in areas such as motivation, openness to diversity and change, critical thinking and moral reasoning, attitudes toward literacy, and the desire to contribute to the arts and sciences (Reder, 2007; Wabash, n.d.). Teaching really does matter. A thriving faculty teaching and learning program shows that a small college takes its mission seriously, making the good teaching that takes place on its campus visible and supporting faculty teaching to increase student learning.

REFERENCES

D'Avanzo, C. (2009, Spring). Supporting faculty through a new teaching and learning center. *Peer Review, (11)*2, 22–25.

Frederick, P. (2007, October). *Sixteen reflections from thirty years of faculty development*. Paper presented at the Professional and Organizational (POD) Network Annual Conference, Pittsburgh, PA. Retrieved March 5, 2008, from http://ctl.conncoll.edu/smallcollege/index.html

Gibson, G. W. (1992). *Good start: A guidebook for new faculty in liberal arts colleges*. Bolton, MA: Anker.

Holmgren, R. A. (2005). Teaching partners: Improving teaching and learning by cultivating a community of practice. In S. Chadwick–Blossey & D. R. Robertson (Eds.), *To improve the academy: Vol. 23. Resources for faculty, instructional, and organizational development* (pp. 211–219). Bolton, MA: Anker.

Love, J. (2008). Meeting the challenges of integrative learning: The Nexia concept. In D. R. Robertson & L. B. Nilson (Eds.), *To improve the academy: Vol. 26. Resources for faculty, instructional, and organizational development* (pp. 263–274). San Francisco: Jossey-Bass.

Marx, J. (2005, September 9). Undergraduate research in the humanities [Letter to the editor]. *The Chronicle of Higher Education*, p. B22.

Mooney, K. M., Fordham, T., & Lehr, V. 2005. A faculty development program to promote engaged classroom dialogue: The oral communication institute. In S. Chadwick-Blossey & D. R. Robertson (Eds.), *To improve the academy: Vol. 23. Resources for faculty, instructional, and organizational development* (pp. 219–235). Bolton, MA: Anker.

Mooney, K. M., & Reder, M. (2008). Faculty development at small and liberal arts colleges. In D. R. Robertson & L. B. Nilson (Eds.), *To improve the academy: Vol. 26. Resources for faculty, instructional, and organizational development* (pp. 158–172). San Francisco: Jossey-Bass.

Peters, D., Schodt, D., & Walczak, M. (2008). Supporting the scholarship of teaching and learning at liberal arts colleges. In D. R. Robertson & L. B. Nilson (Eds.), *To improve the academy: Vol. 26. Resources for faculty, instructional, and organizational development* (pp. 68–84). San Francisco: Jossey-Bass.

Reder, M. (2007). Does your college really support teaching and learning? *Peer Review, 9*(4), 9–13.

Reder, M. (2009). *Assessing faculty development programming on a shoestring: Practical advice and strategies.* Unpublished manuscript.

Reder, M., & Gallagher, E. V. (2007). Transforming a teaching culture through peer mentoring: Connecticut College's Johnson Teaching Seminar for incoming faculty and the Scholarship of Teaching and Learning. In D. R. Robertson & L. B. Nilson (Eds.), *To improve the academy: Vol. 25. Resources for faculty, instructional, and organizational development* (pp. 327–344). Bolton, MA: Anker.

Reder, M., Mooney, K., Holmgren, R., & Kuerbis, P. (2009). Starting and sustaining successful faculty development programs at small colleges. In D. R. Robertson & L. B. Nilson (Eds.), *To improve the academy: Vol. 27. Resources for faculty, instructional, and organizational development* (pp. 267–286). Bolton, MA: Anker.

Shulman, L. S. (1993). Teaching as community property: Putting an end to pedagogical solitude. *Change, 25*(6), 6–7.

Shulman, L. S. (1999). *Fostering a scholarship of teaching.* [Video]. Stanford, CA: Carnegie Foundation for the Advancement of Teaching.

Sorcinelli, M. D. (2002). Ten principles of good practice in creating and sustaining teaching and learning centers. In K. H. Gillespie (Ed.), *A guide to faculty development: Practical advice, examples, and resources* (pp. 9–23). Bolton, MA: Anker.

Sorcinelli, M. D., Austin, A. E., Eddy, P. L., & Beach, A. L. (2006). *Creating the future of faculty development: Learning from the past, understanding the present.* Bolton, MA: Anker.

Wabash National Study of Liberal Arts Education (n.d.). *Effective practices and experiences from the Wabash National Study.* Retrieved November 13, 2008, from http://www.wabash.edu/cila/docs/11.13.08%20Effective%20Practices%20summary%20with%20data%20web%20final.pdf

Zimmer, M. (2005, August 12). How to find students' inner geek. *The Chronicle of Higher Education,* p. B5.

Zimmer, M. (2007, February 16). Guerrilla puzzling: A model for research. *The Chronicle of Higher Education,* p. B5.

19

FACULTY DEVELOPMENT IN THE CONTEXT OF THE COMMUNITY COLLEGE

Helen Burnstad and Cynthia J. Hoss

THE COMMUNITY COLLEGE REPRESENTS a unique institution created origi nally in the United States to serve students transitioning from high school to postsecondary education. In fall 2005 more than 6.5 million students were enrolled for credit in the nation's 1,195 community colleges. These students comprise 46 percent of all U.S. undergraduates, and 39 percent are the first generation in their families to attend college (American Association of Community Colleges, n.d.). Nearly 400,000 full- and part-time faculty members teach in community colleges (Townsend & Twombly, 2007). Initially, community colleges provided only undergraduate education often referred to as "years 13 and 14" in the educational system. During the evolution of community colleges from those first schools established in the early nineteenth century to those established in the twenty-first century, however, the mission of the community college has expanded tremendously. Since the mid-1960s, when one new community college was opening every day on average, the functions have expanded to include academic transfer, career and technical education, continuing education, developmental education, and community service (Cohen & Brawer, 2003, p. 20). This five-pronged function creates special challenges for faculty development in the community college.

Any number of configurations exists to develop, support, and/or maintain faculty development programs. In a 1998 survey ($N = 142$) of

National Council for Staff, Program, and Organizational Development (NCSPOD) member institutions, 13 percent of survey respondents focused only on full- or part-time faculty development programs, with 2 percent serving only the needs of full-time faculty. The majority of respondents (82 percent) offered comprehensive professional development as defined by an array of services, activities, events, and programming for all employee groups (Hoss, 1998, p. 109). According to this research, 95 percent of NCSPOD member community colleges in 1998 offered faculty development. Further, in the 1998 study, "full-time developers existed in 25% of responding institutions, plus staff (5%), plus committees (4%), or programs having both staff and committees (11%) along with the full time developer" (p. 112). In comparison, a 2006 publication providing information about faculty development in community colleges revealed organizational structures having "central units (34%), while the other two-thirds [had] nearly equal numbers of programs that center on an individual (21%), committee (21%), or clearinghouse (17%)" (Sorcinelli, Austin, Eddy, & Beach, 2006, p. 41). In terms of financial commitment, in the 1998 study of community college professional development programs 37 percent of respondents reported that they were supported with 2 to 5 percent of the institutional budget, which is in accord with NCSPOD's recommendation (Hoss, 1998, p. 115). Organization and support was most often determined by size of institution; size of program; years of program existence; number of employees or employee groups; institutional financial capabilities; and, most important, administrative and/or governing board commitment to faculty development.

"Of course, the overarching goal for all faculty development programs is to improve student learning" (Sorcinelli et al., 2006, p. 41). Community colleges do endorse and support this conclusion. In addition, community colleges frequently work to integrate differing staff groups in ways that most other institutions do not. They are concerned about the improvement of institutional functioning and student success, and they expect and require teaching faculty to remain current in changing academic and vocational fields and technology skills. They seek to improve college relationships in the community, increase graduation and transfer rates, improve morale, and respond to legislation and societal changes (Smith & Beno, 1993, n.p.). In sum, community college faculty developers are expected to support a diverse and comprehensive growth and development agenda for faculty and often for other staff members as well.

Community colleges provide services to students ranging in age from fifteen to ninety-five. Faculty members must either be experts in their field, having worked in business and industry, or be prepared with a minimum of a master's degree in their teaching disciplines. They must be dedicated to excellence in teaching and learning so as to promote student success. Community colleges further ask faculty members to provide credit courses not only through face-to-face instruction, but also through online delivery using electronic and television media. Faculty members must be able to function in dual credit environments and must determine credit for prior learning and experience. Technology demands and new delivery modalities require community college faculty to undertake career-long developmental journeys of growth and change.

The context of the community college provides challenges to faculty developers who support faculty members in meeting the needs of special student populations within a climate emphasizing student learning outcomes. Furthermore, community college faculty development is not separate from a larger vision of staff and organizational development. One of the earliest publications on this topic, *Staff Development in the Community College: A Handbook* (Hammons, Smith Wallace, & Watts, 1978), promoted a comprehensive view of staff development and inclusive programs. Building upon the foundation in this handbook, we discuss in this chapter the challenges in the context of community colleges to provide a range of faculty development approaches that address (a) the diversity of student profiles and student goals, (b) the skills needed for effective teaching and learning, and (c) the dimensions of communication through multiple delivery systems.

Background: Student Profiles and Goals

To say that the profile of community college students is extremely complex is an understatement. Most students are commuters as "community colleges tended to be built so that 90–95% of the state's population lived within reasonable commuting distance, about twenty-five miles" (Cohen & Brawer, 2003, pp. 16–17), but a few community colleges do have residence halls available for a small percentage of their population. Faculty members must indeed be willing to contribute to building community among students who live on campus, but it is a far greater challenge to build community within a distance learning environment using Course Learning Management Systems (CMS/LMS, such as Blackboard, Angel, E-College, or Moodle).

The youngest community college students (ages fifteen to eighteen) attend through dual enrollment or "running start" programs that supplement high school offerings with college level courses. Students participate in honors programs, home schooling, or advanced courses not available in their secondary schools. Many students are traditional aged, generally understood as eighteen to twenty-two years old. A prediction of an increasingly significant market share for community colleges is that more "traditional" students (like the ones in the 1960s remembered by faculty) have parents who are now reluctant or unable to pay for four to six years of university education. Traditional students are joined by adult learners who range from age twenty-three to ninety years or beyond. These students may be transitioning between high school and college, work and college, unemployment and college, or retirement and college. Many part-time adult students work full time and juggle to balance work, home, social, and school lives. This demographic mix leads to the phenomenon of many intergenerational community college classes, which presents special challenges as well as joys for the faculty.

A community college tends to reflect the community it serves. Community characteristics might include small and rural, downtown business, online savvy, sophisticated and wealthy, or increasingly international and ethnically diverse. Students' diverse socioeconomic backgrounds create additional challenges in the learning environment. An overriding economic desperation affects many community college students, and this fact overlays their whole experience. Often a student will passively say, "I don't know what to study," followed by the impassioned statement, "Just get me a credential that will get me a job!" Community college students are also especially learning style-diverse. Many of their special needs can be addressed by smaller classes, faculty members dedicated to individual student success, and both service and resource assistance. "Along with attracting students of color, the transfer agreements also bring in older women students, single parents, low-income students and recent immigrants" (Wolf-Wendel, Twombly, Morphew, & Sopchich, 2004, p. 221). Because of demographic diversity, community college faculty members must be prepared to recognize differences at the same time as they seek to establish a sense of community and select appropriate teaching and learning approaches.

Students enter their local community college with varied goals in mind. "Many students who attend community colleges choose to attend not because they are incapable of succeeding at more selective institutions but because they lack what McDonough (1997) calls the cultural capital to select more prestigious private institutions. That is, they do not have the family or schooling background that has introduced them to elite private colleges or provided them with encouragement to attend one of these colleges" (Wolf-Wendel et al., 2004, pp. 214–215). Some seek a degree and intend to pursue a program from beginning to end.

Others attend to complete general education requirements before transferring to a college or university to finish their degrees. They may attend during summer school as "reverse transfer" students (those transferring from a university); this enrollment is one of the fastest-growing groups of students at the community college level. Some attend to complete a program that leads to a credential, certification, or licensure. Others hope to complete a professional or technical program that may be two or three years in length.

Although developmental education is not usually a student-driven goal, community colleges respond to students who need basic skill enhancement in reading, mathematics, English, or English as a Second Language. Because these students need foundational knowledge to be successful, they are usually placed in skill-building coursework based upon initial skill testing or discipline-specific diagnostics. In addition, some seek a General Equivalency Diploma (GED), which equates to completion of year twelve in secondary education systems, in order to continue their formal learning in higher education or to pursue employment.

Many adult learners attend the community college to focus on training or retraining needs. These goal-directed adults have learned that they need different knowledge, skills, behaviors, and attitudes to continue in their current profession or to pursue a new career. Others seek additional specializations in order to advance professionally. Increasing numbers of community college students are pursuing lifelong learning. They take classes to follow an interest or gain knowledge they did not have the time or energy to acquire when they were degree-seeking. Retirees or baby boomers enroll in both credit and noncredit coursework to prepare for retirement, extend their travel opportunities, become part of a college "booster" group of seniors, or attain technological literacy.

Teaching and Learning Expectations

Community college faculty members are hired for their content expertise, knowledge, and preparation. Since community colleges are primarily teaching institutions, faculty skills must include teaching skills that address not only discipline-specific knowledge and skills but also a substrata teaching level that includes assisting students in basic academic study skills, work and career preparation along with general education and personal development. Faculty members who help students learn how to be better students add lifelong learning skills to discipline-specific knowledge.

Community college faculty members need particularly well-developed interpersonal skills to be supportive of the varied student populations they serve. Evidence abounds of the power of community college faculty members taking the time to get to know their students, providing intentional and appropriate feedback, and encouraging each student's success (Community College Survey of Student Engagement, 2007).

Hence, faculty development efforts need to be framed around the development and use of these strategies with students. Since so many community college faculty members teach in career programs and general education courses that support career programs, they need to be prepared to support students pursuing these career paths. Faculty choices are important in helping students learn workplace skills, and faculty members are vital in aiding students to enhance critical thinking, writing ability, mathematical reasoning, and information literacy skills. To that end, faculty development usually supports each faculty member in learning how to use and evaluate assignments to be more effective in learning communities. Online courses have increased the expectation for effective writing and include a diversity of writing requirements with greater demand for clarity, reasonable expression, and succinctness as faculty feedback is mainly available only through the written word.

Faculty development centers and programs, by whatever name, have been at the forefront of curricular change as well as organizational change (Rouseff-Baker in Watts, 2002, p. 35) in support of innovative teaching and learning. Community college faculty development programs also advance civic engagement and social responsibility agendas through service-learning initiatives. Students and faculty participate in international exchanges, community-based projects, and leadership roles and volunteerism—experiences that advance the professional development of all staff in the community college.

Because community colleges are so heavily involved with distance education delivery systems, faculty development centers have been instrumental in encouraging faculty to enhance their skills in engaging students in e-learning. The traditional face-to-face classroom still exists and will continue to do so because learning needs are as varied as educational methodologies. Faculty development endeavors continue to enrich that environment through the advancement of active learning methods, increased knowledge about brain research findings, appropriate and engaging use of technology, and enhanced lecturing. Other learning challenges are addressed with the use of computer-assisted instruction and learning labs.

Many community colleges support faculty who deliver instruction through fully online or hybrid courses, using interactive video or various strategies to hook learners into action-packed media. Emerging technologies and interfaces—such as wikis, blogs, games, second life scenarios, simulations, live demonstrations and real-time connectivity—all offer exciting challenges for faculty members to generate communication and critical thinking applications to current global issues. Technology has become so central to teaching and learning that some community colleges are adding instructional designers to help the faculty integrate emergent technologies into instruction. It is almost beyond "delivery"—it is a different way to situate learning. Learning is on the cusp of a techno-transformation, and faculty developers have seen the shift to the information service age. They are continually scanning for new tools, strategies, ideas, and training to assist the faculty and the organization in meeting the intergenerational learner needs. While this situation applies to higher education institutions of all types, it is particularly evident in community colleges.

Curricula also continue to shift as exhibited through experimentation and establishment of modularized, accelerated, cohort, open entry/open exit, synchronous, asynchronous, and learning community formats. These format changes require faculty training and development as they require rethinking course content packaging. As colleges examine their services to students, some are moving to programming that enables students to take a full load of courses (twelve to fifteen credit hours) while attending classes only one day a week. Serving faculty members who are affected by all these changes has become a great challenge for faculty developers.

Community College Faculty Development Initiatives

Many community colleges use a system of Professional Development Plans (PDP) or Individual Development Plans (IDP), in which faculty members state their wants and needs over time, ranging from one to three years depending on the community college review cycle. These plans must be tied to budget allocation so that needs are met both for the faculty member and the college as a whole. Such plans result in individual development as well as contribute to the growth of the learning organization, the academic division, and the department.

Increasingly, community colleges are integrating faculty development programs that are equally available to both full- and part-time faculty. Depending upon the community college service needs and its location, from 20 percent to 90 percent of credit hours may be generated by part-time (or adjunct) faculty members; thus attention to opportunities for faculty development is equally important for all. Representative community college training and development programs and activities are designed to help faculty learn to teach more effectively, thus enabling them to meet student needs. These include:

○ Initiation and improvement of courses and programs

○ Alignment of instructional goals and objectives with institutional assessment and Continuous Quality Improvement (CQI) strategies

○ Design of instructional delivery systems and multimedia learning materials

○ Individualization and customization of instructional practice

○ Refinement and enhancements of face-to-face or online delivery

○ Simulated realities in the distance learning context

○ Asynchronous and synchronous learning strategies

○ Course assessment strategies

○ State licensure and professional certification assessments

○ Nationally normed assessments (Burnstad & Hoss, 2004, p. 7)

Program development focuses on the improvement of educational and support programs by providing and maintaining the structure, content, and systems at the department level, in keeping with the organizational model. Program development may include:

○ Ongoing development of new curricula and programs to shift with marketplace needs

○ Evaluation and growth of existing curricula and programs in general education, basic skills, career pathways, or lifelong learning skills and competencies

○ Courses and/or program design to refocus learning (Burnstad & Hoss, 2004, p. 7)

Since community colleges seek to respond to the community served, curricular change is an ongoing challenge that faculty development should support. Some institutions have hired curriculum design specialists, multimedia experts, and technologists to help faculty rethink and rework both course applications and delivery.

Organizational needs must be considered to accommodate compliance training, such as the Americans With Disability Act (ADA), the Family Education Right to Privacy Act (FERPA), emergency response systems, safety and security preparation, and sexual harassment prevention. Institutional technology training is required for use of internal systems, for discipline-specific applications, and for individual user office PCs and learning management systems such as Blackboard, Angel, and E-College (Burnstad & Hoss, 2004, p. 8).

Historically, postsecondary education conceived of professional development as content currency, which certainly is embraced and vigorously supported by community colleges. Conference attendance is a major focus of many faculty development programs; some faculty developers have been able to obtain financial support from their foundations to assist faculty with travel and conference costs. Some community colleges are able to provide teaching innovation support through sabbatical leaves that encourage publishing or engaging in grant writing. In addition to conference attendance, faculty members often seek skills enhancement by attending, for example, such programs as StrengthQuest, Appreciative Inquiry training, or workshops on classroom assessment techniques. A few community colleges are building comprehensive support programs for faculty members throughout the distinct phases of their professional lives—from sophisticated new faculty orientation programs to new faculty support, including their ascent into rank and tenure. Programming to meet individual needs in support of mid- and late career faculty is gaining attention. Desired program outcomes are the enhancement of innovation, mentoring relationships, networking, enhanced faculty retention, and high morale throughout the institution (Chang & Baldwin, 2008; E. A. Karls, personal communication, July 25, 2008).

Personal development focuses on whole-life issues and encourages faculty members to focus on self. Such programs may include fitness and wellness programs; financial planning and preretirement seminars; or even occupational, recreational, travel, or social programs (Burnstad & Hoss, 2004, p. 8). Community colleges have long encouraged faculty to participate in community development or continuing education programs, such as countywide leadership programs offered through local chambers of commerce, economic development entrepreneurships and partnerships, and voluntary service to the community through board membership, political office, or soup kitchen support. Programs of this sort are generally coordinated through a comprehensive community college faculty development program.

Innovative Practice

The approaches to faculty development programming as undertaken by community colleges vary from consortial arrangements to in-house-designed programs to programs supported by visiting scholars (Burnstad & Hoss, 2004, pp. 36–39). Commonalities among institutions have been recognized for excellence in faculty development by the National Council for Staff, Program, and Organizational Development, renamed in 2007 as the North American Council for Staff, Program, and Organizational Development. These commonalities include new faculty orientation, faculty technology training, workshops on teaching and learning, Great Teachers Seminars, sabbatical opportunities, centers for teaching and learning, and an assembly of publication and resources. Specific programs illustrate innovative practice and deserve greater explanation; the examples that follow reflect the strategic plans and missions of each institution.

Delta College (Michigan) Professional Development Course Series

One of the most innovative features of Delta College's Faculty Center for Teaching Excellence (FCTE) is its ED 300 professional development course series. This series of fifteen courses (with more in development) was initiated to support the professional development of faculty and staff in a convenient, tuition-supported, colleague-instructed, in-house format. ED 300 courses, offered in various formats (face to face, hybrid, and online), are tuition supported through the programs Delta offers for full- and part-time faculty. All ED 300 courses are transferable as undergraduate courses in Michigan and carry credit toward the Michigan Continuing Teacher Certification. This possibility is a particular advantage to adjunct faculty members, who may be seeking continuing certification at an affordable price. These courses, which are led by Delta's own faculty members, help other faculty and staff members integrate specific curricular programs and the learning-centered values of the college. As a next step in integration, the FCTE is developing a "master teacher" credentialing program with ED 300 courses at its core. Integrated courses provide a "best practices" grounding for individuals who have a strong occupational and/or academic background but who may need further pedagogical study or coalescence with Delta's key curricular practices. Courses such as "Best Practices in Teaching and Learning," "The Adult Learner," and "Writing to Learn" provide grounding in the principles and practices of effective teaching and learning, especially important for adjunct faculty members. Beginning in 2009, adjunct faculty members are recognized for successful completion of this program.

At Delta College, the Faculty Center for Teaching Excellence has examined faculty development over the course of long careers and has developed programming for various ages and stages of academic life. It offers a comprehensive first-year faculty development program through its ED 390 "Best Practices in Teaching and Learning" course for new full-time faculty. This course, initially funded through a Delta College Foundation grant, was created to build on existing professional development opportunities for new faculty while addressing Delta's need for an even more comprehensive, sustained, first-year faculty experience. The course builds a sustainable, positive cohort of new faculty while working to hone teaching practices that foster active learning, reflective practice, and collegial modeling of best pedagogical practices. In addition, it acknowledges the value of institutional history and culture and builds on the positive elements of Delta's organization that can serve as building blocks for future growth. The course extends through the entire first year of employment of new faculty and results in three earned academic credits. For most new faculty these credits result in a pay increase permanently added to the base salary (E. A. Karls, personal communication, August 10, 2008).

Kansas City Kansas Community College Academic Symposium

The Academic Symposium at Kansas City Kansas Community College (KCKCC) began after a faculty member who had been on sabbatical leave went to the faculty development office, looking for a forum to present the results of his work. Personnel determined that other faculty and staff might benefit from having such a forum. Consequently, the Academic Symposium was organized to provide a public forum for faculty and staff members to make presentations of academic or artistic merit. Now six symposia are held each academic year, and they are scheduled for one hour although many run longer. Once six proposals are accepted through a competitive selection process, the faculty development office announces them through the usual flyers and e-mails. Additionally, professional posters are created by the coordinator of the Digital Imaging Program and his top students. The KCKCC symposium generates these positive opportunities:

○ Faculty and staff are making professional presentations outside the classroom.

○ Faculty and staff are observing their colleagues making professional presentations.

○ Students are observing faculty and staff making professional presentations outside the classroom and are participating in discussion and debate with faculty and staff.

○ Cross-discipline and function discussions are occurring.

○ KCKCC's Digital Design program is applying creativity to actual application.

Past presentations have included topics such as the following:

o "Objects in the Mirror Are Closer Than They Appear" (original poetry)

o "The 1829 Big Neck War and Its Impact on Northwest Missouri and Eastern Kansas"

o "Terrorism, Racism, and Black Resistance"

o "Black Death and Syphilis: A Historical Comparison of Contagion Theories"

o "Schizo-world: The Science and Politics of Climate Change"

When this symposium series was started, the anticipated audience was faculty and staff. Increasingly, however, faculty members are asking to bring students to the sessions, and a third to half of the audience now consists of students. These symposia have increased community conversations, building camaraderie among faculty and students. Initially, presenters received no compensation for participation, except feedback from colleagues. Now in its sixth year, the symposium has been so successful that a stipend of $200 is offered for each presentation (B. Hayes, personal communication, August 1, 2008).

San Bernardino Valley College (California) Training for Online Faculty

The mission of San Bernardino Valley College (SBVC) is to "provide quality education and services to a diverse community of learners." One cohort is the ever-increasing number of online learners. The college offers an Associate in Arts degree in a fully online format; and, like many community colleges, it has seen tremendous growth from two online classes offered in 1996 to 110 classes in 2007. These 110 sections encompass twenty-three disciplines, forty-five faculty members, and 7 percent of the FTEs. Students obviously want quality online programs, and SBVC seeks to prepare faculty members to provide "quality instruction and services in an online environment" through quality faculty and staff development activities. In 2003, the college implemented a certification program, which requires faculty members who are teaching online to have completed training and demonstrate competence in the following:

o Course Management System (Blackboard or First Classroom)

o TEACH Act (Copyright Compliance)

o PL 508 (ADA Compliance Issues)

○ Course Organization and Structure (transitioning from face-to-face to online)

○ Pedagogy of Teaching Online

Faculty members can achieve these competencies by attending campus-based professional development or off-campus seminars and workshops. The college offers a seven-week program in two-hour workshops; this training is also available online. Other options for meeting this requirement include participating in @ONE, an online training program free to all California community college faculty members. It is housed at Evergreen Valley College and is sponsored by a grant from the California Community College Chancellor's Office.

In 2007, San Bernardino Valley College determined that the online faculty members desired an opportunity to meet face-to-face to discuss strategies, emerging technologies, frustrations, and success with online teaching. As a result, the Great Online Teachers' Seminar (GOTS) was developed; it is modeled after the Great Teachers Movement and is an appropriate way to address this need. SBVC sponsored the first three-day GOTS seminar in spring 2007 with forty-five faculty members in attendance. Participants shared successes, brainstormed potential solutions for problems, and focused on methods for achieving online teaching excellence. This workshop led to the development of a faculty network for collaborating to enhance online teaching. SBVC now sponsors this event every two years, inviting faculty from other institutions to share expertise, resources, and experiences (K. Weiss, personal communication, August 8, 2008).

Johnson County Community College (Kansas) Adjunct Certification Training

Johnson County Community College offers all adjunct faculty members the opportunity to participate in what is called Adjunct Certificate Training (ACT). ACT provides tools and resources to assist adjunct faculty in becoming more effective educators. Upon completion of ACT, adjunct faculty members are knowledgeable about the college's mission, aware of institutional policies and procedures, comfortable in the college learning community, and equipped with resources to enhance learning. Certification requires adjunct faculty to complete required in-class modules and at least one elective module within a two-semester sequence, but with the option to extend for an additional year.

Required modules include:

○ Orientation

○ Assessment and Test Construction

- Classroom Diversity Issues
- Designing an Effective Syllabus
- Employment Policies and Procedures
- Instructional Design
- Legal Issues
- Microteaching and Classroom Videotaping (lab setting)
- Teaching to the Whole Student
- Technology in the Classroom
- Reflective Journal

Elective modules include:

- Brain Research and Instruction
- Goal Setting Using the Individual Development Plan
- iTeach Online
- Softchalk Jumpstart
- Essential Podcasting
- Master Teacher Workshop
- Learning Outside the Classroom
- Learning Styles
- Teaching Techniques
- Teaching Beyond Technique (J. Gadberry, personal communication, August 30, 2008)

These community college faculty development initiatives reflect the variety of current practices. They accommodate specific faculty populations and meet both program and organizational training and development needs. Lastly, these programs address the needs (a) of mid- and late-career faculty, (b) for faculty and staff research dissemination, (c) for a network of skilled online practitioners, and (d) for adjunct faculty to enhance teaching skills.

Issues of Accountability and Sustainability

The context of the community college dictates a responsibility to evaluate, measure, and share faculty development programs and outcomes. We offer a general recommendation to faculty developers who are creating a standardized form to gather information in response to the following questions.

o What were the goals of the training or activity?

o What were the expected outcomes from the training or activity?

o What competencies were measured?

o How was each competency measured? Did a rubric establish a scale of achievement?

o How effective was the measurement?

o How effective was the faculty development effort?

o How did it reinforce the community college mission? (See also Chapter Nine in this volume, "Program Assessment for Faculty Development.")

Smith and Beno (1993) outlined four levels of evaluation to measure professional development: (1) reaction, (2) learning, (3) behavior and attitude change, and (4) the effect on students and the institution. Additional criteria (return on investment or cost/benefit) were added by Smith et al. in a revision in 2003.

Level 1 measures reactions to events, and the data are easy to collect. The purposes of the assessment are to

1. Determine the quality of the activity

2. Ask if the topic should be further explored in the future

3. Measure the level of satisfaction (positive/negative, like/dislike, good/bad more/less)

4. Determine whether more faculty members should participate in the future

Level 1 is gathered using such instruments as surveys, interviews, focus groups, and participant reports.

Level 2 measures learning and demonstrates knowledge or application gained. The purposes of the assessment are to

1. Determine whether learning has occurred

2. Ascertain whether anything new was learned

3. If not, determine what further activities are needed

4. If not, determine whether the right assessment questions were asked

5. Determine whether participants learned the content, skill, behavior, or change in attitude

Level 2 involves using surveys, samples, interviews, focus groups, and participant reports and may assess learning immediately or several weeks after the activity to measure retention.

Level 3 measures behavior and attitude change and is apparent in word and deed. The purposes of this assessment are to

1. Determine whether change has occurred
2. Identify what changes participants have made
3. Evaluate whether these were the desired changes
4. If not, explore what factors affected the environment
5. Document changes noticed by supervisors, colleagues, and students

Level 3 is accomplished through instruments such as student surveys, self-study, participant reports, and short- or long-term study.

Level 4 measures the effect on students and the institution as a result of the program, training, or intervention; and this area is difficult to evaluate. Impact is determined by

1. Identifying an increase or decrease in morale
2. Evaluating the supportiveness of campus climate for both students and employees
3. Recognizing if and when employees are sufficiently informed to do their jobs
4. Determining the level of involvement in decision making
5. Finding satisfaction levels of the college work climate
6. Ultimately proving that students are learning, or achieving their goals, or completing them in reasonable time, or identifying they are successful
7. Examining how and when students or staff members have problems solved

Level 4 assessment uses climate surveys, measures of student retention, goal accomplishment, complaint reduction statistics, community perceptions, program review, and institutional data.

In the revision completed by Smith et al. in 2003, a Level 5 of assessment was added to measure return on investment or cost/benefit (the most difficult of all to determine). This level is a complex method of assessment used to demonstrate the return on an extensive, expensive intervention such as a multiyear, multimillion-dollar Title III or V grant. Level 5 data are persuasive to legislatures or grant funding agencies. Level 5 asks for answers to two fundamental questions: (1) Did the investment of time and money result in the anticipated outcomes, and (2) how do we know that?

A comprehensive faculty development plan is strengthened by a well-constructed assessment plan that leads to documentable feedback and results that provide guidance for improvement strategies. In some community colleges, faculty development programs are asked to do an institutional program review similar to other programs and support service reviews.

Conclusion

Community college faculty developers need to consider early on how to become force multipliers in their institution, bringing often unlikely sources of support, resource, and enlightenment to the faculty development work. Sometimes the biggest job is listening to others and encouraging them, as most teaching faculty members are essentially motivated to improve the lot of another human being. By and large, community college faculty members take teaching and learning seriously; and they can be easily shaken by problems in the classroom, discouragement in their journey of employment, or significant changes in the methods of instructional delivery.

Faculty developers need to understand the communities from which the students are drawn and represent those cultures meaningfully in the flavor of faculty development; we need to note, however, that this differs college to college. Developers need to be aware of the complexities of sustaining all faculty programming when support structures for full- and part-time faculty vary so widely. Faculty developers should provide an expansive vision of the college as applied to the entire faculty and staff. The work of teaching and learning is not done by faculty members alone; support staff and administrators also have vital roles. This reality is often misunderstood, misrepresented, or ignored—to the potential detriment of student learning.

A rich mosaic of faculty development is needed and offered within the complex environments of community colleges. In this chapter we have addressed the challenges of meeting the multifaceted programming requirements for all faculty members who are at various stages in their expertise, development, and career pathways. Faculty development is further challenged by the diversity in student profiles, motivations, and goals. The challenge exists to meet institutional expectations for ongoing skill enhancement in both teaching and learning, which is compounded by multiple delivery systems. These challenges require a range of faculty development approaches that align each mosaic piece within the context of community college faculty development efforts so as to enhance the lives of faculty, staff, and students.

REFERENCES

American Association of Community Colleges. (n.d.). *Students at community college*. Retrieved October 31, 2008, from http://www2.aacc.nche.edu/research/index.htm

Burnstad, H., & Hoss, C. (2004). *Launching your staff, program, and organizational development program*. Kansas City, KS: National Council for Staff, Program and Organizational Development.

Chang, D., & Baldwin, R. G. (2008). Creating time and space for faculty reflection, risk-taking, and renewal. *The Department Chair, 19*(1), 1–3.

Cohen, A., & Brawer, F. (2003). *The American community college* (4th ed.). San Francisco: Jossey-Bass.

Community College Survey of Student Engagement. (2007). *Committing to student engagement: Reflections on CCSSE's first five years*. Retrieved October 15, 2008, from the Community College Leadership Program, University of Texas, at http://www.ccsse.org/publications/2007NatlRpt-final.pdf

Hammons, J., Smith Wallace, T. H., & Watts, G. (1978). *Staff development in the community college: A handbook*. Topical Paper no. 66. Los Angeles: ERIC Clearinghouse for Junior Colleges.

Hoss, C. (1998). *The mentoring and professional development of part-time faculty*. Lincoln: University of Nebraska Press.

McDonough, P. M. (1997). *Choosing colleges: How social class and schools structure opportunity*. Albany: State University of New York Press.

Rouseff-Baker, F. (2002). Leading change through faculty development. In G. Watts (Ed.), *New directions for community colleges, no. 120. Enhancing community colleges through professional development* (pp. 35–42). San Francisco: Jossey Bass.

Smith, C., & Beno, B. (1993). *A guide to staff development evaluation*. Sacramento, CA: Community College League of California. Rev. in 2003 by Smith, C., DeVol, M., & Stetson, N., as *Evaluating staff and organizational development*. Available from California Community College Council for Staff and Organizational Development at http://www.4csd.org

Sorcinelli, M. D., Austin, A. E., Eddy, P. L, & Beach, A. L. (2006). *Creating the future of faculty development: Learning from the past, understanding the present*. Bolton, MA: Anker.

Townsend, B. K., & Twombly, S. B. (2007). Community college faculty: Overlooked and undervalued. *ASHE Higher Education Report, 32*(6).

Wolf-Wendel, L., Twombly, S., Morphew, C., & Sopchich, J. (2004). From the barrio to the bucolic: The student transfer experience from HSI to Smith College. *Community College Journal of Research and Practice, 28*(3), 213–231.

GRADUATE AND PROFESSIONAL STUDENT DEVELOPMENT PROGRAMS

Laura L. B. Border and Linda M. von Hoene

AS GRADUATE AND PROFESSIONAL STUDENTS move through their programs, they must develop the knowledge and skills required for the academic positions to which they are assigned during their years of graduate study and those to which they may aspire as professors. Historically, the simple completion of a task was considered a sufficient apprenticeship to learn to teach effectively and move on to a faculty position. However, twenty-five years of growth in programming at major research universities in the area of graduate and professional student development (GPSD) demonstrate that graduate students' successful acquisition of skills and knowledge can be facilitated and expanded by an effective support system focused on teaching, research, academic service, and professional development. As programs to support graduate students have blossomed at research universities, graduate and professional student (GPS) developers have begun to conduct research that has resulted in the creation of journals and other publications devoted to the topic. This chapter addresses five areas of graduate and professional student development:

1. The growth of the field
2. The types of programs
3. The knowledge and skills graduate students need to master during their graduate programs

4. The knowledge and skills needed by GPS developers
5. The assessment of graduate student competencies, GPSD programs, and GPS developers

Growth of Graduate and Professional Student Development

After the Second World War, the GI Bill led to a dramatic increase in undergraduate and graduate enrollments. In this same period, universities began to increase their emphasis on research, extending the employment of graduate students as teaching assistants (TAs) and instructors. In the 1960s, the introduction of the Civil Rights Act resulted in another shift in enrollments. By the 1970s, the coalescence of these factors led to the introduction of TA support, particularly in departments of foreign languages, English, speech, and chemistry, which had begun to rely heavily on TAs in laboratories, recitations, and sections of introductory courses. Student unrest and dissatisfaction during the 1970s gave rise to changes not only in the curriculum but also in the evaluation of faculty and TA performance (Border, 2006).

By the mid-1980s, several research universities had begun to initiate programs that addressed the training of graduate students to teach on campus and as future faculty—for example, the University of Colorado at Boulder's Graduate Teacher Program, which was established in 1985. Also in 1985, at the annual conference of the Professional and Organizational Development Network in Higher Education (POD Network), members interested particularly in the training of TAs met and contributed ideas to the first national conference on the training and employment of TAs, held at Ohio State University in 1986. Attended by approximately 300 individuals, including many graduate deans, the conference set in motion a series of five conferences funded by the Pew Charitable Trusts, which fostered broader efforts both in the United States and abroad to prepare graduate students for their roles as TAs, faculty, and as leaders in the private, governmental, and nonprofit sectors. The published proceedings from these conferences (Chism, 1987; Lewis, 1993; Nyquist, Abbott, Wulff, & Sprague, 1991) laid the groundwork for research in the field. At the "Improving University Teaching" international conference held in Germany in 1993, Goldschmid (1993) emphasized the need to prepare doctoral candidates for leadership and management positions as well as for academe, citing "perseverance, leadership qualities . . . rigor, efficiency, energy, autonomy, self confidence, drawn to social contact, social integration, and . . . flexibility" as necessary for "future growth, engagement and adaptability" (p. 533).

By 1995, the Council of Graduate Schools (CGS) and the Association of American Colleges and Universities (AAC&U) had acquired funding from the Pew Charitable Trusts to offer grants for the Preparing Future Faculty (PFF) Program. By 2000, with additional grants from the National Science Foundation (NSF) and the Atlantic Philanthropies to address issues in specific disciplines, the PFF project included seventy-six clusters involving 295 colleges and universities. The program was deemed successful, and the Council of Graduate Schools continues to host the PFF Web site (Council of Graduate Schools, n.d.). In 2000, the POD Network created a subcommittee on TA development, the goal of which was to assure that issues of graduate and professional student development were addressed at the annual POD conference and in POD publications. The "Re-envisioning the Ph.D. Project" initiated at the University of Washington brought a discussion of graduate education to the forefront and highlighted the need to extend the issue of graduate student preparation beyond preparation for teaching as a faculty member to preparation for leadership roles in business, government, and industry (Nyquist & Woodford, 2000). In 2003, POD elevated the original TA development subcommittee to the status of a full standing committee. That same year, the Carnegie Initiative on the Doctorate funded projects in chemistry and education to provide better professional development for graduate students through model (and remodeled) doctoral programs within departments. Subsequently, in 2003, NSF decided to support the preparation of future faculty in science, technology, engineering, and mathematics (STEM) and funded two centers dedicated to improving STEM faculty—the Center for the Integration of Research, Teaching, & Learning (CIRTL, University of Wisconsin, Madison) (2008) and the Center for the Advancement of Engineering Education in 2003 (CAEE, University of Washington) (2008). In 2004, the name of the POD Network TA Development Committee was changed to the Graduate Student Professional Development (GPSD) Committee in order to reflect new influences regarding career preparation and a continued emphasis on teaching as preparation for diverse careers. The Woodrow Wilson Foundation's Responsive Ph.D. Project focused on the appropriate preparation of graduate students for various roles and showcased programs of note in print and online publications (2005).

In the late 1990s, New Forums Press introduced a journal dedicated to the preparation of teaching assistants, the *Journal of TA Development*. Following the publication of ten successful volumes, this journal was renamed *Studies in Graduate and Professional Student Development* to focus more broadly on programs, research, and activities in the field of GPSD. Volume Eleven was published in 2008 under this new title (Border, 2008). In 2009, the POD Core Committee authorized a change in name for the committee to the Graduate and Professional Student Development Committee to reflect more accurately the preparation of graduate and professional students in various schools and colleges for their future roles as academics.

Types of GPSD Programs

Teaching Assistant Programs

During this time of rapid change and development in graduate student programs, Lambert and Tice (1993) produced a catalogue of centralized and department-specific TA programs based on 107 responses to a survey supported by the American Association for Higher Education. At that time, centralized programs were housed predominantly in centers for teaching and learning, although the centers at the University of Colorado at Boulder, Syracuse University, and the University of California-Berkeley, reported directly to the graduate school, thereby acknowledging that learning to teach at the college and university level should be part of graduate education. Lambert and Tice included descriptions of about twenty centralized programs and a similar number of departmentally based programs.

TA training programs function specifically as in-service programs to prepare graduate students for teaching roles on campus; however, a desire to view graduate students as future faculty was soon to follow. Some of these changes are documented in Marincovich, Prostko, and Stout (1998), which provides an excellent overview of the field of TA development at that point in time.

These early programs illustrated the cornerstones of GPSD programs, and they continue as such today: workshops, seminars, and courses on teaching both in centralized programs and in departments; a focus on pedagogy, assessment, and reflection; content that addresses cognition through a learning styles model; an introduction to course and syllabus planning; practice teaching either in collaboration with a professor or as instructor of record; improved oral classroom English training and cultural training for internationals; training in addressing issues of diversity in U.S. classrooms; teaching consultant- or faculty-based observations and consultations on teaching; and the creation and use of locally produced instructional materials.

Preparing Future Faculty Programs

The national Preparing Future Faculty (PFF) project, begun with funding from the Pew Foundation to the Council of Graduate Schools (CGS) and the Association of American Colleges & Universities (AAC&U) (Gaff, Pruitt-Logan, Sims, & Denecke, 2003), extended the interest of graduate student preparation programs beyond the scope of one institution. The major idea behind the PFF movement was to introduce future faculty to an expanded postsecondary environment—that is, beyond the typical research institution—in the hopes of providing an improved teaching staff to liberal arts colleges, community colleges, and specialized colleges. The prototype PFF project brings faculty members from diverse postsecondary environments together to discuss how graduate students can be better prepared to meet future job responsibilities on their campuses, with the goal of aligning preparation with actual future faculty roles. PFF projects encourage graduate students to explore a range of postsecondary campuses, classrooms, and cultures through site visits to partner campuses, mentorships with local or partner campus faculty members, and projects on teaching that benefit both the home and partner campus.

Professional Development Programs

As support for graduate education has matured, some programs have begun to address skills that enhance an individual graduate student's performance as an academic, such as academic writing skills. Some programs train advanced graduate students to serve as consultants on teaching. Others work with faculty to improve their mentoring skills of graduate students. Many have developed a university teaching certificate. Some have developed academic leadership programs, and others have created career development programs to help master's- and doctoral-level students transition to careers outside academe. Others, in response to a more general educational concern about improving undergraduate education, have introduced programs that are directed at classroom or educational research. A discussion of different professional development types follows.

WRITING PROGRAMS FOR GRADUATE STUDENTS. The genres of writing that graduate students must produce in the process of pursuing their degrees are likely to be new to them: grant writing, preparation of conference papers and posters, completion of publishable articles, and the writing of a thesis or dissertation. While training in academic writing is not always seen as the responsibility of graduate and professional student development offices, workshops or courses can be developed based on a substantial body of literature that has emerged on the topic of academic writing. At a minimum, professional graduate student developers should consider providing starter bibliographies like the ones compiled by Soracco (2008) at the University of California-Berkeley on graduate academic writing. All graduate students need to be able to write well, and graduate students who teach need to be able to help their undergraduate students write effectively. Consequently, most programs address academic writing in some fashion via workshops or courses, whether on making an effective academic argument, writing across the curriculum, grading writing, writing a dissertation, or writing within the discipline. Other programs have broached new territory in writing, notably Stanford University's in-depth program to teach graduate students to write for a nonacademic audience and the University of California-Berkeley Academic Services' writing program devoted exclusively to the academic writing needs of graduate students.

MENTORING PROGRAMS. It is expected that faculty members mentor their graduate students, and some institutions have begun to offer development programs to enhance faculty members' mentoring skills. The University of California-Berkeley's Graduate Student Instructor Teaching and Resource Center, for example, holds an annual seminar for faculty members to help them develop the skills they need to mentor and guide the work of graduate and professional students (von Hoene & Mintz, 2002). This seminar helps faculty members fulfill responsibilities articulated in the campus policy on mentoring graduate students. Other universities such as Yale and Wisconsin are planning similar seminars.

CERTIFICATE PROGRAMS. Approximately forty-five graduate and professional student development programs across the United States and in Canada now offer a certificate in college teaching (von Hoene, 2009). The certificates tend to fall along the continuum that matches the programming offered in the centers: for example, a certificate that focuses primarily on classroom teaching, learning, and performance; a more advanced certificate that addresses a wider range of competencies needed by faculty members; or a professional development certificate developed in conjunction with a career services office to prepare for jobs outside of academe.

LEADERSHIP PROGRAMS. The University of Colorado's Lead Graduate Teacher Network goes beyond training for consultation on teaching and prepares fifty graduate students each year for expanded academic leadership roles in their disciplines and in postsecondary institutions. These graduate student "Leads" create a plan for consultation, workshop facilitation, and a legacy project and carry it out under the supervision of Lead Network staff and a home department faculty mentor.

NONACADEMIC CAREER PROGRAMS. GPS developers at the University of Nebraska and the University of Colorado at Boulder have created innovative liaison activities with their local career services programs to provide additional and focused support for both graduate students and postdoctoral fellows. The goal of such programs is to offer advanced degree students career options that they might never have considered. Career Services works with corporations, government, or research groups to set up internships in which the graduate student can try out and learn new skills in a variety of work environments in business, government, industry, or the nonprofit sector (Bellows, 2008).

CLASSROOM OR EDUCATIONAL RESEARCH PROGRAMS. Some institutions have integrated ideas and models based on the original Classroom Assessment Techniques research done at the University of California-Berkeley (Angelo & Cross, 1993); Boyer's model of the scholarship of teaching (1990); or Eric Mazur's (1997) work at Harvard to create graduate student development programs based on reflective teaching, the scholarship of teaching and learning, and more recently teaching as research. Some initial projects have metamorphosed into discipline-based educational research efforts, which study undergraduate student performance based on the level of the instructor involved (Pollock & Finkelstein, 2008). Others have integrated the Scholarship of Teaching and Learning (SOTL) into workshops or certificates for graduate students; still others have created courses and a certificate based on teaching as research (Center for the Integration of Research, Teaching & Learning, 2008).

Skills and Knowledge Needed by Graduate Students

In planning teacher training and professional development activities for graduate students, professional developers must consider the full range of knowledge and skills, including awareness of diversity and academic integrity issues, that graduate students need to succeed in their graduate programs and beyond. With an increased focus on mentored research experiences for undergraduates, graduate students may be called upon to develop skills in mentoring, advising, and even sometimes counseling junior colleagues and undergraduates. In those settings where graduate students participate in departmental or campuswide committees or in activities that have a public service component, they need to learn collaborative skills. For success on the job market, they need to articulate and provide evidence of their training, skills, experience, and career plans.

Beginning Teaching Skills

Graduate students teach in a range of course settings (usually under the guidance of a faculty member): discussion sections, recitations, labs that are part of larger courses, and stand-alone classes in such disciplines as foreign language, composition, and speech. Frequently they are responsible for conducting office hours or providing instruction through online learning management systems. The courses they teach may be at the lower- or upper-division undergraduate level. The beginning skills and areas of knowledge needed in these settings may range from preparing and presenting a lesson plan, classroom management, conducting small group and other active learning strategies, facilitating discussion, giving oral presentations, grading student work, and giving feedback to teaching students on conducting disciplinary research and understanding how students learn. They also need to possess a solid understanding of the professional standards and ethics that should guide the teaching of undergraduates, including how to work with students with disabilities and how to create an inclusive classroom environment. In those classes in which they have greater responsibility, such as foreign language, speech, and composition courses, TAs may, under faculty supervision, develop their own syllabi and course plans. When graduate students teach in courses that include a service-learning component, they need to understand the mutually reciprocal relationships among civic engagement, diversity, learning, and conflict management that is at the heart of community-based action research.

Advanced Teaching Skills

While the skills and knowledge teaching assistants need and learn are essential and basic, those who are pursuing academic positions need more advanced skills and knowledge, as they will have significantly expanded responsibilities when they enter the profession. Thus advanced graduate students may want to explore the skills fostered by typical preparing future faculty programs. Such knowledge prepares them to be "quick starters" in their first faculty positions (Boice, 2000). Professors at research universities, for example, rarely teach the lower-division language courses that are typically taught by teaching assistants; rather they teach litera- ture and critical theory. Professors at liberal arts colleges need to teach a wide variety of courses beyond the beginning sections they taught as gradu- ate students. Thus, different skills may be needed at a liberal arts college than at a research university. One needs only to consider the use of large courses at research universities and the required skills of preparing and giving lec- tures and guiding the work of TAs. Ideally, to be prepared for teaching as future faculty members, graduate students would do well to have a capstone teaching experience, such as the one provided by the Graduate Division at the University of California-Santa Barbara (Academic Services, 2008), which enables graduate and professional students to have the expe- rience of designing a syllabus and teaching as instructor of record. Though only a small percentage have the opportunity to independently design and teach their own courses and function as the instructor of record, all gradu- ate students can benefit from learning to articulate learning outcomes, design activities, and develop and use grading rubrics. The Professional Development Certificate for Preparing Future Faculty at the University of Colorado at Boulder addresses such higher-level skills.

Mentoring Undergraduates and Novice Graduate Students

In addition to the mentoring and advising skills that graduate students use as teachers of undergraduates, graduate students also sometimes function as mentors to undergraduates in formal undergraduate research apprenticeship programs such as the Ronald E. McNair Postbaccalaureate Achievement Program (2008). Many graduate programs train senior graduate students to mentor novice graduate students into the culture of the department. Courses that formally teach graduate students the skills of mentoring, such as that offered by the GSI Teaching and Resource Center at the University of California-Berkeley (2008a), can address this aspect of GPSD.

Research

As they move from graduate student to postdoctoral appointee to faculty member, newly minted doctoral recipients need to develop independent research agendas. In the sciences, they must learn how to write research proposals and secure grants; they must know how to start and manage a lab, oversee the work of a team of researchers that includes postdoctoral fellows, graduate students, and undergraduates, and provide a healthy work environment. It is beneficial to address these skills as part of graduate education, primarily in the home department, and through supplemental support in GPSD programs.

Academic Service

The aspect of graduate student responsibilities that has been least formally taught is that of academic and community service. Often graduate students have the opportunity to serve on departmental or campuswide committees or to coordinate a lecture series or a conference. In some cases, they may serve on editorial boards for graduate student–run journals. For this activity they need copyediting skills and skills in reviewing and judging conference proposals and articles. In participating on campus committees, they need to have knowledge of institutional governance. The National Science Foundation encourages academic service related to disciplinary expertise through K–12 outreach initiatives that place graduate students in elementary or secondary classrooms to discuss their research.

Teaching or Socratic Portfolios

The single most pervasive change in the programming offered for graduate students since the early 1990s is in the area of developing teaching portfolios to document and improve teaching. GPS developers now devote considerable time to workshops and consultations on teaching portfolios, drawing on the foundational work of Canadian scholars (Knapper, 1995) and of Seldin (1997) in the United States. The work of Border (2002) on the Socratic portfolio addresses issues specific to graduate students. Because graduate students are in their formative years, they can benefit most from engaging in a Socratic dialogue with multiple faculty and staff mentors from their departments, their disciplinary associations, their teaching centers, as well as faculty mentors from other campuses throughout their graduate programs as they build their personal approaches to and understanding of postsecondary instruction. The resulting Socratic portfolio contains a narrative and accompanying artifacts that reflect their experiences, discussions, and decisions, as well as a better understanding of the postsecondary environment. Graduate students who explore their academic opportunities in a Socratic fashion are prepared to make better career decisions when they enter the academic job market. Table 20.1 illustrates a sample, albeit idealized, model of graduate student competencies paired with a sequenced continuum of teaching and professional development activities and support.

Table 20.1. Sample Continuum for Graduate and Professional Student Development.

Beginning TA 1st Year		Continuing TA 2nd/3rd Year		Instructor of Record 4th/5th Year		PFF Fellow 5th/6th Year	
GPSD Program	Department	GPSD Program	Department	GPSD Program	Department	GPSD Program	Department
Provides workshops about teaching on campus, classroom management, testing and grading, introduction to ethics, diversity issues and nonbiased teaching, learning styles, leading a recitation, facilitating a lab, assessment and evaluation issues; provides teaching resources, observation, feedback, and videotape consultation on classroom performance; offers academic goal setting and how to begin a teaching portfolio	Faculty mentors supervise and evaluate TAs; teach about culture of the discipline; supervise labs, recitations, or beginning courses; teach methodology course (teaching methods, strategies, learning theory, testing, grading and assessment); introduce teaching resources and appropriate instructional technology; introduce thinking about teaching as a scholarly activity; introduce academic writing and how to begin a teaching portfolio	Provides workshops on active learning, service learning, the university lecture, collaborative learning; expanding knowledge of diversity in teaching, learning, and curriculum; applying technology in the classroom; improving on teaching strategies, expanding knowledge of conflict management, student motivation, and methods of evaluation	Faculty mentors offer an advanced course on teaching in the discipline to teach graduate students how to write a syllabus, articulate learning goals and objectives, imbed assessment strategies into a course; and guide graduate students in drafting a teaching philosophy	Provides workshops on various teaching methodologies: lecture, discussion, active learning, service learning; diversity in teaching, learning, and curriculum; applying technology in the classroom; teaching large courses, managing TAs who assist with large lectures, working with TAs who grade, methods of evaluation; provides observation, feedback, and videotape consultation on classroom performance	Graduate student instructors of record model how to teach upper division courses, give a university lecture, lead collaborative learning, facilitate service learning, engage students in active learning, teach large courses, manage TAs and graders, present a lecture in the field to an upper division or graduate course, and how to present a lecture in the field to high school students	Provides workshops on postsecondary institutions, site visits to partner campuses and departments; identifies faculty mentor for PFF mentorship; provides model report on PFF mentorship; arranges internships for professional students; provides workshops on job interview process, interviewing skills, writing or professional portfolio, writing cover letter and teaching statement for job application; provides observation, feedback, and videotape consultation on job interview; provides workshops on writing for publication and workshops on writing for a lay audience	Graduate student works with faculty mentor in partner institution. Learns how faculty in partner institution work; learns how research, teaching and service are used in partner institution; sits on a faculty committee; prepares an original syllabus; prepares a job application, writes a cover letter, CV, and teaching statement; gives a pedagogical and research colloquium to partner campus faculty; does a mock interview with mentor faculty; reports back to home department graduate students on the experience; reviews job application materials, procedures, and possibilities with departmental faculty; gives a lecture to a lay audience. Graduate and professional students also learn about how their field is used in the private or nonprofit sector or in government

Note: This chart is designed as a potential model. Institutional differences are to be expected and respected.

Knowledge and Skills for Graduate and Professional Student Developers

As GPSD has come of age, so, too, has the need for well-prepared developers. Although similar to faculty development, GPSD requires a different knowledge base and skill set than does faculty development. GPS developers work in different environments when compared to most faculty developers:

- They work almost exclusively in research institutions.
- They must work in coordination with departmental TA training programs.
- Whether or not they report to the graduate school, they must continually liaison with the graduate dean and be aware of issues in graduate education.
- They work with large numbers of graduate students, graduate student groups, and graduate student services offices.
- They must be aware of the literature and funding available for teaching assistant training and preparing future faculty.
- Because graduate students are novices, they must be able to instruct, guide, consult with, and mentor them in ways that address graduate students' specific developmental and career needs.

The first preconference session to focus specifically on the knowledge and skills needed by GPS developers was offered at the 2007 POD Network conference. Follow-up sessions at the Educational Developers Conference in Vancouver and at the biannual conference of the International Consortium on Education Development addressed this topic further and clarified the need for specific support for GPS developers. Based on feedback from participants at the sessions, concerns about the knowledge and skills needed for work in graduate student development fell into eleven categories that are described following.

1. ACADEMIC MANAGEMENT AND LEADERSHIP SKILLS. Because GPSD support offices tend to be housed either in teaching centers or under the direction of the graduate school, GPS developers need to understand their campus culture, the "line" of administrators to whom they report, the schools and colleges with which they work, the decision-making process, and the best way to influence this process. Strategic planning skills (departmental and campuswide) and program planning, implementation, and evaluation skills are necessary. Graduate student developers also need

to be aware of and responsible for implementing policies relating to areas such as discrimination and harassment, research integrity, academic honesty, and the Americans With Disabilities Act (ADA) and to offer programming to help graduate students understand and carry out these policies and standards. For example, at the University of California-Berkeley, all new TAs (approximately 1,300 each year) take an online course entitled "Professional Standards and Ethics in Teaching" (GSI Teaching and Resource Center, 2008b).

2. KNOWLEDGE OF POSTSECONDARY INSTITUTIONS. GPS developers need to have a broad and in-depth understanding of postsecondary environments in the United States and abroad because current graduate students will be seeking positions in diverse environments. As graduate programs continue to become more similar globally, GPS developers have increasingly diverse opportunities to align graduate preparation with actual faculty roles here and abroad (Bellows, 2008).

3. PEDAGOGICAL KNOWLEDGE. While it is unreasonable to expect GPS developers to be experts in more than one discipline, it is essential that they have a solid doctoral-level grounding in a graduate program, the doctoral program process, and experience with choosing a committee, writing and defending a dissertation, and acquiring an academic position. The content of GPSD resides as much in having lived through the experience as it does in a book. If GPS developers are to achieve credibility with doctoral students, they need to be able to ground examples in content-based knowledge and graduate program experiences and use examples derived from teaching in a discipline (pedagogical content knowledge). They need to have a solid grounding in the content and process aspects of teaching and be able to support graduate students with level-appropriate interventions; that is, what a TA needs to know is developmentally different than what an instructor of record needs to master. Rather than expecting GPS developers to be able to conduct workshops on discipline-specific pedagogical methods, it is preferable that they specialize in certain areas and draw on faculty or advanced graduate students to address discipline-specific issues in workshops or courses.

4. CONSULTATION SKILLS. All GPS developers consult with graduate student teachers, whether through drop-in discussions, lengthier one-on-one consultations, or consultations regarding a class that has been observed or videotaped. Effective graduate and professional student developers identify a mode of consultation that serves the needs of the

student, such as an instructor-centered personal growth model or a structured feedback model. The important outcome of consultation is to provide graduate students with the tools and self-reflection skills they need to improve their teaching throughout the current academic term and throughout their careers.

5. INSTRUCTIONAL TECHNOLOGY. It is important for GPS developers to cultivate skills in instructional technology through collaborations with instructional technologists on campus or via experienced faculty members who have already integrated technology effectively into their courses. Building instructional technology into programming, performance, and products helps to assure that technology for the classroom environment is designed to support teacher success and student learning. (See Chapter Sixteen in this volume, "Issues in Technology and Faculty Development.")

6. TEACHING AT VARIOUS LEVELS. The major historical weakness of teaching assistant training is a narrow focus on preparing TAs for their current assignment—teaching assistant—rather than for the full range of roles and courses they will take on as new faculty members. A more effective approach is to provide a developmental program for graduate students as they move through their graduate programs to match the various responsibilities that they have on campus and others that they will encounter later, such as teaching large lectures, upper-division courses, or graduate seminars.

7. STUDENT SUPPORT SERVICES. Graduate student teachers can perform their jobs as teaching assistants, graders, and tutors more effectively if they are aware of various student services offices that are typically found on university campuses. Undergraduates or peers may need to be referred to the counseling center, to academic tutoring support, to a support office for students with disabilities, to a women's center or a child care center, to a gay, lesbian, bisexual, and transgender (GLBT) office, to a student conduct office, or to the ombudsman. Some GPSD programs—the University of Michigan and the University of Colorado at Boulder, for example—offer workshops or interactive theater projects that address conflict management, suicide prevention, and discrimination and harassment issues as they pertain to the college classroom environment.

8. RESEARCH AND PUBLISHING. GPS developers must be cognizant of the requirements, opportunities, and potential venues for attracting research

dollars and for publishing results. It is advisable to create a research plan that covers projects initiated in the program, obtain research approval from the institutional review board, collect data, carry out research projects on their work, and publish in appropriate journals. Understanding research provides GPS developers with the knowledge and skills to build their own programs and bolster graduate students' success in graduate school.

9. HUMAN RESOURCE AND FINANCIAL MANAGEMENT SKILLS. Most GPS developers work with and often supervise office personnel ranging from full or part-time academic or nonacademic career employees to graduate and undergraduate student employees. As a result, GPS developers need to be knowledgeable about human resource policies and develop skills in hiring and managing staff. Developers who oversee budgets also need to possess skills in financial management.

10. KNOWLEDGE OF NONACADEMIC CAREERS FOR DOCTORATES. Publications such as *At Cross Purposes: What the Experiences of Doctoral Students Reveal About Doctoral Education* by Golde and Dore (2001) have pointed to the need to prepare graduate students for positions outside of academe. Because teacher training can be viewed as effective preparation for any career, this is an opportunity to network with local career development personnel who have good connections within the state and regional economies. This collaboration provides the opportunity to bring back as speakers and mentors graduates who have achieved success in nonacademic settings.

11. KNOWLEDGE OF THE PROFESSION. GPS developers need to be aware of the existing body of literature on GPSD, attend yearly conferences to upgrade their knowledge and skills, and network with their colleagues both at home and abroad to maximize their learning and their ability to contribute to the field. Professional development associations exist in nearly all major countries and are a great source of knowledge.

Assessment

GPS developers need to be able to assess three levels of work: graduate student competencies, their own competencies in GPSD, and program effectiveness. Results can be used for formative program enhancement and administrative reports and can be shared with fellow GPS developers via conference presentations or publications.

Assessment of Graduate Student Competencies

Graduate student competencies regarding teaching, research, and academic service can be assessed in multiple ways. Self-evaluations, student evaluations, and faculty evaluations may all play roles. Participation data, certification data, or the production of portfolios is useful. Observations and videotape consultations are powerful ways to determine whether or not a teacher is beginning to master the requisite skills. Mock job interviews, teaching colloquia, or the presentation of teaching-as-research project may be observed and evaluated. Teaching portfolios allow graduate students to conceptualize and articulate their own philosophy of teaching and learning, provide evidence of their growth and success, and detail their past and future as academics.

Assessment of Developer Competencies

GPS developers need to maintain a self-evaluation plan, continually update their own curriculum vitae, and submit term or academic year reports to administration. They can develop professional portfolios that detail the knowledge and skills discussed previously, providing evidence in the appendices of their skill levels. This portfolio presents the individual's philosophy of GPSD and of teaching and learning. A biographical essay outlining one's education or preparation in the field, work experience, participation in campuswide initiatives, workshop facilitation, and consultation experience could follow. An assessment and evaluation section could contain descriptions of how workshops were evaluated by participants and how teachers reflected on their consultation experiences as well as letters of recommendation or evaluation from other GPS developers. Participation in research projects, collaborations across institutions, conference presentations, and publishing in the field could be included. GPS developers may be able to describe service to the institution through interdepartmental committee work and projects, participation and contributions to a professional development association or to their national disciplinary association or service on strategic planning committees, review boards for journals, or granting agencies. The final section of the narrative of the portfolio could describe plans for further personal and professional development and plans to write grant proposals or publications. The appendices should illustrate and provide evidence for items described in the narrative and indicate levels of effectiveness and quality of achievement.

GPSD Program Assessment

Some centralized GPSD programs are assessed as part of their institutions' regular academic review processes; others are not. Departmental GPSD programs or GPSD programs that report to the graduate school may be reviewed and assessed as part of the normal institutional review process or during an accreditation visit.

Because of the visible presence of GPSD programs, the data generated may offer an important picture of the institution. Data falls generally into similar categories on most campuses: satisfaction surveys; participation in workshops, courses, internships, or site visits to PFF-affiliated campuses; graduate student portfolios; feedback from faculty mentors at PFF partner campuses; and interdepartmental collaborations. Data on the number and content of discipline-specific methodology courses that have been developed is important, as are the syllabi for those courses.

At the unit level, assessment needs to be continuous, formative, and based on graduate student, staff, and alumni feedback on the program. Developers use this feedback to update materials and publications, generate new programs, and improve existing ones. It is wise to build any new project on the basis of an approved research proposal plan, so that data can be made public and incorporated into publications. (See also Chapter Nine in this volume, "Program Assessment for Faculty Development.")

Conclusion

As the field of GPSD comes of age, many opportunities exist for developers to write grants, carry out studies, and publish their results. As programs develop internationally, the opportunity for collaboration and research becomes even more interesting. Further research on the knowledge and skills needed by graduate students and GPS developers, the effectiveness of programs, the impact such programs have on alumni careers, and effective ways to provide services and assess outcomes is needed. We encourage our new and experienced colleagues to further engage in the study of these issues and disseminate their findings.

REFERENCES

Academic Services, Graduate Division. (2008). *UC Santa Barbara. Certificate in college and university teaching.* Retrieved November 15, 2008, from http://www.graddiv.ucsb.edu/academic/CCUT/require/index.htm

Angelo, T. S., & Cross, K. P. (1993). *Classroom assessment techniques: A handbook for college teachers.* San Francisco: Jossey-Bass.

Bellows, L. (2008). Graduate student professional development: Defining the field. *Studies in Graduate and Professional Student Development, 11,* 2–19.

Boice, R. (2000). *Advice for new faculty members: Nihil nimus.* Needham Heights, MA: Allyn & Bacon.

Border, L.L.B. (2002, December). The Socratic portfolio: A guide for future faculty. *PSOnline, XXV*(4), 739–743.

Border, L.L.B. (2006). Two inventories for best practice in graduate student development. *Journal on Excellence in College Teaching 17*(1 & 2), 739–743.

Border, L.L.B. (Ed.). (2008). *Studies in graduate and professional student development.* Stillwater, OK: New Forums.

Boyer, E. L. (1990). *Scholarship reconsidered: Priorities of the professoriate.* Princeton, NJ: Carnegie Foundation for the Advancement of Teaching.

Center for the Advancement of Engineering Education. (2008). *CAEE webpage.* Retrieved November 18, 2008, from http://www.engr.washington.edu/caee/overview.html

Center for the Integration of Research, Teaching, and Learning. (2008). *Project background.* Retrieved November 18, 2008, from http://www.cirtl.net/

Chism, N.V.N. (Ed.). (1987). *Employment and education of teaching assistants: Readings from a national conference.* Columbus: The Ohio State University.

Council of Graduate Schools. (n.d.). *Preparing future faculty.* Retrieved November 16, 2008, from http://www.cgsnet.org/Default.aspx?tabid=226

Gaff, J., Pruitt-Logan, A. S., Sims, L. B., & Denecke, D. D. (2003). *Preparing future faculty in the humanities and social sciences.* Washington, DC: Council of Graduate Schools.

Golde, C. M., & Dore, T. M. (2001). *At cross purposes: What the experiences of doctoral students reveal about doctoral education. A report prepared for the Pew Charitable Trusts.* Retrieved November 15, 2008, from http://www.phd-survey.org

Goldschmid, M. L. (1993). Accountability in higher education: The employability of university graduates. *Proceedings: Improving university teaching 18th international conference* (pp. 529–539). Baltimore: University of Maryland and University College.

GSI Teaching and Resource Center, Graduate Division, UC Berkeley. (2008a). *Mentoring in higher education.* Retrieved November 15, 2008, from http://gsi.berkeley.edu/conf_wkshop/mentoring_2009.html

GSI Teaching and Resource Center, Graduate Division, UC Berkeley. (2008b). *Professional standards and ethics in teaching.* Retrieved January 5, 2009, from http://gsi.berkeley.edu/ethics

Knapper, C. K. (1995). The origins of teaching portfolios. *Journal on Excellence in College Teaching, 6*(1), 45–56.

Lambert, L. M., & Tice, S. L. (Eds.). (1993). *Preparing graduate students to teach.* Washington, DC: American Association for Higher Education.

Lewis, K. (Ed.). (1993). *The TA experience: Preparing for multiple roles.* Stillwater, OK: New Forums.

Marincovich, M., Prostko, J., & Stout, F. (Eds.). (1998). *The professional development of teaching assistants.* Bolton, MA: Anker.

Mazur, E. (1997). *Peer instruction. A user's manual.* Upper Saddle River, NJ: Prentice-Hall.

Nyquist, J., & Woodford, B. (2000). *Re-envisioning the Ph.D.: What concerns do we have?* Seattle, WA: University of Washington, Center for Instructional Development and Research. Retrieved November 15, 2008, from http://www.grad.washington.edu/envision/project_resources/concerns.html

Nyquist, J. D., Abbott, R. D., Wulff, R. D., & Sprague, J. (Eds.). (1991). *Preparing the professoriate of tomorrow to teach: Selected readings in TA training.* Dubuque, IA: Kendall Hunt.

Pollock, S., & Finkelstein, F. (2008). Sustaining educational reforms in introductory physics. *Physics Review Special Topics: Physics Education Research, 4*(1), 010110.

Ronald E. McNair Postbaccalaureate Achievement Program. (2008). Retrieved December 29, 2008, from the U.S. Department of Education Web site at http://www.ed.gov/programs/triomcnair/index.html

Seldin, P. (1997). *The teaching portfolio: A practical guide to improved performance and promotion/tenure decisions.* Bolton, MA: Anker.

Soracco, S. (2008). *Graduate writing resources.* Retrieved August 14, 2008, from University of California, Berkeley Graduate Division Web site: http://www.grad.berkeley.edu/acapro/academic_services.shtml#1

von Hoene, L. (2009). *Graduate student teaching certificates.* Manuscript in preparation.

von Hoene, L., & Mintz, J. (2002). Research on faculty as teaching mentors: Lessons learned from a study of participants in UC Berkeley's seminar for faculty who teach with graduate student instructors. In D. Lieberman & C. Wehlburg (Eds.), *To improve the academy: Vol. 20. Resources for faculty, instructional, and organizational development* (pp. 77–93). Bolton, MA: Anker.

Woodrow Wilson National Fellowship Foundation. (2005). *The responsive Ph.D.: Innovations in U.S. doctoral education.* Retrieved November 15, 2008, from http://www.woodrow.org/images/pdf/resphd/ResponsivePhD_overview.pdf

WORKING WITH ADJUNCT FACULTY MEMBERS

Terri A. Tarr

WORKING WITH ADJUNCT FACULTY can be both a rewarding and challenging aspect of faculty development. Many adjunct faculty members are in that role because they enjoy teaching. They are eager to learn more about effective teaching and appreciative of opportunities to be part of the academic community. However, their limited time on campus, weaker connections to their institutions, and low expectations and rewards related to their participation in professional development programs present challenges. With their pivotal role in providing higher education instruction as the number of adjunct faculty increases, institutions must provide appropriate professional development opportunities for this segment of the faculty.

This chapter begins with descriptive information about the adjunct faculty, including percentages of staffing at different institutional types, their faculty characteristics, and issues related to attitudes toward adjunct faculty. It then focuses on considerations for planning programs for and addressing the professional development needs of adjunct faculty members.

About the Adjunct Faculty

In higher education, adjunct faculty members are described as part-time faculty, associate faculty, sessional faculty, contingent faculty, clinical faculty, and with other terms. In this chapter, they are referred to as either "adjunct faculty" or "part-time faculty." Institutions hire adjunct faculty members for a variety of reasons. They may provide expertise not available from within the full-time faculty, or the institution may hire adjunct or part-time faculty for financial reasons, because their salaries are typically lower than those of full-time faculty. Additionally, adjunct faculty are often used to teach classes at less desirable times, such as evenings and weekends; and they may teach online classes. Finally, adjunct faculty members provide more flexibility to an institution in its staffing.

Numbers of Part-Time Faculty

The adjunct faculty represents a substantial proportion of faculty in higher education. According to the 2004 *National Study of Postsecondary Faculty Report on Faculty and Instructional Staff* (National Center for Education Statistics, 2004) in fall 2003, 56.3 percent of the faculty in all institutions worked full-time, while 43.7 percent worked part-time. The distribution of full-time versus part-time faculty varies by institutional type, with fewer part-time faculty in four-year institutions such as public doctoral institutions (77.8 percent full-time and 22.2 percent part-time) and private not-for-profit baccalaureate institutions (63.2 percent full-time and 36.8 percent part-time) in contrast to more part-time faculty in two-year institutions such as public associate's institutions (33.3 percent full-time versus 66.7 percent part-time). Community colleges have had more part-time than full-time faculty since the 1990s (Wagoner, 2007).

The majority of the adjunct faculty is not tenured or on the tenure track (National Center for Education Statistics, 2004). Looking at all institution types, only 4.5 percent of the adjunct faculty is either tenured (3.0 percent) or tenure-track (1.5 percent) in contrast to 68.1 percent of the full-time faculty which is tenured (47.5 percent) or tenure track (20.6 percent) in the same institutions. Not surprisingly, the percentage of tenure-eligible, part-time faculty is higher at public doctoral institutions, where 7.5 percent of the part-time faculty is either tenured or tenure-track, than at public associate institutions, where 4.5 percent is on the tenure track. Without tenure, adjunct faculty members have less job security and less protection for academic freedom, which contributes to greater turnover than in the full-time faculty ranks.

The proportion of full-time versus part-time faculty varies by discipline. Of the nine disciplines included in the 2004 *National Study of Postsecondary Faculty Report on Faculty and Instructional Staff Survey* (National Center for Education Statistics, 2004), education (48.7 percent part-time), fine arts (47.0 percent part-time), and business

(46.0 percent part-time) had the highest proportions of part-time faculty. Agriculture/home economics (21.6 percent part-time), engineering (21.8 percent part-time), and natural sciences (23.5 percent part-time) had the lowest percentages of part-time faculty. In the middle were the humanities (34.6 percent part-time), health sciences (30.3 percent part-time), and social sciences (29.7 percent part-time).

According to the *Digest of Education Statistics* (U.S. Department of Education, 2007), the growth rate has been slower for full-time faculty (22.7 percent growth rate) than for part-time faculty (61.4 percent growth rate) although there has been growth in the number of faculty members in postsecondary institutions between 1995 and 2005. Along with the slower growth rate for full-time faculty, there has been a decrease in the percentage of full-time faculty with tenure from 56 percent with tenure in 1993–1994 to 50 percent in 2005–2006. These changes in employment patterns, the decreased growth in full-time faculty, and the decline in faculty with tenure have aroused concerns in institutions and higher education in general.

Categories of Part-Time Faculty

Adjunct faculty members are a diverse group composed of individuals who choose to teach part-time for a variety of reasons. Although they are commonly portrayed as "freeway fliers" seeking full-time positions while surviving on meager wages and teaching at multiple institutions, part-time faculty often do not fit this stereotype (Leslie & Gappa, 2002).

Gappa and Leslie (1993) described four categories of adjunct faculty that continue to be widely used by others. These categories are useful in considering educational development efforts targeting this group, as they illustrate the variety of reasons why individuals choose to teach part-time and suggest different professional development needs.

1. *Career enders.* These faculty members are those who are either fully retired or in transition from a well-established career to a preretired or retired status in which part-time teaching plays a significant role.

2. *Specialists, experts, and professionals.* These adjunct faculty members typically have a full-time primary career elsewhere. More than half of adjunct faculty members work full-time somewhere else.

3. *Aspiring academics.* These faculty members possess terminal degrees and want full-time academic status. The category includes those who have become full-time part-timers by working at several institutions.

4. *Freelancers.* For this group, part-time teaching is one of several part-time jobs, including those outside of higher education. They also may have jobs doing things such as writing or consulting and are not seeking full-time academic positions.

Comparisons to Full-Time Faculty

As a group, the adjunct faculty differs from full-time faculty in many ways, according to the National Center for Education Statistics (2004).

o Women made up a larger proportion of part-time (47 percent) than full-time faculty (38 percent).

o Part-time faculty were more likely than full-time faculty to be either under age thirty-five or age sixty-five or older.

o The highest degree attained by full-time faculty tended to be higher than it was for part-time faculty. Of full-time faculty, 68 percent had earned a doctoral or first professional degree, 27 percent a master's degree, and 6 percent a bachelor's degree or less. In contrast, only one-quarter of part-time faculty had attained a doctoral or first professional degree, more than one-half had master's degrees, and 21 percent had a bachelor's degree or less.

o The average number of hours worked per week at all jobs was lower for part-time faculty (40.4 hours/week) than for full-time faculty (53.4 hours/week).

o Part-time faculty spent a higher proportion of their time at their institution on teaching (90 percent) than did full-time faculty (61.7 percent), who were likely to spend proportionately more time on research or other administrative activities.

o Part-time faculty had on average 0.5 refereed publications and 4 presentations in the previous two years, which is fewer than the 2.1 referred publications and 5.3 presentations that the full-time faculty reported.

o The average total income reported by full-time faculty was $80,700, whereas the part-time faculty reported a $52,800 income from all sources.

Perceptions and Attitudes Toward Adjunct Faculty

"Strangers in Their Own Land," "Entertaining Strangers," "Gypsy Academic," "The Anomalous Academic," "Will Teach for Food," and "Invisible Faculty" are all phrases in book titles or articles about adjunct faculty. Additionally, derogatory terms such as "frequent fliers" and "roads scholars" are used to refer to adjunct faculty. These descriptors reflect the marginalization of adjunct faculty that contributes to a poor connection between the adjunct faculty member and the institution and full-time colleagues. Employment policies and practices such as low pay, no benefits, lack of long-term contracts, no representation in faculty governance, inadequate or no office space, and exclusion from departmental activities can make adjunct faculty feel undervalued and unappreciated.

As the percentage of undergraduate instruction provided by part-time faculty has risen, concerns about the impact of part-time faculty on the quality of higher education have grown. Although the assumption is often made that adjunct faculty members offer poorer quality instruction, Wallin (2007) reported that most research has indicated that students learn as much and are as likely to be retained when taught by an adjunct faculty member as when they are when taught by a full-time faculty member. Discipline problems and students' evaluations, on the average, were comparable between part-time and full-time faculty (Wallin, 2007). Similarly, Leslie and Gappa (2002) found that full-time and part-time faculty members lecture for a similar amount of time as the primary instructional method, while student discussions and exams comprised about two-thirds of class time for both instructor groups. When looking at more specific aspects of instruction, some differences have been found, which are addressed later in this chapter.

Gappa and Leslie's (1993, 1997) seminal work stated that part-time faculty members are a well-qualified and valuable resource, if properly used, and asserted that the most serious threats to academic quality come from casual, inconsistent employment practices and a lack of institutional support rather than from the quality of the part-time faculty members themselves. Thinking of adjunct faculty members as an asset and investing in them rather than ignoring and devaluing them can lead to increases in their teaching effectiveness and institutional contributions (Leslie & Gappa, 2002).

Although many key issues, such as salary, are out of the control of faculty development personnel, faculty developers can contribute to integrating adjunct faculty members into the academic community by including them in program offerings, welcoming them at events, and providing them with a venue for collaborating with colleagues on instructional matters. Faculty developers also can advocate for adjunct faculty by supporting their inclusion in opportunities for recognition and rewards, by providing departments and schools with resources focused on adjunct faculty, and by speaking up on the behalf of adjunct faculty when they are unfairly portrayed in campus conversations.

Planning Professional Development Programs

Planning professional development programs for adjuncts should begin with the campus units responsible for these faculty members. In some institutions, recruiting, hiring, orienting, evaluating, and continuing professional development are overseen by a central unit. In others, the process is decentralized with, for example, hiring and evaluating done by departments; orientation by departments, schools, and institutions; and continuing professional development provided both by a central unit and departments. Institutional type may influence the structure as well. Community colleges, with their relatively large percentages of adjunct faculty, are more likely to have centralized programs and a tighter connection between the hiring process and orientation. (See Chapter Nineteen, "Faculty Development in the Context of the Community College.")

Regardless of whether responsibility for adjunct faculty is centralized or decentralized, much of the literature (Lyons, 2007a; Murray, 2002; Smith & Wright, 2000) suggests that programs are most effective when they are systematic and comprehensive rather than disconnected and unrelated. Therefore, in contexts in which responsibilities are dispersed, a collaborative approach to professional development programming with good communication and cooperation between and among key stakeholders is crucial. Murray (2002) noted, for example, the following characteristics of effective faculty development programs:

○ Administrative support for faculty development

○ A formalized, structured, goal-directed program

○ A connection between faculty development and the reward structure

○ Faculty ownership

○ Disciplinary support for teaching

Richard Lyons's book, *Best Practices for Supporting Adjunct Faculty* (2007a), highlights effective professional development programs in a variety of institutional types. Comparing the programs, he identified the following four factors as characteristics of successful faculty development initiatives in the context of adjunct faculty members:

1. Early in the planning process, a mission and measurable outcomes were identified.

2. A concerted effort was made to generate support from top administrators, from department chairs, and from faculty.

3. Programs began with a modest budget.

4. Programs generated feedback from participants and fed suggestions back into improving programs on a continuous basis (Lyons, 2007b, p. 7).

Keeping Lyons's four key factors in mind when designing faculty development programs will help insure success.

Considerations for Professional Development Offerings

SCHEDULING. Because many adjunct faculty have jobs elsewhere, evening or weekend programming is common. Using online tutorials or Web sites to provide basic or more in-depth information can make participation more convenient. The best solution may be to provide multiple opportunities and use multiple methods to provide faculty development opportunities that fit adjunct faculty members' varied schedules.

INCLUSION. Another consideration is whether to offer programming specifically for adjunct faculty or to include them in opportunities available to full-time faculty. One concern that arises about adjunct faculty is that they are not sufficiently integrated into the academic community and have not formed connections with colleagues at the institution. Gathering together to discuss common concerns related to teaching provides a wonderful opportunity for adjunct faculty members to get to know and learn from their part- and full-time colleagues.

When including both adjunct and full-time faculty in a program, presenters should be sensitive to the range of academic ranks in the audience. It can be disheartening and uncomfortable for an adjunct faculty member to be in a session on promotion and tenure if it is assumed that everyone in the room is going that route. Thus, if something is relevant only for the full-time faculty, one should be sure either to plan alternate sessions that the adjunct faculty could attend or to frame the session so it is acknowledged that not everyone in the audience is expected to apply the information.

At the same time, it may be appropriate to plan events that target only the adjunct faculty. Sometimes when adjunct faculty members are mixed with full-time tenure track faculty, the adjunct faculty members are at risk of not feeling like "real" faculty members, which can be uncomfortable. At Indiana University, the Faculty Colloquium on Excellence in Teaching (FACET), a community of faculty recognized for excellence in teaching and learning, offers an annual conference for nontenure track faculty, which has been very well received by adjunct faculty members not only because of the programming, but because they feel like they clearly belong in that group. Interaction at the conference among the adjunct faculty, non-tenure track full-time faculty, and faculty from FACET leads to increased respect for each other's pedagogical expertise and provides opportunities for growth. In addition, the community building that takes place at the conference creates more invested part-time faculty. Here are a few faculty comments about the conference (Combs & Lucke, 2003):

- "Meeting and talking to others 'like me' was wonderful. A great place to learn new ideas."
- "Felt more part of faculty and that I have important place in teaching."
- "These conferences are a great opportunity for associate faculty to network and validate our importance to the university."

REIMBURSEMENT. Whether or not to provide reimbursement to adjunct faculty members for time spent at professional development programs is another issue to consider. Part-time faculty members are far more likely to be uncompensated for time spent at workshops or conferences than are full-time faculty members. Expectations regarding participation in faculty development events communicated when an adjunct faculty member is hired are relevant. If a contract stipulates that faculty members are expected to attend an orientation or participate in other professional development programs as part of their responsibilities, then paying them may not be necessary. If a professional development program requires attendance at a multiple day or full-day session, there may be greater need to reimburse adjunct faculty members for their time than if it is a one-hour workshop. Rather than reimbursing faculty for participating in a specific program, another strategy is to develop individual professional development plans and provide bonuses or salary increases dependent in participation in targeted professional development activities. Reimbursement practices vary widely across institutions and depend on the nature of the program, but providing compensation can increase participation.

ONLINE OPTIONS. Online programs are more accessible to those who have difficulty attending face-to-face sessions. This kind of programming can occur in the form of Web sites that provide basic information, tutorials that lead faculty through a presentation of relevant topics, or online discussion forums that provide networking opportunities. At Valencia

Community College, all faculty development programs are offered in two formats: face-to-face and online, thereby giving adjunct faculty the flexibility to participate in whichever format best suits them and at a time that fits their schedule (Jaschik, 2008). The Center for Teaching and Learning for Minnesota State Colleges and Universities has developed a number of online tutorials that are offered as self-directed, step-by-step modules and focus on developing teaching-related knowledge or skills. (See http://www.ctl.mnscu.edu/programs/educ_opp/tutorials.html.) Along with topics such as active learning in diverse classrooms, classroom management strategies, and making grading fair, the center also has an e-handbook for new faculty.

MARKETING AND COMMUNICATION. Marketing programs and communicating with adjunct faculty can be a challenge. Adjunct faculty may not have a campus office and may check their campus mailboxes infrequently, if they even have one. Communicating through e-mail is becoming more common and is much less expensive than printing and mailing materials. One can create an adjunct faculty electronic mailing list or Web site to disseminate information about ongoing professional development opportunities. Perhaps one of the most influential methods of communicating is through department chairpersons or course coordinators. If they are aware of programs and encourage adjunct faculty members to attend, that can be more enticing than simply an informative e-mail sent to the faculty member. Flyers, posters, and handouts distributed at other events and near adjunct faculty mailboxes, offices, or other gathering sites also can be used to spread the word. Once again, use of multiple channels and multiple methods may be the best approach to take when communicating with adjunct faculty members.

Adjunct Faculty Professional Development Needs

The specific needs of individual adjunct faculty members may vary widely as they come to the role with different backgrounds and levels of teaching experience. However, according to Lyons (2007b), the basic needs of adjunct faculty can be summarized as follows:

- A thorough orientation to the institution, its culture, and its practices
- Adequate training in fundamental teaching and classroom management skills
- A sense of belonging to the institution

○ Both initial and ongoing professional development

○ Recognition for quality work that is perceived as appropriate and adequate (Lyons, 2007b, p. 6)

Orientation

A comprehensive orientation is pivotal in helping new adjunct faculty members learn about the expectations and responsibilities of their faculty positions, begin to connect to the institution, meet colleagues, and prepare for their teaching roles. The hiring process is typically less involved for adjunct faculty than for full-time faculty, so adjunct faculty have often had only minimal contact with the institution before they begin their new positions. Moreover, because they are generally at the institution only when they teach, they have fewer opportunities to learn "the ropes" informally from colleagues. These factors increase the importance of orientation for new adjunct faculty.

Adjunct faculty members need to be oriented to institutional, departmental, and course expectations. They also need to find out about how to get a parking permit, computer account, and library access; whom to notify if an emergency arises and they cannot make it to class; and other such logistical matters. In addition, and perhaps most important, new adjunct faculty need to be prepared to teach their classes, which may include learning how to use a course management system and other instructional technology. Many institutions prepare a print or online faculty handbook specifically for adjunct faculty or provide them with a handbook designed for both full- and part-time faculty to ensure they have essential information.

Smith and Wright (2000) have identified key features that should be present in new faculty orientations for part-time faculty. These are as follow.

○ Provide ample opportunity for the adjunct to become familiar with the mission, purposes, and core values of the institution.

○ Acquaint the faculty member with the "nuts and bolts" of the policies and procedures he or she will be expected to follow.

○ Assist adjunct faculty members in forming departmental relationships.

○ Provide opportunities for adjunct faculty to identify and link up with a mentor.

○ Establish a reliable and clearly understood means of communication between the adjunct and his or her departmental leadership.

○ Provide the basic instructional tools that they will need in the classroom. (pp. 55–57)

The format and content of orientations vary widely, as do institutional contexts. When preparing an orientation for adjunct faculty, it is important to be sensitive to the particular needs of the faculty members at different institutions. Getting feedback from current adjunct faculty and from administrators who work with adjunct faculty about what they perceive as the greatest needs can help focus programming. As always with adjunct faculty, it is helpful to offer orientation in multiple ways.

This concept has been implemented at the University of Central Florida (UCF) and has been described by Yee (2007). UCF employs about three hundred adjunct faculty members in a semester. Yee noted three issues related to adjunct faculty development at his institution: steady turnover; diverse disciplinary backgrounds and experiences among adjunct faculty; and decentralized hiring that makes it difficult to identify and contact new adjunct faculty. UCF responded to the challenge by creating "multilayered opportunities for adjunct faculty to receive assistance and attend training sessions of varying lengths and commitments" (Yee, 2007, p. 15). They have created three ways to orient new faculty.

The first is a combination of one-hour workshops designed, as Yee said, to address the important nuts and bolts at the institution. They offer these short workshops just before and right after the beginning of a semester and also provide faculty with a workbook compiled from workshop handouts.

The second offering is a full-day, eight-hour retreat offered on a Saturday near the start of every semester. About one-third of the time is spent on institutional-specific information and campus resources, with the other two-thirds devoted to pedagogical topics. Adjunct faculty members are paid a stipend for attending and given a copy of a book on teaching. Attendees are given a pre- and postsurvey about their knowledge of campus and pedagogical resources as well as a pre- and posttest about their knowledge of general pedagogical principles and specific UCF policies.

The third opportunity is an online course about campus resources and pedagogical topics. This course is designed for self-directed learning and reinforces module content through the use of electronic quizzes, discussion forums, and assignments that can be submitted online for feedback. The course also provides an opportunity to build a teaching portfolio.

Teaching Support

Research that has compared instructional strategies of full- and part-time faculty is mixed, with some results showing no difference between groups and others indicating differences. As noted earlier in this chapter, Leslie and Gappa (2002) found no difference between full-time and part-time faculty in the time they spent in lecturing, discussion, and giving exams. Eagan (2007) analyzed results of the *2004 National Study of Postsecondary Faculty Report on Faculty and Instructional Staff* (National Center for Education Statistics, 2004) related to teaching methods used by full- and part-time faculty and concluded that both groups of faculty were equally likely to use essay and short-answer questions on midterms and finals. Some differences did appear, with full-time faculty being more likely to have students do term papers and group projects. Part-time faculty also were found to use technology less in their teaching than were full-time faculty, particularly in having a course Web site.

Analysis of the results of a survey of community college faculty conducted by the Center for the Study of Community Colleges (Schuetz, 2002) suggested that part-time faculty tended to use innovative or collaborative teaching methods less than their full-time counterparts; and, on average, they interacted less with their students, peers, and the institutions at large. Results also indicated that part-time faculty members were less familiar with the availability of campus services such as tutoring and counseling. The research suggested that adjunct faculty need as much, if not more, teaching support than do full-time faculty, particularly in the use of instructional technology, collaborative learning, and innovative teaching strategies. To the extent that differences between full- and part-time faculty members in their instructional strategies can be attributed to differences in exposure and experience with these strategies, professional development focused on these areas may be able to minimize any differences.

Orientation can equip new faculty with the survival skills they need to get off to a good start in their teaching, but there are limits to how much can be covered and processed by the participants during an orientation. Continued support related to teaching is necessary not only for new faculty but for continuing faculty as they seek to improve their teaching or try innovative strategies. This support can be offered through workshops, symposia, institutes, books, articles, Web seminars, online resources, faculty learning communities, or department-based seminars. The offerings would be very similar to what would be provided for the full-time faculty including, for example, topics such as syllabus construction, first day of class, course planning, assessment, instructional strategies, diverse student populations, instructional technology, and student evaluations of teaching.

An in-depth approach to supporting teaching is to offer a course on teaching. One example of this is the "Instructor Effectiveness Training" course offered at Indian River Community College (Harber & Lyons, 2007). The course begins a week or two before each fall and spring semester and consists of four three-and-one-half-hour sessions held on Saturday mornings. It focuses on course planning, managing the course effectively, strategies for delivering more effective instruction, and evaluating student achievement and teaching effectiveness.

Another example of a teaching course available to adjunct faculty is one called "Teaching in the Learning College," which is offered at Ivy Tech Community College Southwest in Evansville, Indiana (Silliman, 2007). The course uses a hybrid format, delivering course content online for six weeks and two face-to-face meetings during that time period.

Recognition and Rewards

If excellence in teaching is an institutional goal, then finding a way to recognize and reward excellent teaching is essential. Offering teaching awards specifically for part-time faculty at the department and institution level is a way of conveying the value of teaching contributions by adjunct faculty members. Having general teaching awards open to both full- and part-time faculty is also an option, although the part-time faculty may be at a disadvantage when competing head-to-head with the full-time faculty. Leslie and Gappa (2002) found that part-time faculty members were significantly less likely than full-time faculty to have received awards for outstanding teaching.

Another way to recognize excellent teaching is to provide opportunities for advancement or promotion based on excellence in teaching. Some institutions have more than one adjunct faculty rank, so promotion is possible. For example, Belmont College has four different adjunct faculty ranks: instructor adjunct, assistant professor adjunct, associate professor adjunct, and professor adjunct (Lohi-Pasey & Bennett, 2006).

Inviting adjunct faculty to present at teaching workshops, awarding certificates for completing professional development programs, and providing financial support to help pay for travel to professional conferences are additional ways to recognize adjunct faculty. Part-time faculty members rarely have the same access to this type of professional development funding as do full-time faculty.

Conclusion

Adjunct faculty members play a vital role at most higher education institutions, and educational developers play an instrumental role in contributing to the professional growth of adjunct faculty members by ensuring that this group of faculty receives the thorough orientation, opportunity for integration into the academic community, and continued support they need to provide students with the best learning experience possible. For those involved with these efforts, it can be a rewarding experience with tangible results both to the faculty members and their students.

REFERENCES

Combs, T. T., & Lucke, J. (2003, March). *"It's our weekend!": A faculty academy promotes teaching excellence and community-building with part-time faculty.* Poster session presented at the American Association for Higher Education 2003 National Learning to Change Conference, Washington, DC.

Eagan, K. (2007). A national picture of part-time community college faculty: Changing trends in demographics and employment characteristics. In R. L. Wagoner (Ed.), *New directions for community colleges, no. 140. The current landscape and changing perspectives of part-time faculty* (pp. 5–14). San Francisco: Jossey-Bass.

Gappa, J. M., & Leslie, D. W. (1993). *The invisible faculty: Improving the status of part-timers in higher education.* San Francisco: Jossey-Bass.

Gappa, J. M., & Leslie, D. W. (1997). *Two faculties or one? The conundrum of part-timers in a bifurcated work force. New Pathways Working Paper Series, no. 6.* Washington DC: American Association for Higher Education.

Harber, F., & Lyons, R. E. (2007). A proven, comprehensive program for preparing and supporting adjunct faculty members. In R. E. Lyons (Ed.), *Best practices for supporting adjunct faculty* (pp. 186–198). Bolton, MA: Anker.

Jaschik, S. (2008, May 28). Professional development for adjuncts. *Inside Higher Education.* Retrieved November 9, 2008, from http://insidehighered.com/news/2008/05/28/nisod

Leslie, D. W., & Gappa, J. M. (2002). Part-time faculty: Committed and competent. In C. I. Outcalt (Ed.), *New directions for community colleges, no. 118. Community college faculty: Characteristics, practices, and challenges* (pp. 59–67). San Francisco: Jossey-Bass.

Lohi-Pasey, B., & Bennett, C. (2006). *Fostering learning: An adjunct faculty development model for evaluation, development, support and professional advancement*. Retrieved on November 9, 2008, from http://www.oln.org/conferences/ODCE2006/papers/fostering_learning/OCDE%20faculty%20development%20final.ppt

Lyons, R. E. (Ed.). (2007a). *Best practices for supporting adjunct faculty*. Bolton, MA: Anker.

Lyons, R. E. (2007b). Deepening our understanding of adjunct faculty. In R. E. Lyons (Ed.), *Best practices for supporting adjunct faculty* (pp. 1–12). Bolton, MA: Anker.

Minnesota State Colleges and Universities. *Center for teaching and learning tutorials*. Retrieved on November 9, 2008, from http://www.ctl.mnscu.edu/programs/educ_opp/tutorials.html

Murray, J. P. (2002). The current state of faculty development in two-year colleges. In C. I. Outcalt (Ed.), *New directions for community colleges, no. 118. Community college faculty: Characteristics, practices, and challenges* (pp. 89–97). San Francisco: Jossey-Bass.

National Center for Education Statistics. (2004). *2004 National study of postsecondary faculty (NSOPF:04) report on faculty and instructional staff in fall 2003*. Washington, DC: U.S. Department of Education, Institute of Education Sciences. Retrieved on November 9, 2008, from http://nces.ed.gov/pubsearch/pubsinfo.asp?pubid=2005172

Schuetz, P. (2002). Instructional practices of part-time and full-time faculty. In C. L. Outcault (Ed.), *New directions for community colleges, no. 118. Community college faculty: Characteristics, practices, and challenges* (pp. 39–46). San Francisco: Jossey-Bass.

Silliman, J. C. (2007). Supporting adjunct faculty through orientation and mentoring initiatives and an online professional development course. In R. E. Lyons (Ed.), *Best practices for supporting adjunct faculty* (pp. 158–185). Bolton, MA: Anker.

Smith, M., & Wright, D. (2000). Orientation of adjunct and part-time faculty: Exemplary models. In D. E. Greive & C. A. Worden (Eds.), *Managing adjunct and part-time faculty for the new millennium* (pp. 45–69). Elyria, OH: Info-Tec.

U.S. Department of Education. (2007). *Digest of education statistics. Chapter 3. Postsecondary education*. Washington, DC: U.S. Department of Education, Institute of Education Sciences. Retrieved November 9, 2008, from http://nces.ed.gov/programs/digest/d07/

Wagoner, R. L. (Ed.). (2007). *New directions for community colleges, no. 140. The current landscape and changing perspectives of part-time faculty*. San Francisco: Jossey-Bass.

Wallin, D. L. (2007). Part-time faculty and professional development: Notes from the field. In R. L. Wagoner (Ed.), *New directions for community colleges, no 140. The current landscape and changing perspectives of part-time faculty* (pp. 67–73). San Francisco: Jossey-Bass.

Yee, K. (2007). Ensuring an effective start for adjunct faculty: Orientation with multiple options. In R. E. Lyons (Ed.), *Best practices for supporting adjunct faculty* (pp. 13–30). Bolton, MA: Anker.

22

SUPPORTING FACULTY MEMBERS ACROSS THEIR CAREERS

Ann E. Austin

FACULTY MEMBERS MAY ALL SEEM TO ENGAGE in the same kind of work, with the relative weight given to teaching, research, and service dependent on the institutional type. However, the experience of a faculty career varies considerably in relation to the individual's career stage. Particular concerns, challenges, and needs characterize the various stages of a faculty career. Thus, those engaged in planning effective faculty development should have some knowledge of how faculty careers change over time and the kind of faculty development strategies that are most useful and effective for faculty members at particular career stages. While most well-constructed faculty development programs include programs and services relevant to all faculty members, they also offer programs designed specifically for faculty members at particular career stages.

The purpose of this chapter is to explain (1) the typical stages used to conceptualize faculty careers; (2) the characteristics, challenges, and concerns often associated with each career stage; and (3) the implications for organizing faculty development strategies and programs that address the needs of faculty members within each career stage. The chapter begins with descriptions of the three career stages and a brief discussion of how demographic patterns affect the overall pattern of faculty members at each career stage. Three sections follow, each focused on one career stage: early career, midcareer, and late career. These sections highlight key features of each career stage and useful faculty development strategies for each. Informational resources are offered in each section.

Overview of Career Stages

Early career faculty members are sometimes called "new faculty" or "junior faculty," although the title "junior faculty" has become less popular in recent years in recognition of the diverse ages at which individuals may enter the professoriate. Some faculty members, for example, may be early career or new faculty after having worked a number of years in another sector such as business, law, medicine, or government. Typically, early career faculty members are defined as those individuals within the first seven years of their faculty appointments or those who have not yet been awarded tenure. The proportion of early career faculty members is on the rise as retirements increase among senior members of the professoriate. Furthermore, the number of faculty members overall is likely to expand as the number of both traditional-age and older students continues to rise, requiring institutions to employ a greater number of faculty members. Another factor that may result in the hiring of more new faculty members at some institutions is the departure from the faculty ranks among those not yet at retirement age. Recent survey data by the Higher Education Research Institute indicate that at least one-third of the respondents had considered leaving academe (Lindholm, Szelenyi, Hurtado, & Korn, 2005). For these reasons, the proportion of early career faculty is increasing at many institutions. In the United States, 41.3 percent of the full-time or part-time faculty have seven or fewer years in their academic appointments (U.S. Department of Education, 2004).

The early career faculty cohort also is noteworthy in regard to gender, race/ethnicity, and appointment type patterns (Gappa, Austin, & Trice, 2007). The percentage of women in the faculty ranks has been increasing; 44 percent of new full-time faculty in their first six years are women, in contrast to 20 percent in 1969. About one-fourth of new faculty members are from nonmajority ethnic groups, in contrast to about 17 percent of faculty with seven or more years of experience who are from nonmajority ethnic groups (U.S. Department of Education, 2004). Efforts to recognize the specific issues and challenges of early career faculty members who are female or individuals of color and to support them as they become established in their careers are an investment in an institution's quality and future.

A decided shift in faculty appointments is also occurring toward more non-tenure-track positions and more part-time faculty positions. Among the early career faculty group (those with seven or fewer years), 46.1 percent hold non-tenure-track positions. Among those with more years in position, 25.1 percent are in non-tenure-track positions (U.S. Department of

Education, 2004). Of particular note, since the 1960s, the proportion of part-time faculty members has increased. In 2004, only 54 percent of faculty members held full-time appointments, with 46 percent in part-time positions (U.S. Department of Education, 2004). Some institutions take the position that faculty development resources should be invested only in tenure-track faculty members, those likely to spend many years at the institutions. Other institutions, however, recognize that, since non-tenure faculty members carry out important functions and responsibilities, they should also be provided with opportunities that support the quality of their work. Consideration of ways to support the non-tenure-track faculty is especially relevant as institutions employ a growing proportion of these individuals. (See Chapter Nineteen, "Faculty Development in the Context of the Community College," and Chapter Twenty-One, "Working with Adjunct Faculty Members.")

Midcareer faculty members are typically defined as those who have passed the probationary period (typically about seven years at many institutions) and, in those institutions that have a tenure system, have been awarded tenure with its promise of job security. While the end of midcareer is not well defined, those categorized as midcareer faculty anticipate a number of years of work still ahead of them. Due to tight hiring conditions in the 1980s and 1990s, many higher education institutions have a bimodal faculty distribution, with heavier proportions of faculty members at the early and late career stages and relatively smaller proportions in midcareer. Those at midcareer often carry heavy institutional service responsibilities, and they are often tapped for a variety of leadership roles. While they "know the ropes" in terms of the faculty responsibilities of teaching, research, and service, they still face challenges and have some professional concerns that are particularly relevant to their career stage.

The senior faculty members (those in the late career stage) are usually defined as those who see retirement in the near horizon. While there is no official beginning to the late career stage, it is often conceptualized as the period when a faculty member is within ten or twelve years of retirement. As of 2005, in the United States, 50.5 percent of the tenured faculty members were fifty-five years or older (U.S. Department of Education, 2004). Within the ranks of full-time faculty members, more than one-third are fifty-five years of age or older, in contrast to 24 percent of full-time faculty members who were over fifty-five in 1989 (Lindholm et al., 2005). This proportion of senior faculty has been increasing over the past fifteen years; thus the number of retirements is expected to continue at a steady pace in the coming decade. This group of faculty members experiences specific challenges, issues, and concerns that faculty development programs can address in ways that enrich the lives of these colleagues and the quality of their work.

The sections that follow probe in more detail the experiences, concerns, and issues relevant to faculty members at each of these career stages. Each section also suggests specific strategies and programs that institutions can offer in recognition of the changing nature of the faculty career over a lifetime.

The Early Career Stage

The research literature is quite consistent in its reports concerning the experiences of early career faculty members. New faculty members need to have a range of knowledge and skills pertaining to teaching, research, professional attitudes and habits, interpersonal skills, and professional knowledge about higher education (Austin & McDaniels, 2006; Austin, Sorcinelli, & McDaniels, 20007). In regard to teaching, they need to understand course design, how learning occurs, ways to use technology to enhance the learning process, how to encourage students to engage actively in learning, and how to assess student progress and learning. They need to understand how research ideas are developed, executed, and reported. They must have integrity, a commitment to ethical standards, skills in creating professional networks, and an intention to engage in lifelong learning. They also should have some comprehension of the history of higher education, the variety of institutional types and their missions, the nature and responsibilities of different kinds of appointment types, and a sense of emerging professional identity as a scholar. Thus, while the set of knowledge and skills that new faculty are expected to bring to their positions is extensive, research indicates that the graduate experience usually has not prepared them in a systematic way for their new faculty roles. (See also Chapter Twenty, "Graduate and Professional Student Development Programs.")

Studies show, in fact, that many doctoral students aspiring to the professoriate do not feel fully prepared to teach, advise, secure funding for research, or participate as institutional citizens (Golde, 1998; National Association of Graduate-Professional Students, 2001). For most students who have chosen to pursue a faculty career, doctoral education does little to help them understand the different institutional types at which they may find employment, the differing missions of these institutional types, and the implications of institutional differences for faculty work. New faculty members, in other words, usually have a lot to learn about the work they will do. Overall, the literature indicates that doctoral students typically have experienced only limited preparation for the full array of responsibilities—including and beyond research—that they will face as faculty members (Austin 2002a, 2002b; Austin & McDaniels, 2006; Golde & Dore, 2001; Nerad, Aanerud, & Cerny, 2004; Nyquist et al., 1999; Wulff, Austin, Nyquist, & Sprague, 2004).

As they enter their new positions, new faculty members bring much enthusiasm, passion for their disciplines, and commitment to sharing their expertise with less advanced learners. They are motivated by the anticipation of intellectual challenge, the promise of stimulating interactions with students, the expectation of experiencing flexibility in their work, and the opportunity to engage in meaningful work (Austin et al., 2007; Rice, Austin, & Sorcinelli, 2000). Yet, despite their eagerness, passion, and commitment, research shows that those in the early career years consistently report some specific challenges and concerns (Gappa et al., 2007), which are discussed in this section. These challenges relate to the tenure process, collegiality and community, and balance and time among professional and personal responsibilities.

The Tenure Process

One of the most dominant concerns of early career faculty members, not surprisingly, pertains to career progression and, in institutions with tenure, the tenure process (Austin & Rice, 1998; Austin et al., 2007; Boice, 1992; Menges, 1999; Olsen & Sorcinelli, 1992; Rice & Sorcinelli, 2002; Trower, 2005). Early career faculty members worry about the expectations they must meet. They often note that they perceive unclear and sometimes conflicting messages about what they should emphasize in their work. They also report that institutional priorities sometimes seem to shift and that the bar for expectations appears to be continually rising. Furthermore, early career faculty members often perceive that the feedback they receive as they strive to meet expectations is unfocused and not very helpful. Another concern is whether senior colleagues understand the newer areas in many fields in which those just coming from graduate school may be working.

Beyond concerns about expectations and feedback, early career faculty members wonder about the logistics of the review process for reappointment and tenure decisions. When department chairs change, these faculty members sometimes feel disadvantaged if there are changes in the expectations and criteria against which they are reviewed. Similarly, the rotating membership of review committees and the lack of transparency in review processes heighten the worry of those in early career. Tenure review timelines are also a concern for some faculty members. Journal publication backlogs can impede evidence of productivity. In the sciences and engineering, where availability of equipment can be essential to a research program, any delays in initial laboratory set-ups can be problematic. Overall, the tenure process can cause early career faculty members to feel stress, uncertainty, and lack of clarity; and, thus, the tenure process is an area around which faculty development initiatives can provide guidance, information, and support.

Collegiality and Community

A second major area of concern often reported by early career faculty pertains to collegiality and community (Austin et al., 2007; Boice, 1992; Gappa et al., 2007; Rice et al., 2000; Tierney & Bensimon, 1996; Trower, 2005). New faculty members seek to find mentors and friends who will support them as they begin their careers. They particularly hope more experienced colleagues will help them understand the context in which they are working as well as the resources available to them. Instead, many early career faculty often report encountering isolation and competition.

Several features of the academic workplace tend to undermine a sense of community and the time faculty members have available to offer mentorship to new colleagues. Two-career families mean no one is at home to plan social events that would bring faculty members together, as was customary in earlier decades. The pervasiveness of computer use draws faculty members away from gathering places into their offices or enables them to work from home. These features mean that both new faculty members and their more advanced colleagues may be less available for informal interactions and community building. Finding ways to help new faculty members experience colleagueship and community thus becomes another area worthy of attention through faculty development.

Balance and Time

The research literature shows that doctoral students worry about the nature of academic life as they progress through their graduate experiences (Austin, 2002a, 2002b; Rice et al., 2000; Wulff et al., 2004). Their observations of their mentors reveal busy and sometimes hectic lives. Thus, as they enter their first faculty positions, a prevalent question is how to prioritize and balance their multiple professional roles (Austin et al., 2007; Boice, 1992; Gappa et al., 2007; Menges, 1999; Rice et al., 2000; Solem & Foote, 2004; Sorcinelli et al., 2001; Trower, Austin, & Sorcinelli, 2001; Whitt, 1991).

They worry about how to accomplish everything—teaching, research, advising, committee work, service—and about the extent to which their institutions' reward structures parallel the tasks they must fulfill. For example, while teaching and the requisite preparation are often time consuming for new faculty members, the institutional reward structure may emphasize research productivity. Managing this inconsistency, when it occurs, creates stress for some early career faculty members. Interestingly, while faculty members get more comfortable with their teaching over time, their sense of stress about time and balance increases as they grapple with institutional expectations for research productivity and concerns about the impending tenure decision (Olsen & Sorcinelli, 1992).

In addition to finding ways to manage multiple and sometimes conflicting professional responsibilities, early career faculty members struggle with balancing personal commitments with their professional roles and how to manage the stress of this challenge (Austin et al., 2007; Gappa et al., 2007; Gappa & MacDermid, 1997). As dual-career couples become more prevalent and as both men and women seek lifestyles that include time for involvement in family life and personal pursuits, early career faculty members indicate a strong interest in developing effective strategies for achieving a sense of balance across their professional and personal lives. Many early career faculty members seek flexibility in their schedules and sometimes even in the nature of their appointments; that is, for some, there is interest in opportunities to move between full-time and part-time appointments (Gappa et al., 2007).

The issues of finding community, managing time, and handling multiple responsibilities can be especially challenging for early career female faculty members and nonmajority faculty (Rice et al., 2000; Tierney & Bensimon, 1996). Both men and women in the early careers are often starting families, but academic mothers have the added stressor of physically giving birth as they strive to excel in their careers. As discussed in Chapter Fourteen, "Working with Underrepresented Faculty," nonmajority faculty members can feel particularly isolated and report added demands to serve on committees and respond to student needs specifically because they are frequently called upon to be the voice of underrepresented groups (Moody, 2001; Rice et al., 2000).

Faculty Development Strategies to Support Early Career Faculty

A number of authors have written about the array of faculty development initiatives that are especially helpful to early career faculty as they grapple with the need to get established, understand expectations and the tenure and reward structure, find colleagues, manage multiple responsibilities, and seek appropriate balance between personal and professional responsibilities (Austin et al., 2007; Boice, 1992; Gappa et al., 2007; Menges, 1999; Rice et al., 2000; Sorcinelli, 2000; Sorcinelli & Austin, 1992, 2006; Sorcinelli, Austin, Eddy, & Beach, 2006; Tierney & Bensimon, 1996).

RESOURCES ABOUT RESPONSIBILITIES. An important way to support early career faculty is to ensure that they know about institutional resources pertaining to their teaching, research, and service activities, the tenure process, and the management of personal and professional responsibilities. Orientation programs, both initial orientations at the start of employment and those that are organized over the course of the first semester or year, can provide useful information. Some institutions provide CDs and Web sites that organize links to key resources in one place. Department chairpersons should be encouraged to take seriously their role as the first resource to whom new faculty members are likely to turn. Seminars and workshops are often the backbone of faculty development programs, providing useful support as early career faculty members seek to establish themselves as teachers and researchers. Seminars specifically directed at lessening the uncertainty and mystery around the reappointment and tenure process are especially important. Some institutions provide basic information about the reappointment, tenure, and evaluation processes to new faculty, followed up by more in-depth workshops designed for faculty members two or three years into their careers.

STRATEGIES TO PROVIDE SUPPORT AND ENCOURAGE COLLEGIAL RELATIONSHIPS. One-time workshops not only provide useful information; they also provide the opportunity for early career faculty members to meet colleagues beyond their own departments and colleges. Even more effective in helping early career faculty find colleagues and experience community are longer-term programs. Workshop series targeted specifically to the interests and needs of new faculty members and scheduled throughout the year are one example. Another example is the Teaching Fellows Programs at a number of universities, whereby a group of early career faculty members is selected each year to meet regularly to discuss teaching issues, learn about the institution, and engage in projects related to teaching and learning. Some institutions also help faculty members establish collegial relationships by providing monthly social gatherings.

MENTORING STRATEGIES. Mentoring programs can also help new faculty members get answers to their questions as well as establish collegial relationships (Austin et al., 2007; Sorcinelli & Jung, 2006). Some institutions are experimenting with innovative approaches to mentoring, including group mentoring sessions and nonhierarchical arrangements that bring together peers, near-peers (colleagues just a little ahead in years of service), senior faculty members, and chairpersons (Sorcinelli & Jung, 2006). Successful mentoring programs typically involve the establishment of goals, regular meetings, and relationships characterized by reciprocity and mutuality.

STRATEGIES TO ENHANCE BALANCE. In regard to the concerns early career faculty members have for managing multiple responsibilities and balancing personal and professional roles, one of the best forms of institutional support is the easy availability of complete information about relevant policies and programs (Gappa et al., 2007). Web sites and workshops that focus on, for example, policies on leaves, stop-the-clock tenure process options, health care, child care options, sick child support, and options for modified duties, are important institutional strategies. Workshops specifically focused on diverse approaches to managing life responsibilities can also be useful to early career faculty members.

The Midcareer Stage

Far less research has been conducted on the experiences of faculty at midcareer than those at the early career period. As mentioned earlier, even defining midcareer is difficult. Typically it begins when the probationary period has concluded, but where midcareer ends and the senior career begins is blurred. Some researchers conceptualize early midcareer as the period up to five years post-tenure, while later midcareer is understood as the period from five to twenty or so years post-tenure (Baldwin, DeZure, Shaw, & Moretto, 2008). Some faculty members achieve full professor status during this time period, while others continue their careers as associate professors. Many of the challenges and issues that characterize midcareer continue into the late career as faculty members approach retirement.

The recent study by Baldwin et al. (2008) provides data on key issues for midcareer faculty members. Midcareer typically parallels middle age, which for many adults, across career areas, involves some reassessment of priorities and goals. Since few markers of career achievement exist beyond tenure, the midcareer period can raise anxiety around the need to make decisions about goal setting and to assess one's accomplishments. Some faculty members who have achieved tenure report that their career experience becomes less stressful, while others find that the ability to choose long-range projects without operating within the structures of the short-term tenure decision horizon adds to stress. Some institutions require post-tenure review, which provides some opportunities for self- and peer assessment; this process can be supportive and stimulating but can also raise anxiety.

A common challenge for faculty at midcareer is the expectation from colleagues that they will assume more leadership, administrative, and service duties. Early career faculty members are often protected by chair-persons and senior colleagues from heavy expectations for committee work and institutional service. In contrast, midcareer faculty often find themselves stretched thin as they strive to meet expectations that they will chair committees or departments, ensure a steady flow of grant funds into the department, and assume their role in protecting the time of pre-tenure colleagues. Thus, while time management was a challenge during the early career, time pressures can become even greater at midcareer. Work-life balance issues can also become exacerbated, especially for women and men who are juggling the demands of growing families with the expectations of expanding career opportunities and responsibilities. Some female faculty choose to postpone childbearing until after tenure is achieved; in such cases, the early midcareer coincides with the significant demands of having children.

Another major challenge for some midcareer faculty members is maintaining vibrancy and enthusiasm about their work (Baldwin et al., 2008). Faculty members may find themselves teaching the same courses for years and even pursuing research questions that no longer seem exciting. Some also note that the growing gap between their students' ages and their own can make relating to students a challenge. Another aspect of maintaining a sense of vibrancy involves staying current in one's field. This challenge is heightened by the rapid pace of knowledge creation and new techniques, often technologically related, for advancing and disseminating knowledge in many fields (Gappa et al., 2007; Sorcinelli & Austin, 2006; Sorcinelli et al., 2006).

Changes in the nature of the student body and the fast pace of technological developments in recent years also create challenges for midcareer faculty members, as well as for their late-career colleagues (Gappa et al., 2007; Shih & Sorcinelli, 2007; Sorcinelli & Austin, 2006; Sorcinelli et al., 2006). For example, the increasingly diverse student body means that established faculty members may need to learn new strategies for supporting different learning styles, including the learning needs of students of varying ages and backgrounds. Widespread interest in learner-centered teaching can mean that established faculty members face both the excitement of new opportunities to grow professionally and the challenge of shifting away from well-known professional practices. The prevalence of technology is creating expectations and opportunities for faculty members to integrate technology-mediated learning into their teaching and to learn new ways to conduct research and access data. E-mail and other communication devices create expectations on the part of students that faculty members will be readily and frequently available, which may require midcareer and senior faculty members to make changes in their work habits. Each of these changes pertaining to students, learning processes, and technology poses opportunities and challenges for all faculty members, but especially for those who are well into mid- or late career.

Faculty Development Strategies to Support Faculty at Midcareer

What professional development strategies can be particularly supportive of faculty members at midcareer (as well as those in the later years of their careers)? Several of the scholars who study faculty career stages offer suggestions (Baldwin et al., 2008; Gappa et al., 2007; Sorcinelli & Austin, 2006; Sorcinelli et al., 2006). This section highlights the role of chairpersons in supporting faculty at midcareer as well as strategies involving grants and awards, mentoring relationships, and leadership development.

THE IMPORTANT ROLE OF CHAIRPERSONS. Chairpersons have an important role to play in nurturing, encouraging, and challenging mid-career faculty members to stay vibrant. They can do this by listening to the issues on the minds of midcareer faculty colleagues, making explicit the respect that the institution has for these seasoned faculty members, and providing financial support and other resources to help midcareer faculty members stay current or explore new avenues for teaching and learning. Chairpersons might also work with experienced faculty members in developing three- to five-year individual professional growth plans, which address the faculty member's goals and plans in light of departmental priorities. Traditional sabbatical leaves can be rejuvenating as well. One challenge concerning sabbaticals is that the two-career household so common today, coupled with the school-aged children that midcareer faculty members may have, can make taking a sabbatical too difficult in terms of finances and logistics. An innovative strategy is to allow midcareer and senior faculty members the option of developing flexible multiyear work plans that may involve shifting levels of focus to teaching or research (Gappa et al., 2007).

GRANTS AND AWARDS. In addition to encouraging chairpersons to see themselves as "first-line providers" of professional development, institutions can provide additional faculty development opportunities and resources for midcareer faculty members (Baldwin et al., 2008; Gappa et al., 2007) such as seed-grant funds to help them explore new research directions or to support collaborations that bring colleagues from different fields or institutions together. Such awards not only spur research activity but foster new collegial relationships. Teaching awards can be directed specifically to recognize and inspire the accomplishments of seasoned academics.

MENTORING RELATIONSHIPS. As mentioned earlier, some institutions are experimenting with new approaches to mentoring. Mentoring relationships can tap into the generative commitments of midcareer and senior faculty, enabling them to share their experiences with newer colleagues. Such relationships can revitalize established faculty members even as they provide support for those new to the institution. Another variation on mentoring is to provide the opportunity for those in midcareer to receive mentoring themselves (Baldwin et al., 2008).

LEADERSHIP DEVELOPMENT. A few institutions are recognizing the importance of leadership development for midcareer faculty members (Baldwin et al., 2008; Gappa et al., 2007). While leadership development has long been provided at many institutions for department chairpersons, a more recent development is to help early midcareer faculty members develop the skills that help with committee and task force leadership, including, for example, project management, human resources, and conflict management skills.

The Late Career Stage

Faculty members within ten or twelve years of retirement are considered to be in the late or senior career stage. The issues discussed in the previous section on midcareer faculty—particularly, the importance of maintaining vitality over time, the interest in leadership development, and the expectations for meeting changing student needs and gaining competence in the uses of technology—are equally relevant to late-career faculty (Gappa et al., 2007).

The faculty development strategies mentioned earlier can also provide useful support to senior faculty members. Of particular note, however, are the mentoring opportunities, which may be of special interest to faculty members in the later years of their careers as well as to those recently retired. These experienced faculty members, who often have a desire to be generative, have years of experience upon which to draw as they guide new colleagues. At the same time, the mentoring relationship is likely to bring fresh perspectives and new ideas to the senior colleague. For example, while senior faculty members help early career colleagues negotiate departmental politics or offer feedback on manuscripts, the newer faculty members may share recent developments in the field or tips on effective uses of technology in teaching.

A specific area of interest to senior faculty members concerns retirement planning. Some institutions offer phased retirement opportunities, which enable faculty members to change the nature and extent of their employment responsibilities gradually, culminating in full retirement. Faculty development programs can ensure that faculty members in late career have ready access, often provided via seminars and Web sites, to thorough information about policies and options available to them as they plan for retirement. Senior faculty members also appreciate opportunities to talk with trusted chairpersons, faculty development directors, or other institutional leaders about the decision-making process involved as they approach retirement and the implications and issues relevant to completing a fulfilling and productive career.

Conclusion

At each career stage, faculty members are valuable assets to their institutions. Universities and colleges are engaging in wise use of their human resources when they recognize the issues of concern to faculty members as they progress through their careers. Effective faculty development programs offer opportunities relevant to faculty members across career stages as well as programming specific to those at each career stage.

REFERENCES

Austin, A. E. (2002a). Creating a bridge to the future: Preparing new faculty to face changing expectations in a shifting context. *Review of Higher Education*, 26(2), 119—144.

Austin, A. E. (2002b). Preparing the next generation of faculty: Graduate education as socialization to the academic career. *The Journal of Higher Education*, 73(2), 94–122.

Austin, A. E., & McDaniels, M. (2006). Preparing the professoriate of the future: Graduate student socialization for faculty roles. In J. C. Smart (Ed.), *Higher education: Handbook of theory and research, Vol. XXI* (pp. 397–456). Dordrecht, The Netherlands: Springer.

Austin, A. E., & Rice, R. E. (1998). Making tenure viable: Listening to early career faculty. *American Behavioral Scientist*, 41(5), 736–754.

Austin, A. E., Sorcinelli, M. D., & McDaniels, M. (2007). Understanding new faculty: Background, aspirations, challenges, and growth. In R. Perry & J. Smart (Eds.), *The scholarship of teaching and learning in higher education: An evidence-based perspective* (pp. 39–89). Dordrecht, The Netherlands: Springer.

Baldwin, R. G., DeZure, D., Shaw, Al, & Moretto, K. (2008). Mapping the terrain of mid-career faculty at a research university: Implications for faculty and academic leaders. *Change*, 40(5), 46–55.

Boice, R. (1992). *The new faculty member: Supporting and fostering professional development*. San Francisco Jossey-Bass.

Gappa, J. M., Austin, A. E., & Trice, A. G. (2007). *Rethinking faculty work: Higher education's strategic imperative*. San Francisco: Jossey-Bass.

Gappa, J. M., & MacDermid, S. M. (1997). *Work, family, and the faculty career. New Pathways Working Paper Series #8*. Washington, DC: American Association for Higher Education.

Golde, C. M. (1998). Beginning graduate school: Explaining first-year doctoral attrition. In M. S. Anderson (Ed.), *New directions for higher education, no.101. The experience of being in graduate school: An exploration* (pp. 55–64). San Francisco: Jossey-Bass.

Golde, C. M., & Dore, T. M. (2001). *At cross purposes: What the experiences of today's doctoral students reveal about doctoral education*. Philadelphia: Pew Charitable Trusts.

Lindholm, J. A., Szelenyi, K., Hurtado, S., & Korn, W. S. (2005). *The American college teacher: National norms for the 2004–2005 HERI Faculty Survey*. Los Angeles University of California, Los Angeles, Higher Education Research Institute.

Menges, R. J. (1999). *Faculty in new jobs*. San Francisco: Jossey-Bass.

Moody, J. (2001). *Demystifying the profession: Helping junior faculty succeed*. New Haven, CT: University of New Haven Press.

National Association of Graduate-Professional Students. (2001). *The national doctoral program survey: Executive summary*. Washington, DC: National Association of Graduate-Professional Students.

Nerad, M., Aanerud, R., and Cerny, J. (2004). "So you want to become a professor!": Lessons from the PhDs-Ten Years Later study. In D. H. Wulff & A. E. Austin (Eds.), *Paths to the professoriate: Strategies for enriching the preparation of future faculty* (pp. 137–158). San Francisco: Jossey-Bass.

Nyquist, J. D., Manning, L., Wulff, D. H., Austin, A. E., Sprague, J., Fraser, P. K., Calcagno, C., & Woodford, B. (1999). On the road to becoming a professor: The graduate student experience. *Change, 31*(3), 18–27.

Olsen, D., & Sorcinelli, M. D. (1992). The pretenure years: A longitudinal perspective. In M. D. Sorcinelli & A. E. Austin (Eds.), *New directions for higher education, no 48. Developing new and junior faculty* (pp. 15–25). San Francisco: Jossey-Bass.

Rice, R. E., & Sorcinelli, M. D. (2002). Can the tenure process be improved? In R. P. Chait (Ed.), *The questions of tenure* (pp. 101–124). Cambridge, MA: Harvard University Press.

Rice, R. E., Sorcinelli, M. D., & Austin, A. E. (2000). *Heeding new voices: Academic careers for a new generation.* Washington, DC: American Association of Higher Education.

Shih, M. Y., & Sorcinelli, M. D. (2007). Technology as a catalyst for senior faculty development. *Journal of Faculty Development, 21*(1), 23–31.

Solem, M. N., & Foote, K. E. (2004). Concerns, attitudes, and abilities of early career geography faculty. *Annuals of the Association of American Geographers, 1*(4), 889–912.

Sorcinelli, M. D. (2000). *Principles of good practice: Supporting early-career faculty. Guidance for deans, department chairs, and other academic leaders.* Washington, DC: American Association for Higher Education. Retrieved January 2, 2009, from http://www.umass.edu/cft/publications/early_career_faculty.pdf

Sorcinelli, M. D., & Austin, A. E. (Eds.). (1992). *New directions for higher education, no 50. Developing new and junior faculty.* San Francisco: Jossey-Bass.

Sorcinelli, M. D., & Austin, A. E. (2006). Developing faculty for new roles and changing expectations. *Effective Practices for Academic Leaders, 1*(11), 1–16.

Sorcinelli, M. D., Austin, A. E., Eddy, P., & Beach, A. (2006). *Creating the future of faculty development: Learning from the past, understanding the present.* Bolton, MA: Anker.

Sorcinelli, M. D., Austin, A. E., & Trower, C. A. (2001). Paradise lost. *The Department Chair, 12*(1), 1–3, 6–7.

Sorcinelli, M. D., & Jung, Y. (2006, June). *Mutual mentoring initiative: Envisioning a new culture of mentoring.* Poster presentation at the Fourth Annual International Conference on Teaching and Learning in Higher Education, Galway, Ireland.

Tierney, W. G., & Bensimon, E. M. (1996). *Promotion and tenure: Community and socialization in academe.* Albany: State University of New York Press.

Trower, C. A. (2005). How do junior faculty feel about your campus as a work place? *Harvard Institutes for Higher Education: Alumni Bulletin.* Cambridge, MA: Harvard University.

Trower, C. A., Austin, A. E., & Sorcinelli, M. D. (2001). Paradise lost: How the academy converts enthusiastic recruits into early career doubters. *American Association of Higher Education (AAHE) Bulletin, 53*(9), 3–6.

U.S. Department of Education, National Center for Education Statistics. (2004). *National Study of Postsecondary Faculty* (NSOPF:04). Washington, DC: Author. Retrieved January 2, 2009, from http://nces.ed.gov/pubsearch/pubsinfo.asp?pubid=2007175

Whitt, E. (1991). Hit the ground running: Experiences of new faculty in a school of education. *Review of Higher Education 14*(2): 177–197.

Wulff, D. H., Austin, A. E., Nyquist, J. D., & Sprague, J. (2004). The development of graduate students as teaching scholars: A four-year longitudinal study. In D. H. Wulff & A. E. Austin (Eds.), *Paths to the professoriate: Strategies for enriching the preparation of future faculty* (pp. 46–73). San Francisco: Jossey-Bass.

23

ORGANIZATIONAL DEVELOPMENT

Kay J. Gillespie

SINCE THE FOUNDING OF THE Professional and Organizational Development (POD) Network in Higher Education in 1974, organizational development has been a part of the organization's name and its mission statement. This component is currently expressed as follows in the POD mission statement: "The Professional and Organizational Development Network in Higher Education encourages the advocacy of the on-going enhancement of teaching and learning through faculty and organizational development. To this end it supports the work of educational developers and champions their importance to the academic enterprise" (POD Network, 2003). Further, a significant and important element relating to organizational development appears in POD's "stated values," where one finds a clear commitment specifically to the development of "humane and collaborative organizations and administrations" (POD Network, 2003). This organizational development mission and set of values has been internalized by the POD membership as revealed in a recent survey of POD Network members in the United States and Canada. The survey showed that, across all institutional types, educational developers believed they should position themselves as agents and key institutional players in helping their colleges and universities respond to change (Sorcinelli, Austin, Eddy, & Beach, 2006, p. 142).

The ongoing emphasis on organizational development within the POD Network scope of activities also can be illustrated by topical sessions within the POD annual conferences. For example, at the second annual conference held in 1977, the conference program included such sessions as the following:

"Leadership Development Workshop for Academic Department Chairpersons"

"The Inside Job: Consulting with Academic and Administrative Departments"

"A Case Study of a Departmental Intervention"

"Approaches to Administrator Development"

The 2008 POD conference, which was the thirty-third such annual event, also included an array of sessions dealing with organizational matters, as can be seen in such session titles as

"Developing Department Chairs to Create a Culture of Institutional Citizenship"

"Using Facilities Planning to Enhance Organizational Development and Student Learning"

"Building Collaborations Among Campus Offices to Support Professional Development"

"Influencing Organizational Change through Conversation Cafés"

"Risks and Rewards of Being an Organizational Change Agent"

If one accepts the offerings of the POD conference as an indicator of the level of interest in organizational development, clearly this interest has been there since the beginning; and it continues.

Building upon this historical foundation, I offer brief commentary in this chapter on the definition and understanding of organizational development, specifically in the context of educational development; make practical suggestions for providing educational development activities in support of organizational development; and offer examples of implementation. Within the discussion, I address how educational developers might conceptualize the whole of the educational enterprise at the institutional level, be attentive to the importance of building collaborative relationships for the work of educational development, and engage in not only *thinking* but *acting* "organizationally."

The previous chapters of this book have provided a great deal of information and guidance as well as many practical suggestions about the conduct of educational development efforts. We have gone back and forth in this volume among these the terms—*faculty development, educational development,* and *professional development*—because the field is still one in flux and formation; and chapter authors have dealt with detailed matters relating to *instructional, faculty,* and *graduate student development.* Now it remains to raise the umbrella above these topics through the consideration of *organizational development*, which brings us to consideration of the institution as a whole, as a constantly evolving entity.

Readers of this volume include both new and experienced educational developers, faculty members, administrators, and others; and a word of caution is needed, particularly for persons involved in starting a new educational development undertaking or for those persons tapped to implement the effort. Quite simply, no individual can know and do everything that has been mentioned and discussed in the previous chapters or that will be presented in this chapter, and no program can—or should—offer implementation of all the suggestions found in these chapters. One's knowledge and experience evolve and grow as one begins and continues in this work, and programs mature. In fact, experienced educational developers would likely agree that we should never cease growing and evolving in our understanding of this field—just as is the case with traditional academic disciplines or any other area of human endeavor, for that matter. Readers should realize that involvement in organizational development is perhaps on the more advanced side of the spectrum of educational development activities, and it is generally not the starting place for this work. Nevertheless, the organization provides the framework for all that is occurring in educational development, and understanding the import of organizational development efforts is significant even for those just beginning in the field.

Definition and Conceptualization

Within the context of educational development, *organizational development* can be understood as referring to the "organizational structures and processes of an institution and its subunits. Organizational development efforts seek to help the organization function in an effective and efficient way so as to support the work of faculty members, administrators, students, and staff members. Leadership training for department chairpersons; effective use of group processes; review and revision of the institution's mission statement; implementing organizational change processes; and institutional governance are representative topics that fall within the purview of organizational development" (Gillespie, 2002, p. v.). Two foundational concepts are critical to this discussion, in my opinion; and these concepts are *relationship* and *context*.

Relationship

Organizational development is about relationship; that is, it involves relationships between and among individuals and groups and relationships between and among units and subunits of an entity. So, for example, organizational development can be perceived as encompassing personnel matters such as review and revision of tenure and promotion policies and processes, discussion of the faculty roles and rewards system, facilitation of discussions and group processes at the unit level, the appropriate and orderly conduct of searches, and conflict management and resolution procedures. It also involves consideration of relationships within the institution, such as reporting lines for units or alignment of programs and departments within a school or college. Thus, an educational developer is involved with considering both human and structural interactions within the institution and how they affect the functioning of the individual as well as the institution and its subunits. One can then seek ways of making those interactions more effective and more humane.

Context

It behooves us to realize that organizational development works within the broader context in which learning occurs, and the details of this context will vary greatly among institutions. When thinking organizationally, we should recognize how important basic decisions are in the framing and functioning of an organization and how tightly any changes in policy or practices are interwoven into an organizational web. This web can include, for example, decisions about and changes in the format and delivery method of courses; the design and allocation of physical space; the structures for faculty governance; and even the assignments and special interests of members of the institution's board of trustees, to which we perhaps give too little attention. All of these interactions have an impact on the work of all persons involved in the organization, on the instructional setting, and on the context for organizational development, which looks not only at the functioning of the institution as a whole, but also at the relationships between and among its subunits. Baron (2006) expressed these connections quite succinctly as follows: "No campus organization exists in a vacuum, nor can it afford to be an island unto itself. Thus, the functions of faculty development need to be viewed in the context of the entire institution. The effectiveness of faculty development, and sometimes its very survival, are [sic] dependent to a large extent on its ability to influence and participate in organizational development outside of its own confines" (p. 29).

Context also includes consideration of the institutional culture, the importance of which has been stressed in other chapters of this volume. (See, in particular, Chapter Five, "Listen, Learn, Lead: Getting Started in Faculty Development" and Chapter Seven, "Promoting Your Program and Grounding It in the Institution.") Yet its importance merits mention here as well. The culture of the institution reflects its organizational values—stated or unstated, and organizational development must occur within the confines of this culture—whether for good or ill. The culture evolves as change is introduced, or we might alternatively discover that change is introduced as the culture evolves; seldom, if ever, does revolution occur. Consequently, we have to recognize and accept the fact that the implementation of positive change is often a slow process; and sometimes it is arduous indeed.

In his book entitled *The Four Cultures of the Academy,* William H. Bergquist (1992), an early leader in the field of faculty development, provided us with a particularly thoughtful discussion of the concept of culture within the academy; and it provides good background for thinking about organizational development. He initially conceptualized four cultures that work together to form the overall organizational culture. As Bergquist articulated them, these four cultures are

1. The collegial culture, which is rooted in the disciplines
2. The managerial culture, which focuses on tangible educational goals
3. The developmental culture, which emphasizes furthering the growth of all members of the community
4. The negotiating culture, which values the equitable and egalitarian distribution of institutional resources

An understanding of these concepts within the framework of the individual institution is helpful when one is seeking to think organizationally. In discussing "fostering organizational change and innovation," Berquist wrote, "We can do something more to respond to the problems of our colleges and universities than just learn how to improve the status quo" (1992, p. 187). I believe that this comment is an encouragement to educational developers to both *think* and *act organizationally.* (N.B.: A recent revision of this work adds two more cultural concepts—tangible and virtual—to the original four [Bergquist & Pawlak, 2008]).

Organizational Development: Practicality and Action

As an educational developer, one quickly realizes that the very nature of this position places one in the role of acting as a change agent within the academy. Many developers believe passionately that this is a very exciting position in which to be, and educational developers perceive of themselves as both facilitators and leaders of change (Diamond, 2005). This understanding leads to consideration of the practical aspects of educational development work within the organization, that is, translating organizational *thinking* into *action*. All such efforts have as background the internal and external challenges and complexity within the higher education environment and the constituencies and relationships with which educational developers become involved when thinking organizationally.

Challenges and Complexity of the Higher Education Environment

The challenges of the higher education environment have become ever more complex as we seek to respond to the calls for reform coming from different directions, the need for change, the financial and budgetary difficulties we are all facing, the demand for accountability—all the issues that surround us, or perhaps bombard us, on a daily basis. In this kind of environment, it is all too easy to be reactive rather than proactive. The reality is that, as educational developers, we may quite frequently find ourselves acting in both of these ways at the same time, which can create a tension that we must confront.

For several decades the call for reform has been sounded on many fronts; and the academy has responded in many different ways, collectively and institutionally. Government reports and recommendations have appeared; private foundations have disseminated their ideas and fostered innovation; accrediting agencies have modified their standards and expectations; students and parents have made their wishes and sometimes even their demands known; legislators have made laws; courts have made rulings; state systems have mandated changes; institutions have produced and then revised strategic plans; and this list could continue.

When we read the litany of government reports with their recommendations, we may at times argue about them within the academy, most recently, for example, about the findings that came forth from what is commonly known as the Spelling Commission (About the Commission, 2008). On the other hand, sometimes we enthusiastically adopt ideas and recommendations, as we have done with Boyer's seminal work (1990), which stimulated discussion throughout higher education about the nature of scholarship. The response to Boyer's work is also illustrative of the significant impact private foundations can have on our activities in leading to ensuing adaptations such as the Scholarship of Teaching and Learning (Hutchings & Shulman, 2007). We must also respond to external demands, as we did in the 1960s (for example, in the implementation of student evaluations of teaching), and the more recent example of demands for accountability. We must then deal with the positive and occasionally troubling consequences of our responses to these external demands as we implement decisions and assess our actions. Sometimes national associations have championed educational development. The American Association of Higher Education led reform in several areas from the 1970s through 2000, for example, in the murky area of faculty roles and rewards. Regrettably the association was then forced to cease operations for financial reasons. Lawmakers have given us laws about affirmative action; and our courts, campuses, and occasionally even citizen groups have become involved in the often heated discussions around this topic. Our institutions have put new programs in place, and budget cuts may then require us to rethink and recast what we are doing and what we can and cannot do. Again, a listing of our responses to change and the changes such responses have wrought could go on and on.

Whatever our individual lists may include, there is no doubt that we are at work in what is indeed a highly complex environment. If we take our charge as educational developers to enhance teaching and learning and all other aspects of educational development activity in our institutions seriously, it is incumbent upon us to seek to understand this environment and to keep ourselves well informed about it. It is the environment that molds the larger organizational systems and units in which faculty, administrators, and staff work and that influences their behaviors.

If we are thinking organizationally, we then recognize the importance of these organizational structures and seek to contribute to altering them in ways consistent with our values and our missions. We also need to realize that there are no clear lines of separation between the different categories of educational development, that is, faculty, graduate student, instructional, and organizational development. Each area of activity can affect another. Hutchings and Shulman (2007) provide an illustration of the importance of connecting these in our thinking. Pulling together faculty and organizational development, they wrote as follows: "It is heartening to see individual faculty developing examples of the scholarship of teaching; these will become prompts for a next set of efforts (just as they built on work from the several traditions that converge in the scholarship of teaching). *But what's needed as well is a culture and infrastructure that will allow such work to flourish*" [italics added] (para. 26).

Recognizing the challenges and complexity of our environment and its impact might mean we attend to the following.

KNOWLEDGE. First and foremost, we should undertake and maintain our own effort to remain informed about concerns, data, trends, and innovation in higher education at large. This kind of knowledge can be gained and expanded by conference attendance and reading general higher education publications such as the *Chronicle of Higher Education* and *Change* magazine as well as by networking with other educational developers. At the same time, as stressed in other chapters in this volume, we should be well informed about policies and procedures within our own institutions; and significant policy, procedure, and information manuals should occupy a prominent place within every educational development office.

INSTITUTIONAL INVOLVEMENT. We can engage in and positively contribute to organizational initiatives that recognize and explore the complexity of the external and internal environment and that seek to respond to the identified needs for change. Such action is often promoted, for example, by service on the visioning or strategic planning committee of the institution or unit.

THE REALITY. We must also realize that we might face challenges and obstacles, which may include the nature and personalities of persons with whom we work, the structure and culture of our institutional environment, the real or perceived constraints of our mission within the institution, and perhaps our own hesitation or concern about getting involved in this kind of activity.

The Constituencies and Relationships

In *Creating the Future of Faculty Development* (Sorcinelli et al., 2006), developers' visions about the future of the field called for more emphasis on organizational development and change. Specifically, respondents believed that developers should take a stronger leadership role within institutions by working with academic leaders, especially chairpersons and deans; becoming involved in governance structures; and aligning their centers or programs with institutional priorities, which leads us to look at how educational developers might approach such collaborations and relationships.

WORK WITH CHAIRPERSONS AND OTHER ADMINISTRATORS. The department is a critical unit within any institution, and Lucas's body of work (for example, 1994, 2002; Lucas & Associates, 2000) has drawn our attention to the importance of working with chairpersons. She wrote, "My work with chairs during this past decade has led me to select the roles of leader and faculty developer as key to effective departmental functioning" (1994, p. xvi), and "If academic departments are to become the agents of change department, chairs must exercise the leadership, knowledge, and skills to motivate faculty to create quality departments" (2002, p. 157). Connecting work with chairpersons to organizational development, Lucas commented, "Working with departments creates a synergy for faculty development staff, and the number of faculty members whose teaching they can impact increases significantly. Because working with chairs affects the institution as a whole, it is regarded as an organizational development strategy" (2002, p. 159).

With this understanding, department chairpersons become our allies in the work of educational development, and we can be attentive to developing and cultivating relationships with chairpersons because of the critical influence they can have on faculty and instructional development within the scope of their departments. New directors of educational development should take the time and make the effort to meet with all department chairpersons, with a specific agenda for that meeting. Chairpersons are the conduits to the faculty members of the department, and their influence—or absence thereof—can have a strong impact on faculty members' interest in pursuing faculty and instructional development activities and programming. If there are councils of department chairs, one can request to meet with the groups, preferably by offering a special agenda item for discussion and possibly action.

In institutions with advanced educational development opportunities and a high staffing level, sometimes educational developers become involved in, and perhaps even initiate, a chairpersons' leadership series of workshops or seminars, however it might be conceived. There is no end to the topics that are of interest and importance to persons in this position. Such a series could also be conceived as a development opportunity for persons who might be thinking of moving into the position of department chairperson. We know that all too often persons in this mid-level leadership position are poorly prepared and lacking in the critical skills and knowledge needed for effective leadership. A leadership series focusing on the position of chairperson could incorporate such topics as personnel management and procedures, budgeting, conflict management, interpersonal skills, grievance procedures, legal issues of significance, and a wide array of other important areas. The Center for Institutional Change at the University of Washington provides an example of intentional leadership training within an institution through workshops they offer. The focus of this program is "leadership development. Through half-day quarterly ADVANCE Leadership workshops, department chairs, deans, and other faculty are offered professional development workshops to help them become more effective leaders. For each workshop, the Department Chairs are encouraged to invite an emerging leader so that other faculty can be exposed to academic leadership issues" (UW ADVANCE, n.d., para. 1).

There are more modest possibilities, too, that can be undertaken to encourage chairperson development and their connections with pursuit of educational development, specifically their own leadership development. The Center for Teaching at Vanderbilt University, for example, has a segment on its Web site offering Web resources for chairpersons, pertinent print material available in the center's library, and case studies focusing on the kinds of issues that arise within departments. (See http://www.vanderbilt.edu/cft/resources/teaching_resources/specific_audiences/chairs.htm.)

Other administrators, in both academic and nonacademic positions, are also important for our work, and we can cultivate relationships with them. The outcome of this effort is the promotion and enhancement of the educational development work. Whether through formal or informal contacts, we can seek to cultivate relationships with persons in deans' positions, inclusive of assistant and associate deans. These contacts might be formal or informal. One could volunteer, for example, to serve on a particular task force or ad hoc committee if its charge is in accord with the mission of educational development or to assist with a reform agenda of particular interest to the dean. Some institutions have councils of deans, and meeting with these groups can be of benefit because it provides opportunity to inform them about educational development activities and to learn about their particular interests and concerns. The activities of the Office of Faculty and Organizational Development at Michigan State University provide an example of an intentional, internal leadership development effort in that it offers extensive programming for administrative and leadership development. This effort includes orientation Web sites for new administrators and new deans, an Executive Leadership Academy, and a LEadership and ADministrator (LEAD) seminar series (Office of Faculty and Organizational Development, n.d.).

One should be aware of the kinds of development programs or opportunities available beyond the institution for new and experienced administrators. Good information about research-based best practice is available to those in management roles, and they need opportunities to learn about this research and these best practices and develop the requisite skills to implement them competently. If we keep ourselves abreast of this information, appropriate opportunity to share it with others might arise. A good source for this information is the *Chronicle of Higher Education*, which should be on every educational developer's weekly reading list.

Not to be forgotten are the leaders of faculty governance bodies, whatever the body may be called (for example, faculty senate or faculty council). This entity is a critically important organizational structure, and our formal or informal involvement with its leaders can bring opportunities for organizational development and can impact the entirety of our work. Also, at unionized institutions it is of benefit to become acquainted with union leaders, who can be important allies for the work of educational development. (See Chapter Six, "Important Skills and Knowledge.") The POD Network has a long-standing, effective publishing collaboration with the National Education Association, a national teachers' union, and provides a regular column on teaching and learning effectiveness for the association's member magazine.

We should also be thinking organizationally within the structures and units of our own reporting lines. For example, if the faculty development director, whether as an individual or head of a center, reports to the chief academic affairs officer, it is worthwhile to take the effort to become acquainted with the personnel in that office, to be aware of the administrative agenda, and to be ready to serve both proactively and reactively in support of this agenda.

COLLABORATION WITH DEPARTMENTS AND CAMPUSWIDE UNITS. As has been emphasized elsewhere in this volume, the work of educational development is very often done in partnership with other individuals and other units within the institution. If we have cultivated relationships with department chairpersons, we have thereby gained entrée into that organizational unit; but we can go beyond that unit, and the intentional involvement of others in our educational development work offers a variety of possibilities. For example, the chief budgetary officer might become involved in a chairpersons' leadership series by offering a workshop on budget procedures. Through the mechanisms of educational development programming, student affairs personnel might assist in disseminating essential information about policies and procedures impacting students and instructors' behaviors. Physicians might provide wellness information of benefit to all, using centralized educational development structures and programs. Working with diversity or multicultural units can multiply the impact of engagement in the institution's diversity agenda.

If we remain aware of college and departmental interests and change efforts, it is sometimes possible to become involved in the undertaking as advisor, facilitator, or participant by tactfully seeking ways to offer assistance in the effort. Lee, Hyman, and Luginbuhl's (2007) explanation of significant change in undergraduate education provides a good example of group processing at the departmental level and addresses the concept of "readiness" for change within a department.

One can offer to meet with nonfaculty governance groups so as to inform them of educational development programs and activities, perhaps with the suggestion of specific discussion or action items, and to remain informed of their interests and particular agendas. Above all, it is important for us to be respectful of the importance of the contributions of all categories of employees to the mission of the institution. Our attitude can be that of readiness to assist others and to find ways to involve them in the educational development work, as appropriate. Deserving of specific mention are library personnel and persons in offices focusing on matters of diversity.

It is important to realize that these kinds of partnerships have the potential of positioning us to contribute to organizational development in a variety of ways.

COMMITTEE SERVICE AND FACULTY GOVERNANCE. Committee service is often a good mechanism for involvement in organizational development. The educational developer should seek to get involved in those committees that can affect organizational development matters and serve as conduits to involvement in change agency; this involvement can also be a significant public relations activity for the work of educational development.

A particularly good example of important committee work is the institution's strategic planning committee, which charts the institution's direction and has impact on all aspects of its operation directly affecting the teaching and learning environment. Another good example might be the facilities committee of an institution. If a new classroom building is in the planning, from the outset its design is quite critical; and an educational developer can offer advice on teaching and learning needs translated into teaching and learning spaces. Other committees that can perhaps further our work and might welcome the participation of the educational developer include task forces or committees on undergraduate education, general education, the status of women and minorities, faculty roles and rewards, and other academic matters. Service on committees of such import most definitely involves us organizationally. Thus, one should become well acquainted with the committee structure at the institutional and college or school levels as well as within the report-ing division for the educational development unit. If the developer has a regular faculty appointment in a department, there will be opportunity to become involved in the departmental committees. Whatever the com-mittees may be, one must do the homework and be knowledgeable about committee charges and relevant policies and procedures.

Another note of caution is necessary, however, for one should be judicious in determining what kind of and how much involvement is appropriate. For example, service on a strategic planning committee, a facilities committee, or curriculum development committee is likely to be interesting, significant, and beneficial in the context of educational development and also quite time consuming. Service on the athletics committee (or the parking committee) is most likely not appropriate. One, of course, also has to be mindful of the manner in which committee membership is determined; there may be constraints on this, depending on the nature of the developer's appointment. If official membership is not possible, one might still be able to become informally involved as a nonvoting member or advisor.

COMMUNITY AND GROUP PROCESSES. It is a given that all kinds of discussions about many significant topics will occur all the time in any institution of higher education. Change is constantly in process, albeit most frequently in incremental fashion: organizational development is occurring all the time, in one way or another. Indeed, the organization is a "learning organization," whether intentionally so or not (compare Chapter Three, "Establishing an Educational Development Program"). Senge (1990) wrote that the learning organization is "where people continually expand their capacity to create the results they truly desire, where new and expansive patterns of thinking are nurtured, where collective aspiration is set free, and where people are continually learning how to learn together" (p. 3). Could our institutions of higher education be intentional learning organizations in the Sengian sense? Can our work as educational developers contribute to enhancing the intentional learning of our institutions? Can we contribute to building an intentional learning organization, a learning community with these kinds of aspirations? The educational developer's answer to these questions should be a resounding "Yes," which is reflective of a spirit of idealism, positive motivation, and aspirational intent, even though we must recognize that our aspirations will not be perfectly realized.

Yet, clearly there is a tension between idealism and the reality of day-to-day work life in higher education, and this tension can bring us a sense of excitement as well as a sense of frustration. Quite simply, we are confronted with the dilemma of deciding what to do, when to do it, and how much of it to do. With the perspective of the whole academic community, of the whole institution inclusive of its parts, we can seek ways to involve ourselves in organizational processes such as encouraging and developing ways of talking with one another and of resolving conflict that help the institution and its units articulate their shared vision for implementation of the institutional mission. Doing so reflects understanding conflict as something positive. (See Algert & Stanley, 2007; Stanley & Algert, 2007.)

We should seek to foster a culture of respectful inquiry about teaching and learning and intentionally incorporate inquiry into educational development programming. Respectful inquiry and positive resolution of conflict contribute to building community. Reflecting the promotion of this spirit of positive inquiry, the Teaching Learning Center at the University of Nevada, Las Vegas, in partnership with the university's Academic Success Center, offers a program of "Café Conversations" addressing an institutional initiative. In this instance, the purpose of these conversations is to develop a shared understanding of the first-year experience at the university. Five one-hour "cafés" are scheduled, and participants are given two questions for discussion. The questions differ at each café event (Teaching Learning Center, n.d.). An undertaking of this sort can definitely contribute to the building of community within an institution.

We can become involved in the process of the assessment of learning, which should be occurring at the institutional, college, and department levels. A positive approach to assessment and a positive look at the data gathered often leads to organizational changes—for example, alignment of units, resolution of conflicts among faculty members, or reconsideration of curricula and programs. (See Wehlburg's chapter, "Assessment Practices Related to Student Learning" [Chapter Eleven], in which she explains the conceptualization of assessment as "transformative.")

The accreditation or reaccreditation process offers another opportunity for organizational thinking and action through involvement in group processes. An example of a recent change in accreditation standards, likely to have an organizational development impact, is the introduction of the quality enhancement plan, which "describes a carefully designed course of action that addresses a well-defined and focused topic or issue related to enhancing student learning. The QEP should be embedded within the institution's ongoing integrated institution-wide planning and evaluation process" (The Quality Enhancement Plan, 2008, para. I. "Overview").

Working toward the development and implementation of such a plan will likely involve significant organizational change. (See also Southern Association of Colleges and Schools, 2008.)

In our actions, we can seek to cultivate and strengthen the academic value of collegiality. In all possible ways, we can choose to work against potentially negative aspects of institutional climates. Parker Palmer, a distinguished and influential voice among us, has spoken and written a lot about the element of *fear* within the academy, which, if prevailing, undermines the most determined and skilled efforts to build community, to encourage positive group processes and discussions. He has admonished us about the culture of fear within academe in saying, "We are afraid of hearing something that would challenge and change us. . . . We don't want to hear those voices. We carefully wall ourselves off, by means of systematic disrespect, from all those things that might challenge us, break us, open us" (1998, p. B12). Our educational development programming can include workshops for faculty, administrators, and staff on the skills of building and maintaining community including facilitation, listening, and the promotion of positive inquiry and conflict resolution.

In a book entitled *Trustworthy Leadership,* Walsh (2006), the former President of Wellesley College, identified a central leadership responsibility in higher education, which is "to design and sustain communities of meaning and hope, communities that will offer all their members opportunities to learn and grow, to make contributions, and to be seen and recognized for who they are and what they bring" (p. 29). As educational developers, we can contribute positively to this challenging task.

OUR OWN ORGANIZATIONAL DEVELOPMENT. What we do in educational development is determined by the mission and charge for the effort within the specific institutional context; by the nature and type of the institution; and by the many factors, characteristics, and constraints of the organizational context and culture in which we work. As individuals, we may have the possibility of more influence within our own educational development unit than within the entire institution. One's own unit is a sphere of organizational development where we can perhaps more easily and more quickly *act* organizationally than within the institution at large. We can undertake or oversee a strategic planning exercise for the educational development effort, relating it to the unit's internal program assessment efforts and to the institutional agenda, strategic plan, and mission at large. We can take measures to examine the climate within our unit, be alert to potential difficulties, and be ready to make changes, if necessary.

Above all, we should be listening to colleagues and nurturing of others, and I suggest that we strive to be guided by the stated POD value of promoting and developing "humane and collaborative organizations and administrations." This value should guide whatever involvement we might have in organizational development activity (Gillespie, 2000). Of organizational values, Bergquist (1992) wrote as follows: "I propose that when we examine organizational values . . . we are looking at 'tacit knowledge.' We know that these values are present and profoundly influence our life and our attitudes regarding the organization in which we work, yet these values are often not directly known to us. In other words, these values often remain 'unconscious.' They serve as tacitly-held templates against which we measure the 'rightness' and 'wrongness' of behaviors in our organization and the extent to which things have changed in our organization"(p. 353).

Conclusion and Closing Note to Readers

The intent of this chapter has been to encourage persons either working in or interested in the field of educational development to *think* and to *act* organizationally, to provide ideas on the framework for doing so, and to offer practical suggestions for the implementation of organizational development activities to the extent possible given one's individual situation. I have suggested that there are two conceptual pillars for the framework of organizational development, which are *relationship* and *context*; and these concepts are imbedded within the complex culture of the institution.

Upon this foundation, one can then construct an approach to organizational development, weaving it in with what is being done in faculty, graduate student, and instructional development. If the educational development effort is new or recreated or if the undertaking is rather modest in scope, then the educational developer may not be able to do much more than think organizationally. However, *thinking* in this way leads to *acting* in this way. Such action might be rather simple in scope such as arranging meetings with all chairpersons so as to inform oneself about departmental interests and concerns, or it could be far more complex such as proposing and then planning, in collaboration with others, an extended leadership series within the institution. It could be volunteering to facilitate a departmental discussion on a matter of concern, or it could be seeking membership on the institution's long-range strategic planning committee. The choices for action are many and varied, and organizational development can indeed be intentionally included as part of the educational development effort. The first step in doing so is to *think* organizationally, to allow the entirety of the institution and its mission to infuse one's thinking about the educational development effort; in itself that is an *action*.

Thus, this chapter and this book come to a close with an organizational development perspective, which, in a way, invites us to perceive educational development metacognitvely—thinking about our thinking and thinking about all that we are doing, all that we would like to do, and perhaps also all that we cannot yet do. Engaging in organizational development thought and action involves us with all other aspects of educational development in promotion of the goals of higher education and our institutions. This is an exciting opportunity!

REFERENCES

About the Commission. (2008). Retrieved January 30, 2009, from http://www.ed.gov/about/bdscomm/list/hiedfuture/about.html

Algert, N. E., & Stanley, C.A. (2007). Conflict management. *Effective Practices for Academic Leaders, 2*(9), 1—16.

Baron, L. (2006). The advantages of a reciprocal relationship between faculty development and organizational development in higher education. In S. Chadwick-Blossey & D. R. Robertson (Eds.), *To improve the academy: Vol. 24. Resources for faculty, instructional, and organizational development* (pp. 29–43). San Francisco: Jossey-Bass.

Bergquist, W. H. (1992). *The four cultures of the academy: Insights and strategies for improving leadership in collegiate organizations.* San Francisco: Jossey-Bass.

Bergquist, W. H., & Pawlak, K. (2008). *Engaging the six cultures of the academy: Revised and expanded edition of the four cultures of the Academy* (2nd ed.). San Francisco: Jossey-Bass.

Boyer, E. (1990). *Scholarship reconsidered: Priorities of the professoriate.* Princeton, NJ: Carnegie Foundation for the Advancement of Teaching.

Diamond, R. M. (2005). The institutional change agency: The expanding role of academic support centers. In S. Chadwick-Blossey (Ed.), *To improve the academy: Vol. 23. Resources for faculty, instructional, and organizational development* (pp. 24–37). Bolton, MA: Anker.

Gillespie, K. H. (2000). The challenge and test of our values: An essay of collective experience. *To improve the academy: Vol. 18. Resources for faculty, instructional, and organizational development* (pp. 27–37). Bolton, MA: Anker.

Gillespie, K. H. (Ed.). (2002). *A guide to faculty development: Practical advice, examples, and resources.* Bolton, MA: Anker.

Hutchings, P., & Shulman, L. S. (2007). *The scholarship of teaching: New elaborations, new developments.* Stanford, CA: Carnegie Foundation for the

Advancement of Teaching. Retrieved January 30, 2009, from http://www
.carnegiefoundation.org/publications/sub.asp?key=452&subkey=613

Lee, V. S., Hyman, M. R., & Luginbuhl, G. (2007). The concept of readiness in the academic department: A case study of undergraduate education reform. *Innovative Higher Education, 32*(1), 19–34.

Lucas, A. F. (1994). *Strengthening departmental leadership: A team-building guide for chairs in colleges and universities.* San Francisco: Jossey-Bass.

Lucas, A. F. (2002). Increase your effectiveness in the organization: Work with department chairs. In K. Gillespie (Ed.), *A guide to faculty development: Practical advice, examples, and resources* (pp. 157–166). Bolton, MA: Anker.

Lucas A. F., & Associates (2000). *Leading academic change: Essential roles for department chairs.* San Francisco: Jossey-Bass.

Office of Faculty and Organizational Development. (n.d.). Michigan State University. Retrieved January 30, 2009, from http://fod.msu.edu/

Palmer, P. J. (1998, October 9). Melange. *The Chronicle of Higher Education,* p. B12.

POD Network. (2003). *The mission.* Retrieved January 13, 2009, from http://podnetwork.org/about/mission.htm

Senge, P. M. (1990). *The fifth discipline: The art and practice of the learning organization.* New York: Doubleday.

Sorcinelli, M. D., Austin, A. E., Eddy, P. L., & Beach, A. L. (2006). *Creating the future of faculty development: Learning from the past, understanding the present.* Bolton, MA: Anker.

Southern Association of Colleges and Schools. (2008). *Principles of accreditation: Foundations for quality enhancement.* Atlanta: Southern Association of Colleges and Schools.

Stanley, C. A., & Algert, N. E. (2007). An exploratory study of the conflict management styles of department heads in a research university setting. *Innovative Higher Education, 32*(1), 49–66.

Teaching Learning Center. (n.d.). *Café conversations.* University of Nevada, Las Vegas. Retrieved January 30, 2009, from http://www2.tlc.unlv.edu/tlc/reg-istration/winterspring.php?semester=spring&year=2009

The Quality Enhancement Plan. (2008). Southern Association of Colleges and Schools. Retrieved January 30, 2009, from http://www.sacscoc.org/pdf/081705/QEP%20Handbook.pdf

UW ADVANCE. (n.d.). *Leadership workshops.* Retrieved January 30, 2009, from http://www.engr.washington.edu/advance/workshops/

Walsh, D. C. (2006). *Trustworthy leadership; Can we be the leaders we need our students to become?* Kalamazoo, MI: Fetzer Institute.

AFTERWORD

William H. Bergquist

It is a privilege to be asked to prepare an Afterword to a book that is comprehensive in scope and authored by women and men of considerable distinction in the field of faculty development. I suspect that I share with these authors a great devotion to—even a love of—higher education. I also come to the preparation of this Afterword with a second love that is not so obviously aligned with this book, that is, a love for Broadway musicals. As I have engaged in preparing this Afterword, I have been accompanied by reminiscence of the musical *Sunset Boulevard* and the classic movie of the same name, which inspired the musical. In this musical, a former Hollywood star, Norma Desmond, returns to the Paramount studio, the site of her many years of dedicated work. She observes through song that she has much to say about what has changed as well as what has remained the same and that the business in which she worked had "taught the world new ways to dream."

I find myself in a position that is a bit like Norma Desmond. I am returning after many years to a field with which I was affiliated during the last three decades of the twentieth century. In reading the richly insightful and useful chapters prepared for this volume, I notice that some things have not changed during the past two decades, but others have. Furthermore, I continue to be impressed with the extent to which this field of faculty development continues to teach the world of higher education "new ways to dream."

In my return to the field through the writing of this Afterword, I believe I can be of greatest value by focusing on two topics. First, I reflect on what has remained the same and what has changed, using the twenty-three chapters of this book as a base for offering my reflections. I make use of several concepts from the emerging disciplines, or interdisciplinary domains, of chaos and complexity as well as my own analyses of the subcultures that exist in the academy. Second, I propose ways in which the chapters in this book provide us with a basis for considering the diffusion of this exceptional innovation in the higher education community. I borrow terms from Everett Rogers and make use of the alternative terms and metaphors suggested by the Kuhlenschmidt chapter in this volume, "Issues in Technology and Faculty Development" (Chapter Sixteen).

Everything Is the Same and Different

Many years ago, members of the Tavistock Institute in England suggested that organizations tend to replicate certain dynamic patterns that are present at the founding or near the founding of the organization. This principle is often called "subsystem mirroring," suggesting that each subsystem in an organization mirrors or replicates some pattern that is to be found in the overall dynamic pattern of the organization. While this principle never got much notice during the twentieth century, it has been reborn through the more recent studies of chaotic and complex systems. We have come to appreciate the powerful role played by the initial conditions in which any system operates and ways in which these conditions continue throughout the history of the system. The most graphically compelling example of this dynamic is to be found in fractals—and more particularly in those beautiful designs created by Mandelbrot and his colleagues. Fractals are systems that replicate themselves in each or most of their subsystems. The branches of a pine tree, for instance, tend to replicate the structure of the overall tree, as does each of the needles.

Many fundamental issues and tensions that existed when faculty development was first being developed continue to exist and are manifest in the chapters in this book. I need, however, to qualify this somewhat provocative proposition. First, when I comment here on the field of faculty development, I am seeing it through the lens of my own personal experience in the field from 1968 until 1998 and from my perspective as a practitioner who worked primarily with institutions in the United States and Canada. As noted in Ouellett's first chapter (Chapter One, "Overview of Faculty Development") many contributions to the field were made long before 1968. I will be identifying some of them myself. As noted in Chism, Gosling, and Sorcinelli's chapter, "International Faculty Development" (Chapter Fifteen), there are many exceptional faculty development initiatives that have been mounted outside North America.

Second, I fully realize my analysis reveals my own biases, in large part because I played a role (for good or ill) in struggling with many of these early issues. I even helped to create and sustain some of the ongoing tensions in the field. Because I am part of the story, I cannot be an objective observer. However, since I witnessed the conversations and actions, I can speak with some accuracy and with some candor about what occurred "early on" in the then-emerging field of faculty development.

Faculty Development: Means or an End?

An early publication entitled *Facilitating Faculty Development* (Friedman, 1973), the first New Directions monograph from Jossey-Bass, contributed significantly to the evolution of the field of faculty development. The book was not only one of the first to label "faculty development" as a legitimate enterprise; it also provided us with evidence of an initial tension in the field expressed in this question. Is faculty development important in and of itself, or is it a means to some greater or more important end? This early publication focused specifically on faculty, building on the extensive interviews of faculty members at San Francisco State University conducted by Brown and Shukraft (1971) for their joint doctoral dissertation with Nevitt Sanford at the Wright Institute in Berkeley, California. The early work of Jack Noonan and my own work with Steven Phillips came out of this publication and the research done by Brown and Shukraft, who identified ways in which faculty members could be engaged in a manner that was respectful of the unique academic environments in which they work.

The field got quite a boost from the publication of *Faculty Development in a Time of Retrenchment* (Astin et al., 1974). I focus on this publication for several reasons. First, it is remarkable that in 2009 we could easily write a book with a similar title since we are once again living in a time of great retrenchment. How does faculty development relate to the new challenges of retrenchment?

The authors of this seminal book were leaders not only in faculty development but also in higher education in general. Nevitt Sanford was a prime mover behind this book and also *Facilitating Faculty Development* (Friedman, 1973). Both Astin and Sanford played significant roles in building the conceptual and research-based foundation for the nascent field of faculty development. They were instrumental in making a compelling case for the important role of faculty development in addressing the challenges of a higher education community that no longer was living with the ample funds of the late 1960s and early 1970s.

Third, this small book, published by *Change* magazine, promoted faculty development initiatives for many years and helped reinforce the initial and enduring tension in the field. Is faculty development itself a justifiable outcome? While the authors of *Retrenchment* (Astin et al., 1974) were making the case for faculty development as a means to improve the quality of institutional performance during hard economic times, many who were involved in this early project were themselves primarily interested in the challenge of providing ongoing professional development opportunities to faculty members. During moments of candor, many early practitioners, including myself, would admit that they found the "education" of their mature, accomplished colleagues to be of greater interest than the "education" of their unformed, eighteen- to twenty-year-old students. Nevitt Sanford, in particular, was interested in the lifelong development of professionals, as evident in his book *Learning After College* (1980).

The Roles of Instructional and Organizational Development

The next major step came after faculty development programs had been established in several liberal arts colleges throughout North America and teaching improvement centers had begun in several universities such as the University of Massachusetts. This next step was the convening of a two-day conference at the Wingspread Conference Center in Wisconsin. The conference was cosponsored by the American Association for Higher Education (AAHE) and the Council of Independent Colleges (CIC), which were led respectively by two of the major sponsors of early faculty development efforts, Dyke Vermillye and Gary Quehl. The event brought together early leaders in faculty development and several leaders in the related fields of instructional development, including Bob Diamond, and organizational development, including Jack Lindquist. The primary outcome of the conference was the decision to form a new association dedicated to the field of faculty development.

To increase the attendance at a founding meeting of this new association, a faculty development training event run by the CIC was offered at the same time. Additional yeast was added to the brew when a two-day T-Group (sensitivity training) session was scheduled as a team-building exercise prior to the formal meeting. The T-Group was facilitated by Charles Seashore, a major practitioner in the field, and was attended by fourteen persons who later were to form the Professional and Organizational Development (POD) Network. Held in a small room at a woman's college near Cincinnati, this T-Group provided quite an auspicious start to a new association. I keenly remember Bob Diamond sitting cross-legged on the floor (no chairs) and being introduced to the wonders of group dynamics and open disclosure of feelings. I gained a great deal of appreciation for Bob during these two days and admired his willingness to cross cultural boundaries so as to ensure that the field of instructional development was represented in any association dedicated to the professional improvement of faculty.

When the formal meeting was convened, I was elected and served for one hour as executive director of the new association. The group soon determined that Joan North was much better qualified to take on this important leadership task. Our discussion regarding the name of the new organization is revealing of a second tension in the field. Should the field embrace organization development and instructional development as well as faculty ("professional") development? Jack Lindquist argued persuasively and persistently that "organizational" be in the association's name. Though this dimension of the field has often been (or seemed) secondary, Lindquist's insistence at this early stage created the ongoing dialogue regarding the interplay between faculty and organizational development.

Even more broadly, conversations took place concerning the role of institutional planning and development in sustaining and expanding the impact of faculty development programs. Certainly, the analyses offered in the chapters by Ed Neal and Iola Peed-Neal (Chapter Seven), Kathryn M. Plank and Alan Kalish (Chapter Nine), and Kay J. Gillespie (Chapter Twenty-Three) indicate that this dialogue about the interplay among faculty and organization development, strategic planning, and institutional development are still alive. I cannot help thinking, however, that organizational development still plays a secondary role. After all, in this volume there is only one chapter devoted directly to this topic (Chapter 23). Did Jack Lindquist's untimely death mean the loss of advocacy for organization development? Is the tension still present in the field? Has this initial dialogue been often replicated over the past forty years? Is it a fractal?

What about Bob Diamond's efforts to bridge the gap between instructional development and faculty development? Was it worth it for Bob to sit cross-legged through a sensitivity training session? You will notice that instructional development did not make it into the name of POD, which could have been PIOD or (POID). Given the focus of several chapters in this volume, it would seem that Bob's efforts ultimately did pay off. He is referenced many times, and Bob's broader emphasis on locating instructional development and faculty development at the heart of the institution is frequently reinforced. The emergence of a greater emphasis on instructional technology would also seem to have made a difference, although the distinction drawn between information technology and educational development by Robertson in Chapter Three is noteworthy.

Even more generally after reading this book, it seems to me that many faculty developers are quite cleverly linking faculty development initiatives to the educational priorities of their institution. The term *educational development* is used frequently in this book, suggesting that faculty development is being interwoven with instructional development, curriculum development, and even organizational development. Indeed, perhaps the term *educational development* holds the key to categorizing faculty development as a means rather than an end. Or is this just rhetoric about educational development? Perhaps the underlying interest continues to reside in the ongoing professional development of faculty members. Is the means/ends tension a fractal in the field of contemporary faculty development?

Subcultures and Faculty Development

Following the formation of POD in Cincinnati, there was an impressive growth in the number and size of faculty development programs in all sectors of U.S. and Canadian higher education. The chapters in Part Three of this volume provide impressive evidence regarding the engagement of faculty development in many different kinds of higher education institutions. This diffusion, which I shall discuss more fully later in this Afterword, came with a price: faculty development looked and perhaps looks quite different in various settings. The same words were used to describe divergent processes, and quite different assumptions informed the use of specific faculty development strategies.

In working with a variety of institutional types during the 1970s, 1980s, and 1990s, I grew increasingly interested in these diverse perspectives and underlying assumptions. My interest was motivated not only by curiosity, but also by my survival instincts. I needed to know what was happening when my own words were being distorted by my clients and when I needed to adopt different frames of reference in order to gain acceptance for faculty development concepts and strategies. As noted in Gillespie's chapter on "Organizational Development" (Chapter Twenty-Three), I wrote a book (Bergquist, 1992) during the early 1990s about four distinct subcultures in academic institutions: collegial, managerial, negotiating, and developmental. I updated this book recently with the help of my coauthor Ken Pawlak (Bergquist & Pawlak, 2008). We changed the name of one culture (negotiating became advocacy), and we included two other cultures (tangible and virtual).

During the last three decades of the twentieth century, I observed that the collegial culture was winning the day, with the managerial culture coming in a strong second. Much of the faculty development work was being done in liberal arts colleges and in major universities, the heart of the collegial culture. From reading several chapters in this book, notably the chapters on research universities and small colleges, I conclude that these institutions and this culture still play an important role in faculty development—though this culture's focus on faculty development as an end in and of itself may be less credible in the twenty-first century. Community colleges, the heart of the managerial culture, also have a long history of offering faculty development programs, often framed as instructional and curriculum development. I see ample evidence in the present volume that faculty development is tightly intertwined with the managerial culture. Certainly the attention given by Zakrajsek to human and financial resource management (Chapter Six) and by Plank and Kalish to the building of integrating data sets and the valuing of accountability and fiscal stewardship in faculty development programs (Chapter Nine) suggests that the managerial culture is still alive and well.

Unfortunately, faculty development was not very closely aligned with the negotiating (advocacy) culture during the last three decades of the twentieth century. As noted by the authors in Part Two of this volume, particularly the chapters dealing with issues of diversity, there was a focus on service to a very white population of faculty during these decades. Little attention was paid to either professional development for minority (underrepresented) faculty members or to the value inherent in programs that enhance appreciation of diverse perspectives by all faculty members. I suggested in another book (Bergquist, 1995) that education cannot be of highest quality and of greatest value to contemporary students if it does not provide diversity of perspectives. This diversity, in turn, can only be attained with increased access to higher education for potential students and potential faculty members who have faced many disadvantages and diverse experiences in seeking to advance their own careers, knowledge base, and life goals. I am pleased to see chapters in this book that address this interplay between quality and access—in particular I was delighted to read in Chapter Thirteen Stanley's contention that, when faculty developers embrace a multicultural call to action, "we not only enrich the pool of educational resources at our institutions, but the entire academy as well." Tuitt's identification of the Inclusive Excellence Scorecard (Chapter Fourteen) is reassuring, as is Ouellett's attention to power and authority in academic institutions (Chapter Twelve). One hopes that there are other Christine Stanleys, Frank Tuitts, and Mathew Ouelletts in the field of faculty development. With these men and women serving as proponents and guides, the advocacy culture will gain a stronger foothold in the field of faculty development during the coming decade.

There is another dimension of the negotiating (advocacy) culture that received much of my attention when preparing the *Four Cultures* book (1992). This dimension concerned the role played by collective bargaining in higher education—hence the title "negotiating." It is interesting to note that collective bargaining is not the primary focus of any chapter in the current volume though it is briefly addressed by Zakrajsek (Chapter Six). Even back in the 1970s there was considerable confusion about the role to be played by collective bargaining units in the promotion of faculty development. Is faculty development one of the benefits for which faculty unions negotiate, or is it one of those administrative impositions on academic freedom and autonomy that faculty unions are supposed to defend? Certainly, the spirit of collective bargaining and the broader concern for equitable treatment of all faculty members is represented in the chapter about underrepresented faculty members (Chapter Fourteen). This advocacy-related perspective is also evident in Chapter Twenty-One on adjunct faculty members. Yet, I wonder if the advocacy culture is still a second-class citizen in the field of faculty development. Has anything really changed? Has the fractal of homogeneity remained intact? Is there greater openness to the "productive conflict management" that Stanley advocates in Chapter Thirteen?

What about the fourth culture, the developmental? One would assume that this culture is prominent in the field of faculty development given the emphasis in this culture on the ongoing nurturing of both student learning and professional growth on the part of all members of academic institutions. There is ample evidence that this culture exists in many contributions made to this book, such as the emphasis placed by Theall and Franklin in Chapter Ten on formative evaluation (summative evaluation being more closely associated with the managerial culture) along with their attention to the work of notable developmental theorists, researchers, and advocates such as Kolb, Perry, Cross, and Boyer. Similarly, Wehlburg's promotion of transformative assessment in Chapter Eleven is developmental in orientation. When doing my own developmentally oriented work, I wish I had known of her saying: "You can't steer the boat by watching the wake." It offers a compelling metaphor for the forward-leaning strategies of contemporary developmentalists, especially those who take an appreciative perspective.

Despite these contributions, I suggest that the developmental culture still plays a secondary role in contemporary faculty development. I base this conclusion on an assessment of the strong managerial orientation of several chapters in this volume. Clearly, faculty development is accepted and institutionalized because demonstrable return on investment has been calculated, strong administrative support is being provided for those running these programs, and faculty development initiatives have been positioned at or near the center of the institution. The "development" in a holistic sense of students, faculty, and other members of the academic community is clearly hard to quantify—so it is hard to demonstrate return on investment when the "return" is so amorphous. The administrative support for a developmentally oriented program is often hard to "nail down" given that the developmental perspective often calls for peer-based assistance. Furthermore, a developmental strategy calls for the decentralization of services being offered—based on the assumption that "development" should occur everywhere in the institution (leading to the formation of a "developmentally oriented" institutional climate or even an institution-wide developmental culture). All of this produces the exceptional challenge inherent in positioning a developmentally oriented program at the center of the institution.

This does not mean that the developmental culture does not operate in twenty-first-century faculty development. Many of the chapters in this book provide a very sophisticated and compelling analysis of or linkage to developmental theories. Certainly, Wehlburg's proposition (Chapter Eleven) that faculty development must be closely aligned with accreditation processes and her labeling of developers as change agents provide evidence that the developmental culture has become more politically savvy. Furthermore, Austin's chapter "Supporting Faculty Members Across Their Careers" (Chapter Twenty-Two) represents a powerful coupling of research and programmatic design, while the chapters on diversity reveal something about the different developmental issues and styles found among people with diverse life experiences. In addition, it is impressive to see the ways in which faculty development has linked with the student engagement movement, which is clearly embedded deeply in the developmental culture.

Like Norma Desmond, I witness some of the same old issues in the field of faculty development when reading this book. Subsystem mirroring and fractals do indeed seem to exist in this field. Norma put it this way: "It's as if I never said good-bye." However, if a real Norma Desmond were to visit a film studio today she would witness many changes. Similarly, given the content of chapters in this book, I suspect that I would similarly see many changes if I were to visit a faculty development center—more technology, greater administrative support, more concern for assessment and greater emphasis on diversity. Both the continuity and changes in the field of faculty development are signs of vitality.

The Diffusion of Faculty Development as an Innovation

Since the 1960s, a model of innovation diffusion offered by Everett Rogers (1962, 2003), has guided the thinking and perspectives of many persons involved in change initiatives of all kinds (ranging from water purification systems to the distribution and use of contraceptive devices to the introduction of new digital technologies in a "flat world"). While popular, this model of innovation and related research, ironically, has not itself diffused very successfully—that is, until Malcolm Gladwell's *Tipping Point* (2000) was published. It offers a somewhat condensed and some would say distorted version of Rogers's diffusion model. I propose to do some diffusion of Rogers's model, I hope without distortion, by applying it in a preliminary way to the insights offered in this volume as well as the experiences I have had as someone who witnessed the birth of faculty development. In offering this analysis, I borrow from the alternative terminology Kuhlenschmidt uses in Chapter Sixteen.

The Innovators/Explorers

These are the persons who boldly go where no one has gone before (to borrow from the introduction to *Star Trek*). I suggest that there are several kinds of innovators/explorers who either preceded or entered at critical moments in the early history of faculty development. Some of these innovators were major thought leaders of their era—such as John Dewey, Kurt Lewin, Wilbur McKeachie, Nevitt Sanford, Arthur Chickering, Ernest Boyer, and Parker Palmer. Dewey provided the educational underpinnings while Lewin offered the change strategies. McKeachie contributed academic credibility and offered research on teaching, while Sanford contributed research on adult development and provided credibility as a renowned psychologist. Chickering was an innovator in his detailed analysis of student developmental needs, while Boyer bridged the gap between a critical analysis of the academic workplace and the role of leadership in this workplace. Palmer bridged the gaps among philosophy, religion, humanism, and education. While Dewey and Lewin influenced higher education from a distance, McKeachie, Sanford, Chickering, Boyer, and Palmer influenced it directly as active players in U.S. higher education during the last three decades of the twentieth century.

There is a second cluster of innovators. These are the practice leaders, those who innovated not primarily with new ideas but rather with new programs and new strategies for change. I begin this list with Dwight Allen, who first introduced microteaching into teacher education programs. Walter Sykes and Tony Grasha were among the first to use organizational development strategies in higher education, and Don Schön along with Chris Argyris and Peter Senge offered tools for reflective inquiry and metacognitive thinking-about-thinking, as mentioned in Chapter Twenty-Three in this volume on "Organizational Development." The interviewing techniques of Brown and Shukraft were innovative, as were the classroom assessment tools introduced by Cross and Angelo. Others could be added to this list; however, the point to be made is that faculty development has flourished in part because new practices were added that initially were used in other fields, such as teacher education (Allen) and organizational consultation (Sykes, Grasha, and Schön), or for other purposes, such as Brown and Shukraft's doctoral research.

Early Adopters/Pioneers

As Kuhlenschmidt's term suggests, the *pioneers* are those who are willing to "venture West" after the explorers map out the territory. They are willing to embrace or at least try out a new idea, often because in other areas they have themselves been innovators. As a result of their past experiences, these pioneers do not need much convincing. They will try out a new idea or procedure, find its faults, assist in its improvement, and tell the world that it has great potential.

In many instances, they are the "make or break it" folks. If they do not support or try out the new idea, then no one else is likely to get on board the covered wagon as it "heads West." There seem to be several different types of pioneers in faculty development. First there are the funders. They pay for the wagon (and often also for the wagon master/ facilitator). Two key private foundations immediately come to mind: the Lilly Endowment and the Kellogg Foundation. Laura Bornholdt, working at different times for both the Danforth Foundation and the Lilly Endowment, stands out as particularly supportive of and knowledgeable about faculty development practices. Ouellett also mentions the Bush and Ford Foundations in Chapter One. In the public arena, I can point to FIPSE (Fund for the Improvement of Postsecondary Education) and the Title III program for "developing institutions." FIPSE funding was well leveraged even though it was much smaller than the Title III funding base. A FIPSE grant of $100,000 could make a big difference in getting an innovative program started.

The important point to be made is that most of these funding institutions were not interested in support for faculty development per se. They would fund faculty development activities only if these activities led to improved student learning, increased access to education, the preparation of citizen leaders, and so forth. Each funding agency had its own set of distinct priorities, and the clever faculty developer learned how to frame a funding proposal so that faculty development was in the background and the funder's priorities were in the foreground. Thus we see the tension once again playing out between faculty development as an end goal and faculty development as a means to some other goal.

While funding sources were very important during the early stages of contemporary faculty development, there was a second cluster of persons who were invaluable in moving this innovation to early adoption. These were the sponsors of faculty development. In a book I wrote with Jack Armstrong (Bergquist & Armstrong, 1986), we identified the key role played by the college president as a champion for rather than initiator of a new program. Similarly, Art Chickering and Jack Lindquist found in their extensive study of successful innovations in American colleges and universities (Lindquist, 1978) that each innovation needs a strong and skillful champion operating at the top of the organization. I have already identified two of these champions for faculty development: Dyke Vermillye (President of AAHE) and Gary Quehl (President of the Council of Independent Colleges); and I am sure that many other names could be added to this list, though their sponsorship was often not widely known and their invaluable contributions, unfortunately, have often faded from our collective memory. The present volume contains ample references to the many national and international associations that provided support for faculty development initiatives but not much recognition of the specific people working inside these associations who made it all happen.

Closely related to this second cluster are those who actively promoted faculty development. These promoters had neither the money (funders) nor the formal institution position of authority (sponsors) to bring about early adoption of faculty development. However, they were like Johnny Appleseed, moving across the land planting seeds. Harold (Bud) Hodgkinson was one of these early promoters of faculty development. Hodgkinson's colleague, Patricia Cross, was also an early promoter. While Hodgkinson brought the seeds with him, usually in the form of well-used overhead transparencies, Cross located the seeds of innovation that existed in each institution she visited and then brought these seeds to other institutions. She was a cross-pollinator, encouraging leaders to plant these seeds in the soil of own campus. In the community college sector of U.S. higher education. I point to the exceptional early promotional work done by Carol Zion and Lance Buhl. In universities, I point to my colleague, David Halliburton.

A third cluster of persons who help move innovations to early adoption are those who bring order to the innovation and identify how best to administer these innovations. These are the early managers who take over from the often disorganized innovators. Seymour Sarason identified the critical role played by these managers when describing the creation of new settings. In the case of faculty development, I point directly to Joan North, the first executive director of POD. Over the years, Peter Fredrick has been a source of many ideas about the effective management of faculty development programs, especially those operating in liberal arts colleges, as is mentioned in Reder's chapter in this volume (Chapter Eighteen). Many chapters in this book provide guidance in this regard including those authored by Mooney (Chapter Four), Cohen (Chapter Five), Neal and Peed-Neal (Chapter Seven), Ellis and Ortquist-Ahrens (Chapter Eight), Cook and Marincovich (Chapter Seventeen), Reder (Chapter Eighteen), and Burnstad and Hoss (Chapter Nineteen).

Early Majority/Settlers

Members of the early majority, termed the *settlers*, are much more selective than the early adopters. They want some proof before making a commitment, and they will ask questions. "How do I know that this product will work? Can you assure me that this service will be effective and of value to me? Do we have any evidence that this product or service is worth the money we will have to spend in order to bring it to market?" In populating the American West, the settlers wait until they know that there is something to settle into. They wait for reports from the pioneers and check to see if these reports are accurate. They look to the Lewis and Clarks to provide credible accounts of the "true" West.

What are the ingredients that make an innovation "respectable"? How did faculty development become respectable, or is it still at the fringe of the academy? Many authors in this book identify key ingredients that have made faculty development respectable and acceptable on college and university campuses. Four ingredients stand out: (1) building a base of research evidence and interdisciplinary scholarship, (2) constructing solid administrative support, (3) building upon newly emerging institutional norms and values, and (4) establishing a profession to guide the further development of the field. I briefly comment on each of these ingredients.

First, as Rogers (2003) has noted, there has to be compelling evidence of both a qualitative and quantitative nature that is based on reputable research. In Plank and Kalish's chapter (Chapter Nine), we find description of several substantial projects conducted by researchers from major universities, several of whom—for example, Chism, Gosling, and Sorcinelli (Chapter Fifteen) and Austin (Chapter Twenty-Two)—have contributed chapters to this book. This research must be complemented by solid scholarship that is based in several disciplines. In turn, this scholarship must be both theoretically sound and practical. I have already mentioned several of these scholarly contributions to the field of faculty development—for example, adult development (Sanford) and student development (Chickering, Perry). I add the scholarship of critical thinking (Brookfield, Mezirow) and organizational climate and culture (Birnbaum) to this list. In her chapter (Chapter Twenty-Two), Austin provides excellent examples of ways in which research and scholarship can be combined to provide guidance in planning for and evaluating the effectiveness of faculty development programs.

Second, an innovation is much more likely to be embraced by the early majority and is more likely to be sustained if it is well managed. Mooney offers in Chapter Four valuable advice on establishing an appropriate administrative structure for a faculty development program. Robertson (Chapter Three) writes about the importance of budget and financial stability if faculty development is to become an established program in a collegiate institution. There is another element that is just as important: the program should be carefully and systematically crafted so that services are being provided in response to a diverse set of faculty concerns and needs. For example, as discussed in the chapters on graduate students, adjunct faculty, and faculty careers (Twenty, Twenty-One, and Twenty-Two), program offerings should be geared to faculty at all stages of their careers and to both full-time and part-time faculty. These program offerings should be linked to the evaluation and compensation systems of the institution as noted in the assessment chapters and to the distinct institutional characteristics of the college or university in which it is being established and managed as noted in the chapters on institutional type.

Third, the acceptance of a new product or service is often predicated in part on the interplay of this innovation with newly emerging norms and values in the organization. New digital technologies, for instance, are more likely to be embraced because of a broader acceptance of globalization—Thomas Friedman's "flat world" (2008). One needs Skype, Adobe Connect, or some other inexpensive, Internet-based communication tool when talking to friends and colleagues from elsewhere in the world, or one must invest in SurveyMonkey or Zoomerang when collecting opinions from around the world. At the very least, one should learn a second or third language if the entire world has become a community of reference. The chapter on international faculty development

(Chism et al., Chapter Fifteen) certainly illustrates this shift toward a globalized mindset among twenty-first-century faculty members and the emergence of what Pawlak and I have identified as the "virtual" subculture in twenty-first-century higher education (Bergquist & Pawlak, 2008). As Chism, Gosling, and Sorcinelli note in Chapter Fifteen, faculty development must keep pace with, and I suggest can gain energy from, the internationalization and emerging globalization of colleges and universities. Similarly, Cook and Marinocovich (Chapter Seventeen) suggest that the increasing interest in instructional technology among faculty of all persuasions can be used to bring faculty members into faculty development programs.

Another major shift in norms and values is evident in this volume. Specifically, we find throughout this book a new alliance between faculty development and the newly emerging acceptance of peer-based classroom observation and classroom-based research. When I was first starting in the field, there was major resistance to any observation of a classroom; such an activity would violate the norm of faculty autonomy. Given the suggestions offered by Mooney in Chapter Four regarding peer observation of classroom teaching, it would seem that the norms regarding faculty autonomy are changing or are at least being challenged, though Zakrajsek notes in Chapter Six that classroom observation still makes faculty members nervous. Aside from this very understandable sense of discomfort with having one's professional work observed, it would seem that this shift in norms cannot help but increase early majority support for faculty development initiatives. Certainly, classroom assessment techniques such as Small Group Instructional Diagnosis and the classroom assessment techniques originally provided by Angelo and Cross (1993) have become valuable complements to faculty development programming.

Fourth, the early majority often looks to the establishment of a profession if they are specifically considering the acceptance of a new type of human service initiative. Many years ago, Bledstein (1976) proposed that U.S. society, and U.S. higher education in particular, is deeply enmeshed in a culture of professionalism. By extension, other Western societies are also moving toward a culture in which professional credentials are replacing social-economic class structures as the defining criterion for social stratification. This social dynamic is particularly poignant with regard to a newly emerging field like faculty development, given the mission of many collegiate institutions to educate and certify men and women in particular professions such as medicine, law, dentistry, and the ministry. The role played by POD in providing a base for faculty development to become a profession is noteworthy. POD provides not only conferences and workshops, but also publications, a Web site offering many resources, and formulation of ethical standards. More informally, POD offers a social network for the building of enduring interpersonal relationships among professionals, which is an important factor that I revisit at the end of this Afterword.

Late Majority/Burghers

Kuhlenschmidt does not offer a term for this diffusion category, perhaps because we do not have a readily accessible name for the people who move into a town or city after it is formally established. In Europe the term *burgher* was used to identify a person who resided in a formally chartered town. I use this European term because I think it conveys the essence of Rogers's late majority. These people only embrace an innovative idea after it has been fully certified and accepted as a legitimate idea or operation. In the western United States, these are the folks who only move in when the town is "well established" and has the requisite schools, paved roads, general store, and church. Gladwell (2000) used the term *tipping point* to describe the broad-based acceptance of an idea that has been legitimized. The term *bandwagon* is also appropriate in that the acceptance of a product or service by the late majority often means a substantial increase in the number of people using the product or service.

While the "bandwagon" phenomenon can initially be very gratifying to someone who has been laboring for many years to get a new product or service accepted, it can also create major problems because the innovation is typically not fully understood by the late majority and is often misused. This can lead to "casualties." For instance, jogging may become an "in thing"; however, late majority joggers are likely to injure themselves because they do not properly prepare for this new form of exercise. The bandwagon can also lead to failure and anger. "Why doesn't this darn thing work?" Alternatively, uncritical late majority acceptance of a new product or service can lead to neglect or inefficiency. The newly purchased desktop computer, for instance, may either sit on the desk unused or be used only as a glorified typewriter or expensive play station.

In the case of faculty development, we find burghers entering the scene when there is a stable source of funding. This is often a chicken-and-egg phenomenon. There is greater funding because more faculty members are involved, and more faculty members (the late majority) are involved because there is greater funding. Given the financial instability found in many of our contemporary academic institutions, we may find a decline in faculty development funding and a subsequent decline in the number of participating faculty members. The "burgher" faculty may choose to return to safer financial ground (the chartered town). Despite these potential financial challenges (faculty development in a time of retrenchment), this book is written at a time when the late majority might become a focus of attention for those working in the field, with all of the opportunities and challenges associated with engaging this constituency.

Several chapters directly address strategies related to the late majority. Neal and Peed-Neal (Chapter Seven) and Kuhlenschmidt (Chapter Sixteen) identify a set of marketing principles that hold the potential of drawing in members of this group. Neal and Peed-Neal suggest the use of surveys, focus groups, and advisory committees. In each of these instances, it is not so important that one make use of the data gathered from these initiatives; rather these research tools are engaged as marketing tools. Participants in the survey, focus group, or advisory committee get the sense that they are not alone; they realize that other people are involved, too. Furthermore, since they are being asked for their opinions, this activity must be legitimate and mainstream: if it were not legitimate, then they would not be among those being asked. Psychologists have advised us for many years that cognitive dissonance is created if people participate in something that they do not value. Once they agree to participate, these persons must support, at least minimally, the activity in order to restore cognitive equilibrium. Neal and Peed-Neal also note that an effective faculty development program should target several populations, with different communication strategies for each of them. One of these populations can be the late majority, and cognitive dissonance–based marketing can be an effective leverage point for this constituency. Kuhlenschmidt suggests the use of several technologies to bring more faculty members (including the late majority) to faculty development events. She recommends faculty development Web sites that can link faculty members to book reviews, institutional policies, and timely information about events and resources, all of which are attractive to many in the late majority.

At a more fundamental level, faculty development will become an accepted practice if it is associated with other traditions, values, and activities that are already widely accepted and respected by the late majority. A critical role was played at an early stage in the life of faculty development by those who linked this innovation to established products and services. The field should now take advantage of these early initiatives. I have already mentioned Jack Lindquist and Bob Diamond, who linked organization development and instructional development with faculty development. I include Jerry Gaff on this list. He did an exceptional job of joining faculty development with curriculum development. Those who conduct the "Great Teachers" series, which is mentioned in Chapter Nineteen on community colleges, should also be commended. Over the long run, there is probably no one who has been as effective as Gene Rice in broadening the faculty development frame and opening the way for late majority acceptance of this field—appealing to the sixth subculture that Pawlak and I (Bergquist & Pawlak, 2008) have identified (the tangible culture). Rice's impact is evident in the descriptions of and references to his work offered throughout this book. Through his AAHE programs and his presentations and writing about faculty roles and rewards, Gene drew faculty development concerns directly into the core of institutional planning and administrative structures. He talked and wrote about faculty roles and responsibilities, showing how faculty development relates to deeply embedded faculty traditions and values. Along with our colleague, David Halliburton, Gene Rice highlighted the broad-based interest in interdisciplinary dialogue, especially among senior faculty, and suggested ways in which this dialogue can lead to and be incorporated into faculty development programs. Related recommendations are offered in Chapter Seventeen by Cook and Marincovich.

Laggards/Stay-Back-Easters

What about those folks who remain back home? They will not move West under any conditions. They cannot be convinced, bribed, or cajoled into doing so. Often they are actively engaged in efforts to discourage the widespread adoption of an innovation. They might be silent at first; however, once the innovation begins to pick up steam and threatens to be accepted by the early majority, they may become quite vocal.

Often the objections of the laggards and the frequent misunderstanding of them can be attributed to their differing perspective regarding the innovation. Using the model of subcultures in the academy, we could say that the laggards often come from subcultures other than our own within higher education. They view faculty development as representative of a subculture that is alien to the one they prefer. Birnbaum's (1988) views regarding managerial "fads" are illustrative. He might be considered a laggard by those who are promoting managerial "improvements" and "reforms." Similarly, the faculty members and administrators mentioned by Wehlburg in Chapter Eleven who label outcome assessment practices as "scams run by bloodless bureaucrats" might similarly be labeled as laggards with a strong collegial culture bias. I mentioned earlier that some of those faculty members who are aligned with the advocacy culture are inclined to see faculty development as a managerial critique of faculty performance, while those aligned with the collegial culture are inclined to see faculty development as either unnecessary or an intrusion on academic freedom. We can best address these sources of opposition by taking an appreciative approach, recognizing that these alternative perspectives are valuable and that a twenty-first-century academic institution needs all of these perspectives if it is to remain viable. The generative and dialogic tools of Appreciative Inquiry are appropriate, as are the tools of polarity management.

There is yet another source of laggard opposition to a new product or service. Their objections, in many instances, do not arise from the flaws and threats associated with the innovation. After all, we all appear to be laggards with regard to certain new ideas that we consider ill advised or oversold. For many true laggards, the issue is much more personal: these are men and women who were innovators themselves many years ago and were unsuccessful or burned out with regard to this innovation. They chaired a major curriculum reform committee but never saw this reform enacted. They championed the use of a major new educational technology, only to see their colleagues casually dismiss this technology as a gimmick. They devoted many hours to design of a new general education program that was thrown out only four years after being installed in their institution. If a faculty development initiative is successful, then what does this say about the laggard's own past failures as an educational innovator? If nothing else, an important lesson can be learned from the passionate objections voiced by laggards: when we isolate or dismiss an innovator, then we not only lose this person's ideas and potential leadership, but we also create a laggard who can be a persistent enemy of innovation for many years to come.

So what should we do about those laggards who oppose an innovation for these very personal (and usually undisclosed) reasons? We can try to isolate them, but this is rarely effective. Alternatively, we can bring in laggards as historians and advisors, and we can ask them questions. "What can we learn from you about what happened many years ago? What can you teach us? If you were to plan for the successful enactment of this new faculty development program what would you do?" Yes, this is a co-option strategy. Laggards will see right through it if this request is not legitimate and if one does not seriously consider the advice they offer and listen patiently to the stories they tell. As I suggested earlier, there are certain repeated patterns (fractals) that are found in most collegiate institutions. We can identify these patterns with the assistance of our colleagues who happen to be laggards and can effectively leverage these patterns to our advantage and to the advantage of the academy.

Concluding Comments

There are two final questions to be addressed in this Afterword: Why
did I devote so much time to faculty development for three decades; and,
more important, why are my colleagues who have prepared chapters for
this volume doing the hard work of faculty development? I cannot speak
for these authors, but I can reveal something about my own motives. At
the core, these motives all center on something that we in the twenty-first
century call "social networks." Researchers in the new field of social
neurobiology tell us that oxytocin, which is the bonding chemical in
our brain, has produced in *homo sapiens* the most social of animals. We
apparently need other members of our species around us more than other
animals do. I would suggest that faculty development practitioners are
particularly addicted to oxytocin and are primed for social networking.
Several authors in this book would apparently agree when they build
on the observation that faculty development is moving into the "Age
of Network" (Sorcinelli et al., 2006). Maybe this is the real reason why
faculty development is still with us.

I close by offering one example of social networking in action as
a motivating force for faculty developers. I was conducting a weeklong
training program for forty-eight newly minted faculty development
practitioners many years ago under the auspices of the Council of
Independent Colleges. Using funds from one of the benefactors I identified
previously, I recruited five faculty development and academic change-
agent "experts" for this workshop. I have already identified all five of
these experts in this Afterword, but will protect their identity, given what
happened at this workshop. About halfway through this workshop we
focused on change theory, using a survey. All of the workshop participants completed the survey and shared their assumptions about change.
Then one of the participants asked the five experts what their survey
scores were. After some hesitation but with much prodding from the
participants, the five experts revealed their own scores.

In each case, their highest scores indicated that these experts did not
believe that successful change happens very often. It is quite understandable that a minor revolt among the participants ensued. "Why are we
participating in this program if successful change rarely occurs?!" The
five experts offered some of the most candid and insightful comments
I have ever heard in a workshop of this kind. First, they all revealed
that they do this work because the alternative—not trying to bring about
improvement in the academy—was unacceptable to them. All five were
realistic about the chances of sustained change, but they refused to
give up trying to bring about change. They were dedicated to a difficult

cause. Then another level of disclosure took place. They all agreed that they did the work because of friendships established among practitioners in the field. The other four experts in the room were deeply respected colleagues. Each of the five felt it was a privilege and honor to be with their friends. I was one of these five "experts." I find today, in 2009, that I am once again honored to be associated with the authors of this exceptional book about faculty development. Like Norma Desmond in the musical, I feel like I have never said "good-bye."

REFERENCES

Angelo, T. A., & Cross, K. P. (1993). *Classroom assessment techniques: A handbook for college teachers.* San Francisco: Jossey-Bass.

Astin, A., et al. (1974). *Faculty development in a time of retrenchment.* New Rochelle, NY: Change.

Bergquist, W. (1992). *The four cultures of the academy.* San Francisco: Jossey-Bass.

Bergquist, W. (1995). *Quality through access, access with quality.* San Francisco: Jossey-Bass.

Bergquist, W., & Armstrong, J. (1986). *Planning effectively for educational quality.* San Francisco: Jossey-Bass.

Bergquist, W., & Pawlak, K. (2008). *Engaging the six cultures of the academy.* San Francisco: Jossey-Bass.

Birnbaum, R. (1988). *How colleges work: The cybernetics of academic organization and leadership.* San Francisco: Jossey-Bass.

Bledstein, B. (1976). *The culture of professionalism: The middle class and development of higher education in America.* New York: Norton.

Brown, W., & Shukraft, R. C. (1971). Personal development and professional practice in college and university professors. Unpublished doctoral dissertation, Graduate Theological Union, Berkeley, CA.

Friedman, M. (Ed.). (1973). *Facilitating faculty development.* San Francisco: Jossey-Bass.

Friedman, T. (2008). *Hot, flat, and crowded.* New York: Farrar, Straus & Giroux.

Gladwell, M. (2000). *The tipping point.* Boston: Little, Brown.

Lindquist, J. (1978). *Strategies for change.* Washington, DC: Council of Independent Colleges.

Rogers, E. (1962). *Diffusion of innovations* (1st ed.). New York: Free Press.

Rogers, E. (2003). *Diffusion of innovation* (5th ed.). New York: Free Press.

Sanford, N. (1980). *Learning after college.* Berkeley, CA: Montaigne Press.

Sorcinelli, M. D., Austin, A. E., Eddy, P. L., & Beach, A. L. (2006). *Creating the future of faculty development: Learning from the past, understanding the present.* Bolton, MA: Anker.

EPILOGUE

We—the editors and authors of this volume—hope that the reader has found here a sense of history of the field, good information, practical ideas, and encouraging inspiration for the work of educational development, whatever the nature of one's involvement may be. We welcome inquiries or comments, and they may be sent to authors or editors at the e-mail addresses provided in the "About the Authors" section.

For the convenience of the reader and further scholarly pursuits, the complete list of references from this volume can be found under the "Publications" link of the Professional and Organizational Development (POD) Network Web site (http://podnetwork.org/publications.htm).

NAME INDEX

A

Aanerud, R., 367
Abbott, R. D., 328
Adams, K., 235, 236
Adams, M., 187, 189, 191, 203,
   204, 211, 217
Agago, M. O., 233
Aguirre Jr., A., 234
Albright, M. J., 13, 283
Aldrich, C., 265
Alger, R. J., 237, 239
Algert, N. E., 207, 209, 392
Allen, M. J., 177
Allen, W., 185
Allison, D. H., 62
Ambrose, S. A., 281
Amundsen, C., 10
Anaya, R. A., 218
Anderse, M., 188
Anderson, J. A., 185, 188, 203,
   204, 208
Anderson, L. W., 125
Anderson, V. J., 139, 175
Angelo, T. A., 159, 162, 172, 248,
   267, 333
Angelou, M., 218
Antonio, A. L., 186, 225
Ards, S. B., 237
Arneil, S., 265, 266, 267
Arreola, R. A., 159
Asante, M., 208
Astin, A. W., 6, 186, 191
Astin, H., 234

B

Austin, A. E., 4, 10, 11, 14, 23, 37,
   54, 68, 69, 100, 117, 136, 185,
   245, 259, 279, 286, 306, 310, 363,
   364, 366, 367, 368, 369, 370, 371,
   372, 373, 379

B

Bach, D. J., 186, 191
Baldwin, J., 218
Baldwin, R. G., 286, 317, 371,
   372, 373, 374
Bandura, A., 157
Banks, J. A., 186, 208, 217, 219
Banta, T. W., 88, 138, 139,
   176, 177
Baran, J., 10
Barnes, L. B., 233
Barnett, M. A., 186
Barnett, R., 248
Baron, L., 13, 382
Barr, R. B., 6, 248
Bartee, R. D., 187
Bauman, G. L., 187
Bayor, R., 206
Beach, A. L., 4, 14, 23, 37, 54, 69,
   117, 136, 185, 187, 191, 245,
   259, 279, 306, 310, 370, 379
Becher, T., 281
Bekey, J., 160
Bell, L. A., 189, 191, 193, 194, 204,
   206, 217
Bellows, L., 333, 339
Bender, J., 234

Bennett, C., 359

Beno, B., 310, 323

Bensimon, E. M., 187, 368, 369, 370

Berger, J. B., 187, 226

Bergquist, W. H., 4, 5, 21, 22, 383, 394

Berk, R. A., 159

Biggs, J., 248

Birch, J., 122

Black, K. E., 138

Blackburn, R. T., 236, 278, 283

Blackwell, J. E., 235, 236, 237

Blumenfeld, M. J., 204

Boice, R., 121, 186, 334, 367, 368, 370

Bok, D., 278

Boone, L. E., 102

Border, L. B., 11, 327, 328, 330, 336

Borgford-Parnell, J., 13

Borland Jr., K., 13, 187

Borton, T., 211

Bothell, T. W., 142

Boyer, E. L., 84, 162, 248, 333, 384

Bransford, J. D., 84

Brawer, F., 309, 311

Bridges, W., 70

Brinko, K. T., 155, 158, 159

Brooke, C., 140

Brookfield, S., 10

Brown, D., 62

Brown III, M. C., 187

Burdick, D., 22

Burgsthaler, S. E., 186, 188

Burnstad, H., 14, 309, 316, 317

Bustillos, L. T., 187

C

Cambridge, B., 267, 288

Carroll, S., 267

Casey, M. A., 104

Castañeda, R., 204

Cerny, J., 367

Chait, R. P., 225

Chambers, R., 119

Chang, D. A., 286, 317

Chang, M. J., 186, 192, 225

Chattergy, V., 210

Chesler, M. A., 186, 187, 191

Chickering, A., 12, 263

Chism, N.V.N., 8, 9, 13, 60, 138, 139, 142, 146, 159, 161, 187, 206, 243, 249, 279, 284, 328

Cialdini, R., 108, 109

Clark, D. J., 160

Clark, K. E., 5

Clayton-Pederson, A., 185

Clemmons, R., 260

Cohen, A., 309, 311

Cohen, M. W., 67, 69

Cohen, P. A., 156

Colbeck, C. L., 68, 121

Coleman, T., 207

Collins, C., 188

Collins, J., 267

Collins, P. H., 188

Colosimo, J., 175

Combs, T. T., 354

Comstock, C., 6

Cones, H. H. III, 186

Cook, C., 11, 190, 206, 210, 277, 282, 285, 286, 288

Coombs, W. T., 233

Cooper, J. E., 210

Cora-Bramble, D., 233

Cory, R. C., 186, 188

Couturier, L., 243

Cox, M. D., 121, 189

Creamer, E. G., 233

Cross, K. P., 159, 162, 172, 248, 267, 333

Crowfoot, J., 186

D

D'Andrea, V-M., 247
D'Avanzo, C., 304
Davidson, C. I., 281
Dawkins, P. W., 14, 187
de Janasz, S. C., 191
Deblois, P. B., 62
Denecke, D. D., 11, 331
Denson, N., 192
Dey, E. L., 185
DeZure, D., 371
Diamond, R. M., 8, 11, 13, 185, 186, 187, 384
Dillow, S. A., 226
Dore, T. M., 11, 341, 367

E

Eagan, K., 358
Easton, L. B., 120
Eble, K. E., 6, 279, 282
Eddy, P. L., 4, 13, 14, 23, 37, 54, 69, 117, 136, 185, 245, 259, 279, 306, 310, 370, 379
Ehrmann, S., 13, 263
Ellis, D. E., 117
Entwhistle, N., 248
Epperson, D., 6
Erickson, G., 6
Evenbeck, S., 187
Evers, F., 123

F

Famiano, M., 191
Feagin, J. R., 208
Feldman, K. A., 154, 156
Felten, P., 8
Fendrich, L., 175
Ferren, A. S., 209
Fink, D., 41
Fink, L. D., 125
Finkelstein, F., 333

Fleming, J. A., 119
Foote, K. E., 368
Fordham, T., 304
Fox, H., 193, 194
Francis, J. B., 7
Frank, K., 13
Frankel, L., 188, 219
Franklin, J. L., 88, 151, 155, 158
Fraser, E., 190
Frederick, P., 187, 302, 305
Freed, J. E., 177
Frey, S. C., 186
Fuentes, J. D., 186

G

Gadberry, J., 322
Gaff, D. L., 13
Gaff, J. G., 4, 5, 11, 331
Gainene, J., 186
Gallagher, E. V., 293, 295, 296, 300, 302, 304
Gappa, J. M., 349, 351, 358, 359, 364, 367, 368, 369, 370, 371, 372, 373, 374, 375
Garcia, M., 185
Garran, A. M., 191
Garza, H., 235, 237
Gaudelli, W., 120
Geller, W. W., 209
Gibbs, G., 248
Gibbs, J. E., 12
Gibson, G. W., 295
Gillespie, K., 185, 379, 381, 394
Ginsberg, M. B., 203, 204, 219
Golde, C. M., 11, 341, 366, 367
Goldschmid, M. L., 328
Gonzales, D., 10
Gosling, D., 8, 9, 245, 247, 249
Graff, G., 185, 188
Grasha, A. F., 154

Gray, T., 122
Greeley, A., 6
Green, M. F., 219
Greenberg, J. D., 206
Gregory, S., 235, 237
Griffin, P., 189, 191, 204, 206, 217
Gurin, P., 185, 186, 192

H

Hackman, H. W., 204
Hagedorn, L. S., 235, 236, 237
Hammons, J., 311
Harber, F., 359
Hardiman, R., 188, 192
Harper, K. A., 139
Hart, J., 204
Hatch, T., 84
Hativa, N., 281
Hawthorne, J., 180
Hayes, B., 320
Healy, M. M., 55
Heiss, A. M., 5
Henderson, C., 191
Henderson, T., 142
Hendrix, K. G., 188, 187
Herbert, F., 10
Hernandez, A., 234
Higgins, D., 109
Hill, E. K., 234
Hoffman, C. M., 226
Hohenleitner, K., 77
Holmes, M., 265, 266
Holmes, T., 271
Holmgren, R. A., 25, 55, 121, 298, 304
Holvino, E., 204, 206, 219
hooks, b., 188
Hoss, C., 14, 309, 310, 316, 317
Huba, M., 177
Huber, M. T., 120, 248

Hurtado, S., 185, 186, 192, 364
Hutchings, P., 120, 121, 163, 248, 385
Hyman, M. R., 390

J

Jackson, B., 13, 186, 187, 188, 192, 204, 206, 207, 219
Jacobson, W., 13
James, M., 187
Janha, D., 186
Jaschik, S., 355
Jensen, J. D., 69
Johnson, A. G., 188
Jung, Y., 371

K

Kahn, S., 267
Kalish, A., 8, 88, 135, 139
Kallen, H., 206
Kallick, B., 175
Kanter, R. M., 237
Kaplan, M. L., 282, 286
Kardia, D., 194, 207, 208
Karen, D., 185
Karls, E. A., 317, 319
Kashner, J. B., 102
Katz, J., 6
Kaufman, R., 6
King, K. P., 10
Kingston, M. H., 218
Kipp, D., 162
Kitano, M. K., 191, 219, 220
Knapp, S. D., 232
Knapper, C. K., 336
Knight, P., 248
Kolb, D., 10, 153
Korn, W. S., 364
Krathwohl, D. R., 125
Krueger, R. A., 104
Krutky, J. B., 203

Kuerbis, P. J., 25, 55, 298
Kuh, G. D., 76, 154, 157
Kuhlenschmidt, S., 13, 259, 262, 265, 266, 268, 277
Kumashiro, K., 188
Kurtz, D. L., 102

L

Laden, B. V., 235, 236, 237
Lambert, L. M., 330
Latta, G. F., 117
Lawler, P. A., 10
Lawrence, J. H., 236, 278, 283
Lee, V. S., 21, 83, 390
Lees, N. D., 187
Lehr, V., 304
Leslie, D. W., 349, 351, 358, 359
Lewis, A., 186
Lewis, E., 188, 219
Lewis, K. G., 4, 5, 7, 11, 91, 155, 159, 185, 328
Li, C., 10
Lieberman, D., 13
Lindholm, J. A., 364, 365
Lindquist, J., 13
Lindsey, R. B., 187
Lockhart, M., 13, 187
Lohi-Pasey, B., 359
Lorde, A., 188
Love, B. J., 187, 193
Love, J., 304
Lovitts, B. E., 11
Loy, M., 10
Lucas, A. F., 387
Lucke, J., 354
Luginbuhl, G., 390
Luksaneeyanawin, S., 250
Lunde, J. P., 55, 117, 138, 155, 159
Lyons, R., 352, 353, 355, 356, 359

M

MacDermid, S. M., 369
Major, C. H., 12
Marchesani, L. M., 13, 191
Marchesani, L. S., 186, 203, 204, 206, 211
Marincovich, M., 277, 281, 286, 330
Marsh, H. W., 156
Martensson, K., 247
Martin, J. N., 207
Martinez, R. O., 234
Marton, F., 248
Marx, J., 298
Massy, W. F., 76, 121
Mazur, E., 333
McCalman, C. L., 193
McClendon, S. A., 187, 226
McCormick, A., 73
McDaniels, M., 366, 367
McDonald, J., 68, 249
McDonough, P. M., 312
McGowan, J., 234, 235, 239
McKeachie, W. J., 6, 10, 154, 248, 282
McKinney, J. S., 288
McLean, C. A., 193
Melnik, M. A., 6
Menges, R. J., 10, 155, 158, 159, 284, 367, 368, 370
Meyers, S. A., 234, 235
Milem, J. F., 185, 186, 187, 225, 226, 232, 235
Milgram, S., 109
Miller, A. T., 282
Miller, J., 191
Milloy, P. M., 140
Mintz, J., 332
Moody, J., 187, 369
Mooney, K. M., 25, 53, 54, 55, 65, 293, 294, 295, 298, 302, 304, 306

Moretto, K., 371
Morey, A., 191
Morphew, C., 312
Morrison-Shetlar, A. I., 77
Moses, Y. T., 185
Muhtaseb, A., 193
Mullinix, B. B., 42, 43
Murray, H. G., 156
Murray, J. P., 352
Musil, C. M., 185
Myers, S. L., 225, 232, 234, 235, 236, 237, 239

N
Nakayama, T. K., 207
Naylor, S., 84
Neal, E., 99
Nerad, M., 367
Newman, F., 243
Nidiffer, J., 286
Nielsen, J., 269
Nieto, S., 208
Noonan, J. F., 186
Nowlis, V., 5
Nuhfer, E., 162
Nyquist, J. D., 11, 328, 329, 367

O
O'Bear, K., 217
Oblander, F. W., 138
Ogilvy, D., 109
Ognibene, E. R., 219
Olsen, D., 367, 369
O'Meara, K. A., 68
O'Neal, C., 288
Ortquist-Ahrens, L., 117, 129
Ouellett, M. L., 3, 185, 186, 189, 190, 203, 204, 208, 219

P
Palmer, P., 393
Palomba, C. A., 177

Pascarella, E. T., 154, 157
Paul, S. P., 206
Pawlak, K., 383
Peck, M., 13
Peed-Neal, I., 99
Perorazio, T., 288
Perry, R. P., 156, 157
Peters, D., 304
Petrone, M. C., 190
Phillips, S., 22
Piccinin, S., 123
Pingree, A., 8
Plank, K., 8, 88, 135, 139
Pollock, S., 333
Pratt, D., 267
Prosser, M., 248
Prostko, J., 286, 330
Pruitt-Logan, A. S., 11, 331
Purkiss, J., 288

R
Ramsden, P., 248
Rando, W., 10
Reddick, L., 13
Reddy, M., 187, 188
Reder, M., 25, 54, 55, 58, 64, 65, 293, 294, 295, 296, 297, 298, 299, 300, 302, 303, 304, 305, 306, 307
Rice, R. E., 4, 5, 6, 10, 12, 367, 369, 370
Richlin, L., 121
Roberts, H., 186
Robertson, D. L., 35, 45, 78
Robins, K. N., 187
Rock, M., 5
Rocklin, T., 260
Rogers, E., 260, 261, 262
Rohdieck, S. V., 139
Rook, D. W., 89
Rouseff-Baker, F., 314
Rowland, S., 248

Roxa, T., 247
Rozman, S., 14, 187

S

Saddler, T. N., 233
Sagaria, M.A.D., 225
St. John, E. P., 288
Saljo, R., 248
Saroyan, A., 10
Saunders, S., 204
Schilling, K., 177
Schmitz, B., 206
Schneider, C. G., 193
Schodt, D., 304
Schoem, D., 188, 219
Schön, D. A., 10
Schuetz, P., 358
Schuster, J. H., 286
Scully, J., 243
Seldin, P., 161, 283, 286, 336
Senge, P. M., 38, 76, 391
Seubka, P., 250
Seymour, E., 267
Shakespeare, W., 218
Shamdasani, P. N., 89
Shavelson, R., 182
Shaw, A., 371
Sheehan, D. S., 6
Shih, M. Y., 12, 372
Showalter, E., 281
Shulman, L. S., 54, 69, 120, 154, 155,
    163, 171, 248, 288, 293, 296, 385
Sidle, C. C., 43
Silko, L. M., 218
Silliman, J. C., 359
Simpson, R. D., 4, 5
Sims, L. B., 11, 331
Smart, J. C., 156
Smikle, J. L., 206, 207, 209
Smith, C., 310, 323, 324
Smith, D. G., 185
Smith, K. S., 12

Smith, M., 352, 356, 357
Smith, R., 194
Smith-Wallace, T. H., 311
Snyder, T. D., 226, 228
Solem, M. N., 368
Sopchich, J., 312
Soracco, S., 332
Sorcinelli, M. D., 4, 6, 7, 8, 9, 10, 14,
    23, 24, 25, 37, 38, 54, 55, 56, 63,
    65, 69, 117, 136, 141, 146, 185,
    189, 190, 191, 206, 210, 211, 234,
    239, 243, 245, 246, 259, 264, 279,
    280, 281, 282, 283, 285, 287, 289,
    303, 306, 310, 366, 367, 368, 369,
    370, 371, 372, 373, 379, 386
Sprague, J., 11, 328, 367
Springer, A., 236, 239
Stanley, C. A., 186, 187, 190, 192,
    203, 204, 207, 209, 232, 234, 235,
    236, 392
Steadman, M. H., 162
Steward, D., 232
Stewart, D. W., 89
Stockley, D., 68, 249
Stout, F., 286, 330
Sullivan, S. E., 191
Svinicki, M., 60, 64, 91, 154, 192,
    248
Szabo, B., 138, 139, 142, 146, 284
Szelenyi, K., 364

T

Tagg, J., 6, 248
Taraban-Gordon, S., 271
Tarr, T. A., 11, 347
Terenzini, P. T., 154, 157
Terrell, R. D., 187
Theall, M., 88, 151, 154, 155, 156,
    157, 158
Thipakorn, B., 250
Thomas, S. Y., 234
Thoreau, H. D., 103

Tiberius, R. G., 5, 6
Tice, S. L., 330
Tierney, W. G., 54, 100, 368, 369, 370
Tillman, L., 225, 236
Tinto, V., 248
Tomkinson, B., 206
Tompkins, D., 267
Tongroach, C., 250
Torosyan, R., 129
Townsend, B. K., 309
Trice, A. G., 364
Trigwell, K., 248
Trower, C. A., 10, 225, 232, 233, 234, 367, 368
Trowler, P. R., 248, 281
Tuitt, F., 225, 239, 240
Turner, S. T., 225, 232, 234, 235, 236, 237
Tusmith, B., 187, 188
Tuttle, T., 288
Twombly, S., 309, 312

U
Umbach, P. D., 235

V
Vargas, L., 235
von Hoene, L. M., 11, 327, 332

W
Wade-Golden, K. C., 187
Wagoner, R. L., 348
Walczak, M., 304
Walker, A., 218
Wallin, D. L., 351
Walsh, D. C., 393
Walvoord, B. E., 137, 138, 139, 162, 170, 171, 172, 175
Washington, S., 193
Watts, G., 311
Weber, L., 188

Wehlburg, C. M., 11, 88, 169, 172, 174, 176, 392
Weinstein, G., 193, 217
Weiss, K., 321
Wertsch, M. E., 193
Weston, T., 267
Wheeler, D. W., 13, 286
Whitfield, S., 206
Whitney, K., 206
Whitt, E., 369
Wijeyesinghe, C. L., 187, 192, 207
Wilger, A. K., 121
Wilhite, M. S., 117
Williams, D. A., 187, 226, 232
Wlodkowski, R. J., 154, 203, 204, 219
Wolf, P., 123
Wolf-Wendel, L., 312, 313
Wolstenholme, J., 123
Woodard, M., 237
Woodford, B., 329
Wright, D., 352, 356, 357
Wright, M. C., 279, 281, 286, 288
Wright, V. H., 12
Wulff, D. H., 11, 367, 368
Wulff, R. D., 328

Y
Yancey, K., 267
Yee, K., 357
Yeskel, F., 188
Young, A. A., 187
Yun, J., 10, 191

Z
Zakrajsek, T. D., 83, 105, 269
Zhao, C., 73
Zhu, E., 285
Zimmer, M., 298
Zull, J. E., 153, 154, 157
Zuñiga, X., 188, 219

SUBJECT INDEX

A

Academic development,
defined, 32

Academic Leader, 73

Academy of Teaching at The Ohio
State University, 284

Access and equity for
underrepresented faculty, 226,
228-232

Accreditation and assessment of
student learning, 169–170,
176–180, 181–182

Activities: mechanics of running an
event, 124–127; one-time events,
118–120; ongoing programming,
120–124; overseeing ongoing
programming, 128–130

Adjunct Certificate Training, Johnson
County Community College,
321–322

Adjunct faculty members: background
on, 347–348; categories of,
349–350; comparisons to full-time,
350; conclusions on, 360; needs of,
355–356; numbers of, 348–349;
online programs for, 354–355;
orientation for,
356–357; perceptions and attitudes
toward, 350–351; professional
development programs for,
352–355; recognition and rewards
for, 359; reimbursement to, 354;
teaching support for, 358–359

Administration of faculty
development at small colleges,
298–302

Administrators, working with, 92,
373–374, 387–389

Advisory boards, 46, 104

Age of the Networker, 7, 117

American Association for Higher
Education's (AAHE) principles for
program assessment, 137–138

Americans With Disabilities Act
(ADA) guidelines, 111, 316

Assessment, program: AAHE
principles for, 137–138; conclusions
on, 147–148; context and,
135–137; cycle of, 140–147;
importance of, 135; integration
with goals, 138–139

Assessment of student learning:
accreditation and, 169–170,
176–180, 181–182; conclusions on,
182–183; course-based assessment,
172; defined, 170; department or
program assessment, 173–174;
faculty developers' responsibilities
and, 181–182; faculty development
and, 9, 11–12; importance of
assessment practices, 170–171;
institution-level assessment,
174–175; levels of assessment
practice, 171

Assessment of teaching practices:
classroom research, 162–163;
conclusions on, 165; data for
formative and summative uses, 152;
dimensions of college teaching,
156; effects of college, 157;
guidelines for enhancing teaching
and learning, 163–165; student

429

motivation, 157–158; teacher knowledge, 154–156; tools for assessing learning, 162; tools for assessing teaching, 159–162

Attendance at committee events, 64–65

Audience awareness and faculty developers, 106, 208–209

B

Best Practices for Supporting Adjunct Faculty, 352

Book clubs or discussion groups, 120, 129

Books on educational development, 84–85

Branding, program, 46–47

Budget, educational development program, 41–42, 95. *See also* Grant-funded projects, management of

C

Career stages of faculty members: early career stage, 366–371; late career stage, 374–375; midcareer stage, 371–374; overview of, 364–366

Center for Research on Learning and Teaching (CRLT) at University of Michigan, 21, 277, 282, 283

Certificate programs, 122

Chairpersons and other administrators, 373–374, 387–389

Change magazine, 57, 73

Chronicle of Higher Education, 73, 93, 389

Civil Rights Act, 328

Classroom Assessment Techniques (CATs), 162, 172

Classroom observations, 27, 60, 91, 161

Classroom research and Scholarship of Teaching and Learning (SoTL), 162–163, 288–289

Colleges and universities, types of. *See* Community colleges; Small colleges; Research universities

Committee, faculty development: conclusions on, 65; coordination with others and, 58–59; goals, 55; management, 59; membership, 55–56; mission statement for, 54; organizing, 56–58; program ideas, 60–61; questions and answers about, 64–65; subcommittee work, 61–63

Committee service and faculty governance, 390–391

Communication skills for educational developers, 90–93

Community colleges: accountability at, 322–325; conclusions on, 325; faculty development initiatives at, 315–317; innovative practice at, 317–322; student profiles and goals at, 311–313; teaching and learning expectations at, 313–315; as unique institutions, 309–311

Complex roles of faculty members, 9–11

Complexity of higher education environment, 384–386

Conferences, 85, 96, 119, 328, 338, 380

Confidentiality, 46, 60, 91–92, 159, 161

Conflict management skills, 209

Consultations, individual, 26–27, 123, 217

Content knowledge, 154–156

Course-based assessment, 172, 175–176

Course-based multicultural change, 191–192

Culture, institutional: program promotion and, 99–102; size and, 294–295; underrepresented faculty and, 232–234

Curricular innovations, 11–12
Curricular knowledge, 155
Curriculum reform: department-level
(re)design, 123; multicultural,
217–219; at research universities, 285
Cycle of program assessment: closing
the loop, 147; collecting data,
143–145; determining outcomes
and measures, 141–142;
interpreting and reporting data,
145–147; setting goals, 140–141

D

Definitions of faculty development,
7–8
Delta College (Michigan) professional
development course series, 318–319
Directors of educational development
programs: ideal, 42–43; permanent
or rotating, 43–44; at small
colleges, 295
Diversity issues: conclusions
on, 194–195; course-based
multicultural change, 191–192;
faculty development overview
and, 13–14; inclusive practices in
educational development, 187–191;
reflections on personal preparation,
193–194; research universities and,
281–282; systemic approaches to
multicultural change, 186–187;
teaching and, 234–235; terms and
language, 188; transformation,
192–193

E

Early career faculty members, 366–371
Educational developers, skills for:
communication skills, 90–93;
conclusions on, 96–97; general
knowledge, 84–86; human and
financial resource management,
95; institutional issues, 86–88;
organization and time management,

94–95; planning and assessment,
88–90; workshops, 95–96; writing
skills, 93
Educational development, defined, 32
Educational development program,
establishing: advisory board, 46,
104; branding, 46–47; budget,
41–42, 95; director, 42–44;
ethical guidelines, 45–46, 71, 159;
instructional technology, 40–41,
285; mission, 38–40; services,
44–45. See also Program types and
prototypes
Ethical Guidelines for Educational
Developers, 45–46, 71, 159
Events, one-time: evaluating, 127;
mechanics of running, 124–127;
suggestions for, 118–120

F

Faculty, adjunct: background on,
347–348; categories of, 349–350,
comparisons to full-time, 350;
conclusions on, 360; needs of,
355–356; numbers of, 348–349;
online programs for, 354–355;
orientation for,
356–357; perceptions and attitudes
toward, 350–351; professional
development programs for,
352–355; recognition and rewards
for, 359; reimbursement to, 354;
teaching support for, 358–359
Faculty, underrepresented: academic
legitimacy and, 237; access and
equity, 226, 228-232; climate and
culture for, 232–234; conclusions
on, 239–240; growth and
development of, 235; implications
related to, 237–239; inclusive
excellence and, 225–226, 227;
role models and mentors for, 236;
teaching and diversity, 234–235;
unique pressures for, 236

Faculty Colloquium on Excellence in
    Teaching (FACET), 353–354
Faculty development: defined,
    7–8; researching, 71–74. *See also*
    Educational development program,
    establishing
Faculty development committee:
    conclusions on, 65; coordination
    with others and, 58–59; goals, 55;
    management, 59; membership,
    55–56; mission statement for, 54;
    organizing, 56-58; program ideas,
    60–61; questions and answers
    about, 64–65; subcommittee work,
    61–63
Faculty development overview:
    current challenges, 8–9; curricular
    innovations, 11–12; diversity of
    faculty and students, 13–14; history,
    4–5; language and terms, 3–4, 7–8;
    roles of faculty members, 9–11;
    stages, 5–7; technology issues,
    12–13
Faculty learning communities
    (FLCs), 28
Faculty members, career stages of:
    early career stage, 366–371; late
    career stage, 374–375; midcareer
    stage, 371–374; overview of,
    364–366
Family Education Right to Privacy Act
    (FERPA), 316
Focus groups, conducting, 89,
    103–104
Funding for teaching innovations,
    286–287
Funding international development or
    scholarship, 254–256

G
Getting started in faculty
    development, 67–80
GI Bill, 328
Governance organizations, 87

Graduate and professional student
    developers: assessment by, 341–343;
    skills for, 338–341
Graduate and professional students:
    background on training for, 10–11,
    328–329; certificate programs
    for, 332; journal for, 329–330;
    leadership programs for, 332–333;
    mentoring for, 332, 337; Preparing
    Future Faculty (PFF) project for,
    10, 331; sample continuum for
    development of, 337; skills and
    knowledge needed by, 333–337;
    Socratic portfolios of, 336; teaching
    assistant programs, 330; writing
    programs for, 331–332
Grant-funded projects, management
    of, 27, 28, 124
Great Online Teachers' Seminar
    (GOTS), 321
Guidelines for enhancing teaching and
    learning, 163–165

H
HBCU (Historically Black Colleges
    and Universities) Faculty
    Development Network, 14, 72
History of faculty development,
    4–5
Hosting international colleagues,
    252–253

I
Inclusive excellence, 225–226, 227
Inclusive practices in educational
    development, 187–191
Individual Development and
    Educational Assessment (IDEA)
    Center, 154
Individual versus group
    communications, 92–93
Institute for New Faculty Developers
    (INFD), 71
Institution, researching your, 74–78

Institutional culture: program promotion and, 99–102; size and, 294–295; underrepresented faculty and, 232–234

Institutional governance documents, 87–88

International conferences for developers, 251

International faculty development: challenges for educational development centers, 248–249; collaborating on research projects, 253–254; funding international development or scholarship, 254–256; globalization and, 244; hosting international colleagues, 252–253; international overview of faculty development, 245–248; working with colleagues, 252

International journals for developers, 251–252

International professional associations, 249–251

Intrapersonal and interpersonal strengths, 78–80

J

Johnson County Community College (Kansas) Adjunct Certificate Training, 321–322

Journals for educational developers: and graduate students, 329–330; international, 251–252; recommended, 73–74

K

Kansas City Kansas Community College Academic Symposium, 319–320

Knowledge and skills for educational developers: communication skills, 90–93; conclusions on, 96–97; general knowledge, 84–86; human and financial resource management,

95; institutional issues, 86–88; organization and time management, 94–95; planning and assessment, 88–90; workshop presentation skills, 95–96; writing skills, 93

Knowledge of self and multicultural teaching, 207–208

L

Late career stage of faculty members, 374–375

Leadership guidelines for research university center, 280–284

Logo, educational development program, 46, 47

M

Marketing: adjunct faculty and, 355; defined, 102; the "Four Ps", 104–107; institutional culture and, 99–102; market research, 103–104; principles of persuasion, 108–109; promotional methods, 109–114

Mentoring and consultations, 10, 122, 123, 332, 335, 337, 371, 374

Midcareer stage of faculty members, 371–374

Mission, educational development program, 38–40

Models for faculty development at small colleges, 298–303

Motivation and learning, 157–158

Multicultural change: course-based, 191–192; systemic approaches to, 186–187. See also Diversity issues

Multicultural faculty development activities: course and curriculum design, 217–219; domains of multicultural teaching and, 206–207; individual consultation, 217; institutional commitment and, 204–205; program rationale and, 205–206; at research universities,

281–282; responsibilities of faculty developer and, 207–210; syllabus changes, 219–220; workshops, 210–217

Multicultural teaching, four dimensions of, 206, 207

N

Newsletters, periodicals, and helpful publications, 57, 63, 73–74, 84–85, 269

O

Observations, classroom, 27, 60, 91, 161

One-time events, 118–120

Ongoing programming, 120–124, 128–130

Online faculty, training for, 320–321

Online programs for adjunct faculty, 354–355

Online resources for educational developers, 85–86

Online tools for program promotion, 110–113

Open classroom events, 119–120

Organization and time management, 94–95

Organizational development: chairpersons, administrators and, 387–389; committee service and faculty governance, 390–391; community and group processes, 391–393; complex higher education environment and, 384–386; conclusions on, 394–395; context and, 382–383; defined, 381; departments, campuswide units, and, 389–390; relationships and, 382

Orientations, 27, 61, 121–122, 356–357, 358

Otterbein College, description of, 117, 118, 119, 122, 124, 129, 130

Overview of faculty development: current challenges, 8–9; curricular innovations, 11–12; diversity of faculty and students, 13–14; history, 4–5; language and terms, 3–4, 7–8; roles of faculty members, 9–11; stages, 5–7; technology, 12–13

P

Part-time faculty: brief description of, 347–348; categories of, 349–350; comparisons to full-time, 350; conclusions on, 360; needs of, 355–356; numbers of, 348–349; online programs for, 354–355; orientation for, 356–357; perceptions and attitudes toward, 350–351; professional development programs for, 352–355; recognition and rewards for, 359; reimbursement to, 354; teaching support for, 358–359

Pathways into Educational Development, 68–69

Pathways to the Profession of Educational Development, 73

Pedagogical content knowledge, 154–155

Peer observation of classroom teaching, 27, 60, 91, 161

Periodicals, newsletters, and helpful publications, 57, 63, 73–74, 84–85, 269

Portfolios, teaching, 161, 336, 357

Practical suggestions for programs and activities: conclusions on, 130; mechanics of running an event, 124–127; one-time events, 118–120; ongoing programming, 120–124; overseeing ongoing programming, 128–130

Preparing for faculty development work, 67–80

Preparing Future Faculty (PFF) project, 10, 331
Print materials for program promotion, 113–114
Professional and Organizational Development Network in Higher Education (POD): committee development and, 54; conferences, 57, 69, 79, 328, 338, 380; description of, 6, 14, 21, 24, 71–72; ethical guidelines, 46; founding of, 6; membership, 21; mission statement, 379; publications, 57, 85; for researching college teaching, 154; for researching faculty development, 36, 71–72, 128, 284; TA development and, 328, 329, 330; Web site, 24, 40, 71, 73, 85, 270
Professional associations, international, 249–251
Program assessment: AAHE principles for, 137–138; conclusions on, 147–148; context and, 135–137; cycle of, 140–147; importance of, 135; integration with goals and, 138–139
Program types and prototypes: background on, 21–23; categories of programs, 26–29; conclusions on, 33; emerging program types, 29–32; types of centers, 23–26. *See also* Educational development program, establishing
Project Kaleidoscope (PKAL), 192
Promoting a faculty development program: conclusions on, 114–115; definition of marketing, 102; the "Four Ps", 104–107; institutional culture and, 99–102; market research, 103–104; principles of persuasion, 108–109; promotional methods, 109–114
Publications, helpful, 57, 63, 73–74, 84–85, 269

Q

Quick Course Diagnosis, 160

R

Recognition and rewards for adjunct faculty, 359
Research and inquiry skills, applying: conclusions on, 80; importance of, 70–71; researching faculty development, 71–74; researching your institution, 74–78
Research universities: conclusions on, 289–290; faculty development activities at, 284–289; leadership guidelines for research university center, 280–284; teaching center mission at, 278–280
Role models and mentors for underrepresented faculty, 236
Roles of faculty members, 9–11

S

Sabbatical leave, 4, 373–374
San Bernardino Valley College training for online faculty, 320–321
Scholarship of Teaching and Learning (SoTL), 162–163, 288–289
Size and teaching culture, 294–295
Skills and knowledge for educational developers: communication skills, 90–93; conclusions on, 96–97; general, 84–86; human and financial resource management, 95; institutional issues, 86–88; organization and time management, 94–95; planning and assessment, 88–90; workshops, 95–96; writing skills, 93
Skills and knowledge needed by graduate students, 333–337
Small College Committee, POD Network, 293–294
Small colleges: conclusions on, 306–307; defining, 294–296;

guiding principles for, 296–298; models for faculty development at, 298–303; practical strategies for, 303–306

Small Group Instructional Diagnoses (SGID), 27, 140, 160

Society for Teaching and Learning in Higher Education (STLHE), 73

Stages, career: early career stage, 366–371; late career stage, 374–375; midcareer stage, 371–374; overview of, 364–366

Stages of faculty development work, 5–7

Stanford's Center for Teaching and Learning (CTL), 277, 282, 283

Student learning, assessment of: accreditation and, 169–170, 176–180, 181–182; conclusions on, 182–183; course-based assessment, 172; defined, 170; department or program assessment, 173–174; faculty developers' responsibilities and, 181–182; faculty development and, 9, 11–12; importance of assessment practices, 170–171; institution-level assessment, 174–175; levels of assessment practice, 171

Student ratings for assessing teaching, 156, 159–160

Subcommittee work, 61–63

Suggestions for programs and activities: conclusions on, 130; mechanics of running an event, 124–127; one-time events, 118–120; ongoing programming, 120–124; overseeing ongoing programming, 128–130

Surveys, needs/interest, 63, 88–89, 103, 144–145

Syllabi and multicultural goals, 219–220

T

Teacher knowledge and the faculty developer, 154–156

Teaching: four dimensions of multicultural, 206, 207; guidelines for enhancing, 163–165; intentional, 296–297; scholarship and, 297–298

Teaching assistant programs, 330. See also Graduate and professional students

Teaching circles, 27–28, 120–121

Teaching practices, assessing: classroom research for, 162–163; conclusions on, 165; data for formative and summative uses, 152; dimensions of college teaching, 156; effects of college and, 157; student motivation and, 157–158; teacher knowledge, 154–156; tools for, 159–162

Teaching Professor, The, 73, 154

Teaching skills needed by graduate students, 334–335

Teaching styles, valuing a diversity of, 297

TeachingCoach.Org, 73

Technology: administrative activities and, 269–271; assessment and, 266–267; conclusions on, 271–272; digital information literacy and, 264–265; ethical and legal use of, 266; evaluating, 262–263; evaluation of instructors and, 267–268; faculty development activities and, 268–269; faculty members' response to, 260–262; four tasks in using, 259; impact of, 9, 12–13; instructional technology, 40–41, 285; integrating, 263–264; problem-solving skills and, 265; support and training, 62

Technology unit, merging with instructional, 31

Tenure and promotion dossier, 60, 61

Tenure process, 92, 367–368
Thomas-Kilmann Conflict Mode Instrument, 209
Time management, 94–95
"Tomorrow's Professor" listserv, 86, 124
Transformative assessment: accreditation and, 169–170, 176–180, 181–182; conclusions on, 182–183; course-based assessment, 172; defined, 170; department or program assessment, 173–174; faculty developers' responsibilities and, 181–182; faculty development and, 9, 11–12; importance of assessment practices, 170–171; institution-level assessment, 174–175; levels of assessment practice, 171

U
Underrepresented faculty: academic legitimacy and, 237; access and equity for, 226, 228–232; climate, culture, and, 232–234; conclusions on, 239–240; growth and development of, 235; implications related to, 237–239; inclusive excellence, 225–226, 227; role models and mentors for, 236; teaching and diversity, 234–235; unique pressures for, 236
Unionized institutions, 87

University of Michigan's Center for Research on Learning and Teaching (CRLT), 21, 277, 282, 283
University of Waterloo, description of, 117–118, 119, 122, 124, 125, 126

V
Videotaping a class, 160, 161
Voluntary System of Accountability (VSA), 180

W
Web resources and newsletters, 63, 73–74, 269. See also Professional and Organizational Development Network in Higher Education (POD)
Web site, faculty development program's, 110–112, 123–124, 269, 270
Workshops: conducting, 95–96; description of, 26; five-minute 105; for graduate students, 337; as mainstay offering, 118–119; on multicultural issues, 210–217; on a tenure and promotion dossier, 61
Writing programs for graduate students, 331–332
Writing skills for educational developers, 93